Treasures from the Attic

Treasures from the Attic

THE EXTRAORDINARY
STORY OF ANNE FRANK'S FAMILY

Mirjam Pressler with Gerti Elias

TRANSLATED FROM THE GERMAN
BY DAMION SEARLS

WEIDENFELD & NICOLSON
LONDON

First published in Great Britain in 2011
by Wedenfeld & Nicolson

1 3 5 7 9 10 8 6 4 2

Originally published in Germany as *Grüsse und Küsse an alle: Die Geschichte der Familie von Anne Frank* by S. Fischer Verlag GmbH, Frankfurt am Main, in 2009. Copyright © 2009 S. Fischer Verlag GmbH.

A CIP catalogue record for this book is available from The British Library.

Typeset by Input Data Services

The Orion Publishing Group's policy is to use papers that are natural, renewable and recyclable and made from wood grown in sustainable forests. The logging and manufacturing processes are expected to conform to environmental regulations of the country of origin.

Weidenfeld & Nicolson

Orion Publishing Group Ltd
Orion House
5 Upper Saint Martin's Lane
London, WC2H 9EA

An Hachette UK Company

www.orionbooks.co.uk

Contents

Part Three

Buddy Elias, Anne's Cousin (b. 1925)

Treasures from the Attic

Publisher's Note

In 2001, as described in the Afterword, a cache of several thousand letters, photographs, and other documents was found in the attic of the house in Basel belonging to Buddy Elias, Anne Frank's cousin. It was soon realized that these documents were of major significance for the history of the Frank family, and cast a new and clearer light on Anne Frank herself. These papers, organized and edited by Buddy Elias's wife, Gerti Elias—including both previously published letters and documents and some that have never been published—form the basis of the following family history. Mirjam Pressler, who wrote the chronicle that contains them, is the German translator of the Definitive Edition of Anne Frank's diary and a winner of the German Book Prize in 2006 for her literary life's work.

In the German edition, letters are quoted exactly as written, without modernizing the German orthography, correcting spelling mistakes, or filling in abbreviations; punctuation is added for clarity in a few places, and obvious typos in typewritten letters are corrected, but the edition aims to preserve the authentic feel of the personal documents. These features have been carried over as much as possible into the English translation.

Prologue

Sils-Maria, in the Upper Engadine valley in Switzerland—a summer day, 1935. A slim, well-dressed man leaves Hotel Waldhaus, where he has met with an executive of the Pomosin company to report on the progress of their Amsterdam office. The man walks briskly up the road that runs right through the middle of the forest and in a few minutes reaches Villa Laret.

As he steps out from between the trees, it lies before him, in the middle of a parklike field filled with trees, more like a little castle than a villa. The windows are so clean and scrubbed that they flash in the sun.

The man walks up the wide, well-raked gravel road. He smiles when he catches sight of the swing hanging between two tall trees—a wide platform with a railing, big enough to comfortably fit a table and chairs. Two children are jumping up and down on the platform at the moment, making it start to swing. They are laughing and screaming. Two dachshunds hop around under the swing, yapping excitedly, but no matter how hard they try, they can't manage to jump onto the swing; sometimes a dog falls onto its back in its failed attempt and flails around kicking its short legs until it turns right side up, then it starts trying again to jump up onto the swing. The children double over with laughter. The boy is about ten years old, the girl six.

"Not so loud!" the man shouts at the children.

They both stop for a moment. "Daddy, do you know what Auntie O. said this morning?" the girl screams. He steps closer and shakes his head. "Yesterday she asked her maid where her washcloth was, in French of course, and then she wanted Aunt Leni to tell her the German word for it. '*Waschlappen,*' Aunt Leni said. And then this morning, she said to her maid: 'Where is my *wasch-lapin*?' " The children giggled. "Get it, Daddy? She asked where her wash-rabbit was. Isn't that funny?"

He nods. "Yes, that really is funny. But don't make so much noise, so you don't disturb all the ladies and gentlemen."

They both nod. Then they take each other's hands and start playing again, only the slightest bit quieter than before. The children are Buddy Elias and his cousin Anne Frank, and the man is Otto Frank, taking a holiday with his younger daughter at Villa Laret.

About a dozen ladies and gentlemen are sitting on the terrace, at tables covered with porcelain cups and dishes, the ladies with broad-brimmed hats and parasols. The gentlemen, who presumably do not dare to take off their jackets despite the hot weather, are wearing straw summer hats. In any case, the heat is more bearable here, in the middle of the forest, than up on the treeless mountain slopes.

Villa Laret, Sils-Maria

Next to the wide double doors that lead to the salon, two maids with little white aprons and matching white lace caps are standing next to the serving cart that holds the tea and coffee pots and plates loaded with petits fours and cakes, ready to hurry over and serve any guest who signals for them.

Otto Frank walks closer. When the lady of the house sees him and waves at him, he takes off his hat and makes a bow.

The lady of the house is Olga Spitzer née Wolfsohn, a French cousin of Leni Elias and Otto Frank. Every summer she spends a few weeks at her villa in Sils-Maria, a large house with nineteen bedrooms, and she always invites guests to join her. Leni and her mother, Alice Frank, are usually among them, since the family connections are so close. This year Otto has come too from Amsterdam, with his daughter Anne but without his wife, Edith, who went with Margot, the older daughter, to see Edith's mother in Aachen.

Olga Spitzer offers her cousin Otto her hand, and he bends down to kiss it. Then he greets his mother, Alice, and sister, Leni, with affectionate kisses on the cheek before sitting down at their table.

"Did the meeting go well?" Leni asks. In French, of course, since it would be rude to speak German in front of Olga Spitzer, who understands just a few words of the language.

Otto Frank nods. "Yes, very well. It is much easier to do business with someone when he is on vacation. He agreed to everything I suggested."

Meanwhile, the children have come closer, curious. But the adult conversation does not interest them. They each grab a little cake.

"What should we do now?" Buddy asks, chewing.

"I know," Anne says, and she pulls her cousin into the house, through the salon and the hall, up the wide staircase, and into their grandmother Alice's room. "You promised," she says, and points to the armoire. When Buddy violently shakes his head, she insists: "You said you wouldn't chicken out."

Buddy shrugs his shoulders. He knows that there's no point in trying to defend himself. When Anne gets something into her head, she doesn't let go of the idea very easily. And the fact is, he did lose the bet: she had dared to clamber up the tree after all, get a bird's egg from its nest, and come down with the egg in the pocket of her skirt, without breaking it. Then, despite his warning, she climbed back up and put the egg back again.

"Come on, do it," Anne says. She sits down in the armchair and tucks her legs under her.

Buddy wipes his sticky hands on his pants, hesitantly opens the armoire, and takes out a black dress. His grandmother Alice always wears only black dresses. This one has a white lace insert. He pulls it over his shirt and pants, takes a shawl, winds it tight around his waist, and then stuffs two small sofa pillows down the lace neck of the dress. Anne giggles with recognition. He looks at himself in the big mirror next to the armoire. The game is starting to be fun for him too.

He takes a hat with a bouquet of flowers on it out of a hatbox, puts it on, and stands in front of the mirror plucking at the veil until he has it hanging rakishly over one eye. The shoes with the high heels are too big, so he stuffs handkerchiefs into the toes and then prances around in front of the gleeful Anne, who laughs so loud that a maid comes in to see what is going on. The girl, quite young herself, applauds. Buddy, inspired by the effect he is having, lets himself be carried away by the game and starts making even broader gestures—elegantly pursing his lips, jutting out his pinkie and bringing an imaginary teacup to his mouth, then wiping off his pursed lips with an equally imaginary napkin. Then he offers Anne his hand, exactly as elegant and refined as Olga Spitzer when she had given Otto Frank her hand earlier, and Anne gives it a noisy wet kiss.

"Come on, go downstairs and show everyone," she demands, but that is too much for Buddy. He doesn't dare to in this distinguished house. Back home in Basel he would have done it just like that. He takes off the clothes, and the maid puts everything back into the armoire where it belongs. She takes the handkerchiefs he had stuffed into the shoes, to wash and iron them.

"What should we do now?" Buddy asks.

"Hide-and-seek," Anne suggests, even though it's a little boring with only two people. But they have thought up some new rules: the seeker has to wait longer, and if he doesn't find the hider, then he loses and has to pay a penalty, for example, giving the winner his dessert.

They run out through the garden to the forest. "You're it," Anne says. "I was it yesterday."

Buddy agrees. He crouches down under a tree and hides his face in his arms.

Anne doesn't run far—she already knows where she'll hide. During the game yesterday, she discovered a little cavity in the hillside, maybe an abandoned fox hole. She tears off a few branches, crawls into the opening, and pulls the branches over the entrance. Soon she hears Buddy shout that he's ready. He goes past her more than once, but of course he doesn't see her. She knew that this hiding place would be perfect. Hopefully, it really is abandoned; hopefully, a fox won't come and bite her in the behind. Or is it really a fox hole? Maybe it's a rabbit hole, for a *lapin*? She suppresses her laughter as she remembers what Auntie O. had said that morning. Rabbits don't bite, at least she had never heard of anyone being bitten by a rabbit, but foxes have sharp noses and sharp teeth.

Buddy, meanwhile, has got quite nervous. Of course he can't find Anne; she has a special talent for hiding. But eventually it's time for her to come out. "I give up!" he shouts. "Anne, come out!" She doesn't appear, and he shouts louder

Anne Frank in Sils-Maria, 1935

and louder, runs faster and faster. What if she's lost? What if a strange man found her and took her? How could he explain to his mother, his grandmother, and Uncle Otto that it wasn't his fault? He can already hear his mother say: But Buddy, you're much older than she is, it's up to you to be more careful.

He is desperate and close to tears when suddenly she is standing next to him. "I want your dessert when we have ice cream," she says.

Buddy would rather give her a punch in the nose. Or a kiss, because he's so relieved. But he only says: "Look at you, you're all filthy."

It's true. Anne's light summer dress is smeared with dirt, and she tries to knock off the clumps of soil, but it's wet and the stains only get bigger. "Don't worry," Buddy says, plucking a few twigs out of her hair, "Alice is so happy you're here, I'm sure she won't yell at you for long."

"It's a brand-new dress," Anne says.

They start back, a bit dejected. "I could say I fell," Anne suggests.

"You fell on your back and fell again on your front?" Buddy asks. He feels sorry for his cousin.

But in the end it's not so bad. "Look at you!" Alice cries, shocked, when she sees Anne, and Otto asks if she's hurt herself. And Leni goes after Buddy for not looking after his little cousin better. Buddy stands there completely flabbergasted and turns red under the curious gaze of all the guests.

Olga Spitzer, Auntie O., saves the situation by calling her maid and telling her to clean the girl.

"But not with the wash-fox!" Buddy says. "Use the wash-*lapin.*"

A couple of ladies raise their brows in surprise. But Anne smiles again.

After dinner it turns out there is ice cream for dessert. Anne empties her bowl and then shoves it over to Buddy without anyone else noticing, and he fills it up again with his. Then he sighs, but only very quietly, so that no one will notice that either.

The grown-ups are talking about a concert that will happen tomorrow, in the house. The Trio di Trieste will perform. Concerts take place here all the time; Olga Spitzer loves music and is rich enough to pay for private concerts for herself and her guests. Leni said once that no one speaks of money in this house, that the word does not exist in Olga's vocabulary, and that that in itself is the best proof of Olga's wealth.

The sun goes down behind the mountains. The ladies and gentlemen return to the salon, the children are sent to bed, and in the distance the bells toll the hours of the night.

PART ONE

Alice Frank née Stern, Anne's Grandmother

(1865–1953)

Alice Frank with her mother, Cornelia Stern née Cahn, circa 1872

1.

Many Good and Beautiful Things

BASEL, 1935

Alice leans against the window, her arm resting on the windowsill, and looks out onto the street at evening falling in the city. She loves the dusk, the blue hour between day and night, and always has. A man is turning the corner: it's the Italian man who lives in the basement of the house kitty-corner to hers, and he is hauling a sack of either coal or potatoes, she can't tell anymore in the twilight. But she sees the door of the house fly open and two children rush out, a boy and a girl, and she sees the man put his sack down when he catches sight of the children and spread out his arms to catch them and tumble them around, first the girl and then the boy. It's a little painful for her to watch. That's how Michael caught up his children when he came home, and they loved it, screaming and shrieking as much as those two on the other side of the street, whose delighted voices she can hear even through the closed window here on the third floor.

She turns around, stands with her back against the window, and her eye falls on the large oval painting in the heavy gilded frame hanging on the opposite wall. She contemplates the little girl she once was and wonders if she ever greeted her father like that when she was a child. Probably not. August Stern was a sober and serious man, and Alice's governess had always spoken of him with a lowered voice and deep respect. Alice cannot imagine that he ever once tumbled a child around in his arms.

She can no longer see the girl in the painting very clearly, but that doesn't matter, she knows the girl so well that she can see her even with her eyes closed, she doesn't need to turn on the light. She isn't sure anymore how old she was back when Professor Schlesinger painted her in Frankfurt. Maybe four or five, she couldn't have been much older than that. And when the governess pushed her through the door, he would have said, "There's my shweet little girl!" since in Frankfurt all little girls were "shweet." But his cajoling voice and the smile he put on couldn't fool her, she knew how quickly he would turn mean if she didn't keep as still as he wanted her to. His face with its brown goatee would twist into a grimace, and his voice would lose its cajoling tone. Alice can hear it even now, this hard voice brusquely reprimanding her, and can feel the smell of paint and turpentine mixed with pipe tobacco in her nose sixty-five years later, and how she was seized by a longing to get back to her nursery, which rises up before her eyes perfectly clearly, as though she were seeing it in real life: the dolls, the dolls' kitchen with a stove you could turn on, a dining table with real porcelain dishes on it; she sees the bookshelf with all the fairy tales—had *Struwwelpeter* even been published back then? Yes, of course, she can still hear her governess's voice reading her the story of the boy who wouldn't eat his soup—she sees her four-poster bed, like heaven with its clouds of tulle, sees the window with its white lace drapes and the green velvet curtains tied back during the day with gilded ropes.

She can still hear the governess come in and say, "Come along now, Alice, it's time," how she would untie Alice's apron and take off her play clothes, tear the doll from her hand despite her frantic efforts to hold on to it, and put her finger on her lips when Alice began to cry: "Shhh, Mama has a headache, you don't want to make Mama sicker, do you? You're a big girl now."

Even now it frightens her to think about it. Later, when she had children herself, she winced every time the expression "You don't want to . . . , do you?" unintentionally escaped her lips, and she would try, confused, to find other words. Back then, when she was a child, "You don't want to . . . , do you?" had worked on her like a magic spell to break her resistance, like a mysterious potion that paralyzed her. Little Alice let herself be dressed in the

Alice Frank as a child, painted by Professor Schlesinger, the Frankfurt painter, circa 1869

white undergarments with the frilly flounces, the pink slip that was so starched it rustled when she moved, and then the fine lace dress with a sash of the same pink color. She had got the dress only a few weeks earlier, because her old Sunday dress, which had been much more comfortable, was now too small for her—the pretty sky blue bodice was so tight that the governess could no longer hook it closed. Mother had ordered the fabric, sought out the lace, and summoned the seamstress, who in any case was at their house quite often. A redheaded, freckled woman from the Odenwald, she had sewn all day until the new dress was finally finished.

Alice smiles at the painting, a shweet girl, and for a moment she thinks she can feel the white stockings, the gray kid-leather little boots a bit too tight. Strange, how precisely she remembers everything to do with this painting; maybe it is because she has looked at it all her life, longer than anything else, longer even than the pieces of furniture she had brought with her two years ago when she moved from Frankfurt to Basel. It had hung first in her parents' drawing room, then, after that terrible day when she lost her father and had to give up her familiar home and move into her grandfather's house, in her mother Cornelia's room, then after Cornelia's death in her own house, first in Frankfurt, Jordanstrasse 4,* and now here in Basel, Schweizergasse 50. When she thinks about herself as a child, she always sees herself looking the way she looks in this painting.

Little Alice had hated being led in to Professor Schlesinger like that. She knew she would have to stand still, not move her feet even if her legs became stiff and started to hurt, not turn her head to look at a fly, that it was just as forbidden to scratch anywhere if it itched. She had always looked for excuses not to see the professor, but the governess had insisted. "You don't want Papa to have spent all that money for nothing, do you?" No, of course

*Jordanstrasse was later renamed Mertonstrasse; today it is called Dantestrasse.

she didn't want that, Papa had to work hard for his money. Every morning he put his hat on his head and set out to the office, and sometimes, when the weather was so bad that you wouldn't turn a dog out in such a storm, he sighed.

The evening grows dimmer, the shadows rise up in the corners of the room, the hard handle of the window presses against her back, but Alice stays standing, motionless, even if the painting gradually blurs before her eyes and only a few bright patches remain visible. The older she gets, the closer the past seems to her and the more clearly images from her memory that she thought were forgotten rise up before her. She thinks about the sentence her grandfather had spoken so often, "The less future someone has, the more the present loses its meaning," and she smiles at the thought that she had always taken this for idle chatter, the meaningless talk of an old man who doesn't know what he's saying anymore, because what would that mean, life without future? Back then, everything was the future, the whole world, and at least half her thoughts started with "When I grow up . . ." But now?

This might be the moment when an idea comes to her—first vague, then clearer; first a "Maybe," then a "Why not?" and finally a "Yes, that would be good." She goes straight to the light switch, squints in the sudden brightness, turns back to the window, pulls the heavy curtains shut, and in a few quick steps is at her desk, also brought from Frankfurt. She flips open the desk, pulls open a drawer, takes out a black bound notebook, picks up her glasses, and sits down in the armchair. Now she knows what she has to do, and she is relieved that she thought of it in time. It is like an assignment that was given to her some time in the past and that she only now understands. She will write up her life story, for her sons, Robert, Otto, and Herbert, and her daughter, Leni—she will write a letter and give it to them next week when they all come to celebrate her seventieth birthday.

This time it won't be a poem—nothing cheerful, none of the

Zum 20ten Dezember 1935.

Wenn ich Euch, meine lieben Kinder, die ich nach langer Zeit wieder um mich versammelt sehe, heute an meinem 70ten Geburtstag einen ganz kurzen Einblick & Rückblick in mein Jugendleben geben will, so braucht Ihr nicht zu befürchten, dass dies mit einer besonderen Absicht geschieht. Es ist mir nur ein Bedürfnis Euch ein bleibendes Andenken an diesen Tag zu geben. –

Wie wenig wissen doch Kinder im Allgemeinen von der Jugendzeit der Eltern. Die Enkel können sich noch weniger einen Begriff machen, dass wir jung waren, wie sie es jetzt sind. Erst viel später wird ihnen diese Erkenntniss kommen & sie werden dann Vieles verstehen & begreifen können. – Selbst die erwachsenen Kinder wissen meist nur das, was sie als denkende Menschen vor sich gesehen & mit erlebt haben. –

Euer Vater hat Euch allerdings des öfteren von seiner Kindheit & Jugend in dem grossen Familienkreis in dem lieben alten Haus in Landau erzählt. Dort ist die

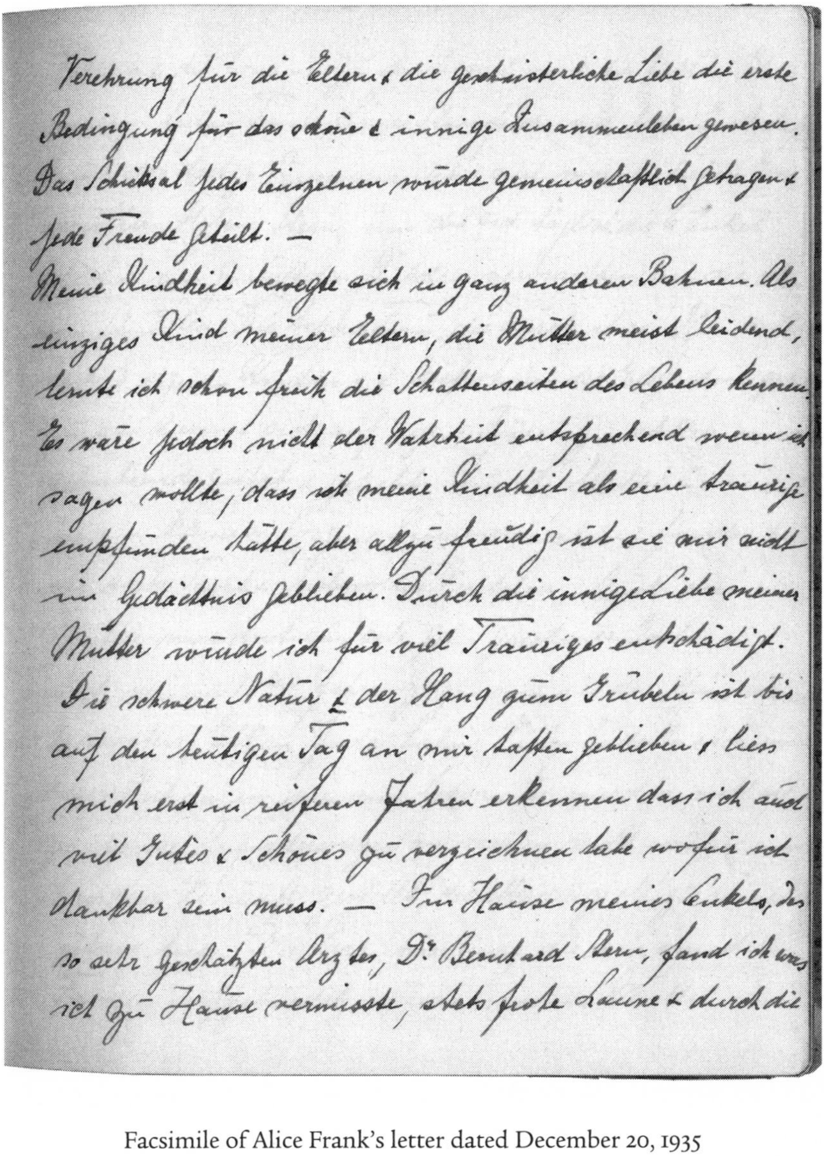
Verehrung für die Eltern & die geschwisterliche Liebe die erste
Bedingung für das schöne & innige Zusammenleben gewesen.
Das Schicksal jedes Einzelnen wurde gemeinschaftlich getragen &
jede Freude geteilt. —
Meine Kindheit bewegte sich in ganz anderen Bahnen. Als
einziges Kind meiner Eltern, die Mutter meist leidend,
lernte ich schon früh die Schattenseiten des Lebens kennen.
Es wäre jedoch nicht der Wahrheit entsprechend wenn ich
sagen wollte, dass ich meine Kindheit als eine traurige
empfunden hätte, aber allzu freudig ist sie mir nicht
im Gedächtnis geblieben. Durch die innige Liebe meiner
Mutter wurde ich für viel Trauriges entschädigt.
Die schwere Natur & der Hang zum Grübeln ist bis
auf den heutigen Tag an mir haften geblieben & liess
mich erst in reiferen Jahren erkennen dass ich auch
viel Gutes & Schönes zu verzeichnen habe wofür ich
dankbar sein muss. — Im Hause meines Onkels, des
so sehr geschätzten Arztes, Dr. Bernhard Stern, fand ich was
ich zu Hause vermisste, stets frohe Laune & durch die

Facsimile of Alice Frank's letter dated December 20, 1935

usual allusions or inside jokes that call forth an understanding smile from the adults and a titter from the children, who of course know the family language perfectly well. This time it will be something to remind her descendants of her when she is no longer there, something to connect her children to a past that was her past too and that she has lost as a result of these barbaric Nazis. For who knows if she will ever get back what she has lost. Sometimes Alice no longer believes that the world will ever be the same again, the way it was—the dark clouds on the horizon are too threatening. In this weather you wouldn't turn a dog out of the house, she thinks, without smiling. She unscrews the inkwell, takes up her pen, dips it in the ink, and begins to write:

*December 20th, 1935**

My dear children, gathered here around me after such a long time apart, on this, my 70th birthday—If I have decided to give you a very short look back & into my childhood life, there is no reason to fear any hidden motives. It is only that I feel a need to give you a permanent, lasting token of our time together today.—

Most children know so little about their parents' youth! And grandchildren are even less able to imagine that we were once young like them. Only much later do they realize it, & there is a lot they can understand & comprehend only then. Even adult children usually know only what they have seen and understood in person, & what they have lived through themselves.—

Granted, your father told you many stories about his childhood & youth with his large family in the beloved old house in Landau. Respect for one's elders and brotherly love laid the groundwork there for a beautiful & devoted life together. The fate of every individual was borne as a group, & every joy and celebration was shared.—

---

*Alice to her children. Frank-Elias Archive. All of the italic passages in this chapter are taken from this document.

Yes, the house is beautiful, Alice thinks with a certain melancholy, even if it did always strike her as a bit run-down. It was built in the Middle Ages and used to be a postal station, a lodge for mail carriages, horses, and travelers, but after 1855, when the Neustadt-Landau railway line was opened and then soon extended to Weissenburg, there were no more postal carriages and the owner of "Zur Blum" gave it up. That is how Zacharias Frank, Michael's father, could buy it for his family in 1870. Of course Michael was already nineteen years old then, so he didn't live there for long. Zacharias Frank, whose father, Abraham, had come as a private tutor from Fürth to Niederhochstadt, about six miles from Landau, moved to the city in 1841 after obtaining a license as an iron dealer. He had run a good business, started lending out money, and become a banker of sorts. Alice had never met him; he died the year before she was married. He and his wife, Babette, had nine children: four sons and five daughters. Michael was the sixth child, and Babette was quite worried about him because he was past thirty and still not married. So she was ecstatic when Michael and Alice got engaged. The whole family welcomed Alice with open arms.

The Frank/Loeb house in Landau-in-der-Pfalz

It was strange for Alice at first, all these people who talked too loud, laughed too loud, wanted too much from her, brought her so close. She would have preferred to hang back, go for walks alone with Michael; she would have been happy to be left in peace to organize her thoughts. But that was out of the question. No sooner had she sat down somewhere with a piece of needlework—she always brought some needlework with her when she visited the family in Landau, as something to cling to—than a sister-in-law would come up to her, an aunt, a cousin by marriage, a neighbor, or even her mother-in-law, to drag her away at the top of their lungs and with an eagerness incomprehensible to her, to join them in some housework or in the kitchen, in a walk to the market, in a visit to a friend.

Babette, her mother-in-law, was a friendly, good-natured woman who liked to eat and ate a lot, cried a lot, and laughed even more. But she was strong willed too, had raised nine children and kept the large house running smoothly despite her age. This woman, who at the time was probably younger than Alice herself is today, never understood how Alice could not know how to cook, how she had never learned and wasn't trying to learn. "The way to a man's heart is through his stomach," she said once,

The children of Zacharias and Babette Frank

before the wedding, and when Alice answered, "We always had a cook, and she did all the cooking," Babette shook her head in disbelief and cast a sympathetic glance at her son Michael. Once, Alice heard one of the sisters-in-law whisper to another: "Michael's bride is too delicate to get her hands dirty." It hurt her feelings, but she pretended she hadn't heard anything.

No, it wasn't easy for Alice to get used to this family back then, but she knew exactly what was expected of a good daughter-in-law and conformed to the expectations. And as the years went by, she learned to appreciate the friendly warmth of the Franks and understand that what she had thought was an uncultivated racket actually expressed vitality and affection, what at first had seemed like meddlesome curiosity later proved to be heartfelt sympathy.

Alice smiles. She dips the pen in the ink and keeps writing:

My childhood followed a very different course. As an only child, and with Mother so often ill, I got to know the darker shadows of life at a young age. It would not be entirely true to say that I felt my childhood to be a sad one, but it does not remain in my memory as particularly happy. The devoted love of my mother was compensation for much sadness. A grave nature & a tendency to brood has stuck with me to this day, & only in my mature years have I come to recognize that I also have many good & beautiful things to record, and which I should be thankful for.—

This tendency to brood is a heavy burden: even today she has to fight against a certain melancholy disposition that she was probably born with; even today she has to make an effort to perceive the "good & beautiful things" that she mentions here. She was never able to just take life as it comes and enjoy herself. Michael was completely different that way, and she learned a lot living at his side, made up for a lot of the pleasures that were perhaps missing from her childhood. Not only was he quite a bit older than she, and so more mature and experienced, but he also possessed an easygoing naturalness and openness to the world that amazed her again and again. It was he who taught her how to enjoy the pleasures of the lighter side of life, and with him, with his death, part of her own pleasure in life had died too.

The handwriting on the paper starts to blur. Does she wipe her eyes with a handkerchief? It's been twenty-six years that Michael has been gone, for twenty-six years she has been a widow, but still she has never fully got over it. Of course it doesn't burn as painfully as it did at the beginning, but a dull ache has never stopped boring into her; sometimes it flares up, and even now she probably thinks, with every decision she has to make, What would Michael say about that? What would he do in this situation?

When I moved in with my uncle, the very highly regarded physician Dr. Bernhard Stern, I found what I had been missing in my old house—a constant good mood & lots of loving company from the cousins and the two sons of my dear aunt Lina Steinfeld.

The connection with Bernhard Stern, the older brother of her father, August, and with the rest of the Stern family had played a large role in her childhood and youth, and was not broken off later. Her cousin Klara (whom everyone called Klärchen), three years older than she was; Richard, the same age as she; and Karl, six years younger, to some degree took the place of the brothers and sisters she never had and always wanted, and then there were Emil and Paul too, the sons of her aunt Lina, her father's and uncle's sister. How gladly Alice accepted every invitation from the Sterns in those years, and how happy were the hours she spent with them. She felt closer to this side of her family than to the other side, the ones in her grandfather Elkan Juda Cahn's house, where she lived after the death of her father. At the Sterns' she was introduced to the kind of cheerful family life that always failed to materialize at home with her ailing mother.

We spent our happiest hours there, because my dear grandmother Helene Stern lived there too, and every day all six grandchildren flocked around her in her cozy little room. This brave woman, who with the work of her own two hands gave three children and two stepsons the opportunity to study & make a name for themselves, was duly honored & loved. We rushed to bring her all our little cares & worries and always found loving consolation and understanding there. Everyone was very happy to see my mother too when she visited.—*

It was this friendly woman, Helene Stern, who bolstered up the thirteen-year-old Alice after the sudden death of her father and the total collapse of her mother. She said that we have to submit to fate but that it is also important to get back up after every blow, just as the grass straightens back up after a storm; and she talked about courage, about trusting your own strength. Even now, Alice can hear her grandmother's voice telling her: "You are still so young. Youth fights and overcomes, age waits and undergoes."

Alice sees before her eyes this woman with white hair under a little black bonnet, sees her small sitting room, which never really got enough light because it extended to the back of the house, and the dark furniture, including the glass cabinet with the Hanukkah menorah, the silver kiddush cup that was used only on the high holy days, and the long-stemmed glasses that were used almost as rarely. Alice almost never saw Grandmother Helene without a piece of sewing in her hand—there was always something that needed patching, darning, or repairing. "Hard work is its own reward" was another of her sayings that Alice never forgot. Silly proverbs often turn out to be wise truths, she thinks now, and you sometimes have to pay a high price to learn that. She dips her pen in the ink and continues writing. Aside

---

*Helene Stern was the second wife of Emanuel Stern, Anne Frank's great-great-grandfather, who died in 1841.

from the scratching of the steel nib across the paper, and the ticking of the clock, all is silent.

In my 13th year we moved to my grandfather Elkan Juda Cahn's house. A lot changed in my life from that point on. Demands were made on me that were probably too great for my understanding, what understanding there was, which in any case left a lot to be desired. The main duty and responsibility that the family placed on my shoulders—to be a support for my mother—was difficult for me. I have borne this feeling of responsibility for her my whole life & gladly too.—

Perhaps Alice feels thirsty at this point. She gets up, fetches a glass of water, and drinks it in long, slow swallows, then sits back down at her writing desk, props up her arms, takes her head in her hands, and gives herself over to her memories.

Her father's death, which struck her out of the clear blue sky, brought far-reaching changes. Her mother, Cornelia, moved with Alice into her own father Elkan Juda Cahn's house on Hochstrasse. Cornelia's mother, Betty, had passed away long before Alice was born. Cornelia's weakened state of health certainly did not improve after this blow of fate: she was tormented with migraines and had such a weak constitution that she often had to take to her bed for days or weeks at a time. Alice suffered, and she had to admit to herself sometimes that she would have been very glad to have a different mother, more lively, more active, better able to give her some support in this new and often difficult environment. One who could have joined her on hiking trips in the Taunus, like the ones she heard about from her friends from time to time, instead of, at best, sometimes taking her to the Palmengarten in Frankfurt to feed the ducks in the lake. Of course she would have quickly shoved such thoughts aside at the time and berated herself for being a bad, ungrateful daughter. She loved her mother above all else, and when Cornelia took her into her arms and hugged her close, Alice could have cried with joy.

Cornelia was a wonderful mother. So what if she didn't go on any hiking trips and rarely went out to see people, Alice had friends of her own. It was Cornelia who taught her daughter needlework and lace making, who showed her how to design a pattern and create sumptuous embroidery. It was also Cornelia who read books with her and told her stories.

Alice raises her head and contemplates the small, oval picture hanging over her desk: a colorized photograph of Cornelia as a little girl, four years old at most. A sweet child, still with baby fat and a much too serious face, a child who seems to look out at the world with suspicious eyes. You can see in this child, into whose chubby little baby hands the photographer had pressed a tendril of ivy and a couple of blue flowers, someone who shrinks back in fear from life. Only in her later years, when she was already a grandmother herself, did Cornelia grow stronger. Alice's gaze wanders to the large photograph hanging on the other wall: Cornelia as an older woman, in her severe widow's clothing. Cornelia still had the same serious look that she had as a little girl.

Cornelia was a good grandmother who was proud of her grandchildren and spoiled them and did everything she could for them. She adored Robert, Otto, and Herbert, but her special favorite was Leni, her granddaughter, who, like Cornelia herself, put a high value on her appearance. A certain vanity revealed itself in Leni very early on, an almost pedan-

Alice Frank's mother, Cornelia Stern née Cahn, as a child, circa 1844

tic approach to her person, and in this respect grandmother and granddaughter were very similar.

Cornelia, too, was always perfectly dressed; even when she lay sick in bed, she took good care to put on makeup and show herself only in a fancy nightgown and lace-fringed bed jacket. Unlike the elegant beauty and sophistication of her granddaughter,

Cornelia Stern née Cahn as an older woman

though, Cornelia's appearance had nothing provocative about it, nothing ostentatious. The difference from Leni was striking. Even as a child, Leni always headed straight at life with an open gaze and outstretched hands, while Cornelia always hung back, like someone who didn't dare walk through a door even if it stood wide open. She had always been fearful and sad, always anticipated terrible troubles. She didn't have the gift of happiness, a talent that no one could deny in Leni.

Ten chimes of the clock on the wall pull Alice out of her thoughts. High time for bed. She wipes the pen on the blotter and screws the inkwell shut. As she stands up and starts to get ready for bed, she thinks over all the preparations for the upcoming party that still need to be taken care of. Franzi, cook and maid in one, has to wash the curtains in the living room, kitchen, and guest room tomorrow; the curtains in the bedroom don't need it for now. She should also put clean sheets on the bed and the sofa in the guest room, so everything will be ready when Otto arrives with Margot.

Anne, the little girl, wouldn't be coming this time, unfortunately—that's what Otto had written—Anne had come with him to Sils-Maria in the summer, after all, and Margot had not, so this time Anne would stay with Edith in Amsterdam. Too bad. Alice has a special affinity with the younger daughter, maybe because she looks so similar to her father. And again she curses the Nazis, who have torn her family apart. Leni and Erich are here in Switzerland with their children, Stephan and Buddy; Robert has immigrated to London with his wife, Lotti; Herbert is in Paris; and Otto lives in Amsterdam with his wife, Edith, and children, Margot and Anne. If it weren't for the Nazis, they would all be celebrating still in Frankfurt, in her large house with enough room for everybody.

Two days go by before Alice sits back down at her desk; on the intervening day, Leni and Erich arrived to discuss the details of the party and decide on the menu. They settled on clear vegetable soup, then a trout au bleu, which Leni especially likes, then roast veal with potatoes and red cabbage, and a plum compote with whipped cream for dessert. Erich will take care of getting some good wine, and apple juice for the children. Alice unscrews the inkwell and lays out the pen. Then she rereads straight through what she has already written before getting back to work.

My mother felt great love & reverence, combined with great respect, for her old father, who was such a support for her. This rather strict man, who had spent his childhood in the ghetto but was not in the least pious, spoiled me in his way & I think back on him with great devotion.

My uncle Julius, who also lived there, was kind enough to give me many cheerful hours, as you would later be able to learn for yourselves. From him I learned a taste for good music, and the evenings with a string quartet, which never met with my grandfather's approval, were a rare joy for me even though I was only allowed to listen from the next room. Very few tastes or inclinations in common united me with my other uncle's son and daughter, even though we associated with each other in the same house every day. Maybe they were jealous that I was our grandfather's favorite more than they were. As a result, my uncle criticized my behavior a lot. There was constant friction, which bothered my mother but which I was more or less indifferent to & which didn't bother me very much.*

Alice has forgotten the causes of these arguments and tensions; they were probably in reality so trivial that there was no point in even trying to recall them. But she can still feel the atmosphere of the house, the complaining voice of her cousin and the reproachful, dejected reaction of her mother, who, although this

*Julius Cahn, one of Cornelia's brothers, later lived at Villa Hattstein in Falkenstein, in the Taunus mountains near the Rhine. The Frank family often visited him there.

became clear to her only much later, depended on the generosity of her father and her relatives. Alice's father had not left enough to guarantee a sufficient livelihood for his family.

My school years, up to my 15th year, were normal, no great expectations were made upon me, & since I had to leave school due to the worsening illness of my mother, my education was definitely mediocre. I caught up somewhat with private lessons that I had with my friends almost every day; I had many friends & we are still deeply devoted to each other, even today. What happy hours we spent in our "little circle"!—I could indulge my tendency to daydream all too easily while working on the many pieces of fine embroidery that were the fashion back then. These daydreams took me far away, to places that were unattainable for me, & my summons back to real life went less than smoothly frequently.

Alice puts down the pen and gently runs her fingers down the new lace collar she recently finished and sewed onto her dark wool dress. Even today needlework is her passion and she can spend hours working on it, thinking up endless new and more complicated patterns: animals, leaves, vines. All of the table linens in her apartment were made by hand—embroidered, crocheted, embellished with homemade lace, hemstitched, with pictures and monograms in delicate white embroidery. Tablecloths and place mats, napkins, doilies, handkerchiefs, underwear, collars on coats and blouses: she made them all herself. Even some of the lace curtains.

Needlework by Alice Frank

She can sit at the window for hours at a time, moving her fingers in an even rhythm. She is happy when animals appear under her fingers—deer, sheep, swans, and fabulous beasts; flowers, branches, leaves, grapes, always another new ornament—and every time another piece is finished, she feels a great sense of satisfaction and pride that comes from within, irrespective of the judgment of others. It is a deep need she has, to produce something that is not only useful but beautiful too, almost as if she were bringing beauty into the world with the work of her hands, and thereby making the world a little bit better. She sometimes thinks that the needle for her is what the pen must be to a poet, and the thread is her ink; sometimes she compares her work to a painter's. If she had not come into the world as a woman, she might perhaps have become a great painter. Sitting with her needlework and dreaming away while something beautiful takes shape under her fingers is her greatest pleasure. But whereas her dreams used to carry her off into unreachable distances, today they tend to carry her into what is—for now at least—a no-longer-reachable past.

If, in later years, I was able to see the foreign lands I had always longed for with my own eyes, I have only the goodness of your father to thank for this happiness.

I attracted his attention when I was only 15, but of course I was much too young & thoroughly inexperienced to think much about it. Still, I happily accepted every proof of his interest in me.—In any case, my thoughts & feelings were going in entirely other directions at that time, which your father well knew but which didn't hinder him from showing me how pleased he was with me.—These events, unforgettable for me, that I mentioned above, I would rather leave unmentioned here, since they affect only me & only call up painful memories in me that should in no way concern and burden you.—

Alice could not remember the exact occasion when she met Michael, but he knew it precisely: it was at a party at the Gymnasium Francofurtanum. He had liked her right away, he told her later, he had even danced with her, a galop, but she hadn't especially noticed him. He chalked up her lack of interest to her youth—she was fifteen, and he was fourteen years older, almost twice her age. She was in love with a boy at the time, for the first time—an unhappy love that caused her much heartache. Later, though, when she kept seeing Michael at parties and receptions at friends' and acquaintances', and became more and more interested in him, and her interest turned to love, and she finally gave in and accepted his proposal, she was grateful that fate had kept her for him. She could not have found a better husband than Michael Frank. It was his love and generosity that opened up the world for her.

I did not lack for admirers, and heaps of flowers and poems flew into the house that was run so puritanically—this caused displeasure in my family, especially since these suitors did not always come from so-called "good society" & therefore had to undergo severe criticism. I didn't care as much about that. I was happy to accept every sign of youthful enthusiasm & the "serenades" connected to it. And how perfect the ground-floor windows were for these serenades, in that house on Hochstrasse that was otherwise so dreary!—I took my first great trip when I was 16, to see my cousin in Bern who was married by then. The great occasion was duly planned, and well-meaning warnings and recommendations were not lacking. The journey that brought us first to Mannheim, where I was invited to a magnificent concert of the then very famous Florentine Quartet in a private residence, was the overture for many lovely & enjoyable hours. I spent almost 3 months with my relatives, in complete harmony, & I met a number of very interesting people there. The old-fashioned city also made a powerful impression on me & so I returned home with many stories to tell. Of course I had also realized that much was lacking in my education, which I then attempted to improve with diligent reading & study, and to some extent I succeeded.

Alice stands up, stretches, and shakes out her cramped writing hand. Klärchen, her favorite cousin, daughter of her uncle

Bernhard Stern, was then, in 1881, newly married, and in fact to another cousin, Alfred Stern. Klara and Alfred lived in Bern. He was already a well-known historian by then, a professor at the University of Bern, and he and his young wife kept a large house. Alice still remembers that he had just finished writing a new book, *The History of the English Revolution*. Alice had admired Alfred, and had even envied Klärchen a little for this clever, eminent husband. The whole family, in fact, was proud of him. His father, Dr. Moritz Abraham Stern, a brother of Alice's grandfather Emanuel Stern, had been the first unconverted Jew in Germany to become a full professor, at the University of Göttingen, after receiving a doctorate from the famous mathematician Carl Friedrich Gauss.

Alice remembers the last time she saw Alfred, two years ago, at Klärchen's funeral. Alfred had grown old, old and withdrawn. For the first time in her experience, he lacked the warmth that had always distinguished him. It was as though with the death of his wife he had lost his soul.

Alice quickly pushes this thought aside and returns to her happier memories of young Klara and young Alfred. The couple, who later had three daughters, Dora, Emma, and Toni, seemed to have had a good marriage—in any case, back then as fresh-faced newlyweds, they were happy. The weeks in Bern, as far as Alice can remember, were marked by laughter and good cheer, excursions and countless invitations. Still, she couldn't help but realize that there were many topics she was unable to join the conversations about. When friends or guests mentioned books, she had often never even heard the name of the author, much less the title. Everyone she met in Bern, literally every person, seemed far more educated than she was, and she often enough turned red and had to lower her head in embarrassment when someone asked her opinion of a play or an actor or a particular staging of an opera.

After returning home, she started to read, to fill in the gaps in her education, and she studied foreign languages more intensively too. The idea of standing there as an uneducated person and making herself the laughingstock of the group was unbearable to her. In that way it was an important and consequential trip for her, entirely aside from how much she had enjoyed her time with Klärchen.

Alice is tired, very tired. She looks at the clock and sees that it is already after ten. She must have been so deep in thought that she didn't hear the chimes of the clock. She will write more tomorrow, tomorrow is another day.

The next evening, Alice turns on the light and pulls the curtains shut early, at six, because Franzi has taken the day off to visit her parents, who are celebrating their golden wedding anniversary. It rained all day. Hopefully, the weather will get better soon. Alice would be happiest if there was a clean, pure white blanket of snow on the ground for her birthday, white as a tablecloth laid out for a special occasion, and a clear blue sky up above, with a cold winter sun. She smiles at this childish wish, which she has had every year for as long as she can remember but which only rarely came true. She sits down at the desk and prepares her things to keep writing.

After my grandfather passed away in 1884, my very unhappy mother and I moved into an apartment in the Trutz. This change brought great transformations to my life once again; now I was thrown back on myself even more & the influence of the family on my mother was also somewhat alleviated. A close relationship with my best friend, Emma [Steger], helped very much to raise my confidence, since she was a very insecure person & clung to me as the younger and livelier friend. As a result I was able to defend myself vigorously when a marriage in England was arranged for me right after my 18th birthday. I would*

*A street near the Eschenheimer Tower.

never have agreed to such a separation from my mother, especially since I was bound with every fiber of my being to my homeland.

Home . . . Her home is Frankfurt, the city of her childhood, her youth, and her years as a wife and mother. She would never have moved away from Frankfurt of her own free will, if this wretched Austrian had not come to power there, this screechy little troublemaker who is far too frightening, though, for her to be able to laugh at him.

And not just frightening to her! On many, many long evenings she sat with her sons Robert and Otto and discussed the situation. It had got more and more difficult after the bank that Michael had founded lost almost everything in the great stock market crash on October 25, 1929. Erich was the first to come to the appropriate conclusion, and he quickly found a position in Switzerland, in Basel. Two years later, Leni and little Buddy had followed. Leni left their older son, Stephan, who was already in school, with her, Stephan's grandmother, for a time. He was to follow his mother and brother after the school year was over.

The financial situation was beyond difficult. Otto had even had to give notice at his apartment on Marbachweg, and he and his family lived with her again, on Jordanstrasse, which had already been renamed Mertonstrasse. But without the political developments it would probably have never reached the stage of their all being forcibly separated. After the local election of March 1933, however, when the Jewish mayor, Ludwig Landmann, was forced out and the Nazi party member Friedrich Krebs became the new mayor of Frankfurt, they realized that they had no future in Germany. When Leni's husband, who worked for Pomosin in Switzerland, arranged a position for Otto as the company representative in the Netherlands, his choice was clear: to move to Amsterdam with Edith and the girls. Robert wanted to try to open an art gallery in England, and Herbert, the problem child, wanted to stay in Paris.

They had talked about Palestine, too, to which many Jews now wanted to immigrate, but it wasn't an option for them. "What would we do in a country that's just a desert? No theater, everyone speaking a foreign language, it's so hot that you can't walk down the street, if there even is a street," Alice had said. And Leni added, "A country where you can't give children any culture."

They all agreed. Otto said, "We don't belong there. We Jews have lived here in Germany for almost two thousand years. We are educated, cultured, we are Jewish of course but not Orthodox. We have nothing in common with those eastern Jews, the merchants and factory workers who are largely Zionists because they have no other choice. We have absolutely nothing to do with those Eastern European rabbis. No, we could live in another European country, or America, but not in Asia."

For Alice it was clear from the beginning that she would follow Leni to Switzerland. A mother belongs near her daughter. And now she has been here in Basel for two years already. But this city has never become her home—it is too provincial, the pace of life is too slow. And how can you compare the theater, the opera, the whole cultural and social life here in Basel with the one she knows from Frankfurt? Not to mention the frightful Swiss German everyone speaks here, which she can still barely understand—this guttural croaking that sounds so much more unfriendly than the much softer Frankfurt German she knows so well. Alice sighs and picks up her pen again.

Almost 2 years followed that I would probably call the most wonderful & carefree years of my life. Love and friendship were shown to me from every side, and to some extent that is still true, & I responded with all of my heart.

For a long time your father had not ceased to direct his attention toward me. This got back to my mother & since she saw that I was deeply fond of him too, the family consulted and took the decision to remove me for a while from this apparently dangerous environment.

Even though in truth we could only be together on relatively rare occasions, & then it was usually possible only with great difficulty & with the help of trusted dear friends, nonetheless we were certain of our mutual love & had decided to bind ourselves together for life. But when it would be possible—that was far from clear to us . . . I took a trip to Switzerland in good spirits with my cousin Richard, felt very happy there & in no way exiled, and with my cheerfulness and good mood I put on a façade of forgetting. It was not true in the least, but was met on all sides with a sigh of relief & the goal of the trip was considered fully accomplished.

Soon after I got back, we surprised all the relatives with the fait accompli of our engagement, without having asked anyone for advice or permission. This caused a great sensation at first, of course, & my mother had to withstand a heavy flood of accusations which she in no way felt up to. You can guess how hard it was for her to accustom herself to the thought that she would have to let me go, you who knew her well yourselves. But later she had your father to thank for many good & beautiful things.—At first it was extremely difficult for me to get used to the duties one has toward brothers and sisters, since of course I had never had any, & it was only after a considerable length of time that I learned to understand what this unconditional belonging together really means. How deeply in later years I grew attached to and loved all these dear people. You as well have had only good & beautiful experiences with all of them.

Not much more remains for me now to tell you & report about my youth.

You have grown up into thinking people, you had a sunny & happy childhood. We did everything in our power to make your lives & your childhood beautiful & happy. These memories have stayed with you and remain today, & may they stay faithfully in your minds, more than ever, since the serious times have separated us & each of you has had to travel your own path.—I hope I can still accompany you for a little while longer, but I cannot give you any more help or support. But knowing that my deepest, most heartfelt thoughts are always with you will give you, I hope, something stable to rely on, something you can always feel surrounding you even though you are all mature, grown people yourselves.—Even when countries and oceans separate you, never forget the beautiful childhood you had together, which was meant to give you & did give you a guiding thread for your whole lives. Always keep as a valuable treasure the memory of the family home, filled with love, & do not let the image of it fade in your minds.

Your Mother

Basel, December 1935

Two days later they arrive, Otto and Margot. Franzi has prepared a light supper, and Margot, worn out from the long train ride, has gone to bed early. Franzi has tidied up the kitchen before withdrawing to her attic room, and Alice and Otto sit together for a while longer. Alice examines the new photographs her son has brought with him from Amsterdam, especially the pictures of Anne.

Otto also tells her that his business is slowly but surely getting off the ground; the sales reps have sold significantly more pectin in the past six months than in the whole previous year, he says, and they have had a very good autumn. The business outlook is getting better and better, and the children are a great joy to them. It is harder for Edith to get used to living in the Netherlands than it is for him, though. She is having greater difficulties with the foreign language and is not making new friends. Even now, after two years, she still feels homesick. But it's going very well for the children; it is truly a joy to watch them grow up. They speak Dutch like natives, he says, and Anne is happy in school.

Alice could listen to him talk for hours, but Otto looks exhausted, the long journey was hard for him too. So she does not protest when he withdraws. Before she goes to sleep, she stays standing at the door to the guest room for a little while, listening. She can't hear anything—father and daughter are both asleep. Alice smiles. What a beautiful, clever girl the nine-year-old Margot is. And so tomorrow is the great birthday celebration.

Alice goes to her bedroom, takes the letter she had finished out of the desk drawer, and adds something more at the end, a P.S. for her grandchildren Stephan, Buddy, and Margot:

And now to my little ones, with our little Annelein missing, unfortunately. I would like to imprint this day especially into the memory of the three of you. Not because of outward presents but because of all the love & devotion that you have experienced today with us grown-ups, December 20th should be & remain a day for you to remember. You must all know that no one except your parents loves you as much as

Your
Grandma

2.

Where We Come From

Alice had the good fortune to be born into a family where many stories were told and much was handed down from one generation to the next. In her letter to her sons, Robert, Otto, and Herbert, and her daughter, Leni, she wrote that her grandfather Elkan Juda Cahn had still lived in the ghetto as a young man. It was he who had passed the memories of Judengasse, or "Jews' Alley," the Jewish street in Frankfurt, down to the family.

These images of the past must have lived on in his daughter Cornelia and his granddaughter Alice, because what grandfather does not tell his children and grandchildren how different life used to be back then, back in his day, especially when the economic and social relations were so drastically different, as was the case between Elkan Juda Cahn and his descendants? Only in later generations do the images start to fade, the stories lose their vitality, until finally only a couple of memorial objects remain. For example, Buddy Elias, Anne Frank's last living cousin, has hanging in his house a hand-tinted photograph of Elkan Juda Cahn and his wife, Betty, and the family possessions include a twenty-four-place set of silverware, hand forged from real silver, bearing the initials EJC. That is what remains of him. How he lived, what he dreamed, and which dreams he was able to make come true—no stories are told about any of that anymore.

But Alice doubtless grew up with stories of Judengasse. Her

grandfather would have told her about the old days sometimes; he would have said: "I didn't have it as good as you do." And then he would have described the little alley, only four or five blocks long, surrounded by walls and so narrow that no cart could turn around in it. Only north of the synagogue that stood at the middle of the Judengasse was it a little wider, but even there not wide enough for any light, air, or sunshine to make its way in.

Starting in 1462, all the Frankfurt Jews, who had previously lived in the middle of the city, most of them near the cathedral, had had to move into the newly built houses along the medieval city wall. There were gates at both ends of the alley, which were locked in the evenings and on Christian holidays, and there was also the Judenbrückelchen Bridge near the middle of the street. Every time Elkan Juda Cahn spoke of the gates, he emphasized that the gates and walls not only locked the Jews in but also protected them against enemy incursions and raids. In fact, in some cities, such as Speyer, the Jews had been petitioning for centuries to be allowed to enclose their quarter in walls.

In Frankfurt, on the other hand, the city council had forced the Jews to move to the Judengasse. The houses were spacious enough for all 110 people to live comfortably at first, but in the sixteenth century the number of inhabitants multiplied many times over, and it grew more and more crowded. The city council nevertheless refused to grant permission for any expansion.

"When I was a boy," Elkan Juda Cahn said, "the northern part of the Judengasse had already burned down, but my father, Nathan David, always told me how it was when he was young. Back then, unbearably cramped conditions were prevalent. Back then, more than three thousand people lived in the Judengasse, and they built on every inch—every courtyard, every little garden, the cemetery, everything, everything was built on, and whatever could be added to and built up higher, was. Every Sukkot arbor had been turned into a house, and they even built more houses on the roofs of the other houses. The rooms had got so small and narrow that you could put a bed only on the long side. You can't imagine how cramped and crowded everything was."

Alice couldn't really imagine it, of course, even though in her own childhood in the eighth decade of the nineteenth century the remains of the Judengasse were still standing: pitiful, narrow houses, where she never would have wanted to live. When her grandfather talked about how his father, Nathan David, and the

Elkan Juda Cahn and his wife, Betty (Anne Frank's great-great-grandparents)

other Jews had lived, she always pictured in her mind the anthills in the Palmengarten, which Richard, Klärchen's brother, used to poke around in with a branch he had broken off. Even less could she imagine her own grandfather, this respectable and prosperous businessman, and his father, Nathan David, whom she knew only from stories, as dirty little boys in the Judengasse, when he described the filth and the stink that you could never overcome. "The open sewers that the inhabitants had for their needs were always clogged, and the street was so narrow that you could barely get enough air to breathe. The stink was horrible. No wonder the children were pale and thin and suffered from scabies, cradle cap, impetigo, and the like. Even though they played and ran around in the street the way all children do, until they were old enough to take on their share of obligations."

But Nathan David, his father, had had it better than the other children, Alice's grandfather went on. Already as a young man he often went with his father as a peddler to the surrounding villages: to nearby Taunus, to Wetterau, and as far away as the Odenwald. They had dealt in old things—junk, used clothing. The Jews were not allowed to practice any handicrafts, because that might have cut into the guilds' business and they blocked all possible competition. Aside from butchering and baking for their own needs, the only trade left to the Jews was in old, used things—officially, anyway. Even back then, the residents of the Judengasse had begun to make new clothes and sell them; there were more than enough people there who could sew.

"My father loved to go wandering as a peddler," Alice's grandfather said. "It was the only way to get out of the stink and the cramped conditions, and see other things. Other faces, red from the sun, animals, birds, trees, fields, meadows. And the sky. In the Judengasse you could never really see the sky, he said. Peddling was a joy for him, he could move around and finally breathe some fresh air for once. He was healthier than most of the others. And then he always told us what a splendid experience it was for him to pick an apple from a tree. Or go looking for wild strawberries, which they never, ever had at the Jewish market."

Sometimes he was gone for days and came home only just before the Sabbath. Then his father would put the little money that he had earned on the table and head off to the ritual bath in the cellar of one of the houses, to purify himself before the Sabbath started. Nathan David would stretch out on his bed, and his mother would rub his swollen feet with oil. "The rich Jews who traveled to other countries to sell their wares had horses and carriages, of course, which they kept outside of the Judengasse, or they rented them for the journey. But everyone else had to go on foot. Sometimes someone would take pity on them and bring them part of the way in his wagon or oxcart, but most of the time that didn't happen, they were more often spat on. It was hard work to go from village to village, from house to house, to knock on strangers' doors and offer their wares."

"Why didn't they have a store?" Alice asked once. "It's a lot easier to sell things in a store."

"Jews were not allowed to have stores," her grandfather answered.

Until the ghetto was dissolved, it was prohibited for Jews to own stores outside Judengasse. It was forbidden for the rich Jews too, the pawnbrokers and money changers, although of course they found ways to get their wares from the Judengasse to the Christian part of the city, through middlemen. Especially in spring and fall, when there were the great fairs in Frankfurt and things were being bought and sold throughout the city, when merchants and sellers poured into the city from the surrounding areas, near and far. Many Jews dealt in "foreign trade"; in other words, they took long trips, as far as England, and sold fabrics, silks, brightly patterned brocades, lace, jewelry and other decorations of embossed silver, and whatever else the rich aristocrats and patricians needed for their lavish lifestyles. And since a ban on usury was imposed upon the churches and cloisters in the

Middle Ages, the Jews had, from early on, resorted to money lending and collecting interest. The large number of small states and principalities, and the desire of the princes and noblemen to keep a lavish court, made money lending necessary even aside from all the wars that needed to be waged. The Jews were traders, merchants, and bankers; they specialized in high-risk credit and short-term loans; and the noblemen not only tolerated high interest rates but demanded them, because then their profit was higher too, from taxes. The "Jew profiteer" typically made his money from the poorer city residents and farmers, of course, which stirred up hatred against the Jews. But from changing money, and loaning money against collateral—money that often could not be repaid, so the collateral was forfeited—arose great warehouses, stockpiles, and finally businesses. And from the earlier money-lending businesses grew the banks, especially in the seventeenth and eighteenth centuries. They were founded, went bankrupt, and made way for new establishments. The chain of Jewish money changers in Frankfurt remained unbroken down to the Rothschilds. And the military supply business gave rise to a brisk trade in horses.

"The life the Jews led was really hard. There were plenty of times that they didn't have enough to eat," Elkan Juda Cahn said. "If my father's name had been Rothschild, or Speyer, it would have been a different story, but his name was just Cahn."

"Why are you saying that?" Alice protested. "You usually always say that we should be proud to be descendants of the Cahns."

"Yes, all Jews named Cahn or Cohn or anything like that are *cohanim.* They belong to the priestly caste and descend from Aaron, Moshe Rabbeinu's brother. Aaron was the first high priest of our people, chosen by God, a peaceful man whose rod made flowers bloom."

Alice had heard this many times before; it didn't interest her, at least not at the time. "Tell me about the rich Jews," she pleaded. "Tell me about the Rothschilds."

"I knew one myself, old Mayer Amschel Rothschild, who founded the great banking house M. A. Rothschild & Sons and later managed the finances at the court of the Hessian landgrave. The Rothschilds lived in the Haus zum Grünen Schild, the House of the Green Shield, across from the Judenbrückelchen. Mayer Amschel started making coins and medallions, and later became the main military contractor. He dealt in textiles with England, changed money, and finally moved into the banking business with loans to the state. Aside from all that, he married well. Meyer Amschel's wife, Gutle, was the daughter of Wolf Salomon Schnapper, the court chamberlain, and she belonged to one of the old Frankfurt families. His sons settled all across Europe and founded affiliate banks in Vienna, Naples, London, and Paris. Even so, they always came back to Frankfurt—their roots were in the Judengasse, and they never tried to hide it. These weren't the only rich Jews, there were also the Speyers, the Rindskopfs, the Mayers. Of course rabbis and Torah scribes lived in the Judengasse too, learned and educated men, but there were many more servants, day laborers, and beggars. In truth, there was everything, occasionally great riches and more often poverty and misery, sickness and hunger."

Alice thought about what her grandmother Helene Stern had told her and Klärchen about the old days: the many children who never had their own room, or toys, or nice clothes, and who had to sleep two to a bed, or three, or sometimes four—two at the head and two at the foot. About the women who often didn't know how they were going to feed their many children, who had to do all the housework themselves, who had no maids or cooks, and who were so weakened by their many childbirths that they sometimes died in childbed. "Like your grandfather's first wife," Grandmother Helene always said then. "May the earth on her grave be light, her life was heavy enough." After these words, she always raised her hand and wiped her eyes, and Alice and Klärchen looked away, embarrassed.

Grandfather went on: "Life was merciless and hard. The only diversion was the holidays. The Jewish children looked forward to Purim all year."

Yes, Grandmother Helene had told stories about all the fun Purim games too: about how they would march through the Judengasse singing and dancing. She also told stories about the fires, though, that sometimes broke out because everything was so cramped and crowded. And about the hooligans who would tear through the Judengasse on the Christian holidays. The mothers would bring their children indoors and hide them in cupboards or under the beds until the danger passed.

Alice's grandfather had kept talking, even though she wasn't listening—had described how the children dressed on Purim and the plays they would put on. Now he was saying: "When I was a boy, there was still Purim Vincent."

"Purim Vincent?" Alice asked. "What's that?"

"In memory of the Fettmilch uprising," he said.

"*Fettmilch?* Whole milk?" Alice was confused. "Why not sour beer or skim milk?"

"Fettmilch was someone's name," her grandfather explained, and began another story. "At the beginning of the seventeenth century there was an uprising of the people of Frankfurt against the city council."

The uprising, named after its leader, Vincent Fettmilch, broke out in 1612 when the coronation of Emperor Matthias took place in Frankfurt and the council, in accordance with a regulation of the Golden Bull, required the guilds to pay for the protection of the prince. The guilds countered with demands of their own, including a reduction in the number of Jews and a retroactive decrease in the interest rate on loans by Jews from 12 percent to 8 percent. The council, and even the emperor himself, rejected these demands, and a gang of rebels banded together under Vincent Fettmilch. Even when the interest rate was, in the end, actually lowered, they were not satisfied. Now they were demanding that every Jew who possessed less than fifteen thousand guldens' worth of belongings leave the city. Since Emperor Matthias took the side of the Jews, Fettmilch and his followers turned to violence. They invaded the Judengasse, ransacked the houses, laid waste to the synagogue, and forced 1,380 Jews to leave the city, abandoning all their possessions. These Jews were taken in by the neighboring towns, such as Offenbach and Hanau.

The rebel bands terrorized the city for almost two years until they were finally defeated and the Frankfurt Jews were officially welcomed back into their houses. Fettmilch and five other ringleaders were hanged that same day. An earlier emperor had mortgaged the Jews to the city of Frankfurt; now Matthias placed the imperial coat of arms on the gates of the Jewish quarter, with the words "Protectorate of His Roman Imperial Majesty and the Holy Roman Empire." He thereby emphasized his overarching authority, without dissolving the mortgage, so that a sort of double authority over the Jews—the city council and the emperor—remained in place. On Matthias's orders, the city of Frankfurt had to pay the Jews 175,919 guldens in compensation.

"The Jews celebrated the day of their return, 20 Adar,* as Purim Vincent for a long time," Elkan Juda Cahn concluded the story. "But as time passed, the custom was forgotten. You see, there was enough suffering in the Judengasse during the centuries of its existence. In 1819, when I had already moved out of the Judengasse, there was another pogrom that started in Würzburg and spread through all of Germany. Frankfurt was not spared. With shouts of 'Hep-Hep! Die, Jew!' Jewish homes and businesses were ransacked and destroyed. The attackers broke windows, in the Rothschilds' bank too, and beat Jews on the street in broad daylight."

"You too?" Alice asked.

Her grandfather shook his head. "No, I was lucky."

*March 10.

"And how was it when the Judengasse was dissolved and the Jews were allowed to live anywhere?"

"It started in 1796, the year I was born. Napoleon ruled in France and he gave Jews the same rights as all other citizens. After the French Revolution, the demands for liberty, equality, and fraternity spread. In 1796 the French troops laid siege to Frankfurt and conquered the city. Fires broke out everywhere, the worst in the Judengasse. About a hundred residences in the northern part of the street were destroyed, and almost two thousand Jews were suddenly homeless. They rented apartments from Christians, and that was the beginning of the end for the Judengasse, though it took until 1812 before the Jews were finally no longer subject to the *Stättigkeit* and—at least in part—received the rights of citizenship. But they paid heavily for it."

"*Stättigkeit,* I don't know what that word means."

"That's what they called the regulations applying to Jewish residents in Frankfurt. The *Stättigkeit* also stated how much they were required to pay for the right of residence, and what they were allowed to do, such as where they could do business. More than anything, it set out what they were not allowed to do: live outside of the Judengasse, go for a walk in the city parks, marry when they wanted—there was a set number of weddings allowed too, just like the set number of Jews who were allowed to move to Frankfurt from elsewhere. That all changed under Napoleon."

In 1806, Napoleon declared Frankfurt the administrative capital of the Confederation of the Rhine and made Prince Primate Karl von Dalberg the ruler of the city. Dalberg was a man of the Enlightenment, and he admired Napoleon, but he did not want to start a fight with the citizens of Frankfurt, who vehemently opposed equal rights for Jews. As a result, he enacted the New Stättigkeit and Protective Regulations for the Jewish Population of Frankfurt am Main in 1807. According to the new laws, Jews were required to live in a Jewish quarter that comprised the Judengasse and adjacent areas. Their education and schools were tightly regulated. And the protection money they were required to pay annually was raised to twenty-two thousand guldens. It was a serious setback for the Jews. Only when Dalberg's government ran into grave financial difficulties, in 1811, did he sign an edict of emancipation in exchange for 440,000 guldens. In this Highest Decree Concerning the Civil Rights of the Jewish Community of Frankfurt, it stated: "Henceforth the Israelite inhabitants of the city of Frankfurt shall enjoy the same civil rights and privileges under the same obligations as the other, Christian citizens, and all prior regulations, decrees, and customary laws concerning the previous inequality of rights and levies are hereby abrogated and no longer in effect."

"One hundred and fifty thousand guldens had to be paid right away," Elkan Juda Cahn told Alice, "or else Dalberg would not have signed it. I was fifteen, and I still remember how hard it was for us to come up with the money. Everyone gave what they could, but without the help of the Rothschild bank we would never have managed it. The community paid interest on the loans until 1863, even though the Jews' equal rights were rescinded only four years after they were proclaimed. Even so, there was no going back to how it was."

No, there was no going back. In 1812, three Jews attained public office: Mayer Amschel Rothschild was elected to the Wahlkollegium;* Dr. Joseph Oppenheimer took over the office after Rothschild's death, and the following year became municipal councilor and a member of the city school board; lastly, Ludwig Börne, then still named Löw Baruch, a well-respected man who published books and newspapers and fought against anti-Semitism and for freedom of the press, was appointed police actuary (clerk of the law court). Even if a few years later, when the old restrictions on Jews were put back into effect, he had to fight

*The Wahlkollegium was an electoral college of 75 citizens who chose slightly more than half the members of Frankfurt's legislative body.

for his position and was eventually retired with a pension, such a thing had never existed before. Napoleon's troops had spread the idea of emancipation and civil rights through all of Europe, and it could no longer be withstood. Frankfurt withstood it a bit longer than other places, in any case, since the Christian citizens did not want to grant Jews equal rights. But the Judengasse was never built up again, even though many Frankfurt citizens demanded it. There was a constant oscillation between hope and disappointment, from the failed National Assembly and all the quarrels that went with it up to the founding of the monarchy.

"But in the end we got our rights," Alice's grandfather said triumphantly. "Now we are free citizens, just like the Christians. You are lucky, Alice. You were born in a better time than I was."

"Back when you were allowed to leave the Judengasse, was that when you bought this house?" Alice wanted to know.

"No," her grandfather said. "First I lived on Langestrasse. Your mother was born there. I only bought this house much later. But some Jews had magnificent, elegant houses built, even under Dalberg—real palaces. For example, the banker Zacharias Wertheimer whose house, the Red Tower, had been destroyed in the fire of 1796, had a palace built ten years later. And in the burned-out part of the Judengasse, the Rothschilds built a new office building on the foundations of five houses that had burned down; that was at the top of the street, by the Bornheimer Gate, where the north gate of the Judengasse used to be."

"When you lived in the Judengasse, were you still Orthodox?"

Elkan Juda Cahn shook his head. "We were not Orthodox. I don't know why, that's just how it was with us. But if you want to know more about that, you should ask your uncle, Bernhard Stern, the doctor—he studied in school, he knows a lot more about all that than I do. The Sterns are an old, respected family, and I was really very proud when your mother married your father. Ask Uncle Bernhard."

And Alice did. The next time she was sitting with Klärchen in the elegant salon of the Stern house, she noticed the portrait of

Süsskind Stern from 1671, the very first portrait of a Frankfurt Jew, as her uncle Bernhard liked to point out again and again. "Did the Sterns use to be pious Jews?"

Uncle Bernhard, sitting at the table smoking his pipe, nodded. "Yes, they were always good Jews, you would have to say that, at least in earlier times. Your great-grandfather, Abraham Süsskind Stern, was a scholar. He was a bookseller, but in truth he dedicated his life to studying the Talmud. I myself saw very many books with countless notes and annotations in his handwriting at the house of his son, my uncle, Moritz Abraham Stern. He thought of Moses Mendelssohn as his model. Moses Mendelssohn was a great philosopher who translated the Jewish Bible into German so that his brethren who didn't know Hebrew could read it as well. He was interested in science and art but still strictly followed the laws of the Torah."

"And what about my grandfather?" Alice asked. "Did he also strictly follow the laws?"

Uncle Bernhard laughed. "No. Moritz was very different from his brothers, Jakob and Emanuel, who would hesitate even to eat in a Christian household. Your great-grandparents, though, were truly religious, especially your great-grandmother Vögele Eva Reiss. I definitely have to tell you about her.

"She was twenty-one years old when her family lost their house and all their possessions in the fire of 1796, but she didn't let that stop her. She got silk fabric from an uncle who was a silk dealer and sold it at a profit, mostly to French émigrés. That earned her enough money not only to support her family but to put together a dowry for one of her sisters. She was an extremely capable and fearless woman. When she heard that Bavarian soldiers were ransacking the Judengasse, she got a high-ranking Bavarian officer to accompany her there. The looters were disobeying their commander and drawing their weapons when Vögele, the young Jewess, walked right into the thick of the melee and didn't budge until at last Herr von Bethmann arrived with a company of Cossacks to drive off the Bavarians. She was a strict woman, but

Portrait of Süsskind Stern, 1671

fair and generous. No beggar left her doorstep empty-handed. And when a maid, Jitel Dudelsheim, who had worked for her for decades, grew old and sick, she took her in and took care of her like a member of the family. And she was truly religious. Even in her old age she fasted on the Day of Atonement. I can still see her now, sitting in her simply furnished living room on Allerheiligengasse: a small, venerable woman, hair covered in a black scarf and a white cap. Or standing, already a very old woman, in her little shop between rolls tied with silk ribbons and bundles of pencils. As children we never once left her presence without her putting her hands on our heads and blessing us.

"She and her husband, Abraham Süsskind, took the raising of their sons very seriously, especially their son Moritz Abraham, who showed great intelligence from early on. Uncle Moritz had a huge effect on my intellectual and moral development. As a young man I lived in his house for more than three years, while I was a medical student in Göttingen. I was his favorite nephew—he said so again and again—and his influence on me can absolutely not be overestimated. His parents didn't let Uncle Moritz go to a public school, as other Jewish children were already doing at the time; instead, he was taught at home, by tutors. He learned Latin and Greek, he is a superb Hebraist, and he is deeply familiar with German literature as well. Even as a young man he loved Schiller and Goethe and was inspired by Fouqué's novels. He is truly an extraordinary man. Wait a minute, I want to read you something."

Uncle Bernhard opened a cabinet, took out a thick notebook, and opened it with reverence. "My cousin Alfred, who was only a boy when I was living with them in Göttingen, once secretly showed me his father's, Uncle Moritz's, diary. I know that it was wrong to look, but I was curious, and then I copied out the beginning because it made such an impression on me. And it inspired me to keep a diary myself. Uncle Moritz was sixteen when he wrote this, younger than you are now, Klärchen. Listen:

My Diary
Dedicated to myself

For a considerable time now I have entertained the desire to compose a diary, in which I might have as it were a mirror to keep myself perpetually in view by setting down my innermost thoughts, observations, conversations, &c., and then later, in cold blood, precisely investigating these data to determine what is good in them and what is bad, with the firm determination to root out the weeds that deprive the flower of virtue of its soil and thus enable that flower to sprout up in its fullness all the more resplendently. Only by repeatedly reviewing one's mistakes is it possible for the resolution to improve oneself to take root; otherwise it is all too quickly blotted out of our minds as soon as a new pleasure appears, just as the straight road vanishes from the eye of the wanderer whenever he lets himself be led astray by the glittering shimmer of the will-o'-the-wisp. Even the smallest deeds should not be exempt. For can Man, stumbling blindly into the future, seeing only the present, truly say with any certainty that this or that deed is insignificant? The book of history shows us thousands of examples that contradict this idea. A single word, a movement, a breath can have the greatest effect on our whole lives and bring joy or sorrow. Now this thought has reached maturity, and I plan to, God willing, follow it throughout my entire life.

Today I have turned 16 years old, I am no longer a child, and I have begun to have more serious thoughts and to look to the future with a more focused gaze. Still, relying on God and His assistance, I will always be happy so long as it pleases Him to grant me my health. May it please Him to let me become a good man, so that I might be a joy to my parents in their old age—they to whom I owe so much and who have had so much trouble on my account, who have been so patient with me—and also that I might be of some use to the rest of my fellow men. Amen.

Uncle Bernhard lowered the notebook and looked at the two girls. "Can you imagine what kind of man this boy would become, and why his influence on me was so great?"

The girls nodded, although Alice simply could not imagine her great-uncle Moritz as a sixteen-year-old. She knew him from his visits to Frankfurt: he always stayed with Uncle Bernhard, and Alice avoided visiting the Sterns when he was there. Uncle Moritz was a strict old man with penetrating eyes; when he was around, Alice always had the feeling of looking wrong, saying the wrong thing, and not behaving the way she should. Klärchen, too, was a little afraid of him and always glad when he left.

"He has an indomitable personality," Uncle Bernhard continued. "Some people call him stubborn too. He began quite early on to doubt the sacred character of many of the traditional forms of Jewish practice. A friend told me that Moritz had a secular book under his prayer shawl in the synagogue once—Goethe's *Faust*—and was reading it while everyone thought he was deep in prayer. Then he studied mathematics in Göttingen, under Gauss, and that was where he met up with his brother Emanuel again, your grandfather, Alice. Emanuel had gone off on adventures to South America after the firm he was working for, Wolf, went bankrupt. Young Emanuel was a good musician; he became choirmaster for a battalion of the French civic militia and met a traveling recruiter whose job it was to find soldiers for the Brazilian government. Emanuel followed the call and set off for Brazil. He caught yellow fever not long after he got there and was taken to the military hospital, but he survived. A businessman who knew him from Frankfurt helped him get out of the army and paid an English ship's captain to bring his protégé back to Europe as a 'sick sailor.' Emanuel showed up in Göttingen with a sunburned face and his clothing in tatters—his money had run out. So Uncle Moritz supplied the necessary funds and sent him back to Frankfurt, while he himself stayed in Göttingen. He couldn't become a professor at first, because he was Jewish, but he did become a lecturer at the university."

Moritz Abraham Stern never cut his ties to the Judengasse, and even though it took almost two days to travel by post coach from Göttingen to Frankfurt, he often returned home, especially when the Jewish Reform Society invited him to work with them. He was convinced that the Jews not only needed to put aside the strict observances of their religion but should even give up their hope in the coming of the Messiah, and he felt that their homeland was nothing more and nothing less than the country where they were born, their secular fatherland. In a letter to a friend that was later published, he expressed himself this way:

When I ask myself what it is that obliges me to work for the Jews and their betterment, I am constrained to answer that it is in no way a sense of religious fellow feeling with the great majority of the faithful, since for a long time I have doubtless been as far removed from the Jewish faith as from Christianity. I cannot even say, like you and others, that I share with them a pure monotheistic belief. What binds me to Judaism and makes me feel closer to its believers than to others is purely a filial sense of duty. I am simply oriented toward the camp of the religion in which I grew up and whose teachings I learned, the same as I am toward my mother, my family, my fatherland . . . It is my duty to defend the interests of the Jews; that is a bedrock principle for me.

Then Uncle Bernhard told the girls about how Uncle Moritz had got married, which had turned out to be rather difficult, since the *Stättigkeit* stated that only fifteen Jewish weddings per year were permitted in Frankfurt. Moritz and his bride got around the prohibition by having their wedding in Bockenheim, in Hesse. Six years later, after the birth of their third child, a girl, the young woman died. In 1859, Dr. Moritz Abraham Stern finally achieved the goal he had worked so hard for and became the first unconverted Jewish professor in Germany. In later years other Jews became professors, but he was the one who opened the door.

"He never gave up," Uncle Bernhard said. "And every time younger people like us complained that the quest for equal rights was going backward instead of forward, he would say, 'You have no idea how it was when I was young.' "

Uncle Bernhard shut the notebook and put it back in the cabinet.

Two years later, Klärchen, just nineteen years old, married the son of the man that Uncle Bernhard had described so enthusiastically: Alfred Stern, a historian and by then a professor at the University of Bern.

3.

Family Life

It was a certain Michael Frank, a successful businessman, who paid court to Alice Stern. Michael Frank was from Landau-in-der-Pfalz. Alice's family, who had never heard of the Franks, were not enthusiastic about the match; they would rather she had found a groom among the well-known Jewish families in Frankfurt, or even among their relatives, for example, Richard, her cousin. That was common practice at the time—Klärchen, after all, had married her cousin Alfred.

But Alice didn't care what her family said. She felt flattered by the interest that Michael showed in her and found every possible way to meet him, usually with the help of her girlfriends. Michael was suddenly invited into a home where he had never been invited before, or he was brought along somewhere by Alice's friends' helpful brothers. Even in a relatively rigid society, like Jewish Frankfurt at the time, couples in love always found ways to see each other, secretly exchange a few words, look each other in the eye. It is not entirely clear why Cornelia Stern was against Michael Frank as a son-in-law at first, but her resistance must not have been all that heavy, since when Alice presented her mother with the fait accompli and said that she had firmly decided to marry Michael and no one else, Cornelia gave way.

The planned betrothal led to a busy correspondence between members of the two families. So, for instance, Léon Frank,

Michael's brother, two years younger than Michael, felt compelled to write a long letter to his brother from Paris, on October 17, 1885, in which he first congratulated his older brother but also offered to come to Frankfurt in case Michael felt the need to discuss his plans further with someone in the family. Even though this was not the best moment to leave Paris, with the stock markets as they were, still he would gladly come to Frankfurt for a few days, perhaps also to discreetly inquire into the circumstances of Michael's intended. The letterhead said, "Frank, Wolfsohn & Co. / DÉPÊCHES / Wolfsohn-Bourse-Paris. 21, Rue Saint-Marc."

The letter from Alfred Stern, the professor in Bern, to his cousin Alice was very different:

Dear Alice! When I came home just now, Dora [his young daughter] yelled out while I was still in the hall: "Alice is engaged!" It was clear that this must be happy news, since she yelled it in a bright loud voice despite a bad cold and runny nose. Indeed it was. May all the good and beautiful things I wish for you come true, many times over.

Give your bridegroom my heartiest greetings, even though I haven't yet met him. [. . .] I am deeply glad for your happiness.

Yours,
Alfred Stern

Michael Frank, circa 1880

Alfred's father, professor emeritus by then and living with Alfred, congratulated Alice and Michael and signed the letter too: "Your Uncle Stern."

Klärchen added something as well: "I can't believe I'm not there with you, to share in all your celebrations! But when it's time for the wedding!! I hope I'm invited?? I'll come and give you both a great big hug. Your Klärchen."

Rebekka Loewi, Michael's oldest sister, who at thirty-four was already a grandmother, wrote from Paris on October 26, 1885:

My dear Alice! For a long time now it would have been right for me to introduce myself to you as your sister, I hope dear Michel has already done so, I have not been well or else I would have sent you my congradulatory wishes already. You probably have not missed them, the first days there are so many demands on you that I feel sorry for every new bride and groom. But now, my d. Alice, even if they're late I hope you accept my deepest congradulations and believe me you are a lucky child to be able to make my d. brother Michel your husband and lifelong companion. It's not because I have any sisterly illusions about my brother that I say Michel is the best and most agreeable man with the finest character and more able than anyone to make a wife happy. I dont want to say too much, it looks so strange to praise your own brother, but I will say this, since Im firmly convinced that a happy, beautiful future awaits you. [. . .] For many years we made a happy, comfortable home and have been joined to each other with family ties that few other brothers and sisters can have taken so much pleasure in. Each of us lives for the other & I hope to God that it will stay the same in future too, because my d. Rosa tells me that you dear Alice are a good creature too who will have no problem joining us in our family.*

Especially moving is the letter that Babette Frank née Hammelfett sent on October 22, 1885, addressed to her future daughter-in-law Alice while including a congratulatory note to her son Michael.

*Rosalie Loewi née Frank, a sister of Rebekka and Michael Frank, married to Ottmar Loewi in Frankfurt.

Most dearly beloved daughter!

Thank you, oh thank you, for your so darling letter, I truly cant wait for when I can press you to my heart, dearest daughter, not only because you have made my good Michael so happy, you have made me just as happy since his hapiness is my hapiness it was always my deepest wish to see him with a wife like he deserves and with Gods help he has found one in you, my dear Karolina cannot write enough about you, my dear child, and so I am already eqsited from this joy. I cant expres my feelings very well I am so beside myself that my saintly dear father did not live to see this day please ecxuse me for my short note and I cant wait to see you and congradulat your dear mama in person may dear God give her the gradest joy and you to my dearest children—Michael will always striive

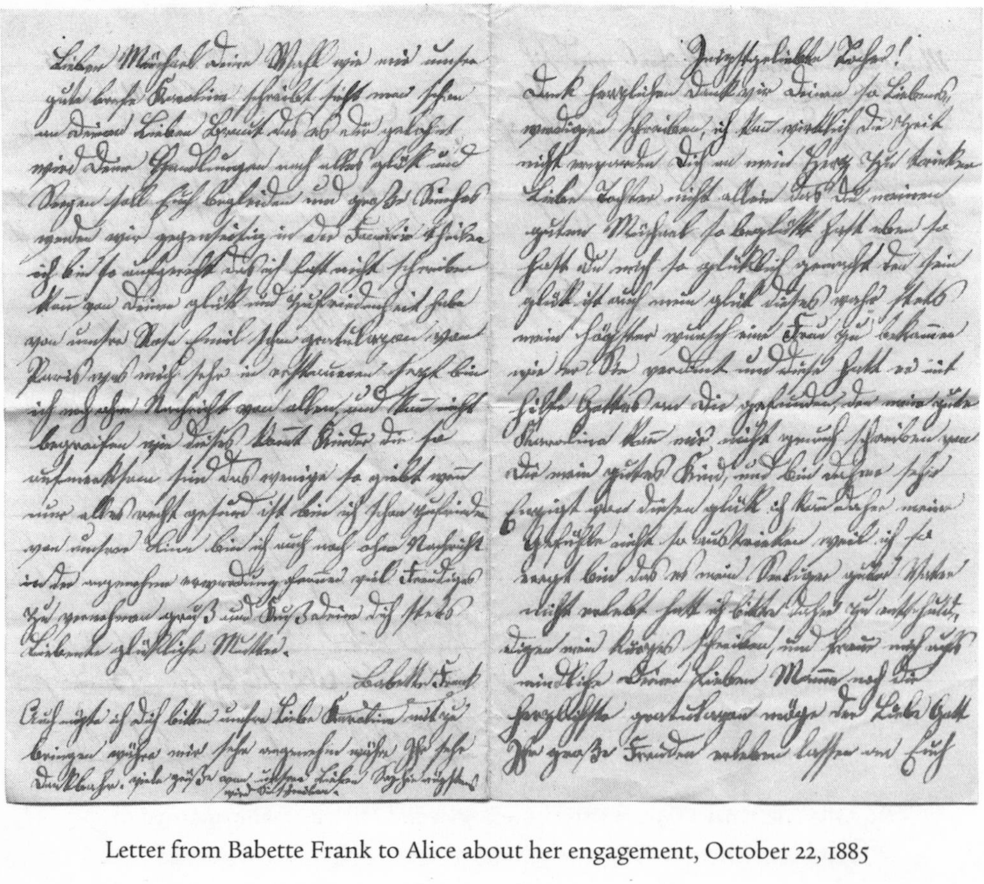

Letter from Babette Frank to Alice about her engagement, October 22, 1885

to be a good well-behaved son just like you a good daughter and please say hello to your dear relattives for me and give my congratulazons [. . .] Goodbye and hugs & kisses from the bottom of my heart from your happy and always loving mother. Babette Frank

Alice would have read this letter with mixed feelings. The childish style and many mistakes would probably have embarrassed her, coming as she did from a family that put so much value on education. At the same time, she must have been deeply moved by this woman's straightforward affection and goodwill.

She would definitely have discussed this letter with her mother, Cornelia, and Cornelia would have told her that the simpler sorts of Jews used to speak Yiddish, or Jewish-German, a language that was like German but substituting many Hebrew words and, most important, written in the Hebrew alphabet. That was probably the language that Babette Frank knew as a child, and where would she have learned German spelling? Besides, the education of girls was not seen as very important. It was expected of boys that they would study the Torah and the Talmud their whole lives (which is why a synagogue is also called a shul), but for girls it was usually enough to teach them the alphabet. They had to be able to read the prayers; it wasn't important that they understand them.

Cornelia would have advised her daughter not to take Babette Frank's mistakes too seriously. Her son Michael, after all, was not uneducated; he was an intelligent businessman who would offer his future wife a comfortable, carefree life.

In any case, Alice no longer had much time for reflection. The betrothal took place on October 21, 1885, and the wedding was planned for January 3, 1886. The trousseau had to be finished by then, and there were all sorts of other preparations to take care of.

As was common at the time among well-to-do families, it was a large wedding with numerous guests—relatives, friends, and acquaintances, both Michael's male friends and the bride's girlfriends.

The menu for the reception has not been preserved, unfortunately. There might have been pâté as an appetizer, then soup,

Alice and Michael Frank shortly after their wedding

then trout au bleu, roast veal, coleslaw, sauerkraut, maybe even wild boar with mountain cranberries to emphasize how far removed they were from the Jewish dietary laws? And would dessert have been chocolate mousse or orange parfait?

What has been preserved are the songs and poems written for the young couple, and the friends' comments ribbing Michael about his bachelor days and how he liked to enjoy a good glass of wine and other pleasures:

In Landau-in-der-Pfalz
Was born our noble Frank:
Wherever lots of wine and malts
Were found, there lived our man.
He liked his wine and beer
And liked his beer steins roomy—
He knows them well from all the years
He stared down into them, never gloomy.
Down goes
His nose
Into the glass;
A barfly's life
Free of wife
Is how it was.

Further on in the song came hints that Michael had been in love once or twice before, but these were only "false alarms" that "he always knew weren't true." His true love was clearly Alice, and everyone there had nothing but good wishes for the young couple.

It would have been after the banquet, over wine, that the friends performed their poems and told their stories and anecdotes, and there would definitely have been a lot of laughter and chatter in the hall, remarks flying here and there, innuendos that the bridegroom might not have been unreservedly happy to hear in the presence of his bride and their families. But goodwill and good cheer prevailed.

A flyer that his friends made up is also amusing:

Let it be known to all that the heretofore single ***Alice Stern,*** *hereby granted right of domicile, has left her parental residence under conditions which seem to imply that she does not intend to return thereto for extended periods of time.*

She has been seen in the company of the so-called "stockbroker" ***Michael Frank*** *(with whom she appears to have certain intimate relations) and furthermore bedecked in a white dress among other similar veils, garlands, &c.*

The aforementioned Stern has the legal authority to have meanwhile exchanged this outfit for one more comfortable on long journeys.

One presumes that the many times aforementioned ***Stern*** *and her accomplice* ***Frank*** *have made off via railroad toward Bavaria or Austria.*

The authorities have been notified thereof, and are hereby instructed to keep the couple under close surveillance and, should any embarrassing circumstances arise, to smoothly and unobtrusively facilitate their journey.

Signed:
For the Examining Magistrate:
Dr. A. Mox

Alice had in fact exchanged her wedding dress for a more comfortable traveling outfit, but her honeymoon brought her not to Bavaria or Austria but to Paris. The young couple had originally planned to continue their trip to London, but the weather made them change their plans.

Cornelia wrote a letter to the two of them:

Dear Children, At last I have received the letter I long hoped for, confirming my suspicion that you had changed your travel destination and remained in Paris due to inclement weather. I am certain you will enjoy it there as well, dear Liza, I am only afraid that your expectations are too high. I know my little social butterfly too well [. . .] in any case, I hope very much to hear from you how you are enjoying married life. Is it better to be a Mrs. or a Miss?

The answer to her mother's question must have come very easily to Alice: of course it was better to be a Mrs., a wife, the spouse of a successful husband who earned enough money as a businessman to give her and the children she would no doubt be having soon a comfortable life. He had become self-employed and offered his services as a broker. He invested any profits in other lines of business, so, for example, he owned a food-processing plant in Bockenheim and was a partner in the Sodener mineral tablets company. He bought a cigarette store, Engelhardt & Co., and was involved in the travel agency in the Hotel Frankfurter Hof. In 1896–97, he sold all his property except for his share of Sodener Tablets and founded the Michael Frank Bank as a publicly traded company specializing in securities exchange and foreign currencies. The Franks were not among the truly rich, but they were certainly well-off.

Alice enjoyed the new freedoms that marriage offered her. Michael had to work hard, true, but her life had its share of pleasures. They attended concerts, the theater, and the opera. They gave dinner parties and were invited to others'. They led the life of people possessing full civil rights. There was nothing to remind them of their parents' and grandparents' time: they had broken free from the ghetto, and the degrading limitations of the *Stättigkeit* had been overcome.

Of course, as Jews, even prosperous Jews, they did not belong to high society—only noblemen, patricians, and high officers and civil servants under Kaiser Wilhelm truly belonged in those circles. Even Professor Moritz Stern, Alfred's father, had no access there because he had not been a member of one of the fencing societies as a student and thus could not count on the support of former fraternity brothers. Anyone without the intricately interwoven strings of ancestry and connections to pull had no way to enter the true upper class, and an invisible sign seemed to hang above the stairs leading upward: "No Jews Allowed." Even the old, established business families were not seen as truly belonging, as possessing truly equal rights—the age of the guilds was still too recent, even if they no longer expressed their scorn and contempt as openly as before because in this period of rapid expansion in Germany, people wanted to do business. In socioeconomic terms, Michael and Alice Frank fell somewhere between the upper class and the rising tide of factory workers, small farmers, and craftsmen, not solidly in either camp.

But even if you don't quite belong, you can lead a comfortable life if you have enough money. And in the end, they were not alone—they had far-flung families, relatives who had married into other families, friends, business colleagues, and fellow bankers with unsatisfactory family backgrounds just like them.

Twenty-five years of married life were granted to Alice and Michael Frank—twenty-three years in which the world changed forever. Municipal electricity came to Gutleutstrasse in early 1895. There were still mostly horses and carriages on the streets, but the horse-drawn streetcars established in 1872 went electric in 1899, and there were more and more automobiles. Candles, kerosene lanterns, and gas lamps were replaced by electric lights; soon the first vacuum cleaners appeared, and the better sorts of people managed to get telephones put in. The Franks were among the first in Frankfurt to get a telephone: their phone number was apparently 82. Even more important for economic and social life was the construction of the railway network: more and more cities in Europe could now be reached by rail. There was first class, second class, and third class, of course, but if you had enough money, your journey was entirely comfortable, in luxurious dining cars and well-appointed sleepers.

The Franks traveled often, not only for business or on vacation but also to visit friends and family. Old relationships were fostered and new ones formed. No wonder that Alice, the "social butterfly," as her mother had called her, lived it up and sought out all sorts of enjoyable new experiences. There were lots of parties, even within the tight social constraints of the time—receptions, tea parties, dinners, soirees—there were billiard games, and the children learned riding and tennis. Their letters tell of excursions into nature together, so-called country parties. Social life blossomed—it was really very impressive. The homes were correspondingly well furnished, with heavy furniture, heavy curtains, and even heavier carpets. Gradually, the somewhat gloomy luxury of the late nineteenth century gave way to Art Nouveau and, later still, to the functionality and clear, clean lines of the Bauhaus. Alice never quite accepted this new style, though, and surrounded herself until her death with dark, somber furniture, ornate and elaborate, that was closer to Biedermeier than to Bauhaus.

Alice's life was good, especially when the children arrived.

On October 7, 1886, precisely nine months after the wedding, Robert was born. He was artistically gifted and many of his letters are adorned with drawings, sometimes very beautiful drawings. He was the one who later opened an art gallery in London and rediscovered the painter John Martin (1789–1854). He found two of Martin's large canvases by chance in an attic, *The Plains of Heaven* and *The Last Judgment*, and bought them; in 1974, long after Robert's death, his widow Lotti gave both paintings to the Tate Britain (formerly the Tate

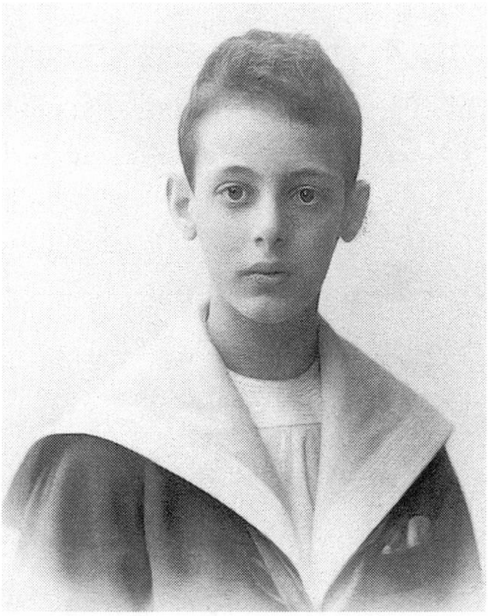

Robert Frank, around ten years old

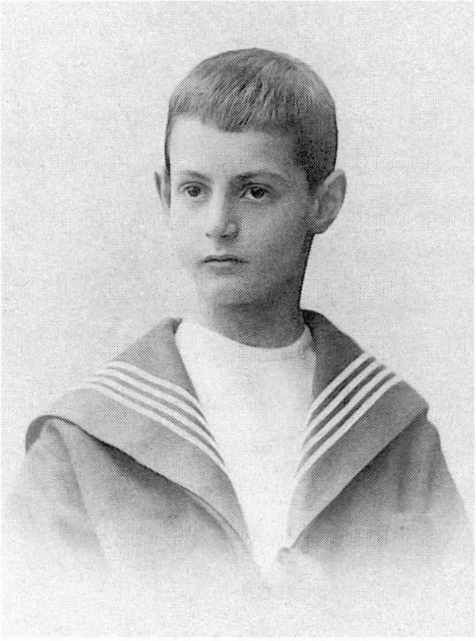

Otto Frank, around ten years old

Gallery of British Art). The paintings are still shown there today, and labeled "Bequeathed by Mrs. Robert Frank."

Three years later, on May 12, 1889, their second son, Otto, was born. Otto Frank was to be Anne Frank's father—Anne who was born, like her ancestors, in Frankfurt am Main but who fled the Nazis with her parents, to the Netherlands. When the Nazis occupied the Netherlands and she and her family had to go into hiding, in a secret annex above and behind Otto's office, she would keep a diary for two years that would make the Frank family world famous.

After another two years, on October 13, 1891, Herbert was born, who would be Alice's "problem child" when he grew up. She worried about him her whole life, and when she felt close to dying, she gave her daughter, Leni, the responsibility for continuing to take care of him.

Portrait of Leni Frank, around five years old

Alice and Michael longed for a daughter, but the three sons came first; finally, on September 8, 1893, their wish was fulfilled, and Helene was born. Alice, herself so powerfully shaped by her mother-daughter relationship with Cornelia, must have been ecstatic. And Helene—whom everyone affectionately nicknamed, whether Leni, Lener, Lunni, or Lunner—was a strikingly pretty child. Alice was so proud of her that she later had her portrait painted. Helene was around five years old at the time, maybe as old as eight, and magnificently decked out for the occasion. Alice loved Leni, and Leni loved Alice; their relationship was presumably as warm and close from the beginning as the relationship Leni's son Buddy Elias would later see for himself.

Helene was not given a middle name, but the sons were. Noticeably, none of the names was biblical, or traditionally Jewish. Michael's grandfather, who had moved from Fürth to Niederhochstadt, was called Hersch Frenkel until 1810, when he started to call himself Abraham Frank. Well into the nineteenth century, when the Jews were forced to take on one of a set list of family names, they were traditionally named X, son (or daughter) of Y, although occasionally there would be names indicating family or origin, for example, Stern (from the Stern family) or Frenkel (from the Franks, the inhabitants of Franconia) or Cohn (the descendants of the *cohanim*). Many Jewish family names were taken directly from the family's birthplace: Bamberger, Frankfurter, Wormser, Holländer. And there were also simple translations of Hebrew names, for example, Wolfsohn from Ben Se'ew (son of a wolf) or Hirsch (deer) from Zwi. When people turned to German names, they often tried to keep the same initial as their Jewish name, for instance changing Moshe to Moritz or Zwi to Zacharias. Still, when they gave their children middle names, it was customary to choose biblical ones. But even this suggestion of religiosity had vanished in the Frank family: the boys were named Robert Hermann, Otto Heinrich, and Herbert August. They were German, they considered themselves German, and they no longer had much of anything to do with their ancestors' history.

At first the Frank family lived on Leerbachstrasse; with the birth of their second son, they moved to nearby Gärtnerweg; and in 1901, Michael Frank bought the house at Jordanstrasse 4, not far from the Palmengarten. They rented out only the mansard, and Cornelia, Alice's mother, moved into the third floor.

The house was big enough for everybody; later there was even room for Leni's and Otto's families. And surrounding the house was a lovely garden where the children could play. It was easy to find servants who would keep everything spick-and-span: more and more poor girls were flooding the city from the countryside and looking for work from the rich. Alice didn't have to work; she only gave orders. We can assume that never once in her life did she touch a cleaning rag or dry a plate, and that her daughter, Leni, didn't either. Leni's daughter-in-law, Gerti, would later relate: "If there was a stain on the table, Leni would point at it and tell me, 'Please, wipe it off!' She would never have done it herself." Buddy, Leni's son, said: "My mother could barely boil water for tea."

The Frank family house, Jordanstrasse 4 (later Mertonstrasse, now Dantestrasse), in Frankfurt

Happy years followed. How would Alice and Michael have raised their children? No doubt as was typical for the time: Children had to obey, to be seen and not heard, and to bother their parents as little as possible. Proper behavior was the highest goal of child rearing, and was strictly enforced. But no less certainly, a loving, tender relationship between parents and children existed in the Frank family—as is proven by the many surviving letters. There are letters from the children to their parents when the parents went off on another trip, leaving the little ones in the care of their governess, Fräulein Auguste Serg, whom everyone called Fräulein; the cook, Trauda Ullrich; and their grandmother Cornelia. Unlike the names of the maids or serving girls, which were not passed down, the names Auguste Serg and Trauda had a firm place in the family and were never forgotten.

Their children's education was very important to Michael and Alice. They all had music lessons—Otto played cello, Herbert violin—and naturally they owned a grand piano. There was a Miss to teach them English, a Mademoiselle for French, and Italian lessons too. Leni's daughter-in-law would later tell stories about how, when the family entertained—for example, at Leni's famous tea parties—the language spoken at the table would constantly shift according to which guest you were talking to or whether you were giving instructions to the Italian housekeeper.

The children were apparently encouraged quite early to express themselves in writing, without being forced into strict forms, as was common at the time. Not only Robert's many drawings in his letters show this, but also the early attempts at poetry from all the children. Robert was only eight when he put together these New Year's rhymes in 1894:

Dear Parents,
May this year be your happiest yet!
Of children you now have a quartet,
And they should bring you nothing but joy,
May you be happy with each girl and boy.
New Year's wishes from your eldest.

Robert, Otto, Herbert, and Leni Frank, circa 1895–96

Alice loved coming up with rhymes and poems for every special occasion, and her children knew, of course, that their mother would be especially pleased with a couplet or poem. Leni, for example, wrote this for her parents for Christmas 1901:

Little Christ child, decorate
The Christmas tree anew,
So every child will know to wait
For a Christmas visit from you.

She must have copied out the poem—it is too polished to have been written by a child of eight—but even so, the beautiful handwriting is striking, and proof that the children were very often encouraged to write.

So the Franks celebrated Christmas. It would be wrong to conclude from this that they were in any way becoming Christian; that was surely not the case. They were not religious at all; they just took every chance to celebrate that offered itself.

At the turn of the century—which, on Kaiser Wilhelm's orders, was celebrated in Germany on January 1, 1900, a year earlier than everywhere else in the world, which celebrated it on January 1, 1901—Robert sent his mother a postcard illustrating "German Fashion, 1800–1900." The printed text runs:

Everything in fashion
Always comes around again,
Especially what was prettiest,
What pleases everyone the best.

Robert continued by hand:

But that's not so important here—
With me and all the rest
You act how you are and will always be
And that's what pleases me the best.

Den
lieben Eltern.

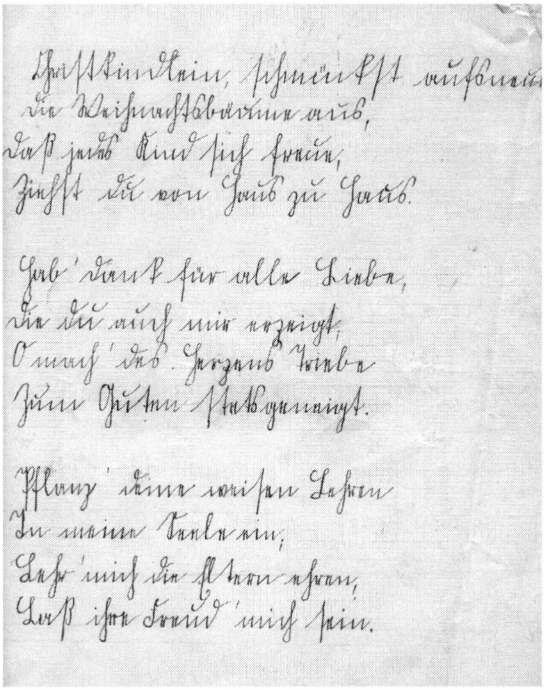

Christkindlein, schmückst aufs neue
die Weihnachtsbäume aus,
Daß jedes Kind sich freue,
Ziehst du von Haus zu Haus.

Hab' Dank für alle Liebe,
Die du auch mir erzeigt;
O mach' das Herzens Triebe
Zum Guten stets geneigt.

Pflanz' deine weißen Rosen
In meine Seele ein;
Laß mich die Eltern ehren,
Laß ihre Freud' mich sein.

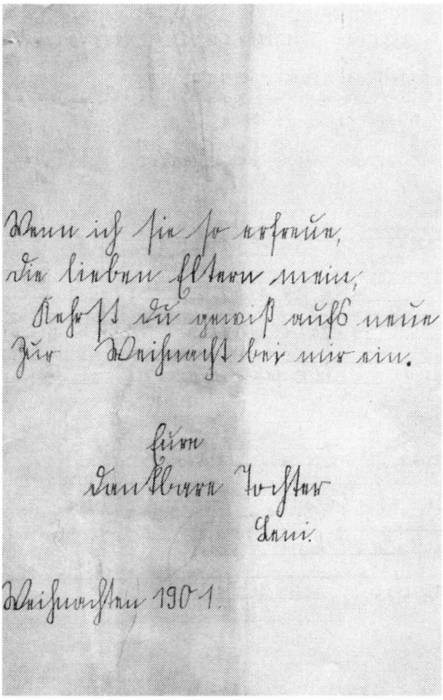

Wenn ich sie so erfreue,
Die lieben Eltern mein,
Kehrst du gewiß aufs neue
Zur Weihnacht bei mir ein.

Eure
dankbare Tochter
Leni.

Weihnachten 1901.

Christmas poem by Leni, 1901

What an enchanting declaration of love from a thirteen-year-old to his mother! Yet we can no longer describe him, the oldest, as a child—he took on responsibility for his younger brothers and sister at an early age, and only three years later he would start to work in an antiques store during his vacations and free time.

The Franks seem to have had a cheerful, companionable family life. Alice was no doubt responsible for that, since she so enjoyed hosting parties—her daughter, Leni, would later say so again and again. In the surviving documents, there are also various pieces of evidence to confirm it: invitations to parties, to Carnival celebrations, to Christmas, to New Year's, most of them adorned with a little poem. For a costume party where all the guests were to dress up as children, Alice wrote this rhyming invitation:

Mardi Gras should always be merry
So Mr. and Mrs. Frank, to every
One of our friends, extend a hearty

Postcard from Robert Frank to Alice, 1900

Invite to a jolly party!
And since kids always have most fun—
Babies, schoolboys, every one,
Teenage girls included too—
We would like to ask of you:
Dress as a child, and don't be late
When Saturday 19th is the date;
RSVP from east and west
To make our Children's Party the best!

For the party, Alice dressed her four children in costumes that she described in her black notebook: "blue long pants, checkered vests and skirts, white carnations in the buttonholes, broad red paper top hats."

There were also parties for the children. One invitation to a party on February 19, 1898, reads:

Peace and calm are virtues, in truth,
Not often practiced by our youth.
But today no squabbles or breaking ranks
At the children's party at the Franks'.

The celebrations did not only take place in the private sphere. The frequent mention of concerts and plays in Robert's letters to his parents shows the extent to which even the children took part in the cultural life of the city: "Mademoiselle just left for a concert (*Creation*) . . . I'm sending Fräulein to *La Traviata* tonight with your season ticket, and if you're not back by Saturday, I'll let Otto go to *Robert and Bertram* . . . Otto and Herbert went to the cinematograph . . . Tonight the children are off to *Joseph and His Brothers,* and I'm going to see *Tricks of Love* and then fetch the children from the opera after the theater gets out." On one occasion, Robert wrote, "Tonight I'm probably going to see *Hamlet,* and I'm very much looking forward to it," and on another: "*A Doll's House* is playing at the Playhouse on Saturday. May I use your ticket to go?" Once, after seeing *The Robbers* with Josef Kainz in the role of Franz Moor, he wrote: "It was a brilliant production, and it was very interesting to observe how the leading actors would gesture and express themselves." In another letter, he told his parents: "Otto, Herr Böttcher, Fräulein, and Edgar performed two beautiful piano quartets by Beethoven and Mozart here at home last night. It was really very lovely." And once, when his parents were about to go to Venice, he reminded them: "Take a good look at the Titians and the other paintings so you can give me a full report."

Most of the letters from the children are addressed to their mother, who missed them terribly when she was traveling. Their relationship to her seems to have been closer than their relationship with their father. That was not uncommon, when the unquestioned role of the father within the family was more strictly defined as being the authority, which naturally brought with it a certain distance. The father ruled the household, he decided what would or wouldn't happen, with the mother having more influence on everyday life and smaller concerns.

Still, there is an especially beautiful card that Robert sent his father. It is addressed to "Michael Frank, Esq., London, Hotel Cecil," and it contains a poem and a drawing of the whole family sitting at their table. The card was signed by everyone, and it says a lot about the domestic life and the free and open manners that must have held sway at the Frank household:

We sit at the table, not too late,
With all the asparagus we just ate
And roast beef, each has cleaned his plate,
And thinks of Father, for whom we wait!
We hope your time in London was great
And that your return will be first-rate,
But enough of this little poem so ornate—

Lots of kisses will land on your pate
From Grandma, Lisel, Robert, Otto, Herbert, Leni.
Best wishes until that date . . .

Most of the letters come from Robert's pen. He seems to have taken it upon himself to keep his parents informed about what was happening in the house, perhaps so that they wouldn't be worried; in any case, he wrote not only about himself but about the others as well. So, for instance, a letter of November 1898 told them about his dance class, then emphasized that all the children could imagine "how much you are enjoying yourselves and we are happy for you with all our hearts. It must be wonderful, the sea before you and the mountains behind you and all the beauty everywhere." He went on to say that he had had lunch with Grandma, Cornelia, who, whenever anyone asked her how she was doing, said "terrible!!!" but was otherwise "cheerful and merry." Otto had set up a little store or a lottery and wanted "to make some money." Another time, Robert reported that Leni had started school "and, unbelievably, wasn't sick with a cold this time." He didn't say much about his own experiences in school, mentioning only once the corporal punishment that was still common at the time: "Nothing special happened in school today, only that our teacher has bought a new cane and already today he broke it in, on two boys."

School played a much greater role in Otto's life. He was attending Lessing High School too by that time, and he reported his grades to his parents time and time again: a 3 (B-) in a Latin *extemporale,* a 1-2 (A-) in German dictation, a 2-3 (B) in Latin, "Good overall" in home ec. His letters were not particularly long and tended to be objective and informative: whether he had had lunch with Grandma or an aunt, or that he had practiced the cello while the Miss listened. Sometimes he also described his outings—where he had ridden the train to, and where he had gone on foot. All in all nothing very intimate or emotional. The very man who would later write such gripping and empathetic letters started off as a child with a much more reserved, even cold, writing style, especially compared with his brother Robert's letters. Otto's most entertaining comments were limited to the fact that Leni "didn't have an accident in her bed" or that there were no "smell events" today and that Grandma had plans to "take a bath today."

Card from Robert Frank to his father in London, 1902

Herbert, the other brother, wrote even less often than Otto, mostly about food, for example: "Today we got soup with too much salt, so we didn't eat it, a nice leg of venison that was very, very tasty, and the most excellent bread dumplings in the world. Other than that, I don't know what else to tell you." Once, he did send his parents a poem:

Happy and healthy as can be
Like jolly fishes in the sea.—
For you I have a little plan:
Bring me some chocolate and marzipan.
From everyone who's here at home
Much love goes with this little poem.
Your little Bertie who misses you
Sends extra special kisses too.

Leni wrote the least of all the children, no doubt because she was much younger: seven years younger than Robert, four years younger than Otto. In one early letter, she writes to her father: "Herbert always sleeps in your bed and in the morning he comes in and then we play Salesman from Paris. Kisses, your Lener."

And there is one poem that she sent to her parents when she was ten—the only proof we have that Michael also put rhymes together sometimes:

Dear Mom!
For your postcard a great big thank
From your daughter Leni Frank!
I was happy to get a card from you
And surprised that Daddy makes rhymes too.
He did it well, he deserves high praise.
I think that it's only a few days
Before you're back, then you can tell me
If it was nice in Italy? (yes?)

It's already getting late at night
Soon time for Leni to go right
To her soft bed and fluffy pillow too,
And there she'll dream sweet dreams of you.
Hugs and kisses, Dad and Mom
From your little daughter here at home.

Alice and Michael were in Italy celebrating the engagement of Arthur Spitzer and Olga Wolfsohn—the same Auntie O. who would later invite everyone, especially Leni and Alice, to her magnificent Villa Laret in Sils-Maria.

Robert commented on this engagement as follows:

J'étais tout à fait baff!!! *[. . .] When Leni heard, she said: "Oh, Spitzer? I would have snapped him up too in Olga's place." Otto and I are visiting Aunt Rosa and Aunt Karoline, of course, to give our congratulations. When I went to the main post office yesterday to send our telegram and told the man behind the counter that Palanza was in Italy, not South America, he answered: "Yaah, I know. Therr've binna tonna telegrams goin there awready t'day. Summ big engagement."*

For the wedding itself, Robert sent a letter saying that they would be celebrating in Frankfurt too: Aunt Rosa, Michael and Rebekka's sister and the mother of the bride, had invited the whole family. Below his peppy signature, he added a sketch of the bride and groom at the altar that shows the boy's real artistic talent.

At the time, Robert was working in his spare time and during vacations at Herr Ricard's antiques store. He was sixteen and already acted very grown-up—as the biggest, the oldest, the role clearly came naturally to him. He must have impressed others as being very mature too, because Herr Ricard was prepared to leave him, the teenager, in charge of the business. Robert wrote to his parents once that Herr Ricard was traveling, and that he, Robert,

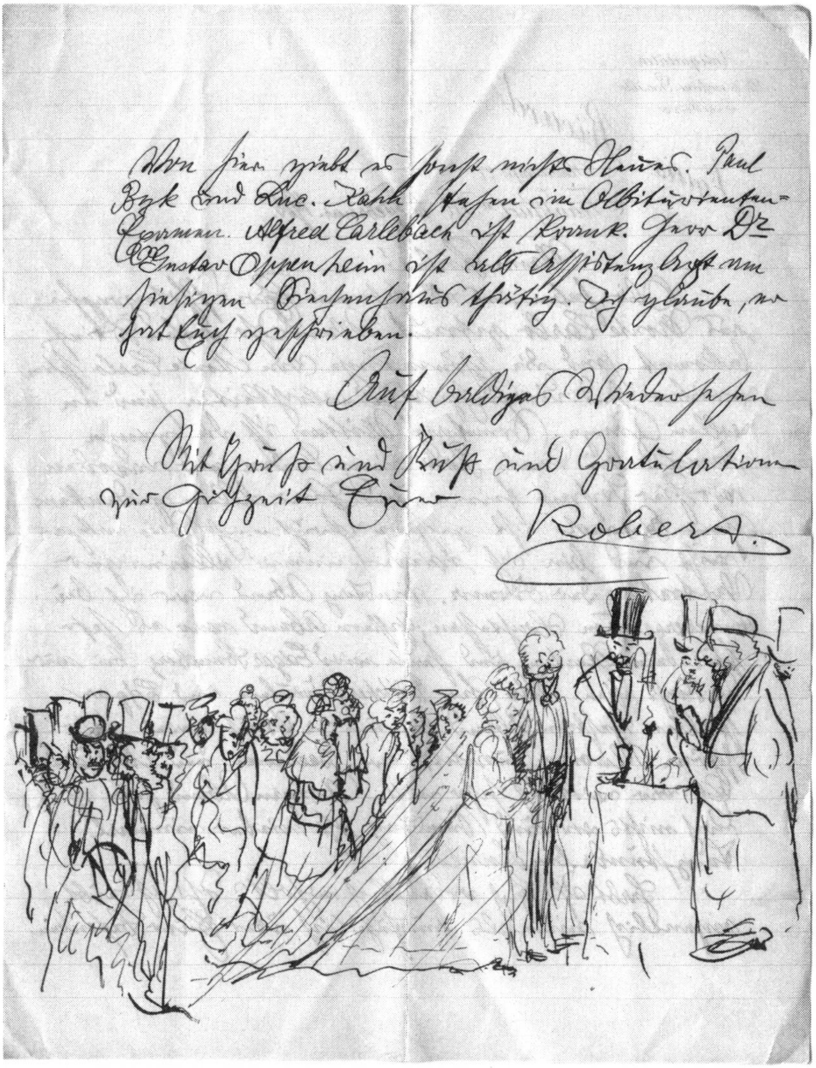

Letter from Robert Frank on the wedding of Olga Wolfsohn and Arthur Spitzer, February 16, 1905

had much more to do in the store than usual, when Herr Ricard was there. The day before, for example, he had not even had time to eat lunch. Another time: "Yesterday I went with Herr Ricard to see Director Cornill in the museum, to help with the taxes on the paintings."

In another letter, he wrote:

I'm sitting here in the store after I've just seen a photographic apparatus that Herr Ricard plans to buy for photographing objects and paintings. It is a very good machine and I'd be glad to have it. [. . .] I've invited a few friends for a billiards contest tonight, and ordered a keg of beer and some sandwiches for it. [. . .] May I permit myself the most humble and obedient question to Mama, if there might be any circumstances in which I could see The Valkyrie *with Fräulein [Auguste Serg]? I most patiently and respectfully await your reply.*

He is almost grown up—inviting people over, ordering food and drink. Robert was so reliable and his parents put so much trust in him that they traveled even when the house was due to be repainted. Robert took care of everything, as his letter from August 20, 1903, shows:

Dear Parents! The long-awaited workmen are now here! Two huge guys crawling around on ladders in the empty rooms, smearing the ceilings. All the walls are covered with rags and the whole house smells of this pleasant material and a few other things. We men are sleeping upstairs in the guest room, and I slept quite badly in my first night on the guest bed, because it squeaked and meowed all sorts of ways every time I moved a muscle. I dreamed of cats all night long. Now I've had them bring my own bed upstairs and I sleep undisturbed. Last night I went to see Talisman, *which was a lot of fun. It's pretty quiet in the store.*

Two days later, in his next letter, it already said: "Since Mother asked how things look around here, I can only say 'frightfully unpleasant.' Wherever you go, you trip over a workman crawling around on the floor or swinging from a chandelier and now it smells of white, blue, and green paint along with the rotten rags."

"We men," he wrote, rather wittily when you consider that

the "men" were sixteen, fourteen, and twelve. But his letters show that the Frank children were raised to be independent and responsible, and show how great the mutual trust between parents and children must have been.

In a letter to his mother from July 19, 1904, while she was enjoying a trip to Engelberg with the rest of the family, Robert wrote that he had worked all week at the store owned by Herr Ricard, who was doing better. He had got into the habit of sleeping with the shutters and windows open, and having his breakfast on the veranda, "and it's so nice there that I can imagine I'm on a summer vacation in the country too." He also reported on his visits to various people, a bicycle ride to Ginnheim, the fact that he had moved his "English conversation" from Wednesday to Tuesday, that Ricard had invited him over for Friday, and that he thought he might go with Arnold and Edgar Sonneberg to the Summer Theater in Bockenheim on Saturday.

Now you have my whole schedule, and you can see from it that I am making myself quite comfortable here. Nothing is lacking. Grandma feeds me very well [. . .] Yesterday there were strawberries and cream, and today there'll be diplomat pudding. Quelle embarras de richesses?! By the way, you can see that I'm also taking care of the housework, at least insofar as it affects me personally. About the rest I couldn't care less. As far as I'm concerned the moths can devour the whole salon. In any case, Trauda runs around with a paddle every day in the salon, on the hunt. It's amazing that she hasn't yet managed to swat even one [. . .] Tell Father that there's nothing to report on the business front. What does he do to amuse himself all day? [. . .] Anyway! I think the gift of the gab has given quite enough for today, don't you? Enough for the next two weeks. You are hopefully satisfied with my eagerness to scribble. Best wishes to Father, Otto, Herbert, Leni, and Fräulein and kisses to you from Your, Robert Frank.

All the letters and other evidence attest to Alice being a happy wife and even happier mother, loved by her children. Buddy, her grandson, would later always stress how much he loved and admired her. Life offered her many comforts and amenities, and she presumably felt that it would always continue to do so, at least for many years.

Michael Frank, circa 1908

But then, on September 17, 1909, fate struck a blow. Michael, just fifty-seven years old, died suddenly and without warning, just as her father had when she was twelve. His death hit Alice hard. She was only forty-three when she became a widow—a woman in the best years of her life, even in that era.

A rabbi who apparently knew Michael as a young man gave a moving eulogy at the funeral. Alice, sunk in her cares and sorrows, presumably did not catch much of the rabbi's speech, but maybe she reread the eulogy later, for she always kept it with her. The rabbi said, among other things:

Two days ago he was happy still, and healthy, prepared to take another business trip, and now he has suddenly set off on a journey to the dark land from which no one returns. Before his loved ones could take their farewell, before they could think through what it would mean to lose him—he was gone. [. . .] And when I call forth an image of the dearly departed before my eyes, there rises up a long-departed time as well—more than forty years past—images of happy days vanished long ago; I see the dignified figures of his good parents, and the dearly beloved street in the friendly hometown where he lived, right next to the ancient synagogue.[. . .] I see him as a half-grown youth, standing out already from the other boys his age due to his effervescent, lively spirit, his sunny good cheer, his intelligence, and his energy and initiative. And what the boy promised, the man delivered. From closefisted life he wrestled success upon success. He was a businessman of unusual ability, full of enterprising spirit, as cautious as he was adventurous, always sharp and practical. And he kept his sunny, golden good cheer as well, the bright and happy spirit of the Pfalz region he was from, the charm that won your heart and the happy natural confidence of his own, which offered itself to you as it was—direct, open, true, and unreserved. But those were only the outward characteristics of his nature. On the inside was a true, golden heart that was goodness itself. [. . .] It was hard for him to turn down a request from anyone. [. . .] Where was there a better, warmer, more selfless husband? A gentler, more loving, more devoted father? How his eyes shone whenever he spoke of his children! Where was there a more faithful brother? [. . .] To all of us who were close to him, he was a dear friend, and it seems to me that each one of us must lament his passing like David that of Jonathan. [. . .] Let us console ourselves with the thought that he is beyond all suffering now. Childlike—a young man despite his gray hair—and without pain, free from the torment of sickness and apprehension, he has been called back to his eternal home. [. . .] In truth, we do not mourn for you—yours was the most beautiful possible death, at the height of your powers, without pain and struggle! May you gently rest in peace. The thought of you will live on, unforgotten, in the hearts of your loved ones, and your memory shall remain for them a peaceful, unclouded image, a rich and sacred blessing. Amen.

The Sterns wrote Alice a condolence letter from Zurich, where Alfred had become a professor. It is especially clear from Klärchen's letter how well she knew her cousin, with whom she had had a sisterly bond since early childhood. She wrote that she could perfectly identify with Alice, whose soul felt that life would hold no further joys:

Even your closest ones must feel far away, since they (luckily for them) have not withdrawn from active, happy life as completely as you have, and that you feel even lonelier as a result, maybe even abandoned and misunderstood [. . .] And the children have a lot of Michael's personality, who even in his own times of greatest suffering was simply unable to let it totally and completely overwhelm him [. . .] There were not many things he was proud of, but he was proudest of everything about his marriage to you. So you should be grateful if the children resemble him in their love of life and lively natures. When you've got past the worst of it, that will certainly be a consolation to you.

It took a long time before Alice found the consolation Klärchen wrote about, if indeed she ever found it at all. It must have felt to her as though all joy had left the once-carefree house

The Frank siblings, circa 1907

for good. Her children had the worst of it behind them—even the two youngest, Herbert and Leni, were seventeen and sixteen.

Robert was grown-up, had studied art history, and become an executive secretary in Ricard's antiques business, which Michael had bought for him and then later sold. Otto, who had likewise chosen to study art history in the summer semester of 1908, broke off his studies to travel to New York and visit his schoolmate Charles Webster Straus, whose family owned Macy's department store. Charles changed his name to Nathan Straus Jr., but for Otto he was always "Charley." Otto wanted to "check out the business." He was en route when his father died, and he heard the news only when the ship reached New York harbor. By then, Michael was already buried.

No letters from Michael remain today. Maybe the situation was so traumatic for Alice that she destroyed them all in a fit of melancholy after his death, so as not to have to be constantly reminded of him. But that is pure speculation. Buddy Elias says,

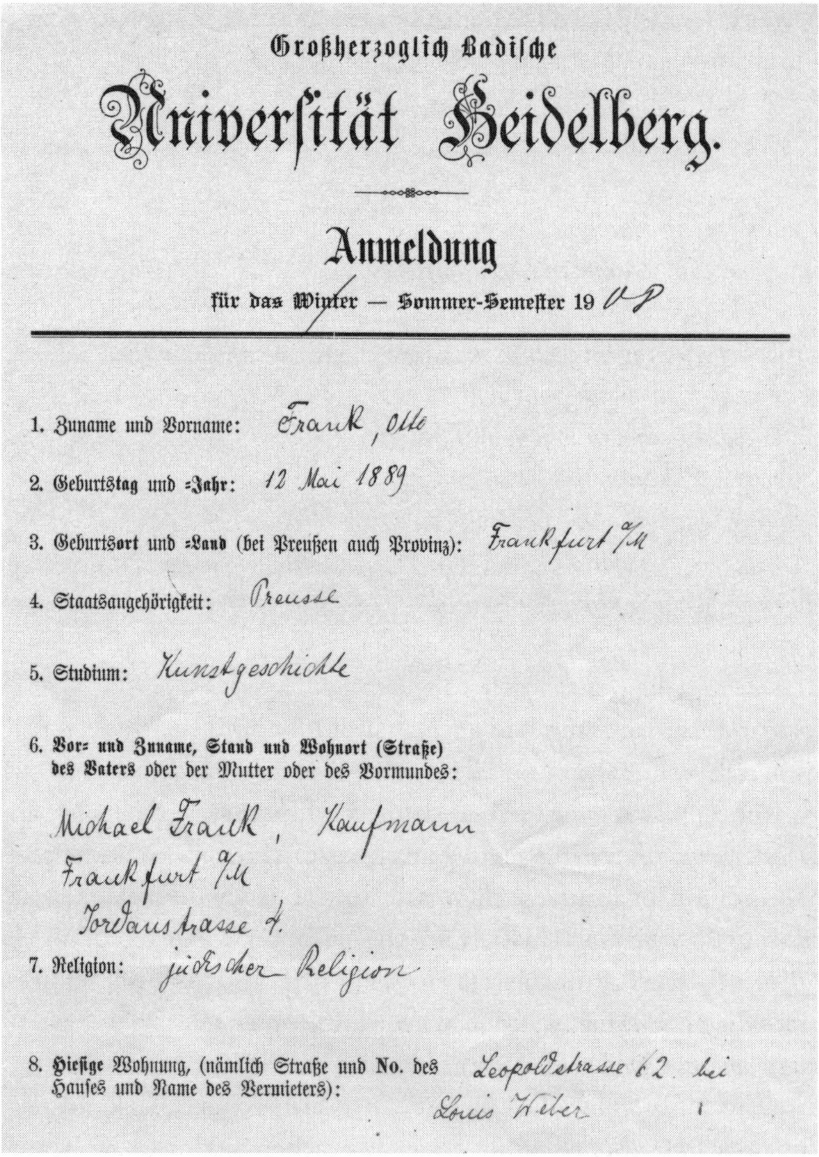

Großherzoglich Badische

Universität Heidelberg.

Anmeldung

für das ~~Winter~~ — Sommer-Semester 1908

1. Zuname und Vorname: Frank, Otto

2. Geburtstag und -Jahr: 12 Mai 1889

3. Geburtsort und -Land (bei Preußen auch Provinz): Frankfurt a/M

4. Staatsangehörigkeit: Preusse

5. Studium: Kunstgeschichte

6. Vor- und Zuname, Stand und Wohnort (Straße) des Vaters oder der Mutter oder des Vormundes:

Michael Frank, Kaufmann
Frankfurt a/M
Jordanstrasse 4.

7. Religion: jüdischer Religion

8. Hiesige Wohnung, (nämlich Straße und No. des Hauses und Name des Vermieters): Leopoldstrasse 62 bei Louis Weber

Otto Frank's university enrollment form, 1908

in any case, that Alice practically never spoke of Michael—his name was never mentioned. Alice seems to have fallen into a kind of depression much like the melancholy of her childhood years.

It was obviously hard for her to see the "good & beautiful things" in life anymore, just as it had been for her before.

A letter that Otto wrote to his mother on January 22, 1910, further elucidates her state of mind:

I think it is absolutely not right to want to withdraw further & further into yourself. You mustn't, for your own sake & for your children's sake. I know that you are reserved by nature & would rather take care of everything on your own, but you mustn't let this natural characteristic override your will. I believe you when you say that you find no distraction or enjoyment from your visitors, that it's painful to let people see you in this state, and hard to see how they can get used to everything when you yourself can't. You must know, though, that this is the way of the world & that it can't be otherwise. The world must go on & people want to live and they have to work. It's no wonder that you feel so empty & hollow, but if you crawl back into your suffering, that won't bring you any peace. You mustn't do it & you mustn't want to do it. Don't forget that you still have obligations; you're not fulfilling them right now, but you do still have them. Did our dear father leave nothing behind on this earth entrusted to your care? He had 1000s of ideas & gave you a broad outlook on the world & got you used to real life, and even if all that is now dormant in you, Mother, it must be there, as a sacred inheritance from dear Father. You mustn't let it all atrophy away & you need to fortify yourself & carry on. I keep reminding you again and again of Leni & the conversations you and I had about her. Don't close yourself off, open your eyes again & make sure that at least some of all the experiences you've been holding back for a long time will live again & put down roots. Work on something, not mechanically but because you want to do something that has a purpose. How many people did Father help? Can't you help too? Each according to his abilities! But everyone can help and support others & if you answer that you can't help anyone, that you're helpless yourself, then I say that it's not true. If nothing else, the pain you feel lets you understand others' pain better & help relieve it. Where there's a will there's a way. Be well. I'll write again later about the rest of what you said in your letter.

Many loving kisses from
Your faithful son, Otto

It is clear from this letter how much has changed. Otto's letters to his parents used to be dutiful, written because it was expected to write letters in his family; this letter shows that at only twenty he was extraordinarily mature with a deep understanding of his mother. It is as though he had stepped out from under the shadow of his older brother, Robert—the imaginative, gifted young man—and now was showing what he had in him. He obviously felt responsible for the family—had taken that responsibility upon himself. Unfortunately, the letter from his mother that Otto refers to has not been preserved. But presumably it had told him about the black pit into which she had fallen after Michael's death, about her despair and failing courage.

The next year, on the anniversary of Michael's death, Otto wrote to his mother:

As you can see from my letter of the 3rd, I remembered the date. I'm sure countless memories are rushing through you and we all have been amazed at how quietly you bear everything alone, without ever discussing anything with us or with Grandma. Amazed at it and sometimes regretting it too. We had a beautiful childhood and we all know it, I not the least, and my young life is also rich in memories, it's probably from you that I got my inability to forget. It's just that I have a happier nature & don't brood so much—as of course I did before now.

I am also lucky enough to be able to express my thoughts freely to others, especially to you and my brothers and sister. I know that I have my parents to thank for my happy childhood and am always grateful for it. I hope we can talk more about this later in person, at greater length.

It was her children that gave Alice the strength and courage to bear the difficult years that lay ahead—the years without Michael, as a widow.

Alice Frank, circa 1910

4.
The Siblings

Otto was grown up, and now it was clear how close he was to his family, how tied to them, with bonds that would shape his whole life.

His relationship to Leni, which had always been good, grew more intense after Michael's death. He all but took over the father's role for his little sister. In 1909 he wrote a letter containing these wise, almost precocious sentences: "For every person is different & the more people you meet, the more different lines of thought you get to know & that is how you form your own thoughts. You know how I always like people, just because they are people & so they show me how life is. And life interests me. You are now also at an age when the friendships you form will last & maybe for life."

His comments on Leni's reading are in the true style of an older brother: "Keep writing to me diligently & even if you've read novels you're not supposed to read. But don't go too far with such things, they really are pointless & can only harm you. They work you up and get you excited, but you have to be reasonable & know what you're doing. Mörike is very good. I have his complete works on my shelf. If you read them, please don't get them dirty because the covers are white & in good shape."

The special affection between Otto and Leni would last their whole lives. Leni's relationship with Robert, on the other hand, seems to have been more difficult. Leni wasn't the sweet, spoiled little sister anymore; she had grown up into her own independent person, and Robert seems to have had problems with that. Unfortunately, there are no letters from this period except from Otto, though there must have been a many-sided correspondence at the time.

A melancholy poem that Alice wrote in early June 1912 has been preserved:

Oh, Mother, how it felt to spy
Our garden, after the years gone by,
Where once we were so full of cheer,—
The time so far, the place so near.
I walked right by the little cabin, where
The lilac bloomed on the wall, just there.
My eyes were already dimmed with pain:
My turbulent feelings sought it, in vain.
Still, the apple tree's branches spread
Out even more sturdily than they had,
And near the trellis on that ground
We so often walked past, gazes down,
I saw your roses, red and round.
Instead of the nearby pathways, though,
Snaking through the meadows twain,
(Our meadows! so well tended, oh!
So closely mowed and well maintained!)
Where a child's foot barely dared to go
Now weedy wildernesses grow!
But back behind the garden house
It's almost the same as it was before:
The red steps where we used to carouse,
Jump up and down in days of yore;
The brown gate so oft opened wide;
And greeting us like well-known eyes

The flashing windows look down at us all
Under shoots of old ivy on the wall.
Overhead and arching free,
Was the dome of the mighty chestnut tree.
The days and years a many-linked chain
Winding gratefully, painfully back again
To the dearest places of the past,
I stood a long time brooding, lost.
I felt the overflowing pleasures
Of youth, I felt the quiet treasures
Of an easy heart in my breast, I was
So blissfully touched, so enveloped in
The peace you and father made for us
Which held us like the vault of heaven.
The riches of our childhood were
Like paradise lost, but we had to endure;
On the gate the angel's word did burn:
"Never again will you return."
Slowly, my eyes dim with tears and sadness,
I wandered back through the wilderness.
I greeted the old swing, with a thousand
Happy memories wound around it.
I saw the basin of the fountain,
The tender slope of the Bergelchen mountain,
Looking back down, my gaze passed by
The castle wall where the white trees were
That stretched their branches in days gone by
Over festivals in the open air.
They came to my mind, I don't know how.
Longing backward, I walked ahead
And all the treasures that once were ours
They silently filled my heart and head,
They came without bitterness, they were pure
More joy and sorrow than I could endure.

And then I walked through the garden gate,
Turned the old key with gentle care,
Stood there remembering till it grew late,
And thought: at home I would find you there.

This poem shows the gloomy, melancholy mood that Alice was sunk in after Michael's death and only with difficulty ever emerged from. But life went on. Alice had inherited the bank and was now responsible for supporting the family—she had to manage to find new routines, a new life not only for her children and her mother but for herself.

Robert had no interest in the banking business, only in being an art dealer. Otto returned home from America, but he apprenticed with a businessman and then got a job at a Düsseldorf metalworks company. An attorney was in charge of running the bank, and Alice took on a supervisory role. Michael had apparently always discussed his business activities with her. Still, the new role must have been difficult for her. And yet she filled it well, because the bank continued to succeed, suffering setbacks only as a result of World War I and later the worldwide economic crisis of the 1920s.

In 1904, France and England resolved the conflicts stemming from their colonial endeavors and reached an entente, while Russia and England too had come to an agreement with respect to their interests in Asia. Germany felt surrounded. The conflict flared up when the Balkan peoples tried to complete their unification into nation-states by breaking off parts of the Austro-Hungarian Empire that had been conquered from Turkey centuries before. These efforts collided with the economic and geopolitical interests of the European Great Powers, and the Balkan situation developed into what was soon called the fuse on the "powder keg of Europe."

Then, when the Austrian crown prince, Franz Ferdinand, and

Anfang Juni 1912.

Wie wird mir, Mutter, da ich nach Jahren
Den alten Garten nun wiederseh,
Wo wir so jung einst u. glücklich waren —
So ferne die Zeit, die Stätte so nah.
Am Wolf'schen Hüttchen ging ich vorüber
Da wurden mir schon die Augen trüber,
Den Flieder, der dort an der Mauer geblüht,
Sucht' ich umsonst mit bewegtem Gemüth
Doch mächtiger noch als zu unseren Zeiten
Sah ich des Apfelbaums Äste sich breiten
Und bei dem Läubchen in der Mitten
An dem wir, die Blicke abgewandt
Vorsichtig oft vorübergeschritten,

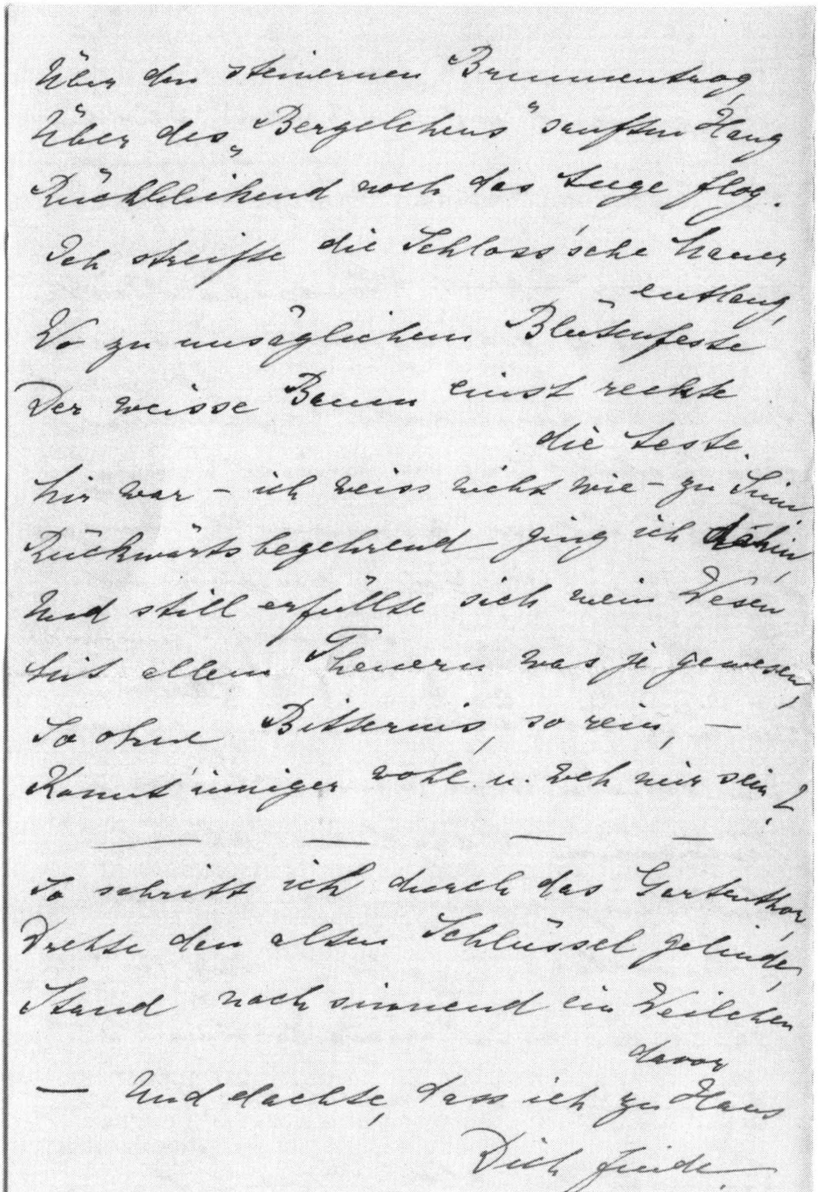
Über den steinernen Brunnentrog
Über des „Bergelchens" sanften Hang
Rückblickend noch das Auge flog.
Ich streifte die Schloss'sche Mauer entlang
Wo zu unsäglichem Blütenfeste
Der weisse Baum einst reckte die Äste.
Mir war – ich weiss nicht wie – zu Sinn
Rückwärts begehrend ging ich dahin
Und still erfüllte sich mein Wesen
Mit allem Theuren was je gewesen,
So ohne Bitternis, so rein, –
Kann's inniger wohl u. doch nie sein?

— — — —

So schritt ich durch das Gartenthor
Drehte den alten Schlüssel gelinde,
Stand nachsinnend ein Weilchen davor
— Und dachte, dass ich zu Haus
Dich finde.

Poem by Alice Frank, June 1912

his wife were assassinated by a Serbian nationalist in Sarajevo on June 28, 1914, Vienna wanted to resolve the Serbian question once and for all. That would only be possible, however, with the help of its German allies. Meanwhile, England and Russia were allies, and the Russians backed Serbia against Austria's July Ultimatum. With the Russian mobilization of July 31, the die was cast in Berlin for a military solution, and so began the war that would later be called the First World War and that led to a decisive break in history and in the life of mankind. In August 1914, the "good old days" came to an end, and the era of horrific twentieth-century warfare was born.

At first the soldiers went off to war as though to a picnic in the countryside–singing, sticking flowers in their rifles, and promising to be back home by Christmas at the latest. No one suspected that the war would last for four long, hard years with staggering losses of life on all sides. By autumn, after the conquest of Belgium, the German advance was already brought to a halt, at the Battle of the Marne. The yearlong trench war at Verdun, in northern France, and in Flanders, took the lives of millions of soldiers. The battles remained outside the German borders, with the German armies laying waste to the neighboring countries and using poison gas for the first time in history in the Battle of Ypres; for the French and the Belgians, on the other hand, the *Grande Guerre* with its slaughterhouses of Verdun and Flanders remains a living memory down to this day. While the German men gave their lives "on the field of honor," the women were asked to give their all "on the home front": their enemy was the lack of food, which grew worse and worse and eventually led to widespread famine.

Until they were granted equal civil rights, the Jews had not been allowed to serve in the German army. Now, with the outbreak of World War I, a large number of German Jews hoped that by proving their patriotism and voluntarily enlisting, they could finally assert a German national identity and assimilate fully into

German society. Despite the slander spread by anti-Semites that the Jews would shirk active duty, in truth the percentage of the Jewish population that voluntarily enlisted was higher than the national average. A hundred thousand Jews fought in World War I, and thirty thousand were decorated for "bravery in the face of the enemy." Twelve thousand died for their "German fatherland."

What happened to the Frank family in World War I? They too felt themselves to be German—they *were* German. Nevertheless, they could not have been as enthusiastic about the war as many others were. They had relatives in England, relatives in France. As recently as the summer of 1914, Michael's brother Léon Frank had come to visit Mertonstrasse in Frankfurt with his wife, Nanette, and their sons Oscar, Georges, and Jean-Michel. The great fear they must have had, that cousin would have to take up arms against cousin, was now bitter truth. When their first and then their second son fell in battle against Germany, Léon Frank jumped out of a window in despair and Nanette had to be sent to a sanatorium. Only Jean-Michel, twenty years old, remained behind. Herbert would later visit him in Paris and probably stayed with him for a while in his apartment on Avenue Kléber.

Front: Nanette, Jean-Michel, and Léon Frank; rear: Oscar and Georges

Right at the start of the war, Alice Frank had signed up as a volunteer nurse at the Kyffhäuser military hospital in Frankfurt, according to a certificate from the "Hospital Personnel Employment Office" dated September 21, 1914. In June 1917, she was awarded the honorary medallion for volunteer nurses. There is also a pass from Reserve Hospital X granting Nurse Alice Frank permission to leave Frankfurt am Main for Travemünde, valid from July 1 to August 1, 1917, at midnight. "All authorities are hereby requested to permit the bearer to travel unhindered and give the bearer any aid and assistance that should be necessary. Signed: Head Doctor." Underneath it says: "1. This pass must be shown to the window attendants freely and voluntarily when purchasing a military train ticket, must be shown upon demand during the journey, and must be handed in upon returning from leave. 2. Do not answer any questions! Do not discuss any military matters! (Espionage hazard!) 3. For travel on personal business, purchase only public rail tickets." One additional document survives: "Frau Alice Frank, recommended by Dr. Grünwald, is hereby authorized to wear Red Cross Armband #581." Later, Leni too would sign up as a nurse at the military hospital.

It goes without saying that Robert, Otto, and Herbert also took part in World War I. Robert served in the First Squadron, Cavalry Regiment, on horseback. Herbert was in the Eighteenth Army and left Frankfurt in early December 1914 for Lüttich. Otto was drafted into a Rhineland infantry artillery regiment in 1915. He sent numerous letters from his barracks in Mainz, the first of which, from August 7, 1915, displays a naive and carefree attitude that is hard to even imagine today:

Dear everyone, You would have enjoyed my calling-up yesterday as much as I did. After a very good meal in the main train station, we drove here and arrived at 11:00 a.m. in our bunk, i.e. straw sack, 19 people in a room for 8. Today we were split up, clothed, & had to thoroughly clean house. My job was to wash the windows & put my boots in order etc. On the whole I believe I am very lucky to be here.

Unlike with Robert, almost everyone here is older and rather fat and cut a lot of slack, & so the training here should be pretty easy. The sergeant is very quiet & friendly, in short everything's fine for now.

In two weeks I should be allowed to live outside the barracks. The food is very good here, but feel free to send stuff anyway—eggs, cigars and cigarettes, no clothes yet except a pair of socks.

Five days later he wrote again, to say that the training was indeed very easy, he was never even tired; his muscles were sore sometimes, but that wasn't a bad thing. Aside from that, he said how much he was looking forward to their visit, it would definitely be especially interesting for Helene to get to see the inside of a barrack.

Otto's letters to Leni during the war are particularly affectionate and worried about her. He calls her Lunner, Lunni, Leni—children who are loved have lots of names.

On one occasion, he wrote: "You write, 'Now I'm doing something else.' What else? If you stay single, then I'll stay single too, and we'll keep a wonderful house together, right? Dummy! What a thing to contemplate now."

Less than a week later:

Your letter was so sweet and sincere that I don't want to wait long to answer it. I'm glad that you can write to me that way, you know how important it is to me that we be able to live in perfect harmony and how glad I am to mediate whenever it's a question of clearing up misunderstandings.

We've probably had fewer misunderstandings than most people, don't you think? because our personalities are kind of similar & so I'm glad when I see that you trust your brother Otto & that we can still talk to each other freely, the way we always did. That is worth a lot, dear Lunni, I often think and have often thought that mothers and siblings are the only people in the world you can truly rely on—at least that's maybe how it is with us Jews.

With Robert you'll never be like you are with me, and that's only natural, but where there's a will to understand or at least recognize the other point of view, then understanding is possible. You yourself could observe that many times, between Robert and Mother too. Whenever anything goes wrong, Robert is there and ready to help out. That's the best sign, since it's in the most difficult times that people show their true nature openly, while in daily life everything is muddled & every passing mood or impression is reflected in their behavior.

How clearly we can see here the Otto Frank who would later, in the Secret Annex, always try to mediate between people and strive for mutual understanding and sympathy. When we read his letters, it is impossible to avoid the thought that Anne Frank inherited much, much more from her father than just her external appearance. His spirit, his love of others, and his humanistic principles shaped his daughter as well.

Otto mentioned the relationship between Leni and their brother Robert again and again in his letters. It was apparently not always a happy one, but a card that Robert wrote to Leni for her twenty-third birthday demonstrates that the discord was not truly serious. The card showed Sergeant Robert Frank on horseback and is addressed to "Miss Leni Frank, Munich, Bayerischer Hof." (Did Leni really take a vacation to a Munich hotel in the middle of the war?)

Otto's letters to Leni grew more and more intense and heartfelt. For example, on Christmas 1916, to his "dear Lunni":

Thank you for the two letters, and I'm glad you're being reasonable and sticking by Mother and Grandma as best you can. I'm also very glad you put up with Robert better this time, you know I'm a little [illegible] when it comes to family. Herbi really has had the worst luck and is in by far the worst situation of the three of us. I feel tremendously sorry for him, poor guy, but of course that doesn't do much good in these terrible times. [. . .] It can't go on much longer, even if the Entente Minister can't seem to shut his trap.

Things were apparently not going well for Herbert. He was serving in the Fifth Army, Western Front, Second Company, 149th Reinforcement Battalion. His grandmother Cornelia wrote to her grandson, her "Dearest Herbelchen" (he was twenty-five years old at the time), on December 28, 1916:

I'm so terribly worried about you and sadly with good reason. Your last letter sounds a bit more satisfactory T.G. [Thank God] as far as rations are concerned but everything else seems to leave a lot to be desired. Believe me, my golden boy, that I miss you, your soup plate is always standing ready, but Leni, who wants to take your place, is not always punctual and so your place is often empty. [. . .] Don't lose courage, it looks like better days are on their way, stay healthy, that is what I hope for more than anything.

The following year, August 28, 1917, Robert wrote and told his mother how good it was that Herbert could now stay at home. This letter also contained a drawing that Robert titled "Cross Section Through My Room Under the Churchyard Wall," a surreal drawing that uncannily depicts the dangers of war, death lurking everywhere around the soldier in his exhausted sleep.

Robert Frank as a soldier in World War I

From a distance, from the battlefield, Otto was also concerned about his sister's love life, which apparently gave rise to a lot of discussion. On May 19, 1917, Otto wrote to his "dear Lunni" about a certain K. and Leni's feelings for him: "I've now heard all sorts of things and there's nothing unflattering about K. in Mother's letters, but only now in your letters do I see how serious you are. I can only say that I find your inclination to wait and see & consider to be thoroughly reasonable & at the same time I can't imagine how you feel." Otto tries to advise his sister, and talks about feelings and the language of the heart, "since if a girl marries a man she doesn't really love she can have only half a life & you know that yourself."

In a later letter to Leni, staying in Travemünde at the time, Otto writes about their grandmother Cornelia, who "suffers so much from nerves and from the fact that you are not there with her now & neither is Robert. When she's in an excited state there isn't much anyone can do to help her, but still the feeling of being left alone is always depressing for her." In the same letter Otto also mentions that, try as he might, he cannot share Robert's unhappiness at the sale of one of their paintings, an Adam and Eve; he is glad "to have the naked couple out of the house at last. Nowadays you have to be happy with any 'cash' you can get, because who knows what's coming next.[. . .] I devour the newspapers & hope that the Russians will get a good thrashing so that we can finally be done with all this. I don't think Russia will last another winter & I'm sticking to my optimistic point of view."

The further progress of the war showed how wrong Otto Frank (now a sergeant major) and his optimistic opinion were. But the letter is significant for two other reasons. First, Cornelia was suffering "from nerves" again—in other words, her multiple illnesses should be considered as falling within the range of symptoms categorized as "neurasthenia" at the time, which today we would probably call depression. Second, the Franks, whose bank specializing in foreign currency exchange was obviously doing very little business in wartime, were apparently forced to sell valuable objects from their house, which hurt Robert's artistic sensibilities but prompted Otto, always much more pragmatic, to comment that in these times people were happy with whatever cash they could get.

28. August 1917.
Liebe Mutter! Das ist aber eine schöne
Überraschung, daß Herbert jetzt zu Hause
bleiben kann. Ich hatte gerade einliegen-
den Brief an ihn eingeworfen, als die

Letter from Robert Frank to Alice, August 28, 1917

On August 31, 1917, he then wrote a very beautiful, sympathetic letter to Leni, who was struggling with an unhappy or at least unsatisfactory love affair. This letter also shows how openly the Frank family would discuss their problems among themselves.

Dearest Lunni,

I am finally resolved to answer your letter, first of all because I've just got some free time & second since I've received letters from both Robert and Mother mentioning E.S. [Ernst Schneider]. Mother writes to say that you've given up the correspondence with him & Robert gave me his opinion based on his conversation with you, so now I need to write and relay it to you again, since it's precisely our open and honest conversations with each other that lay the foundation for our mutual trust. Robert has the impression that you think about this man much too much & that in spite of your assurances to the contrary you secretly harbor the hope & idea that something might come of this after all. And he thinks it's so self-evident that this would meet the strongest resistance not only from Mother but also from him &, he assumes, from me and Herbert that we don't even need to talk about it.

Dear child, we don't live in an ideal world. I believe you & I can't and don't want to pass judgment on this man. As I wrote to you before, I don't see any point in preserving a relationship that can't lead to anything healthy. Think of it this way: It was something beautiful. Consider it as an interlude, a brief, beautiful, ideal time in these war years during which happy, pure souls like you miss out on much more than many other people. But draw a line under the episode & don't let there be nasty aftereffects. Let what was beautiful remain beautiful. Ideals are ideal precisely because they can't be achieved.

In a later letter, Otto returned to the problem again: "As for Ernst, I already told you that I value him as a person. I don't think he was right for you, even aside from the pecuniary and familial requirements he is not suited by nature to guide and direct you. A man you can trust [. . .] but not, it seems to me, someone strong enough to carry out what he attempts. A friend, but no husband. He has certain similarities to me, actually, in his understanding, his softheartedness."

Otto Frank thus feels himself similar to this man in understanding, and in softheartedness. His self-assessment is even clearer in a later letter to Leni: "What you write about me is too flattering to be true. I have as much ego as anyone, I just express it in another form. The same time I got your letter I received a few lines from Elsa R., who also sings my praises. It's just that it makes me happy to make other people happy, & so both parties benefit. There's nothing to thank or praise me for, I just do what my reason & conscience tell me to."

This letter brings to life the Otto Frank whom his daughter Anne worshipped without it ever being entirely clear why from her diary. He must really have been as tolerant, balanced, and civilized as his contemporaries described him as being—a serious, thoughtful man. At the same time, these letters show his tendency to withdraw or keep himself out of the limelight, a quality which would distinguish him later in the Secret Annex, and which must have been an important part of his personality. In any case, he was writing these letters from the battlefield, under outward circumstances that must have weighed heavily upon him—his life was constantly in danger—and yet he worried about his sister and her love life, keeping quiet about his own problems. This self-effacement can also be seen in a letter to his grandmother Cornelia:

If wishes could make you better then you would truly have nothing to complain about, but as it is, we can only hope as always that you can relax a little & that in better times you will get pleasure again from us & from life. You mustn't lose courage, even when things look bad.

Everything's fine with me & there's no reason to worry about me at all, I'm not worrying about myself. Yesterday I went to church with Lieutenant Sch. & was looking out at the countryside when I noticed a pair of pigeons in the corner. Today we delivered the pigeons to their proper destination—they were carrier pigeons that had got lost. I thought of you & a delicious roast squab, but you have to let carrier pigeons fulfill their destinies. So I am now in search of some chickens, & hope I'll manage to get hold of a couple somehow.

Otto wrote nothing about life as a soldier, mentioning neither his fears nor the death that reigned all around him—there was not a word about his own despair. Only once do we get a hint of how he probably felt. In a letter to Leni, he wrote: "When can we finally start our comfortable life? I've really started thinking again & a man really does miss women, that's how it is, a man alone is half a life. So my thoughts roam here and there, but they don't settle on anything. You think of the past & you plan for the future & it's all a useless game, it's a strange feeling." In a birthday letter to his grandmother Cornelia, he wrote: "I never once thought about 'New Year's' [Rosh Hashanah, the Jewish New Year]. What is there to celebrate? I'm very sorry to hear that Trauda has lost another nephew. How many people are suffering like that, day after day? You can't even understand how anyone's still left to carry on the fight."

Otto Frank as a soldier in World War I

Otto obviously was always thinking about his family; they were at the center of his thoughts, and their well-being was more important to him than anything else. Otto's character comes through especially clearly in a letter he sent to his mother on the anniversary of his father's death:

My thoughts fly to you with these lines & to everyone else there too, coming together in your thoughts of Father. A few months ago I had counted on being able to be back home with you on this difficult day, but it didn't work out & I can only be at your side in my thoughts. You know my thoughts without my needing to go into any details. It's not the goal of these words to lose myself in gloomy memories. On the contrary. We should hold tight in our memories to the happy, uplifting things, and call back the good times, now when everything dark around us is so much darker than usual. And you don't lack happy memories any more than we do. We're all living off the past, really. The uncertain future wavers before us like a dream, the present and its demands consume all our superfluous thoughts, only the past refreshes our spirits. So anyone who has good years behind him and can spin unbreakable threads from his memories of those years has to count himself lucky. And we all have good memories, thanks to the example you've set for us & the joys & pleasures you have let us take part in. So even the 17th mustn't only be a day of mourning for you. What you & we have lost, we know that. But did Father lose anything by not living through these times? My thoughts are wandering, I'll stop here. Your Otto.

The longer the war lasted, the worse the situation got in terms of provisions. Furthermore, thousands of wounded and maimed men were coming back from the front, despite the steel helmets that were introduced in 1916 after the terrible head wounds of the first years of the war. There was not enough food, enough bandages, enough medicine.

Otto was called to the western front and served in a light rangers artillery troop in the Cambrai sector. He must have experienced the first major tank attack of the war—the first in history—in November 1916, and in 1918 he was promoted to lieutenant and received the Iron Cross, although he doesn't mention that in his letters. Only his family mattered to him. On August 8–11, 1918, the English forces broke deep into the German positions with 450 tanks; August 8 has ever since been "the black day for the German army," and it contributed significantly to their final defeat. On November 11, 1918, the armistice went into effect. All three of the Frank sons had survived.

On December 15, 1918, Dr. M. Katzenstein of the medical corps wrote to Alice Frank. The document is not only a doctor's reference for his assistant but at the same time a thank-you note to someone who had shared his suffering:

For 4 years we have spent many worrisome hours together but also many satisfying hours that spurred us on to new labors, and when I think with satisfaction that it was granted to me to have helped in some small way so many of our poor soldiers, to have dried a few of their tears and alleviated some of their suffering, this is thanks in no small part to your

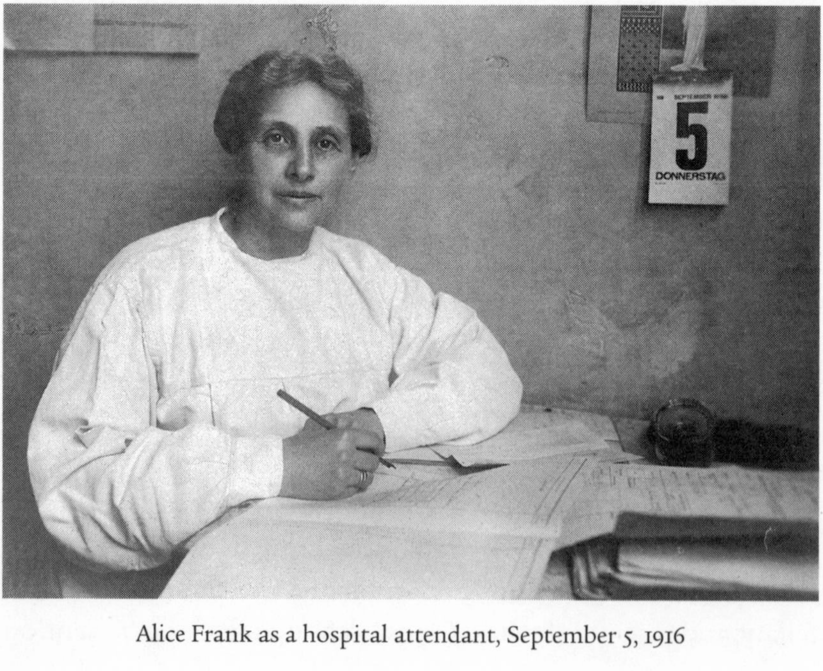

Alice Frank as a hospital attendant, September 5, 1916

self-sacrificing assistance. You have not only sacrificed your valuable time, sometimes more than the conscientious housewife in you could well spare, you have also given of your bodily and mental strength, and above all you always attended to the task at hand with your whole good heart, and all of this has made it possible to say today after 4 years that we did it for the fatherland. It is indeed an official duty of mine to acknowledge your great services properly, but since certain things in this respect are different than we had imagined, due to the new political conditions, you will no doubt find your greatest reward for everything good you have done for our wounded in the fact that you can think back on your actions during Germany's darkest hour with satisfaction and with the knowledge that you have faithfully fulfilled your duties.

By these "new political conditions," Dr. Katzenstein no doubt meant the abdication of Kaiser Wilhelm II on November 9, 1918; the debate about the form in which Germany would continue to exist after its defeat; the confusion of the 1918–19 revolution; and the proclamation of the German Republic. The revolutionary unrest lasted almost a year, until the constitution of August 11, 1919, laid the foundation for the Weimar Republic.

The Franks were certainly faithful to the kaiser. This is proven by an invitation to a charity ball in October 1901 that the Franks received on the occasion of a Prussian princess's visit: "Sir! Her Royal Highness the Princess Friedrich Carl von Hesse, Princess Margarethe of Prussia, will be honoring our International Fair with her presence, and we therefore invite you to arrive punctually on Thursday afternoon at 1:30. Black tie. Faithfully yours, the Select Committee, Georg Adelmann, L. Krebs-Pfaff."

And in 1907, "Banker Michael Frank in Frankfurt a.M." received a thank-you note signed by Kaiser Wilhelm himself:

Through the generous contribution that you have put at my disposal for the purposes of founding a convalescent home for officers in Falkenstein in the Taunus, you helped me to fulfill a wish I have long treasured and at the same time have helped lay the groundwork for a project that, God willing, will redound to the benefit of thousands in my army.

In expressing my most heartfelt gratitude for your spirit of sacrifice, I have ordered a bust of me, modeled by Professor Manzel and manufactured in my majolica factory in Cadinen, to be sent to you forthwith as a sign of my appreciation.

Berlin, January 27, 1907
H.R.H. Wilhelm

One reason for the Franks' faithful service to the kaiser was no doubt their gratitude for the form of government that had brought the Jews equal civil rights. In addition, their social position presumably made them far more conservative than socialist. Thus Alice Frank, like many of her patriotic German fellow citizens, had bought war bonds with her private funds and lost a lot of money. Still, it is safe to assume that Alice Frank and her sons were in accord with the new form of government, the republic. They were in a position to be interested in politics only insofar as it had a direct influence on their own lives.

For the time being, they had other concerns, and also other things to celebrate. Leni, after her unhappy affair with E.S. (Ernst Schneider), fell in love with Erich Elias, a Jewish man from Zweibrücken. He had taken part in the war as well: the cache of documents includes an authorization form for one year of voluntary service, from the examination board in Speyer, dated May 1, 1915. He too received an Iron Cross.

The love between Leni Frank and Erich Elias must have been passionate, because beautiful, exuberant love letters from Leni to Erich survive. He too came from a very close-knit family. For example, his father, Carl Elias, visited his new relatives in December 1920 and afterward wrote a grateful letter to his son: "I've more or less recovered from the strain it was a bad follow-up to the delightful days I spent with your new relatives, they were all

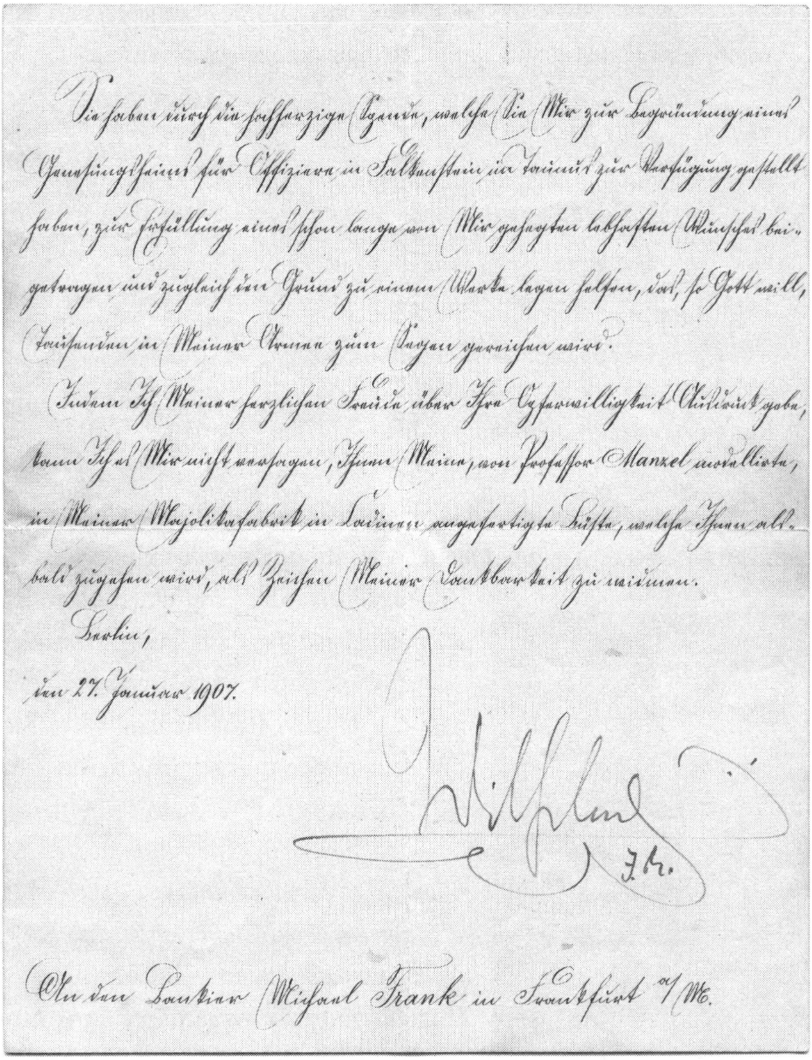

Sie haben durch die hochherzige Spende, welche Sie Mir zur Begründung eines Genesungsheims für Offiziere in Falkenstein im Taunus zur Verfügung gestellt haben, zur Erfüllung eines schon lange von Mir gehegten lebhaften Wunsches beigetragen und zugleich den Grund zu einem Werke legen helfen, das, so Gott will, Tausenden in Meiner Armee zum Segen gereichen wird.

Indem Ich Meiner herzlichen Freude über Ihre Opferwilligkeit Ausdruck gebe, kann Ich es Mir nicht versagen, Ihnen Meine, von Professor Manzel modellierte, in Meiner Majolikafabrik in Cadinen angefertigte Büste, welche Ihnen alsbald zugehen wird, als Zeichen Meiner Dankbarkeit zu widmen.

Berlin,

den 27. Januar 1907.

Wilhelm I.R.

An den Bankier Michael Frank in Frankfurt a/M.

Letter of thanks from Kaiser Wilhelm to Michael Frank, 1907

so nice and considerate to me; there has been so much work to do here at home that I have not yet had a chance to thank them for all their consideration."

Erich Elias and Leni Frank were married on February 16, 1921.

In a poem that Alice recited at the wedding, she mentioned that Helen Schuster, a childhood friend of the Frank children, had introduced Leni and Erich. The six-stanza poem gives many details of the childhood of the bride; in the second stanza:

Then when our little girl was born
Everything was turned upside down.
The child was small but our joy was great,
Her arms and legs were so little and sweet.
Trauda was scared to give her baths
Or hurt her by taking off her clothes.
She may not have always got her way
But we have our naches now today.

Yiddish words come up very rarely in the family's letters—they apparently spoke a pure German with nothing of their Jewish heritage in it—but the word *naches* is an exception: it means "joy, pleasure."

Erich and Leni's wedding photograph, February 16, 1921

One of the few surviving documents from Paul Elias, Erich's brother, who was murdered in Auschwitz, is this wedding poem:

Since Elias, as we all know,
Was a great prophet long ago,
And since everyone in this family
Has a habit of always speaking frank-ly,
I will prophesy today:
That this couple will be happy always.
For pure love binds them to each other
And that is the best way to ensure
A true and faithful life together.
So now we wish for the youthful pair
That the sun of happiness will always
Shine upon them as it does this day . . .

Alice had thus married off her daughter, but in the same year she lost her mother. Cornelia died in June 1921, another hard blow of fate for Alice since she and her mother were so close. There are no documents attesting to her loss; presumably the fact that her daughter was pregnant consoled Alice a little, and helped her get over the loss of her mother. Leni and Erich's first son, Stephan Carl, was born on December 20, 1921, a wonderful present on Alice's fifty-sixth birthday. Three and a half years later, on June 2, 1925, came their second son, Bernhard Paul, nicknamed Buddy—only Otto Frank and his family would call him Bernd.

There is a lot of evidence to show that Leni and Erich had a good marriage. Not only their younger son, Buddy, but Gerti, Buddy's wife, report that Leni and Erich's life together was harmonious and tell stories about Leni's gentle, affectionate teasing. She was apparently the stronger of the two.

The following year, two more weddings took place. On April 12, 1922, Herbert August Frank married an American, Hortense Rah Schott, living in Aachen. The marriage produced no children and ended in divorce on August 16, 1932. The judgment reads: "She, the respondent, left him, the petitioner, in September 1930. A legal judgment of March 31, 1931, required her to return to the married state, but this judgment has not been obeyed . . . The marriage is therefore dissolved and respondent is held to be responsible." And on July 18, 1922, Robert Frank married Charlotte Witt, whom everyone called Lotti. Neither letters nor poems related to either wedding survive.

The next important wedding took place in 1925, when Otto Frank married Edith Holländer, daughter of the Aachen industrialist Abraham Holländer and his wife, Rosa née Stern. For Otto, who was by then working in the family bank, Edith's dowry may have played a significant role, since financially Michael Frank's banking house was not doing well after Germany's defeat and the Holländers were a very wealthy family.

Not much is known about Edith's childhood. She was born

in Aachen, a city near the Dutch border, on January 16, 1900. As the name Holländer suggests, her ancestors had emigrated from Amsterdam to Germany, in around 1800. Benjamin Holländer, Edith's grandfather, began as a scrap metal dealer, quickly found success, and later owned several metalworking factories. Edith's father, Abraham, was born in 1860 in Eschweiler, one of nine children. His own children were Julius (b. 1894), Walter (b. 1897), Bettina (b. 1898), and finally Edith. Abraham took over the family business and proved to be a successful businessman.

The Holländers were not Orthodox, but Abraham was a prominent member of the Jewish community in Aachen. Compared with the Franks, they were religious. They kept a kosher household and regularly went to temple, where Edith's oldest brother, Julius, sang in the choir. Edith attended the Victoria School, a Protestant girls' high school that also accepted students of other faiths. She is described as a shy girl, but is also said to have had many friends. She played tennis and paid a lot of attention to fashionable clothing.

The year 1914 was a turning point in her life, because her sister, Betti, died at only sixteen years old, of complications from appendicitis. To honor her memory, Edith would later name her firstborn daughter Margot Betti. During the war, Edith took her exams and helped her father in the office. Her brother Julius was wounded with a gunshot to the arm and put on the disabled list.

Edith's parents knew about Otto Frank's financial difficulties, but it probably would have pleased them that their daughter was marrying into one of the best-known families in Frankfurt. Most likely, their main concern was that the Franks were known to be among the assimilated Jews, and anything but religious. Edith didn't keep a kosher household, but her daughters, especially Margot, still learned about Jewish life at their grandparents' house. Edith herself was an open, liberal-minded woman, as is clear from the "modern educational methods" that later, in the Secret Annex, would rub everybody else the wrong way.

Edith Frank née Holländer, the mother of Margot and Anne Frank, circa 1925

Edith and Otto Frank's wedding photograph, May 12, 1925

In the noticeably tight-knit network of the Frank and Elias families, Edith seems to have been somewhat off to one side. Possibly she chose this position herself, although her own prominent sense of family, her close relationship with her mother, and her love for her brothers would seem to suggest the contrary. Perhaps the Franks were simply too dominant, and too focused on themselves, to make room for her, even though she no doubt deserved it.

The wedding took place on May 12, 1925, Otto's thirty-sixth birthday, following the Jewish custom in accordance with the wishes of the bride's parents. After the ceremony, the reception was celebrated in the Great Monarch luxury hotel in Aachen. A so-called "fairy tale" printed in a newspaper-style wedding announcement, the *Aachen-Frankfurt Daily Paper*—"first and only edition"—tells how Otto and Edith met:

Once upon a time—that's how fairy tales always start, but this time what I have to tell is a true story. Once upon a time in San Remo, in 1925, under blossoming flowers and in the laughing sunshine, a family from the Rhineland was taking a stroll by the deep blue sea. The family consisted of three ladies and a gentleman whose youthful appearance made it impossible to guess that he was the father of the family. Further sharpening people's curiosity, since of course it is well-known that most people on vacation occupy themselves primarily with observing their fellow travelers, a slim young man from Main country had joined the Rhineland family. The beautiful beach of San Remo must not often have had the opportunity to observe together a daughter of the Rhine with a son of the Main, whereas the green meadows can tell far more tales of their affiliation with the river children. The Rhine Maiden's parents cast their eyes discreetly aside, while the goddess Flora, curious as goddesses all too often are, caught every glance of love that passed between the young couple with great delight. After a torturous delay, the young people declared themselves to be engaged and public opinion was duly calmed. All entered upon the return trip to the Main and the Rhine. The couple, eyes magically drawn to each other's, forgot their surroundings and leaned, blessedly entwined, against a gate which a ghost's hand opened; only the powerful protection of the parents prevented them from sinking into the underworld. The goddess Flora enveloped the two lovers in the cloak of love until they reached the destination of their journey.

Today we see them happily united, and I hope that they will often tell this tale of blessed days on the sun-drenched landscape of the Riviera to their children, grandchildren, and great-grandchildren.

Of course no one could know that Otto and Edith would never have grandchildren or great-grandchildren. In 1925, the world was still as it should be, and the future was promising, even though Adolf Hitler had already written his book *Mein Kampf.*

The menu with Alice Stern's name on it has been preserved: "Pasta romana–Soup and side dish–Rhine salmon with mayonnaise–Roast beef and fresh vegetables–Sweetbreads ragout with fresh truffles and stuffed morel mushrooms–Young duck with various compotes and salads–Ice cream–Pastries–Mocha." The rhymed commentary to the menu, presumably by Alice, runs:

It's crucial for a wedding's mood
To solve the problem of the food–
The menu this is writ upon
Has solved it with masterly aplomb!
Above all with the meal, methinks,
One mustn't forget the needed drinks.
And in between the different dishes
Come cheery songs and thoughtful wishes:
That's the only way we can
Tackle the next course on the plan.
Host and guests, we all combine
To make the party a happy time.

It's filled with love and filled with teasing
And all the food is choice and pleasing!

It must have been a magnificent party. After the honeymoon, which took the couple to San Remo once more, Otto and Edith moved in with Alice, in her house at Mertonstrasse 4, where Leni and Erich were living as well. They were still living there in 1926 when their first daughter, Margot Betti, was born.

In 1927, Otto, Edith, and Margot moved into half of a duplex in Marbachweg 307, and in June 1929 their second daughter was born: Annelies Marie, called Anne. The reason for the move may well have been that Otto and Edith, with "modern" ideas about how to raise their children, wanted to avoid any interference from the family. Otto held the humanistic conviction that the only way to make the world a better place was to implant the seeds of goodness in children's souls. He explicitly insisted that he wanted his children to grow up "free," which meant as well, of course, that he aimed toward a liberal environment, free from social constraints. In any case, there was not a rift between the families: the children often visited Grandma Alice, as her nursery maid later reported. Buddy too remembers having seen his cousins often. The family relations were and remained close. Everyone was united in mourning when Trauda, Alice's cook, passed away, and the death notice in the newspaper gives the names of every member of the family.

Am 18. Juni verschied nach kurzer Krankheit unsere liebe

Trauda Ullrich

im 67. Lebensjahre.

Seit 40 Jahren hat sie in treuester Pflichterfüllung in unserem Hause gewirkt. In dieser langen Zeit war sie mit ihrem ganzen Fühlen und Denken mit unserer Familie auf das Engste verbunden und hat stets Freud und Leid mit uns geteilt. Ihr Hinscheiden ist für uns ein unersetzlicher Verlust und wir werden ihr Angedenken stets in hohen Ehren halten.

Alice Frank
Robert und **Lotti Frank**
Otto und **Edith Frank**
Herbert und **Hortense Frank**
Leni und **Erich Elias-Frank**
und drei Kinder.

Frankfurt a. M. (Mertonstr. 4), den 19. Juni 1927. 170

Death announcement for Trauda Ullrich, the Frank family's cook for many years

Meanwhile, both Otto and Erich Elias, Leni's husband, had joined Herbert working for the Michael Frank Bank. It might well have been a matter of necessity: by virtue of the reparations that the defeated Germany had to pay, and the worldwide economic crisis on the horizon, the economic and political situations were growing more and more serious. The New York stock market collapsed on October 24, 1929, and four weeks later the Nazi Party won nine seats in the local election in Frankfurt, up from four, receiving just over 10 percent of the vote.

Erich Elias was the first to draw conclusions from the altered economic and political circumstances. In 1929 he accepted an offer to set up a Swiss office for the Opekta Works and moved to Basel, where Leni joined him two years later. In 1931, the Michael Frank Bank suffered another setback: Herbert was arrested by the authorities for tax evasion. He was accused of breaking the new regulations on securities trading with foreigners. Upon his release he moved to Paris, and at the judicial hearing that pronounced his innocence he was not even present.

Also in 1931, the anti-Semitic owner of the apartment on Marbachweg gave notice that Otto Frank would have to move out, so the Franks moved into a smaller and less expensive apartment on Ganghoferstrasse. But the economic situation only got worse. A quarter of the population was without a stable income. In the Reichstag election of 1932, the Nazis won 230 of the 608 seats. The rise of the National Socialist German Workers Party (NSDAP) to national prominence seemed unstoppable in Frankfurt as well.

Not only the banking business was going badly; the factory in Bad Soden felt the effects of the Depression, and the dowry Edith brought with her into the marriage had already been spent. At the end of December 1932, Edith and Otto gave notice at their apartment on Ganghoferstrasse and moved back in with Alice on Mertonstrasse, to save money on rent.

January 30, 1933: The president of the Reichstag, Paul von Hindenburg, proclaims Hitler the Chancellor of the German Reich. Soon afterward, on March 12, the Nazis win the local elections in Frankfurt am Main as well, and therefore expect to "legally" take control of city hall. On April 1, SA commandos are stationed in the entrances to Jewish warehouses and businesses, and others prevent anyone from entering the offices of Jewish lawyers or doctors. This preplanned "boycott" had the function of subliminally reinforcing the idea that all Jews were bankers, merchants, doctors, or lawyers.

The Franks' financial situation was dire. Alice traveled to Paris once more, to ask Michael's nephew Jean-Michel Frank, an increasingly successful furniture designer, for a loan so that she could pay the mortgage for the large house on Mertonstrasse. Jean-Michel gave it, but it was soon clear that this was just a drop in the ocean. As a result, after long and painful discussions, they decided to leave Germany.

It was a logical choice: under the present economic and political conditions, there was no hope for reviving their banking business. Another important reason, for Otto, was that Margot, who was in school by then, was being forced to sit on a separate bench in the back of the classroom with the other Jewish children. The idea that his children would have to experience such exclusion and ill will must have been unbearable for him. The last straw was when Otto heard the SA gangs marching by outside the window of the bank, loudly singing: "When the storm trooper marches into fire, / Oh, what a brave heart has he, / And when Jew blood spurts from under the knife, / Oh, that's even better to see." He later always described this incident to his nephew Buddy Elias as the main reason he decided to emigrate.

Otto Frank decided on the Netherlands. First, he had friends there, since he had once tried to establish a branch of the bank in Amsterdam (which came to nothing, as it turned out). Second, his brother-in-law Erich Elias helped him get a job setting up a branch of Opekta in the Netherlands. Edith took the children to her parents' house in Aachen, and Otto traveled to Amsterdam to start his new company. In early 1934, he brought the family to Amsterdam.

For Alice, probably ever since Erich's decision to move to Switzerland, it was clear that she would eventually move to Basel as well, to be near her daughter, Leni, and grandchildren, Stephan and Buddy. With the sale of the Frankfurt house to a businessman from Lorraine, she had burned her bridges. On September 21, 1933, Alice left the city where she was born, where she had spent her childhood, her youth, and her years as a wife and mother—the city where her roots extended down so deeply. The history of the Frank and Elias families in Frankfurt am Main had come to an end.

5.

But the Ones Who Stayed Were Scattered to the Winds

So Alice moved to Basel, into a four-room apartment on the second floor of a house on Schweizergasse that Leni had found for her. The statutory declaration she had to give the German authorities upon her emigration is an interesting document, especially the three-page list of all the pieces of furniture she was bringing along "for personal use."

Alice had a housekeeper in Basel as well. She arranged her new life there, but Basel never truly felt like home, which was only natural: she was sixty-eight years old, no longer a young woman, and even though she had all the furniture she knew and loved around her, it must have been hard to move from a large house she had always shared with a large family to a fourth-floor apartment with a small balcony. It was surely also difficult to have to exchange a cosmopolitan metropolis for a tranquil Swiss city in which there was so much that seemed provincial. Everything was strange, foreign, and not what she was used to. Alice must also have missed her extended circle of friends and acquaintances from Frankfurt—even if she was a rather introverted person, it is still easy to imagine how lonely she must have often felt. A woman with her place in society had turned into an exile, a foreigner. And this turning point in her life was one she had to face alone: without Cornelia, without Michael. She was not the type to whine and complain; she must rather have withdrawn

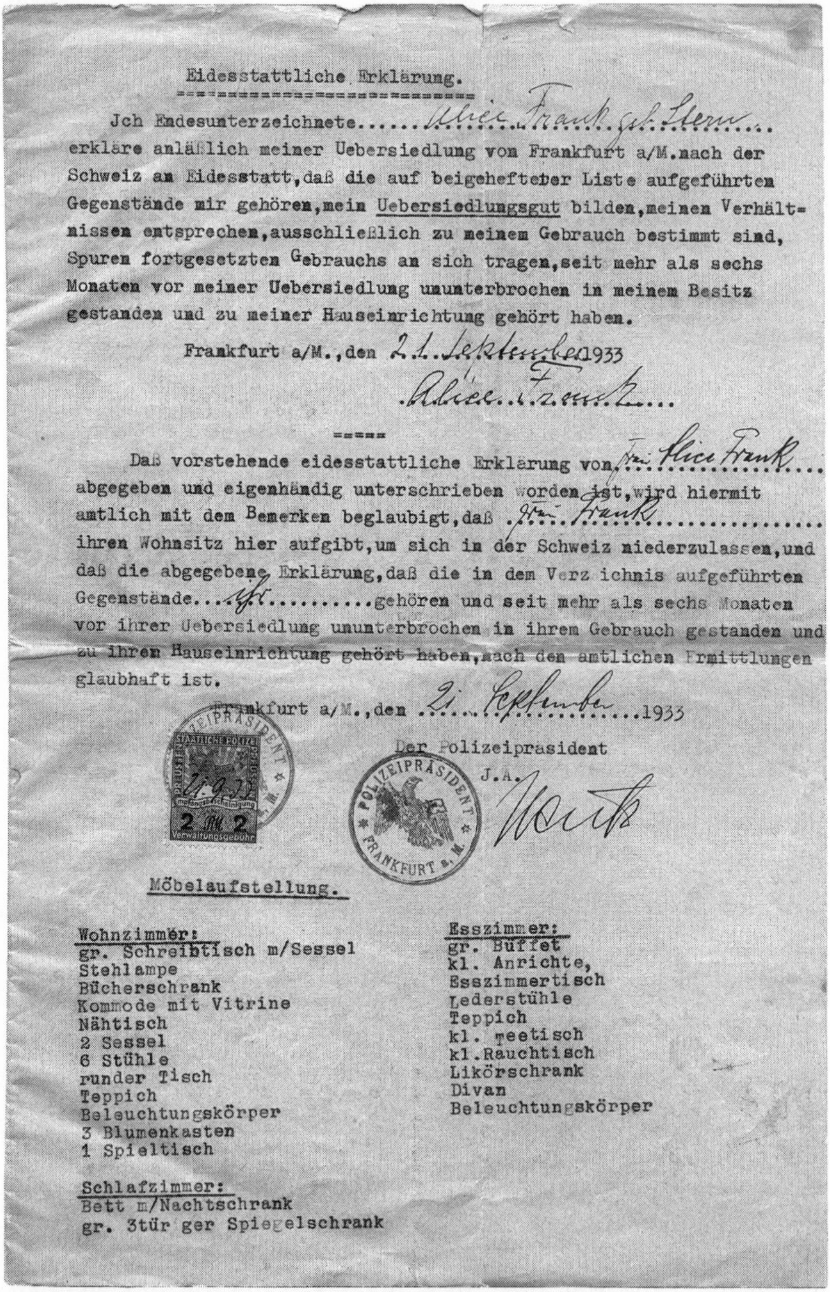

Eidesstattliche Erklärung.

Jch Endesunterzeichnete.....Alice Frank geb. Stern.....
erkläre anläßlich meiner Uebersiedlung von Frankfurt a/M. nach der Schweiz an Eidesstatt, daß die auf beigehefteter Liste aufgeführten Gegenstände mir gehören, mein Uebersiedlungsgut bilden, meinen Verhältnissen entsprechen, ausschließlich zu meinem Gebrauch bestimmt sind, Spuren fortgesetzten Gebrauchs an sich tragen, seit mehr als sechs Monaten vor meiner Uebersiedlung ununterbrochen in meinem Besitz gestanden und zu meiner Hauseinrichtung gehört haben.

Frankfurt a/M., den 21. September 1933

.Alice..Frank....

=====

Daß vorstehende eidesstattliche Erklärung von Frau Alice Frank.... abgegeben und eigenhändig unterschrieben worden ist, wird hiermit amtlich mit dem Bemerken beglaubigt, daß .Frau Frank................ ihren Wohnsitz hier aufgibt, um sich in der Schweiz niederzulassen, und daß die abgegebene Erklärung, daß die in dem Verzeichnis aufgeführten Gegenstände.....ihr..........gehören und seit mehr als sechs Monaten vor ihrer Uebersiedlung ununterbrochen in ihrem Gebrauch gestanden und zu ihrer Hauseinrichtung gehört haben, nach den amtlichen Ermittlungen glaubhaft ist.

Frankfurt a/M., den 21. September.........1933

Der Polizeipräsident
J.A.
Wirth

Möbelaufstellung.

Wohnzimmer:
gr. Schreibtisch m/Sessel
Stehlampe
Bücherschrank
Kommode mit Vitrine
Nähtisch
2 Sessel
6 Stühle
runder Tisch
Teppich
Beleuchtungskörper
3 Blumenkasten
1 Spieltisch

Schlafzimmer:
Bett m/Nachtschrank
gr. 3tür ger Spiegelschrank

Esszimmer:
gr. Büffet
kl. Anrichte,
Esszimmertisch
Lederstühle
Teppich
kl. teetisch
kl. Rauchtisch
Likörschrank
Divan
Beleuchtungskörper

Alice Frank's statutory declaration upon her emigration from Frankfurt to Basel, September 2, 1933 into herself. It would once again have been her needlework and handicrafts that filled her many uneventful hours and days. If Klärchen had not died so young, Alice might have felt less alone in Switzerland.

Of course there were bright spots too, above all Leni and Erich and their two sons, Stephan and Buddy, who often visited her and whom she regularly went to see in turn on Gundeldingerstrasse. But a grown woman with children of her own has her own life to live—Alice knew that—and Leni was a very social person. She struck up acquaintances easily, and there was no shortage of German émigrés in Basel. Many of them remained in the city for only a short while before they had arranged their further travels, and they went to see Leni, asked her advice.

Letters from Amsterdam gave Alice a certain amount of consolation and diversion as well, even if they did not arrive as often as she might have liked. The next generation, her grandchildren, had started to write—first Margot, who was already going to school, and then Anne. Margot's letters were limited at first to "How are you? I hope you're doing well," or thanking Alice "for the lovely things" and sending "hugs and kisses from Margot and Anne." One letter, addressed "Dear Grandma," runs: "How are you? I hope you're doing well. I hope Aunt Leni gets better soon. Love to everyone, Your Margot." Later the letters grew longer. For example, there is this touching letter that Margot sent from Amsterdam to Alice in Basel in 1936, still in a child's handwriting:

Dear Grandma,

How are you? Thank you very much for the beautiful present, it just arrived today and was a lovely surprise; also, thank you + Aunt Leni for your letters. I got very many presents + a lovely chair from Grandma. For your present, Mommy bought me a swimsuit with a jacket + pants, and with the rest of the money I'm getting my bicycle fixed. Many thanks to Uncle Erich too for the chocolate. Warm hellos to Stephan, Bernd, Uncle Erich + Aunt Leni. Hugs + Kisses, Margot.

P.S. When are you coming to visit? We are so looking forward to seeing you.

Eight months later Margot reminded Alice in a birthday letter that no one was going to be able to visit from Amsterdam. "But this year the family is not as big as usual." She also, in her letter to Stephan, whose birthday was also on December 20, mentioned Alice's seventieth birthday that they had celebrated together the previous year, in 1935. And she asked: "Do you still remember the summer when you were in Zandvoort [in Holland, on the coast near Amsterdam], and the winter before that when we were all with Grandma in Basel? This year you're celebrating without us, but with a lot of presents I'm sure. I hope we see each other again soon. Greetings to Bernd and best wishes from Your, Margot."

Even aside from the occasional stays at Villa Laret in Sils-Maria, Otto often visited his mother in Switzerland, sometimes with both children and sometimes with only one. Buddy remembers a few things about these visits, for example, that Margot and Anne went with him to the skating rink and watched him skate. He thinks that Edith rarely came to Basel, though; presumably, she visited her family in Aachen instead.

The year 1938 brought great changes. Erich wanted to bring his widowed mother, Ida Elias née Neu, from Zweibrücken to Basel. Since the apartment at Gundeldingerstrasse 139 was too small for another person and the children were growing up and needing more space anyway, they decided to rent a house for the family and move in together.

They found one at Herbstgasse 11—a corner house in a row of six houses, built around the turn of the century, not especially big but with three stories and an attic floor added on. There was a small, pretty garden adjoining the gardens of the surrounding houses. The ground floor had a kitchen and a dining room with double doors that led to a living room, which Leni insisted on calling the "salon." A few steps went down from a small veranda to the garden. The second floor had Leni and Erich's bedroom with a nice balcony, then a child's bedroom and a small room for the housekeeper. Alice had her room on the third floor—a large room with a view of the garden—and Grandma Ida was to move into the small room next to the stairs, above the housekeeper's room. A steep set of stairs led up to the attic floor, which had a room for someone to live as well. Every room, including Leni's bedroom, had a cord with a bell that would call the housekeeper. The house was very pretty, though much smaller than the old house on Mertonstrasse, and the rooms were certainly not large. Nevertheless, it was a refuge and a home for everyone.

Alice must have agreed right away when Leni and Erich told her about the plan to move: it meant the end of her solitary life on Schweizergasse. In difficult times, people always feel the need to be closer to one another. And of course the money from the sale of the house in Frankfurt was gradually melting away, despite their frugal lives.

The news from Germany sounded ever more threatening. The German pogrom that the Nazis called Kristallnacht, or Night of Broken Glass, took place on November 9, 1938: synagogues were destroyed, windows shattered, businesses looted. Today the estimates are that at least four hundred Jewish persons were killed or driven to suicide on that night, and of the nearly thirty thousand Jews who were arrested and sent to the concentration camps in Dachau, Sachsenhausen, and Buchenwald, another several hundred met their deaths in the following days and weeks.

If Alice had sometimes felt homesick before—felt any melancholy longings for everything she was used to in her past—then now, by November 1938 at the latest, she must have realized what good fortune it was for her and her family that they had left Germany in time and were safe. Of course no one could know at the time that the Nazis would catch up to Otto, Edith, Margot, and Anne.

Adam 14-2-'36

Liebe Omi,

Wie geht es Dir? Ich dan-
ke Dir vielmahls für das
schöne Geschenk, es ist
erst heute angekommen
das war noch eine schö-
ne Überraschung; auch
danke ich Dir + Tante Le-
ni für die Briefe. Ich
habe sehr viel bekom-
men + einen schönen Stuhl
von Oma. Für Deiniges Ge-
schenk kauft Mutti mir
einen Schwimmanzug mit
Jacke + Hose, für das über-
bleibende Geld lasse
ich mir mein Rad in Ord-
nung machen. Ich danke On-

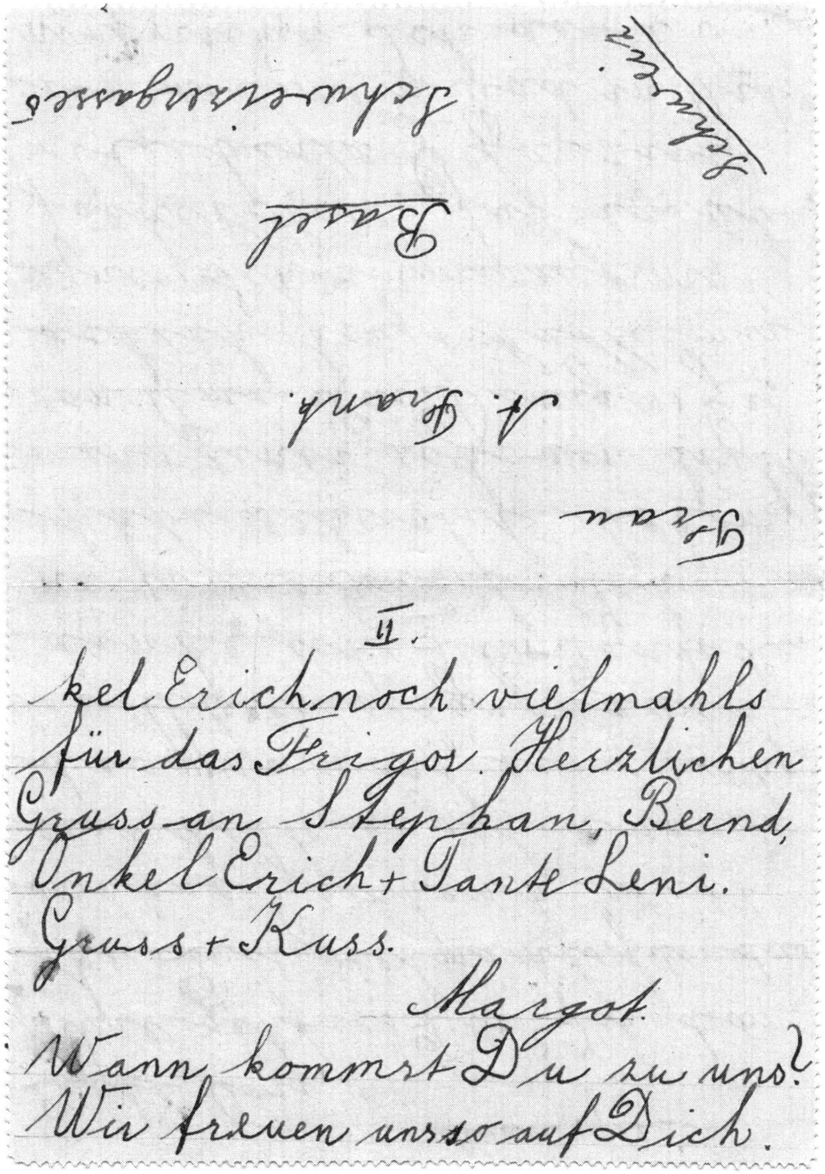

Frau
A. Frank
Basel
Schweizergasse
Schweiz

II.
kel Erich noch vielmahls
für das Frigor. Herzlichen
Gruss an Stephan, Bernd,
Onkel Erich + Tante Leni.
Gruss + Kuss.
Margot.
Wann kommst Du zu uns?
Wir freuen uns so auf Dich.

Letter from Margot Frank to her grandmother Alice, 1936

When the pogrom in Germany took place, Alice was in Amsterdam visiting her son Otto and his family. Unfortunately, she fell sick there and was slow to recover. Robert wrote from London to Amsterdam while she was convalescing: "That was a pleasant surprise, to get Edith's darling card this morning with a note from you included. It's a good sign that you can get out of bed every day now and that you're feeling noticeably better and stronger. [. . .] Just be careful, and patient, so that you'll get all your strength back. Be careful what you eat! I can't say yet if and when I'll be able to arrange to come to Holland, because first I have to try to do some business here, which is otherwise not only difficult but almost impossible."

Robert's worries sound minor compared with the ones the German pogrom unleashed on the Jewish émigrés. There is a letter from Alice to Basel, after Leni and Erich had telephoned her in Amsterdam. She mentions many people who wanted to leave, or who had left, or whom no one knew about, showing the unease and fear after November 9, 1938, among the Jews who had left Germany. In Holland the concerns were apparently greater than in Switzerland. Alice wrote:

Dearest children,

I can't tell you how happy I was yesterday to hear your voices! & I think you felt the same! If only the reasons for the teleph. call were not so unspeakably sad. Otto is running his legs off about Walter. [Julius?] is still free, they'll probably leave him alone as a wounded veteran. The news we hear here is not to be described. It's as much as I can do to summon up the least bit of selfishness, since I <u>*want*</u> *to travel back as soon as possible. Anyway, the sun has to be good to me first & I have to be out of the house at least 2–3 x. The stairs will be difficult, but I won't have to go downstairs much at Herbstgasse & so it'll go better there.*

Today Elsa N. visited me, it was a miracle, she arrived by airplane & today has already flown off for L. In Berlin it's unspeakably terrible. Anne Kater visited me too today, & Frau Goslar. It wears me out a bit

& I should be having a lot more rest than is possible here. My nerves give out now and then, but otherwise it's going very well for me, except for the little place that I'd love to get fully healed. I'm not taking anything, and haven't taken any coramine for a long time, & I hope that I'll be there before long, maybe not looking like a 50-year-old but at least like a 60-year-old. [She was 72.] Rob. wrote today that he is trying to write an application for Edgar & Nellie with Ilse, Edgar & Ernst are in Weimar [that is, Buchenwald] & how many others? What have you heard about Paul? There are not nearly enough facts to think concretely about & so you turn them over and over in your mind. [. . .] Can't Ivo look in on Grandma Ida? How is Lotti doing? Rob? Steger is at home, no word from Helen & Lisel. Max & Titty are already in London, Adolf and [illegible] too. Franz W. was on a trip and so escaped being brought in, Fritz Et. we haven't heard anything about. It is absolutely not necessary that anyone come and get me, I don't want you, dear Leni, to spend even 1 hour here, there is only unbearable news that I'm striving to avoid, luckily I can hear see & write well. The letter from Lili is horribly sad, I wrote her a few lines yesterday. You can keep the letter to Helen. Otto is calm needless to say, Edith is also doing what she can in her way. The nurse is not coming anymore & I consider myself really almost entirely better, it's like a miracle! Soon hopefully I can sit at my desk chair and listen to Butzelein & you practice your Fr., Bübü [a pet name for Stephan]. Margot has an enormous amount of homework. Both the girls are darling and very considerate. I hope I won't need to write so often anymore & that we'll see each other soon, maybe in 8–10 days, I don't want to take any chances & I'll be fine for that long. I also wrote Rob. that he definitely should not come, he writes to me every day. All my love to everyone there,

*from I.**

*Alice was usually referred to in the family not by name but by her nickname, I. The explanation for this nickname has not been passed down; Buddy Elias also doesn't know the reason behind it.

Alice recovered and returned to Basel, to the Herbstgasse house, where Grandma Ida, Erich's mother, soon moved as well. Life went on once more.

Margot wrote a letter to her "Dear Granny" for her birthday on December 20, 1938, and both the handwriting and the style clearly show that she had grown two years older. She was twelve.

Many happy returns to you on your birthday, if it even counts as a birthday, but I'm sure you'll be spending it with Leni and Erich, and Stephan will definitely spend the day with you.

It's very cold here, but the wind from the east is as always the coldest. We went ice-skating with Daddy today behind the Apollo Hall. Mommy came too but didn't go out on the ice. We went fast but then it was too cold and we warmed up at home and then kitty-cat came and joined us. I don't know what else I can write. This letter is for Stephan too. Many happy returns to him too, and lots of hugs to Leni, Erich, and Bernd. Especially lots of birthday kisses from Your Margot.

It was for this birthday too that Anne, then nine years old, wrote the first letters by her that survive, one to Alice and one to Stephan.

Dear Granny,
Many happy returns on your birthday. Is it as cold there, here we can hardly stand it, it is 8 below during the day, 11 at night. Is Pussi back again and is Stephan carrying her on his shoulder again. Was it Hanukkah there too, we had Hanukkah and there was a lot of "snoepen" [Dutch: "gulping down candy"]. We go to the ice rink a lot and I have learned how to skate too, I fel a lot at the begining now its better, I like it. Lots of hugs to everyone and kisses to you.

The letter is signed "Zärtlein," Anne's nickname (meaning, "delicate little one").

To Stephan she wrote:

Many happy returns to you too on your birthday. Its very cold here. Do you go skating a lot, we do I learned it too. did you get lots of presents. Is Granny doing better, I hope she is. Is it nice living together. Granny told us alot about it. This isnt much of a birthday letter but I hope you like it, hugs to everyone most especially to you also to Berndt.

Anne

It is worth noting that Anne wrote this letter in German, a language that she apparently knew better in 1938 than she did later. Or possibly someone wrote out sentences in German for her to copy. In any case, her later letters were all written in Dutch and accompanied by translations (not always very good ones) from Otto.

What was the family's life like, together on Herbstgasse? Alice had a room where she could have her own furniture, probably including a fold-out card table since the family liked to play a lot of games. We know that they often played cards and that everyone liked solitaire. Leni had a regular bridge circle on Wednesdays, which she continued to participate in even after she started her antiques business and became the family's main breadwinner. Alice spent a lot of time in her room doing needlework; even today the house is full of tablecloths, place mats, napkins, and linens that she hemmed, embroidered, or embellished with lace or monogram. The traces of her agile hands are everywhere. She didn't go out much, apparently, but where should she have gone? She was not the type to just go for a walk.

No mementos of Grandma Ida, Erich's mother, have been passed down, and strangely there are only a few photographs of her as well. Buddy says that she was an inconspicuous, modest woman with few needs; no one noticed much of anything about her, except that she was constantly cleaning "somewhere upstairs," to the point that Erich, her son, sometimes asked her to stop. She and Alice had little in common. "You cannot imagine two more polar opposites than my two grandmothers,"

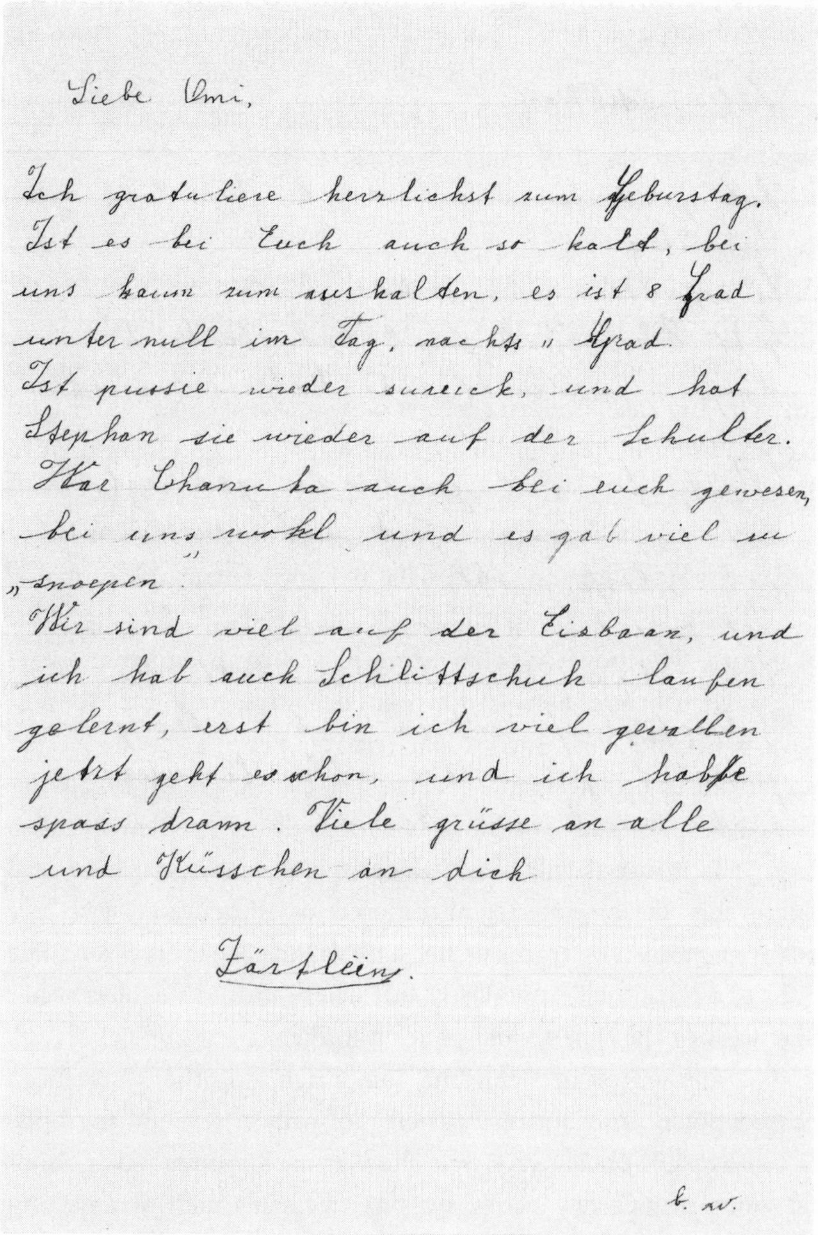

Liebe Omi,

Ich gratuliere herzlichst zum Geburstag.
Ist es bei Euch auch so kalt, bei
uns kaum zum aushalten, es ist 8 Grad
unter null im Tag, nachts " Grad.
Ist pussie wieder zurück, und hat
Stephan sie wieder auf der Schulter.
War Chanuka auch bei euch gewesen,
bei uns wohl und es gab viel zu
„snoepen".
Wir sind viel auf der Eisbaan, und
ich hab auch Schlittschuh laufen
gelernt, erst bin ich viel gevallen
jetzt geht es schon, und ich hoffe
spass daran. Viele grüsse an alle
und Küsschen an dich

Tärtlein.

b. w.

Letter from Anne Frank to her cousin Stephan Elias, December 1938

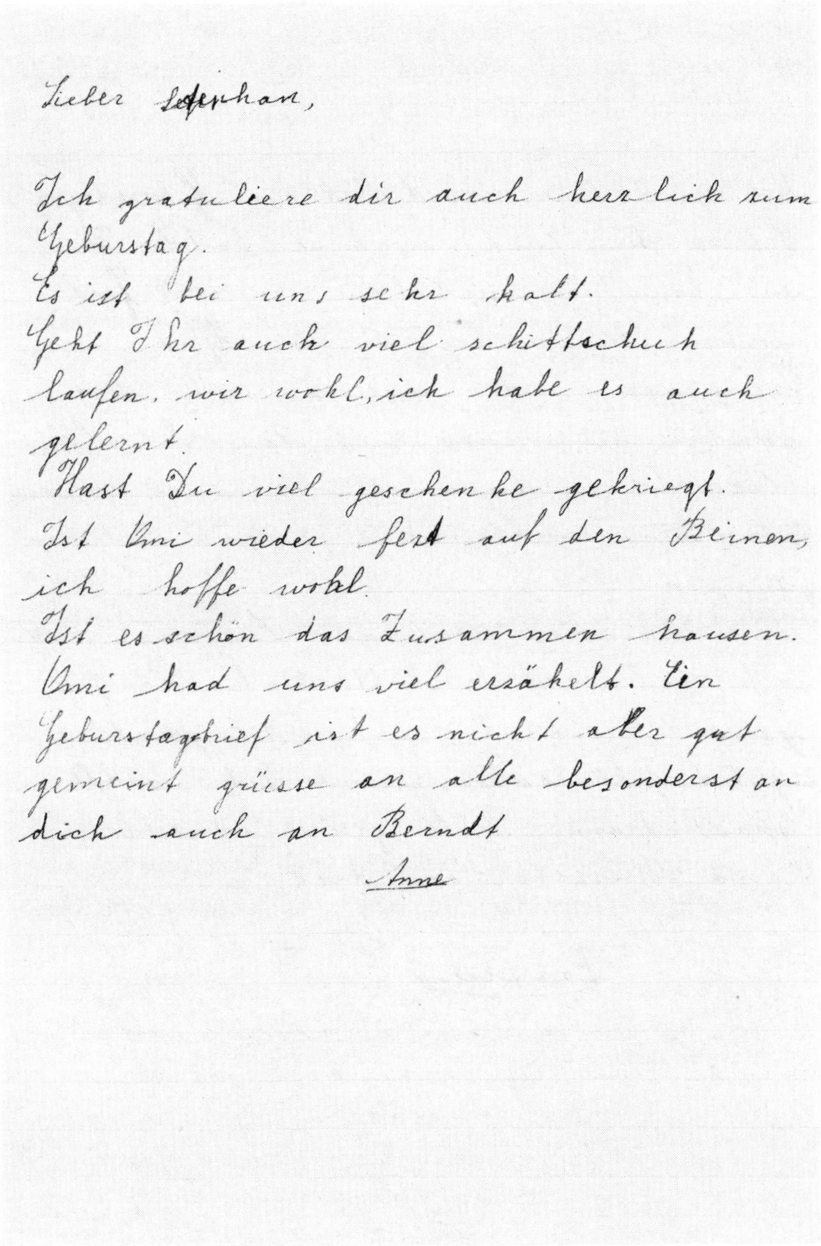
Lieber Stephan,

Ich gratuliere dir auch herzlich zum
Geburstag.
Es ist bei uns sehr kalt.
Geht Ihr auch viel schittschuch
laufen. wir wohl, ich habe es auch
gelernt.
Hast Du viel geschenke gekriegt.
Ist Omi wieder fest auf den Beinen,
ich hoffe wohl.
Ist es schön das Zusammen hausen.
Omi had uns viel erzähelt. Ein
Geburstagbrief ist es nicht aber gut
gemeint grüsse an alle besonderst an
dich auch an Berndt
Anne

Letter from Anne Frank to her grandmother Alice, December 1938

Buddy says, although he doesn't remember any fights or conflicts between them. Maybe in that whirligig of a house, with two growing boys and two rather dominant women, Grandma Ida didn't have many chances to stand out. It could also well be that Alice—"the Queen," as the family often called her (in English)—and Leni simply intimidated her and that she therefore kept herself well in the background.

While the family in Basel was busy working out these new arrangements, life in Amsterdam went on as well—not without cares and worries, but to a certain extent normally. After the German pogrom, Edith's two brothers escaped to America and her mother came to join the Franks in Amsterdam. Among the cache of documents there is a letter that Edith wrote to Hedda Eisenstadt, her former neighbor, on December 24, 1937. It shows that Edith was worried and that Otto may have tried to arrange their immigration to England:

Dear Hedda,

Finally! is what you'll say and you'd be right! But you know how it always is with these endless excuses for not writing, there's no time during the day and at night you're too tired . . . We're well, everyone is healthy. Anne is going to school half days, which she loves, the nervous little thing needs a lot of quiet time. Margot has got big and sturdy and loves school and studying. She went to Aachen on Wednesday, and since Otto and Anne have been in Basel for a week, I have some peace and quiet (so I can write this letter!). Otto is coming back tomorrow morning, he's been mostly on the road since September and is working hard on the thing with England: whether that will work out is unclear, but unfortunately the business here is not doing well and we have to get something extra, maybe we will move on too . . . We see friends very little, since I hardly ever go out alone and Otto is always too tired. The new orders that Jews can neither travel to——nor visit from abroad have affected me very much. and I'm worried about my family . . . I think that all German Jews are scouring the globe now and can't find a way in anymore.

It is not clear how this letter ended up with the family correspondence, likewise the following letter that Otto wrote to Edith on May 12, 1939, their fourteenth anniversary and his fiftieth birthday, which gives us a glimpse into their marriage. Otto presumably brought it with him when he moved into the Herbstgasse house after the war.

Margot and Anne Frank with Grandma Holländer, circa 1939

Dear Edith, You know that I don't in the least like celebrating and especially not "being celebrated," but I must admit a 50th birthday is a special occasion, and even more so since it coincides with our anniversary. So we should be especially happy today and celebrate, in the spirit of our "agreement," not loudly and in a big group but in our own little circle with each other.

We should also be happy that despite being in such a difficult situation for so long, we are all still healthy, none of our close relatives remained back in Germany, and we have everything we need, for now.—Our 14 years of marriage have certainly not lacked for twists of fate, and when you think back on the whole length of time, from San Remo to today, you can truly appreciate the changes that have affected everything. Still, even the most difficult circumstances could never disturb the harmony that exists between us. From the beginning, you showed a strength of character that is rare indeed, a sense of solidarity that has given you the power to carry on through thick and thin.

Aside from temperament, upbringing and one's parents always play an important role, and we both should be thankful for what our parents have given us.

So it should also be our goal to transmit to our children that same sense of solidarity, feeling of comfort, and sense of mutual responsibility.

No one knows what the future will bring in terms of the outside world, but we know that we can avoid making life worse with squabbles and petty conflicts.

May the coming years of our marriage be just as harmonious as the years so far. I want to thank you, especially today, for all the love & care you have given in these 14 years. If we stick to our tested agreement, nothing can go wrong.

Your O.

Then, on September 1, 1939, World War II began—a great catastrophe that no one could imagine the extent of, neither in Holland nor in Switzerland, two countries that had been neutral and experienced the last great war only from afar. For the time being, the correspondence makes no mention of the war. "The times are difficult," true, but there is not the slightest suspicion of the disaster that awaited them. For instance, Alice wrote another poem for Stephan, her grandson, on his eighteenth birthday, December 20, 1939:

On the day that you were born
What happiness did my soul adorn!
And I have always given you
A thousand good wishes and blessings too.
The burden, but also all the other
Things it means to be a grandmother:
That it was you, my darling boy,
Who gave me these things was a pure joy.
I don't feel like I belong
With other old people—I feel young
And want to share your life with you,
Delight in all the things you'll do,
Grow with you, and every day
Help you as you make your way.
Some of these things have come to be:
We've seen the mountains and the sea,
Experienced beauty shoulder to shoulder—
You in your youth and I much older.
What ties us together and joins our fate
Is not just the accident of a date—
Your birthday, which is the same as mine—
It's that, as you've felt so many times,
The love of a grandma, your very own,
Is always with you, wherever you roam.—

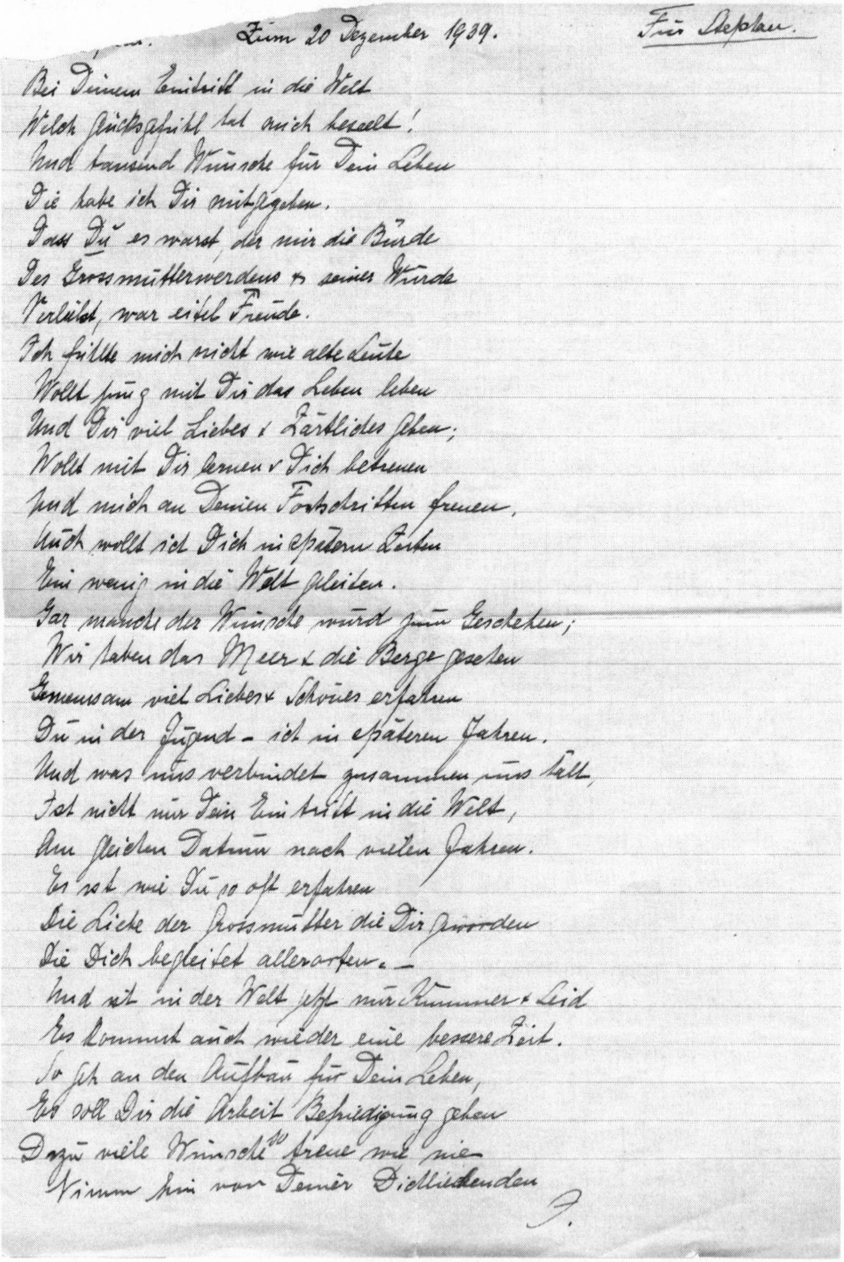
…pau. Zum 20 Dezember 1939. Für Stephan.

Bei Deinem Eintritt in die Welt
Welch Glücksgefühl hat mich beseelt!
Und tausend Wünsche für Dein Leben
Die habe ich Dir mitgegeben.
Dass Du es warst, der mir die Bürde
Des Grossmütterwerdens & seine Würde
Verliehst, war eitel Freude.
Ich fühlte mich nicht wie alte Leute
Wollt jung mit Dir das Leben leben
Und Dir viel Liebes & Zärtliches geben;
Wollt mit Dir lernen & Dich belehren
Und mich an Deinen Fortschritten freuen.
Auch wollt ich Dich in spätern Zeiten
Ein wenig in die Welt geleiten.
Gar manche der Wünsche wurd zum Geschehen;
Wir haben das Meer & die Berge gesehen
Gemeinsam viel Liebes & Schönes erfahren
Du in der Jugend – ich in späteren Jahren.
Und was uns verbindet zusammen uns hält,
Ist nicht nur Dein Eintritt in die Welt,
Am gleichen Datum nach vielen Jahren.
Es ist wie Du so oft erfahren
Die Liebe der Grossmutter die Dir geworden
Die Dich begleitet allerorten. –
Und ist in der Welt jetzt nur Kummer & Leid
Es kommt auch wieder eine bessere Zeit.
So geh an den Aufbau für Dein Leben,
Es soll Dir die Arbeit Befriedigung geben
Dazu viele Wünsche freue wie nie
Nimm hin von Deiner Dichliebenden
J.

Poem by Alice Frank for her grandson Stephan Elias's birthday, December 20, 1939

The world may often be sorrow and strife,
But carry on and build your life:
Better times are on their way,
Hard work is its own reward today.
And take many wishes, truer than ever,
From she who loves you. Yours forever,
I.

Despite the strict neutrality maintained by the Netherlands, the German troops invaded the country in 1940 and occupied it within five days. The royal family and the government went into exile, and the Dutch army capitulated on May 14, 1940.

A strange and moving coincidence of dates makes it worth reproducing a postcard here that Alice received from Luxembourg in May 1940, from her nephew Arnold Frank, a son of Michael's brother Emile. Buddy still remembers Arnold well: he was crippled, and he visited the family in Basel rather often. Arnold Frank wrote:

Dear Aunt Alice! You are very right indeed when you say that the calm of my humble self is merely external, because in the unconscious we can never really be free from the pressure of events. Certainly our spirits here have been more or less soothed, but a lot of people's are not yet in order. * *Others have simply packed up and left. Olga is staying in P[aris], of course, since all her furniture keeps her tied down there. [. . .] I've had a few lines from Edith, & Otto writes to me too. He says that he thinks we'll pull through and he feels confident. Now there's more than enough to worry about in Holland too, but in my opinion the well-armed Swiss have nothing to fear. I'm glad that Stephan is holding up & I hope Erich is doing all right as well. I often think about Leni, who has had to live with these annoyances for 7 years & whose wishes have still*

*It was already clear at the time that there would be war between Germany and France. Germany had cut off the delivery of coal to Luxembourg, to force that country to support Germany.

not been granted in that matter. * *She'll get it someday, but probably not for another 2–3 years. If you go to Geneva, dear Aunt Alice, say hello to St[ephan] for me. I feel healthy & and am very comfortable here in Hotel Conti. The weather is nice & it's lovely in Letzeburg.*

Very best wishes & all our love, Yours, Arnold

Arnold wrote this card on May 9, the day before he died—on May 10, the same day that the Germans invaded the Netherlands and Luxembourg.

Even aside from the pathos of this coincidence, his letter shows the general unease and uncertainty that was everywhere in those days. No other correspondence remains between him and Alice, which proves that the cache does not contain all the documents that there were—whether the missing ones were carelessly misplaced or intentionally removed can no longer be determined.

The Germans now occupied the Netherlands and installed Reichskommissar Arthur Seyss-Inquart as head of the civil government. As in all the occupied territories, anti-Jewish regulations were put into effect in the Netherlands as well, beginning with the removal of all Jewish civil servants from office and ending with completely depriving the Jews of their civil rights before the deportations began in 1942. These measures have been described often enough; Anne Frank herself documented many details in her diary. As a result, the discussion here will be limited to the Frank family in particular and say less about the general conditions. We may take as one sign of the family's unease the fact that the number of letters sent from Amsterdam to Basel rose sharply in these two years. Anne wrote much more frequently. Still, only nine of her letters written between 1940 and their going into hiding have survived, and only two of Margot's. Anne wrote her letters in Dutch with a German translation supplied by Otto.

*Arnold presumably means Leni and Erich's failed attempts to gain Swiss citizenship.

In one letter to her "Dear Granny," Anne wrote:

I'm getting a new dress now, it's terribly hard to get fabric and you have to use a lot of ration cards for it.

Hanneli is sick, she hasn't been as good as me in school for a long time, she has fallen behind, and I'm not exactly the best myself. [. . .]

Anne Frank with her friend Hannah (Hanneli) Goslar, Amsterdam, 1939

Papa has a lot to do at the office, he's moving soon, it's too small for him on the Singel so the company is now on Prinsengracht. I go and meet him at the streetcar a lot. It's really nice to sleep with Papa, but still I'd like it better if I had another reason for sleeping downstairs and the times were back to normal again . . . My hair has got rather long, you probably saw that already on the photos, Papa and Mama want me to cut it, but I'd much rather let it grow.

How is everybody there? I'd love to see Bernd on the ice again, hopefully that will be possible sooner than we all think.

I'm taking French and in that class I am the best, we're getting grades for it too but only after the Christmas break. There are no Hebrew school classes at the moment, and in the winter I don't think I'll be able to go either, because I'd have to come home in the dark and I don't want to do that and am not allowed to either. I have a little device in my mouth and braces, I have to go to the dentist every week now, then it falls out again the next day, it's been like that for 8 weeks already, it's a big nuisance. I have to stop writing now because it's my bedtime. Lots of love to Uncle Erich, Aunt Lenie, Stephan, Bernd, and Grandma Ida, and lots more kisses to you from your Anne.

In the birthday letter that Margot wrote to Alice in 1940, the only hint of the changed situation came in her comments about school. She wished her dear granny a happy birthday, a very special one since after all you only turn seventy-five once, and then she expressed her wish to be able to see her again on December 20 sometime soon.

Since it's so dark in the evenings now we almost never go out and I play a lot of cards with Mr. Wronker, our lodger. Anne and I like to go see Goslar's baby, she already knows how to laugh and she's sweeter and sweeter every day. Anne is going tomorrow to the skating rink they have in the Apollo Hall now, much closer. Is Bernd still skating a lot or does he have too much work to do?

At our school a couple of the teachers are gone and we don't have French anymore, also no math teacher. Now our school starts at 9:45 instead of at 8:30 and we have shorter classes too.

On Saturdays I usually go with Mama into the city and now, before Hanukkah, you can always buy something.

So best wishes to you and of course to Stephan too from your Margot.

In her own birthday letter to Grandma and Stephan, Anne also expressed her hope to celebrate with them in person again soon. Hopefully, this would be the last *naarest** birthday.

This afternoon we had dictation and I made no fewer than 27 mistakes, you all would have laughed if you read it I'm sure, but it's no wonder, because it was very hard and I'm hardly an ace at dictation.

I'm really looking forward to tomorrow because I'm going to the skating rink (first time this year), and it's not as far away anymore, it's in the Apollo Hall. I'm sure Granny knows where that is, I think you had a coffee there once in the cafeteria. And tomorrow afternoon I'm going to an auction with Daddy.

Margot got very good grades and I'm very proud of her, I don't think that I'll get all 8s and 9s [roughly B to B plus] later.

Gabrielle Gosslar is a cute baby, Margot and I are sometimes allowed to be there when she's given a bath.

Margot has put up all the blackout curtains just now, it's <u>the troubles</u> these days, and I'm awfully angry about it, we don't have to yet and it's finally such nice weather outside, now Margot has left the room and I've simply taken them all down again. I wish you all the best for this new year. Lots of kisses to everybody, but especially

to Granny.

Yours, Anne

**Naar* is Dutch for "repulsive, unpleasant, nasty, disgusting."

Anne wrote her next letter as soon as January 1941, this time addressed "Dear Everyone." She thanked Bernd for his letter and then took up the topic of ice-skating again.

I'm at the rink every spare minute. Up until now I've always had the old skates that Margot used to have. You had to screw them on with a little key, but all my friends on the rink had real ice skates that are attached to the shoes with nails so that they don't come off.

I wanted skates like that awfully badly and after long and grueling efforts I finally got some. I'm taking skating classes regularly now, where we're learning how to dance and jump and everything else.

Hanneli has my old skates now and she is happy about it so it worked out well for both of us. Hanneli's little sister is terribly cute, I'm allowed to hold her on my lap sometimes, she laughs at everything now, all the children are jealous of Hanneli because of Gabi. How is everyone there? I've written all this time about myself and the skating rink, but please don't take it badly, I'm just very excited about it. I hope that I'll learn to skate as well as Bernd someday. It's going well here (I mean at school), I don't have much free time in the week except for the days when there's ice outside. I have French on Mondays, Wednesdays, and Thursdays and don't get home until six. Tuesdays and Fridays I have homework too and so there's only Saturdays and Sundays for ice-skating.

Bernd, maybe we can skate as a pair together someday, but I know I'd have to train very hard to get to be as good as you are.

Love and lots of kisses to everyone

Yours, Anne

Remember that Anne Frank was eleven when she wrote this letter, eleven and a half to be precise. In her next letter, in March, the ice-skating phase was already over: Jews were no longer allowed to play sports in public. Most likely there was a sign hanging on the entrance to the skating rink: "No Jews Allowed!" Like the signs everywhere then: on libraries, theaters, cinemas, cafés, and restaurants. Anne thanked the family for a photograph of

Bernd that she thought was very funny, because all the spectators were laughing, and she said that she had hung it over her bed. "I would really love to start skating again, but I need to have a little patience until the war is over, if Papa can still afford it, then I'll get skating lessons again, and if I get good, Papa promised me a trip to Switzerland to see all of you."

At the end of the letter, she described her "very big" room: "We have a dresser and a washstand, and a closet and Mama's secretary that we've set up as a cute little writing desk, and then there's Margot's fold-out bed and another little bedside table, and a couch where I sleep, and a table in the middle with a big armchair, and all my pictures and photos, including the one of Bernd."

That summer, she wrote to thank the family for the birthday letter from Basel that she had received only on June 20—her birthday was postponed that year because Grandma (Edith's mother) had had to go to the hospital and have an operation. Anne listed all her presents: an atlas, a bicycle, a new schoolbag, a beach dress, stationery from Margot, and lots of other little gifts. During her summer vacation she was planning to go with Sanne Ledermann to visit Sanne's family, then spend another two weeks in a summer camp. "I have hardly any chance to get a tan because we're not allowed to go to the swimming pool, it's a shame but there's nothing we can do about it."

Apparently the swimming pools too were off-limits to Jews by then. And she describes all these restrictions as so apparently self-evident.

Buddy Elias, ice-skating

A card followed from the summer camp in Beekbergen, with greetings from Anne and signatures as well from Sanne and Hanneli, two friends of hers. The card is addressed to Alice Frank, c/o Spitzer, Villa Laret, Sils-Maria. In a later letter from the vacation home, Anne asks if it's nice in Sils-Maria and says that she and Sanne are always playing with a sweet little boy.

Edith's mother died in January 1942. There is no mention of the event in the correspondence, and only one in Anne Frank's diary: "No one will ever know how much she is present in my thoughts and how much I love her still."

No one on Herbstgasse knew that Otto was desperately trying to get a visa for Cuba. But Nathan Straus, whom Otto had turned to for help, was unable to manage it. No visas for the United States were available in the Netherlands; the only chance anyone had to reach a neutral country was by a detour through another country like Cuba. Here is an excerpt from a letter that Otto wrote in English on October 12, 1941, to "Charley":

Spain or Portugal do not give any visas before one can prove that one can leave again. Cuba is the only Country giving order to their Representatives that visas can be given to certain people at Bilbao and Berlin and I have seen telegrams to this respect coming from New York. Only after having received a cable of this sort one can apply for the permit to leave Holland and after having received this, one gets the Transitvisum Spain. It is all much more difficult as one can imagine and is getting more complicated every day. I do not know your intentions and I am grateful for all you do. As far as I see there are difficulties too if I would go alone as I was told, that permission to enter the U.S.A. will not be given if members of the family remain in occupied territory. I am sure that my brothers-in-law will do all to help and they certainly will pay à fond perdu the amounts necessary to get the Cuban visas for all of us. As far as I know this amounts to $530,—. They certainly will not be able to deposit money necessary to get the visas, even if this money will *be refunded later. As you see there is no chance for me to do anything without a Cuba visum. If it is not possible to act for all of us it might be for me alone or with the children. Both of them are below 16 years of age, but as Margot is going to be 16 in February I would not like to leave them here under the present conditions, even if Edith would have to stay here with her mother. She prefers this as she regards it more urgent for me and the children to leave, as for herself and her mother.*

In the meantime I had orders to liquidate my business and shall not be able to continue my work. The situation is getting more difficult every day and you can imagine that I am anxious to get your further news as I know I shall never be able to leave without your help.

On December 1, 1941, Cuba actually did issue a visa for Otto Frank, but it was canceled as early as December 11. It was too late—the Franks were trapped.

Only a few weeks before going into hiding, Otto wrote a postcard on his birthday, May 12, 1942: "Dearest Mama, we are not especially celebrating today but not wallowing in thoughts of the past either, since we also don't want to forget the lovely and dear things."

One of the last letters before going into hiding bears the date July 4, 1942. By then he had already prepared the Secret Annex and knew that he and his family would soon have to move into hiding.

Dear everyone,

Mother's card from 6/22 arrived & all the news made us happy, especially her good health. Everything is fine here too, although things are getting more and more difficult from day to day here as you probably know. But don't be worried about anything, even if you don't hear very much from us. Even when I don't go to the office there is a lot to do here & a lot to think about & you often have to make difficult decisions.—The children are on vacation now, both of them got good grades,

Anne better than expected, she is working very hard. What else should I tell you. You can tell Herbert that Mr. Koch has [illegible] died. Aunt Lina writes that her trip has been postponed & she is grateful for every day she can stay. She's jealous of Grandma, and we are happy about her circumstances too. Blanche wrote a short card too. He . . . is still in F.—We think of you all the time & know that you're thinking of us, but you can't change anything here & you have to take care that you make it through yourselves. With much love, as always,

Your O.

With this, the correspondence between Amsterdam and Basel came to an end. The dark years had begun.

Alice was seventy-six years old. She had had many life experiences: had grown from a melancholy child into an upper-middle-class wife, had seen most of the great cities of Europe, and had raised four children. She had shaped her children's personalities, passing along her love of language and of self-dramatization. She had given them more than just a typical upbringing, done more than just foster their education in the usual way.

She had grown out of her role as daughter into the role of wife and mother, then into that of a widow, and finally that of a grandmother. Her family had always been her center—everyone else, no matter how much she loved them, had circled like planets around the sun. At first her mother had been the focus, then it was her husband and the children, now the grandchildren had taken over that role. But that December, on her seventy-seventh birthday, she would not get any letters from her granddaughters—nor on her seventy-eighth birthday, or her seventy-ninth. Never again.

There were eleven years remaining for Alice, years in which she no doubt experienced some joys here and there, but also experienced the greatest loss of her life.

PART TWO

Helene Elias née Frank, Anne's Aunt

(1893–1986)

Leni Frank, around ten years old

6.

Daily Life and Distant Longings

Late July 1942. Leni is sitting in her room in lower Basel, between piles of used clothes, shoes, books, lamps, and small pieces of furniture. For the past two hours not one customer has appeared, she is restless, and on top of it all it's much too hot. She sold one single dress that morning, nothing more—an evening dress for which the customer, a wealthy Basel businesswoman, wanted to pay only twenty francs. Twenty francs for a dress that was worn only once, that Frau Horowitz, four years ago, paid ten or twenty times as much for in a Dresden atelier. Leni wipes the sweat from her forehead with a white handkerchief. If only it wasn't so hot. She opens the top button of her blouse.

Someone knocks at the door. "Come in," Leni says, and raises her head expectantly. She knows, even before the door opens, that it will be a woman: she has got into the habit of guessing from the knock who is going to come in, and she is almost always right. This time too. It is Frau Schwarz, wife of a doctor and former professor at the University of Berlin. Or was it Dresden? A former professor in any case—almost all the Jews in Germany were now former somethings. The woman has a rather big brown leather suitcase in her hand, she is sweaty, and there are two perfectly round red spots on her cheeks. Leni notices for the first time what deep wrinkles she has between her nose and the corners of her mouth.

Leni closes her blouse button, stands up, and offers the woman a hand. "How may I help you, Frau Professor?" she asks, and helps the visitor lift her suitcase up onto the table.

Frau Schwarz takes a little key out of her purse, slowly and laboriously unlocks the suitcase, flips open the lid, and takes out two furs, a mink stole and a fox. Leni had often seen her last winter wearing the fox fur coat—it's a beautiful piece, and a classic cut, although the sleeves are a little worn. It'll be easy to sell the mink stole; Leni can already picture the fat Swiss wife who will let out a little scream of joy when she finds the luxurious present under her Christmas tree.

Even so, she hesitates. She fetches a glass of water to gain a little time. Frau Schwarz thanks her and drinks the water standing up.

"I can't sell a fur coat in the middle of summer," Leni says. "Not now. Please, sit down." Leni sits down at the table, and the woman sits down on the one free chair opposite her; the others are covered with items of clothing.

"We're leaving tomorrow," the woman says. "Heaven be praised. We have a visa, my cousin in Argentina sent us a visa. I don't need a fur coat in Buenos Aires, and we desperately need money, my cousin doesn't have very much."

"All I can do is take the coat on commission," Leni says, "and send you the money when it sells."

The woman nods. "I trust you, Frau Elias, you're a dependable woman."

"And you know that I take 15 percent?"

She nods again. "Yes, of course." She grips Leni's hand. "Couldn't you at least give me a little in advance, the same as what I'd get if I brought the coat to a pawnbroker's?" The woman's voice grows soft, and she lets Leni's hand go, turning her face to the side, trying to hide her shame. She can't go to a pawnbroker—they are illegal here, and she knows that Leni knows it.

The silence is unbearable. Leni's reason battles her pity.

Finally she picks up her purse and takes out the envelope with fifty francs in it that she'd tucked into the zippered side pocket yesterday when the Swiss antiques dealer bought the little Biedermeier secretary that he would resell for a profit. Dr. Marcus, the owner of the secretary, would just have to wait a little while longer for his money—he doesn't need it as urgently as Frau Professor Schwarz. Leni opens the envelope, takes out the banknote, and holds it out to her.

The woman thanks her effusively, puts away the money, and stands up. "I'll send you our address right away, as soon as we arrive," she says. "God bless you, Frau Elias."

Leni wishes her and her husband a safe trip and the best of luck for the future. Then the woman takes her now-empty suitcase and leaves. Leni stays standing in the doorway and waits until she hears the hall door close.

About a year ago, the professor and his wife appeared one day at the house on Herbstgasse, which had gradually turned into a sort of way station for people fleeing not only from Frankfurt but from all of Germany and Austria. Two helpless individuals, no longer very young, each with a suitcase and a rucksack, trying desperately to keep an attitude that displayed what was left of their former dignity. Leni invited them into the house, and while Vreni made tea, Alice came downstairs and joined them. Alice was wonderful when it came to helping people over their embarrassment, and giving them back their pride and human worth, which had been taken from them on the other side of the border. Giving them something like hope that better times would come again. Alice of all people, who herself was so often gloomy and depressed. But when she needed to, the Queen played her role perfectly. The professor and his wife were both truly calmed by Alice's presence, and Erich, friendly and helpful as ever, took care of finding a cheap room and even helped them, with his business contacts, try to find the address of that cousin in Argentina. Successfully, it turned out. Erich will be glad to hear it.

Still, Leni is sorry that she let herself make this generous gesture—the fact is, they need every franc on Herbstgasse too. But somehow or other it will all work out; up to now it always has, somehow.

She pulls on her white gloves that she never leaves the house without, puts her hat on her head, and sets out for home. The sun is blazing in the sky, and Leni is happy to reach the garden gate. It's comparatively cool and shady in the house; Vreni didn't forget to pull all the curtains closed so as not to let the heat in.

"Vreni, would you bring my tea out to the veranda?" Leni calls, as she takes off her hat, pulls off her gloves, and slips out of her high-heeled shoes. She slowly walks out to the veranda, sits down in the garden chair, and stretches out her tired legs.

It doesn't take long before Vreni comes out with a tray with the tea things on it. Next to the teacup is a card, a card from Amsterdam. Leni recognizes the handwriting at a glance—her brother Otto's. She snatches up the card.

"Dearest Lunni," she reads. "Happy birthday! We're all sending you our best birthday wishes today . . ." She lowers the card and shakes her head in confusion, and takes a sip of tea. A birthday card in late July? Strange. Her birthday is September.

Happy birthday! We're all sending you our best birthday wishes today, since we want to be sure that you'll get them in time & we won't have a chance to send them later. All our love from the bottom of our hearts. We are healthy & together, that's the main thing. Everything is hard for us these days, but sometimes you just have to take what comes. Hopefully, peace will come this year so that we can see each other again. We can't correspond with I. and with you all anymore, which is regrettable, but there's nothing we can do about it. She must understand. Again, warmest regards, Your O.*

---

*"I." is his mother, Alice, who, as mentioned earlier, had that nickname within the family.

A chill comes over Leni. What is that supposed to mean, "We can't correspond with I. and with you all anymore"? What is Otto saying, and why this cryptic formulation, especially from Otto, who usually expresses himself so precisely?

Edith, Margot, and Anne also added short messages. Anne had written in Dutch on the front of the card, left of the stamps, in the block letters she always used when it was important that it be legible: "I can't write a vacation letter now. Hugs and kisses from Anne."

Leni knows only a few words of Dutch that she picked up in Amsterdam, but she understands that Anne can "*niet schrijven*" her holiday letter. Underneath Anne's message are "All the best, Your Edith" and "Best wishes, Margot." And on the bottom, the sender: "O. Frank, Merwedeplein 37, Amsterdam."

Leni reads the card again, then a third time. The strange feeling grows within her that Otto was trying to communicate something very different from birthday wishes. She puts the card in her handbag before standing up. Lunch will be ready soon. She goes upstairs to her mother's room, having decided not to mention this strange card around Alice, at least not at first. She doesn't want to worry her unnecessarily.

Leni had not gone into business voluntarily, and ended up in this line of work quite by accident. Since 1936, when the Pomosin Company headquarters in Cologne had inquired whether the executives and board of directors of Rovag AG were "pure Aryan," Erich's workplace situation had got worse. In 1938, he had been stripped of his authority as director of Rovag. "Furthermore, the business activities of Rovag are hereby reduced to a minimum, i.e., bookkeeping only, which you will continue until further notice. We reserve the right to take further measures concerning this question." Then, in January 1939, Rovag Glarus, a subsidiary of Pomosin AG in Cologne, sent definitive notice removing Erich Elias from the board of directors. The time of financial difficul-

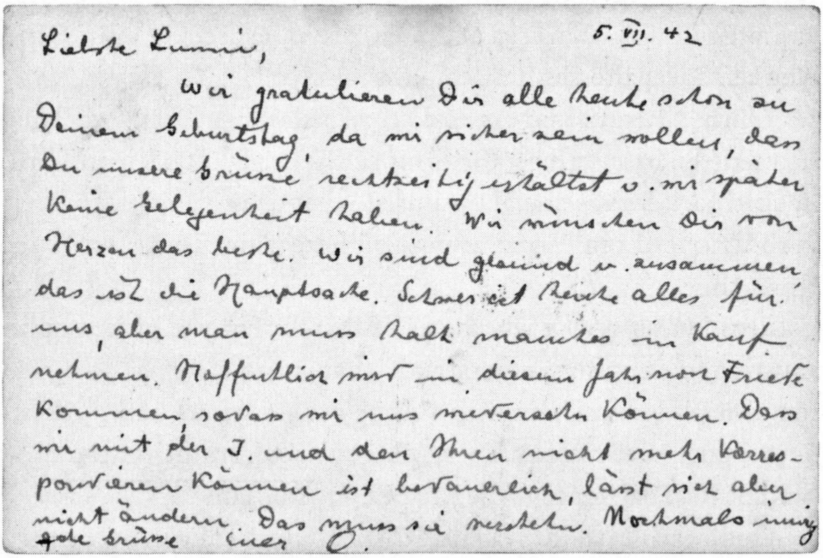

Liebste Lunni, 5. VII. 42

Wir gratulieren Dir alle heute schon zu Deinem Geburtstag, da wir sicher sein wollen, dass Du unsere Grüsse rechtzeitig erhältst u. wir später keine Gelegenheit haben. Wir wünschen Dir von Herzen das beste. Wir sind gesund u. zusammen das ist die Hauptsache. Schwer ist heute alles für uns, aber man muss halt manches in Kauf nehmen. Hoffentlich wird in diesem Jahr noch Friede kommen, sodass wir uns wiedersehen können. Dass wir mit der J. und den Ihren nicht mehr korrespondieren können ist bedauerlich, lässt sich aber nicht ändern. Das muss sie verstehen. Nochmals innigste Grüsse Euer O.

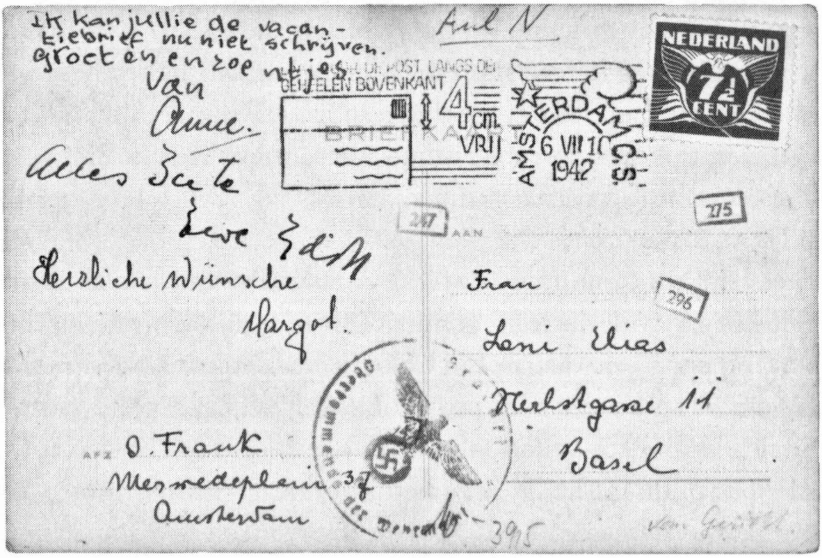

Ik kan jullie de vacantiebrief nu niet schrijven. groeten en en zoentjes van Anne.

Alles Gute Love Edith

Herzliche Wünsche Margot.

AFZ O. Frank Merwedeplein 37 Amsterdam

AAN Frau Leni Elias Herbstgasse 11 Basel

NEDERLAND 7½ CENT

AMSTERDAM C.S. 6 VII 10 1942

Card from Otto Frank to Leni, written before going into hiding on July 5, 1942 ties began. Erich did manage to find a job at another Pomosin subsidiary, Unipektin in Zurich, where he worked in the lab but at a much lower salary, even aside from the costs of commuting between Basel and Zurich. It was impossible for Erich to look for another job because, in spite of all of his efforts, he had still not succeeded in becoming a Swiss citizen, only a legal resident. And not only did Switzerland continue to refuse him citizenship, but in the previous year Germany had revoked his citizenship as well.

At the same time, more and more emigrants appeared at the house on Herbstgasse who had heard from others that Leni was always ready to offer a cup of tea and some good advice. Many of them were in financial difficulties of their own and asked Leni to help them by selling some of their things, offering her a commission. She started doing so as a favor to them, out of pity, but of course she could also certainly use the money: the fact is, it was not cheap to keep a household of so many people—she and Erich and their two sons, Stephan and Buddy, plus Alice, Grandma Ida, and Vreni the housekeeper. In addition, they were trying to bring Paul, Erich's brother, to Basel, and also Herbert, the black sheep, who hadn't succeeded in anything and whom Alice still felt responsible for. That's a lot of mouths to feed, with no immediate improvement of the situation in sight.

At first the commissions were just a little extra income, but gradually they became the main part of their support. Not only was the word out among the emigrants that Herbstgasse was a good address when you had something you needed to sell, but more and more Swiss who wanted to buy started to know Leni's name, including a lot of bargain hunters who took advantage of the fugitives' desperate situation. The business side was simple: Leni didn't buy the things, since she didn't have enough money—she took them on commission. If the items sold, the owners got the money in cash if they were living in Basel, or else she sent it on, minus 10 or 15 percent commission, depending. A business like that requires trust. Leni's capital was her honesty and good name. People brought her more and more things—clothing, shoes, jewelry, everything imaginable. It got crowded in the house, with boxes and packages standing around in the rooms and bundles of clothing everywhere. She found by accident a cheap room on the second floor of a house in lower Basel, the part of town on the other side of the Rhine Bridge, and there she set up what she called her "flea market."

Of course back when she had met Erich, she had pictured her life rather differently. When she told him "I do," the world looked very different. The terrible war that they would later call World War I had seemed, with all its constraints and anxieties, to be behind them for good; the family had lost money, like almost everyone in Germany, but a sense of optimism was in the air and the future seemed bright. People believed in a new beginning; people wanted to enjoy life. For Leni, the war years seemed like nothing more than an interruption to the hopes and dreams that had suddenly returned. A carefree future seemed to lie before her, and she, the spoiled only daughter, believed that she had a self-evident right to it; she was young and pretty, in love with a very handsome man who admired her, who was outwardly as well as inwardly what they call a gentleman, and who met with her family's approval, which was important to her. Especially that of Otto, her beloved, then still unmarried brother. It was not only for sentimental reasons that Leni did not want to go against the will of her family, of course, there were financial reasons as well—as the daughter of a bourgeois house she had never been trained for a career and had remained, in a sense, "the child" while her brothers had grown up into men.

It was especially important to her that Otto agreed with her choice. Otto was her favorite brother, and was always the one, even as a child, whom she could come to with everything. He had never looked down on her, made fun of her, or teased her, as Rob-

Leni Elias, circa 1919

ert sometimes had. Otto had the gift of taking people seriously: he liked people, as he had written once in a letter to her from the battlefield, and as Leni already knew. For her, Otto was not only the admired older brother but also the very model of an upstanding human being, someone she no doubt measured everyone else against. After the death of her father, the role that this brother played for both her and Alice had only grown more important.

That is why it mattered so much to Leni that Otto liked Erich. Even if he may have welcomed this new love only because he saw it as proof that Leni's unhappy affair with Ernst, which he was so worried about, was over for good. In any case, Erich, unlike Ernst, was not engaged to someone else, and was Jewish, not from a well-known family but his father was not poor, he owned a grain and feed factory in Zweibrücken. He was neither a starveling nor a religious fanatic, as Otto had once put it in the presence of others—within the family he called such people "religious nuts." He would not have liked to have one as a relative. Then, when Erich's father came to Frankfurt to meet the Franks, he had even won Alice over to his side, despite her initial resistance. "A pleasant man," she said, and Leni's happiness was complete.

The family was no doubt relieved that Leni was getting married at last. She was twenty-seven years old and not inexperienced, and given how things were back then, it was high time for her to marry if she did not want to end up as an old maid. The fact that Leni of all people, beautiful and admired by all, was still single could not have been entirely the fault of the war, or the financial situation after Germany's defeat, which must have cut rather deeply into her dowry. In any case, the relief must have been great about the planned wedding, presumably in Leni herself as well.

Erich Elias, circa 1920

But there is no question that she was also in love with her Erich.

"There is something so beautiful about this life," she wrote to him right at the beginning. "I don't want to come back down to earth, because the everyday world with its worrisome cares understands only too well how to drag us down from the heavens & give rise to a sensation that I don't want to wish on my dear ones. I need you, I long for you."

The letters she wrote to Erich, in which she spoke of their future life together, were passionate, for example this letter from Munich on October 20, 1920:

A train trip like this, 10 hours long, is designed to send your thoughts on a journey too & I don't need to tell you where mine wandered off to, do I. A thousand dear things that we've never talked about yet came to mind & when I think about how someday we will be able to share all our joys with each other, my mood grows so happy & sunny. I don't want to think anything about sadness, even though I'm sure it will come up too in our lives together, but when two people are together they can help each other & everything is easier to bear. You are an idealist & I, who have unlearned my idealism a bit, I am starting to view life and people from a better angle again & I firmly believe in great, great happiness. The two of us still don't know each other nearly well enough, of course, but what we do know promises a harmonious life, and we can't be wrong about that. Actually there's no point in constructing big theories, in practice it always turns out differently, but I look forward to the future & am not afraid to put my life in your hands. The main thing is to love each other & this principle gets you further than anything else, don't you think, Erich?

She did not want to think about sadness, she wrote; she had a firm belief in great happiness. When Erich went to Zweibrücken to tell his parents about their intention to marry, a letter from Leni was already waiting for him there. She wanted him to have a few words from her right away, she wrote. "You left me alone today, to smooth my road to your parents & you can be sure that my thoughts are constantly with you. I feel like I need to come to you, to be with you, so that your dear ones can also see that my highest goal is to make you happy, you who deserve it more than anyone else. As for me, I have the definite feeling that I have found my happiness—you and I are in harmony, trust each other & love each other. What more can anyone want?"

Especially moving is a letter that she wrote to him six weeks before the wedding, which was to take place in February 1921:

You're still here, it's true, & I can see you, talk to you & maybe kiss you too a few more times, but my thoughts have already hurried ahead to greet you when you arrive in Berlin. Erich, my dear heart, I have so much to say to you and don't know where to start. Life rages on all

Leni, pregnant, with her in-laws Ida and Carl Elias, summer 1921

around me, I make my face look the way it has to look, following all the necessary rules, I'm friendly to the people I know and grumpy to the ones I don't like & I put on an act for everyone else. I occasionally put on a piece of theater for myself, which might not be anything to scoff at in my condition but I'm afraid I just can't—I have to admit it, to you at least—I do not give a damn about anything in the world at the moment except you, it's almost ridiculous. I'm a little off balance & I hope I regain it soon, before you're back—in any case <u>*you*</u> *shouldn't have to suffer because of this. I'm very rarely in a bad mood because I'm an optimist by nature, only the war broke down my optimism a little & now I've fully & completely won it all back again. And as soon as the* <u>*sun*</u> *shines again everything is sheer joy & shining light for me, because I have it in my heart & want to give you so much of it that you'll never feel a chill in our whole life together.*

It is certainly not easy to enter into each other's lives so deeply that it doesn't turn into a habit but we wouldn't want to live without each other. But I'm not afraid to try, after all we're both adults and both understand how to accommodate ourselves to each other a little, if we're torturing each other, we don't need to share every joy & sorrow! The disappointments I have felt up to now in you & your character are still bearable, although I <u>*do*</u> *have high expectations of people! And I want you to expect things of me too.*

Goodbye for today, Erich, I kiss you with all the warmth and tenderness I have.

Leni

Then, in February 1921, the wedding took place—a celebration exactly as Leni had hoped. She wore a dress from the most expensive atelier in Frankfurt, the guests were numerous, and the presents were too. Leni was in seventh heaven, and the early years of her marriage seemed to be everything she expected them to be. She might have taken it as a bad omen that her grandmother Cornelia died four months after the wedding—Leni loved Cornelia, and her death was a hard blow—but she was three months pregnant by then, and her joyful expectation of a child was probably great enough to push her grief into the background.

Her happiness seemed complete when her son Stephan was born on December 20, 1921, precisely on Alice's birthday—she would take pleasure in this birthday gift for the rest of her life—and then her son Bernhard (Buddy) on June 2, 1925. Erich had meanwhile joined the bank, like Herbert and Otto, and everything looked rosy for a while. But gradually the economic situation grew more tense, Michael Frank's banking firm went downhill, and the family had to cut back more and more. Erich's decision to move to Switzerland and set up Rovag AG for Pomosin seemed promising. Even if not all the hopes that Erich and Leni had about Switzerland were to be fulfilled, even if some of them turned out to be illusions, Switzerland nonetheless offered sufficient security during the years of persecution and in the end turned out to be a great good fortune for the family.

The long months of living alone with the two children in Frankfurt were difficult for Leni, as evidenced by the many

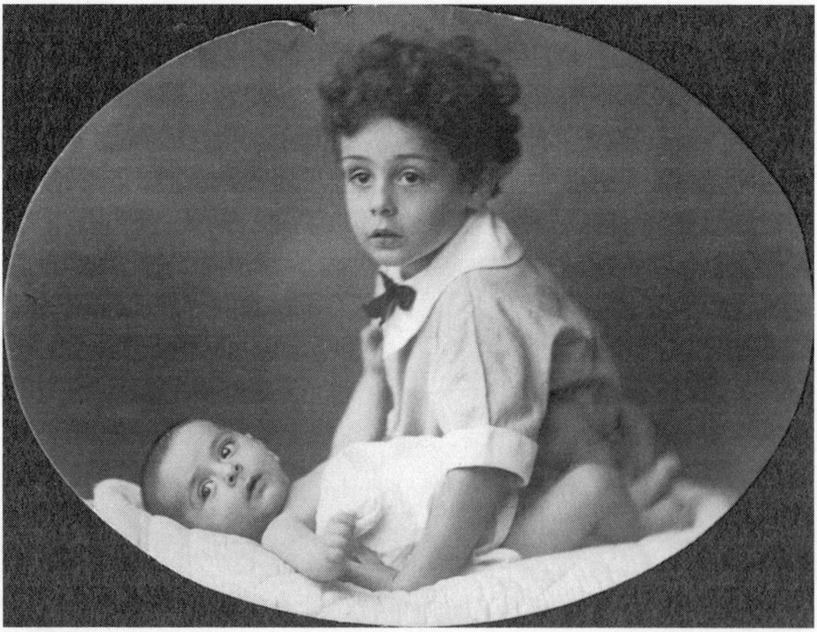

Buddy and Stephan Elias, 1925

letters she wrote to Erich telling him about her everyday life and the children. Stephan called himself Bübü, and so did everyone else while he was young, and then there was Buddi (spelled with an *i* at first, only later with a *y*). Leni often felt overwhelmed by daily life alone with two children, although of course she had a nanny, Dadi, whom Buddy loved very much and whom he describes even today in the most glowing terms. On June 1, 1929, Leni wrote to Erich:

My darling, Yesterday you made me very happy with your long detailed letter, thank you very much for it. I had a busy day & I'll tell you about it. Since the maids were cleaning like crazy & no stone was left standing on another, I decided to go out to eat with Dadi & the children. It was quite a party. In the morning I went first to the city to see Helen, Irma May, & Dadi had Buddi's hair cut. Then she took him straight to the lodge and I drove home to meet Bübü, who was coming home from school. I packed our bathing suits & then Bübü & I were off to the lodge, where we ate a delicious & cheap lunch, were very content, & thought of you. After lunch Dadi drove home & I took the boys to the pool, where it was wonderful. Our little otters were a great joy, I missed you very much, the boys were so excited and very cute. At 6:30 we were back home, Bübü had to do his homework, and I went to the Stegers later. They welcomed me and were as nice as ever.

The letter ends: "That's it for today. I have to go get some money from the office."

It is striking how little Leni apparently noticed the political situation, the developments in Germany, the gradual change in mood and growing anti-Semitism—or at least she didn't write about it. Not a word about the increasing number of unemployed, about the Brownshirts who were growing ever louder. In late April 1929, the Reichsbanner members Heinrich Koch and Heinrich Schmidt, twenty-one and seventeen years old, were murdered by the Nazis: the first deaths from the Nazi campaign of street terror. Leni did not write about that either; she did not even mention that Otto and Edith had moved to Marbachweg. Was this a sign of her single-minded concentration on her own family, or simply a class-specific, self-involved way of seeing the world? Did she really, as she had written, "not give a damn about anything in the world" other than Erich and her children?

The very next day, on Buddy's fourth birthday, June 2, 1929, she wrote the following letter to Basel:

Darling,

I would have hurried to you at top speed this morning, if I could have, first because you seemed to be seriously homesick & second because I had an indescribable longing to be with you especially on Buddi's birthday that we had to celebrate without you. I bawled my eyes out, but then I noticed that it wasn't doing any good & instead prepared a happy day for my little one. He was very sweet & excited & got a wonderful pile of birthday presents with 2 charming suits & a stunning model streetcar from "Mama Dadi," a fire engine, a soccer ball, socks, stockings, a jacket, games, a little hat, underwear, it was really a mountain, he's spoiled on all sides. His party was a great success and the children were sweet & very well behaved. The afternoon flew by. Mother phoned from Paris, very happy, I told her she should visit you, but I don't think she will. She was very glad to get your nice note. She won't be back before Thursday or Wednesday night & I leave Saturday at 9:42 a.m.—(3:52 p.m. at Basel Station) if nothing goes wrong. I've made magnificent preparations since we'll have Sat. & Sun. to enjoy together & I can look forward to that all week. Oh, darling, I think about you so much & I'm so sad every day I can't be with you.

I know how much you miss the children, but there we have to be reasonable, it will be that much better later. Edith was in the hospital yesterday, false alarm and she's better today, but I hope for her sake that the little bundle arrives soon . . . I was very glad to get your nice note from yesterday and the card to Buddi too, I read it to him. You write so deeply*

*Ten days later, Anne Frank was born.

about how we feel about the children . . . Anna and Dadi are having another fight, Anna is a real ninny. Bübü keeps wanting to go to Basel & asks about you all the time. Can't you visit on business? . . . Should I bring your trunk? I have no idea where I can stow my own things. Can you ask? I want to stay longer with you. Just write if I should bring anything.

Leni visited her Erich regularly, even though the train took a lot longer then than it does today. Erich sometimes came to Frankfurt as well. Business was not going well enough in Basel yet—Erich simply didn't have the money to bring his family to Switzerland. But the hope remained. On November 20, Leni wrote:

My beloved,

It's rare to have so much happiness & pain at once & I can hardly describe what I'm feeling. Your letters give off so much love & warmth & longing that I feel terribly happy & sad at once. Of course I would have loved to be with you long ago, but I think that 1. you'd rather I spend a little time with the children and 2. I haven't been feeling especially well in the past 2 days & I made an appointment with Dr. Gottschalk today. I have a lot of aches and pains, but since Dr. G. didn't take them seriously, I've gradually stopped worrying about them too. But since the pains in my back & side are getting worse, I want to talk to him today and hear if that's normal, I can't believe it is. I'm dying with longing for you & if I didn't mention our engagement anniversary

Buddy and Stephan Elias, circa 1928–29

the other day, it was mostly so that I wouldn't mention a special occasion that we couldn't celebrate together & so that our hearts would not be made heavier. But since you were sweet enough to send me my beloved red carnations and a letter with dear words & 20 francs, now I want to send heartfelt thanks & express my wish that we can soon be together in peace & not need to be apart. You write that 9 years ago was our most carefree time. We didn't feel it then, and aside from that the true love & camaraderie that today helps us get through our wretched situation was missing . . . Bübü was in raptures this morning about the zeppelin, he went to the airport with Herbi, Rudi, and Lou, it was apparently very interesting, it flew over the building 2x and you could hear everything on the radio. Bübü isn't back yet. Your letter to the children was so sweet, naturally I cried and cried, it's like I'm made of water when it comes to anything to do with you. I can't help it, I could cry my eyes out whenever I think of you . . . What do you think about the collapse of the international banks? It could turn out in our favor. I'm so proud of Basel! I hope, oh, I hope and hope you will be successful there soon, so that—I can't finish the sentence . . . I'll use your 20 francs for my new winter hat, that will be great. Buddi just gave me his Sunday kiss, he is really too sweet & has such a colorful imagination. You should have heard him going on and on about the zeppelin, you would have died laughing.

The world economic situation had grown more and more acute, culminating in the market crash of October 25, 1929. This time, Leni did mention the worldwide catastrophe after all, but only in passing: "What do you think about the collapse of the international banks? It could turn out in our favor." Did she really see the world through such rose-colored glasses? Could it truly have never occurred to her that the collapse might have difficult consequences for her own family's bank?

Leni's letters are full of longing and ever more insistent in tone. She wanted to be with her husband, and life in Frankfurt was becoming unbearable for her.

My everything,

Je suis navrée [I am brokenhearted]. It was monstrous of me to make you more depressed, you have enough to worry about these days, but I only wanted to take the burden off you as you need, & do you a favor. I'm fretting of course because it really doesn't make sense that we're a family & that we can't be together. Dictation: Dear Papa, Why aren't you coming back, I'd like it so much if you did! (It shouldn't have been allowed!) Wasn't the other letter I wrote you nice? Do you still know how Maleni looks? (Beautiful!) Do you still remember how I look? Best wishes from BUDDI *[the name is written in awkward block letters, clearly by Buddy himself]. He is so sweet! He just said: "But I always write great letters because I'm such a wonderful Bertje!" Yesterday he said to Mrs. Speyer: "I really want a little sister but my Maleni doesn't want one, so I'm not getting one!" On that subject, there was a big ruckus at Speyer-Ellissen, they let go 43 people, some of them very old, & the scenes that played out there must have been terrible. You can feel that I'm sad & I can't hide it from you, but I have hours when I'm satisfied too & when I'm with you again I'll be happy and content with everything.—I just heard that Rudolf R. Bauer went bust, that's a hard blow for the construction industry & Herbert is beside himself. How will it end? I think you should thank God & A.S. that you're in Basel, even if you're short of funds, that will change soon there, here there's nothing to be done anymore.—It's not so easy for me to raise the children but I'm trying my best & when we think what good little souls they are we can feel satisfied. Lucie says "As long as you have your health" & she's right.*

This time she wrote about layoffs and bankruptcies, even if she did not directly relate them to herself. For her, the issue was her children, her state of mind, and her longing. It is easy enough to imagine that she was missing the physical side of her marriage as well; in one of her last letters before moving to Basel, she wrote:

My dearest darling, Today I found a few letters from you while I was straightening up, where you told me about your candy stick & other lovely things like that! It made me feel so ancient & made me desperately want to get my head carefree enough that I can enjoy thinking about the lower half of my body again. What do you think of that? I love you so much, but what good does it do me if I have to scratch around with my pen point on a sheet of paper all the time to give you a sermon on my love? I can't ever see you darling & over the phone everyone is always in the room & never budges & so we never have any privacy to talk. It'll be over soon, I'm sure of it & today when I packed up 4 boxes of china & glasses I thought about how long I'd probably have my things in those boxes. Till September at the latest, I think, but I'd prefer July!

It did take a long time, however, before Leni could finally move to Basel. She brought her younger son, Buddy, with her but left Stephan in Frankfurt for the time being, with Alice: for one thing, he was still in school, and Leni wanted to look for the most appropriate school in Basel first; for another, Alice thought it was better for her daughter to bring only one child at first, that would make it easier for her to start over in Basel, and furthermore they didn't have a place to live yet. And Stephan? Stephan loved his grandma Alice and probably didn't mind the arrangement at all.

Erich, Leni, and Buddy lived in a hotel for a few months before they found the apartment on Gundeldingerstrasse. At last they could set out and use the furniture from Frankfurt and unpack the boxes of "china & glasses." Leni and Buddy settled into Basel, and soon Buddy was speaking such good Swiss German that Leni had to always be after him to speak High German.

But the family was still torn in two, between Basel and Frankfurt. Only when Stephan moved to Basel in 1932 and Alice in 1933 did they finally more or less reestablish their normal life.

There was a tennis court behind the house on Gundeldingerstrasse, which a coating of water in winter transformed into a skating rink for the children. Did Buddy get his first ice skates that first winter, or the next one? He no longer remembers. But there are a couple of things he knows for sure: he was happy the first time he had skates on his feet, and his greatest joy was when they built a real skating rink across the street. From then on, his winters were devoted to ice-skating—and not only his winters, also his brother Stephan's.

The boys spent the summers either with Leni and Alice in Sils-Maria, at Auntie O.'s, or up in the mountains at a summer camp called Alpmorgenholz, near Laus in the Graubünden Canton, which Buddy remembers extremely fondly. Obviously, it was a summer camp for boys—coeducation was not common at the time—and Buddy didn't mind that in the least. On the contrary: he liked life with so many other boys, taking hikes and playing sports, putting on plays, singing and playing around the campfires. They bathed in the open air and ate very simple food, but everyone was full at the end of the meal. Every other day, two boys were sent down to the village with panniers on their backs to replenish the camp's provisions. As a reward for the long hike and the hauling, they were allowed to buy an ice cream in the village confectionery, and this privilege was enough for the boys to get into fistfights over.

Leni was fully occupied with settling into Basel, meeting people, and getting to know her new surroundings. Of course she had help around the house in Gundeldingerstrasse as well: Sophie Schmidt, a brawny woman from Baden who, Buddy recalls, spoke in dialect with a thick accent. A good-hearted woman, but extremely energetic. When she called the children to the table, she would always say: "Hey, cripples, go wash your hands!" Buddy also says that he and his brother, on Erich's wishes, received religious instruction for a while from a Polish man who spoke only broken German. Stephan always used to mimic him: "Rachel, sssee was a beauuutiful gull." They were not religious, but Erich went to temple on the High Holidays and fasted on Yom Kippur. Leni never did either, of course.

Leni quickly struck up an acquaintance with the women she would play bridge with once a week, and whom she would also sometimes meet at the pastry shop in the afternoons. In addition, she had to take care of her mother, Alice, who was having an unexpectedly difficult time getting used to life in Basel. A daily routine developed that was very different from what Leni had expected, but life in general was much more peaceful than in Frankfurt. No one knew what would happen in Germany, but the hateful slogans about Jews were impossible to overlook; they even reached Basel. At least the family was together again. Erich's business was not going as well as Leni had hoped. "It's better to get rich slowly than quickly," she had written in one of her letters—but this was definitely *too* slow. They got by, but they certainly were not rich.

Still, none of them were homesick for Germany.

The fact that Erich started applying for Swiss citizenship very early shows how serious he was about his life in Switzerland. At first he received only a residence permit, then permission to settle in Switzerland, but on April 2, 1936, the Basel Canton Depart-

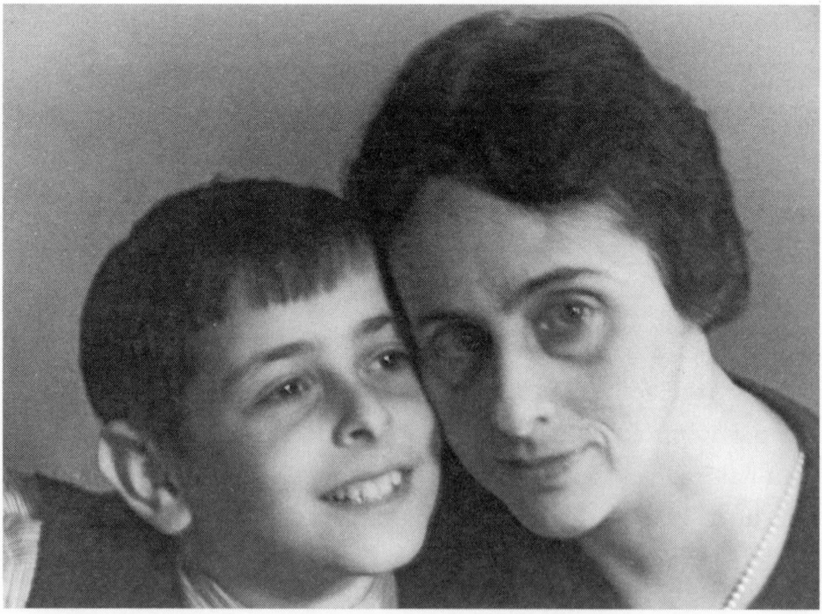

Buddy and Leni Elias, circa 1933

ment of the Interior refused his application for citizenship due to his "still insufficient assimilation"—whatever that might mean. His hopes for a Swiss passport would remain unfulfilled for a long time to come.

Why would a Swiss passport be so important to him, if he was living with his family in Basel and there was no threat of deportation? Shouldn't that have been enough? But a passport means more than merely the right to live somewhere: it defines its possessor; it says where he or she belongs, to what group, in what place. A passport also defines who is responsible for the possessor's welfare, if it should be necessary to provide any services. At least that's how it is in a state ruled by laws. Furthermore, Erich would have needed a passport to take business trips for the company. And it would soon become clear how right he was to pursue a Swiss passport. Nazi Germany was not a state ruled by laws, and a regulation of November 25, 1941, revoked the German citizenship of any Jews living outside of Germany. They were now without a passport, without a state, ineligible to claim any social services—in short, without the right to a homeland.

In April 1942, the German consulate ordered Erich Elias to send in any identification papers in his possession. The notice was addressed to Mr. and Mrs. Erich *Israel* Elias, Herbstgasse 11, Basel: according to a regulation dating from August 17, 1938, all male Germans of Jewish background had to have the first or middle name Israel, and all female Germans of Jewish background had to be named Sara; their passports were marked with a large stamped *J*. Buddy, sixteen years old at the time, still remembers the day when he came home and his father had just got the news that he had lost his German citizenship and had to give up his passport. He says he almost never saw his father so angry. Erich took his son to the consulate and slammed his passport onto the table, then took him out for a beer at the pub on the corner. That was the first time Buddy ever had a beer with his father.

In February 1942, the now-stateless Erich Elias reapplied for "Procurement of Authorization from the Swiss Confederation for the Granting of Citizenship." He received a request to appear "at 8:15 a.m. on October 30, 1942," together with his wife, "to supply information to the town clerk about your state of health and the medical background of your family." It sounded promising. Erich and Leni went to the city council offices at Stadthausgasse 13 with high hopes—their state of health was good, after all—but on June 25, 1943, almost eight months later, Erich was verbally informed that his request was once again denied "due to insufficient assimilation." This time he submitted an appeal, for the following reasons:

Since 1929, that is for 14 years, I have lived in Basel without interruption. I received permission to settle in the Basel-Stadt Canton in 1936 and kept that permission until 1942, when it was withdrawn solely because I became stateless as a result of a German regulation. During my many years in Switzerland, I have grown intimately familiar with the local customs and circumstances and have learned to treasure my host country in the highest degree. As I can substantiate with numerous references, I have completely assimilated here and have no relationships whatsoever with my former native country. This is especially true, in addition, of my two sons, Stephan (b. 1921) and Bernhard (b. 1925); as you can see from the attached autobiographical statements, both have spent the majority of their lives in Switzerland. Neither in language nor in mentality are they in any way different from their Swiss contemporaries. Especially in Swiss sports circles, both are well-known and well liked.

I myself have worked for years in the pectin industry, specifically in the laboratory of Unipektin Corp. in Zurich. It is primarily at the request of my company that I have decided to submit this appeal. As stated in the enclosed letter from Unipektin Corp., Zurich, which I hereby expressly declare to be an attachment to this argument for recourse, it would be of great significance to the company, one that is not unimportant in the national economy, if you were to grant my request.

I therefore hope that you consider the point of view put forward by Unipektin Corp. as you take my request for appeal under review with all due consideration.

But this protest failed as well. A letter from Erich to the citizenship office reveals why the process went so badly for him: he had learned from one of the unfavorable reports in his file that it was due to "underhanded business dealings in financial transactions with Jews in Germany."

Erich countered as follows:

My only relationship with Germany, during the past 12 years, consisted solely of the fact that I had previously established a foreign subsidiary of the most important German pectin factory (Pomosin Works), made up of businesses that manufactured and sold pectin and pectin products (e.g., the well-known "Opekta") combined into a holding company with the deceased national councilman Dr. R. Gallati, from Glarus, on the board of directors. The company also had a line of business exporting Swiss pomace, and I can claim to have been the first to pioneer this export industry. Financial transactions took place only within the framework of this business, never with myself or anyone else acting as private individuals. In Basel alone, my employees in the office, the factory, and travel have numbered as many as 35 persons. During this entire period I have never once done any private business, neither with Jews nor with Christians and neither in Germany nor anywhere else.

As a result of conflicts with the National Socialists who joined the executive team of the company in 1937–38 and with their local representatives in Switzerland, I have been removed from a leadership role in the company.

The unfavorable report given to you about my activities is objectively untrue and can only have come from someone's intentional efforts to malign me. I am able and eager to supply references to prove my unimpeachable business conduct.

I have also learned that my older son has been described to you as a "disingenuous shirker." I can only conclude that this characterization likewise was made with malicious intent, or else by someone who simply does not know my son, since it describes the exact opposite of the person he truly is.

Without being guilty of flattery, I may say that he is the sincerest and most honest person you could imagine, and diligent and hardworking like few others I know. The last school he attended, at the Commercial Union, graduated him with honors. He takes part in numerous athletic competitions and his teachers and schoolmates can all attest to his probity.

A letter from a lawyer, Dr. Naegeli, to Erich Elias on November 23, 1943, shed light at last on the real reason Erich's citizenship requests were denied: Switzerland's reluctance to admit too many Jews. "The boat is full" was the phrase heard far and wide at the time. The lawyer reports that he had discussed the prevailing practice with the officials in charge of requests for citizenship, obviously without naming any names.

Buddy and Erich Elias, circa 1944

Then I received the strange explanation that the Executive Federal Council had given instructions simply not to grant any more requests from Jewish applicants born abroad . . . I am afraid that in fact the practices described to me by the official in charge are how in fact things are done these days, and no matter how astonished I am by this position, there is nothing I can do at the moment to change it . . . When the war reaches its end and the many immigrants currently living here without papers have found new homelands elsewhere, in other words when the danger of our needing to permanently shelter so many Jewish refugees has passed, that will no doubt be the time to resubmit your application and have it granted.

(It would take until 1952 before Erich and Leni became Swiss citizens.)

The autobiographical statements put together by Stephan and Buddy Elias, and included in Erich's 1942 appeal submission, show the course that their lives were taking.

Stephan Carl Elias: Autobiographical Statement

I was born on December 20, 1921, in Frankfurt am Main. I attended primary school there for four years. Then I moved to Basel to rejoin my parents, and attended high school here for six years. Afterward, I attended technical school for one semester, but then changed my original career goal and started commercial training, during which time I simultaneously attended the business college of the Commercial Union for three years. I passed my final exams and am currently a sales employee at a Basel firm.

As a member of the Red-White Sport Club, I compete in track and field in the summer and ice hockey in the winter. I am the goalie of the Basel team and was once even offered a place on the Swiss National Team by the Technical Committee of the Swiss Ice Hockey League.

In my entire way of life, thought, and feeling, I am Swiss.

Bernhard Elias: Autobiographical Statement

I was born on June 2, 1925, in Frankfurt am Main. I lived there for four years before moving with my mother to join my father in Basel. I went to kindergarten every day and attended primary school for four years, starting when I was 6. After scoring well on the entrance exam, I transferred to the high school, from which after just 4 years I transferred again to the canton commercial high school, from which I graduated. In May of this year I entered an optician training program.

In the athletic sphere I am mainly active in winter in figure skating, and have performed in skating exhibitions and variety shows on almost all the rinks in Switzerland. In addition, I am a member of the R.T.V. Track and Field association. I am also a member of the "Quodlibet" theater troupe, and always take part in the public performances of plays in dialect.

My deepest wish is to become a Swiss citizen.

These autobiographical statements sound so "normal," so harmless—as though there were nothing in their lives besides school and sports. And sports really did play a great role in both boys' lives, with acting as well as sports for Buddy. Buddy says that when Stephan's hockey team was playing in another Swiss city and the game was broadcast on the radio, the whole family gathered around the radio to listen, and every time the announcer said the goalie's name, "Elias," they all clapped and cheered and almost burst with pride, even Alice, who didn't care much about sports.

These were completely normal things to do for two completely normal young men. Still, from today's perspective, it does sound rather odd when you think about how, while they played hockey, performed variety shows on ice, and acted in dialect in an amateur theater, all around them—all around Switzerland—millions upon millions were dying. In 1942, when these autobiographical statements were written, the large concentration camps already existed, and the first killings with poison gas had already begun at Auschwitz. But they knew nothing about that; they couldn't know anything about it.

7.

The Time Without Letters

What was life like safe in Switzerland, surrounded by warring nations, by the thunder of cannon whose echo you felt like you could hear even if they were miles away? What was life like under the droning of warplanes, the bombers with their deadly cargo? Even in Basel they must have sometimes heard the planes—the borders of France and Germany are not far away, and there were probably bombs meant for one or the other that accidentally fell on Swiss soil. At least that's what Buddy says today.

The family received its first shock in March 1941, when they learned that Jean-Michel Frank, Leni's cousin and a well-known furniture designer, had committed suicide in New York. The motive is not known. He was one of the Germans who fled from Paris to America because he felt doubly unsafe there—the Nazis not only persecuted Jews but also mercilessly persecuted homosexuals. At age forty-six, he jumped out the window of his apartment in Manhattan. His friend Jean Cocteau said Jean-Michel's death "was like a curtain falling between the world of light and the world of darkness." The news of his death struck the family hard, and awakened memories of Jean-Michel's brothers, Oscar and Georges, who had died fighting against Germany in World War I; and of their father Léon's sad end, when he heard about his second son's death and likewise committed suicide; and of their mother, Nanette, whose despair was so great that she had to be sent to a mental institution, where she had since died as well. The family in Basel must also have been struck by the fact that Jean-Michel had chosen the same way to die as his father so many years before—jumping out a window.

Then, in 1942, no more news reached them: the time of letters was over, for a long while to come. The family, who were used to hearing about everyone, suddenly didn't hear anything. Apparently, no one on Herbstgasse learned that Robert was among the hundreds of German Jews sent to prison on the Isle of Man that summer by the English government, "in the interest of national security." It took his wife, Lotti, weeks to find out where he was being held, and several months before he was released and allowed to return home.

Instead of family news reaching Herbstgasse from London or Amsterdam, there arrived only reports of deportations of Dutch Jews to the infamous camps in the East whose names were gradually becoming known: Auschwitz, Majdanek, Treblinka, Theresienstadt. At the same time, rumors reached Basel that countless Dutch Jews had gone into hiding to avoid deportation. They heard nothing about Otto, Edith, and the children, on Herbstgasse, but they knew Otto, knew how prudent and foresighted he was. If anyone could manage to keep himself and his family safe, it was Otto. But doubts and fears must have remained. How was it for them? How did they live with uncertainty, not only about Otto, Edith, Margot, and Anne's fates, but also about Robert and Lotti, since the Germans had not stopped bombing London?

Jean-Michel Frank, circa 1925

As brutal as it might sound, people get used to everything. And they calm themselves, they convince themselves that everything is okay, they build walls of straw to protect themselves against the dangerous outside world. People flee from a reality that they cannot or do not want to imagine into a daily routine which presses into the foreground all too easily with its demands. Of course they did not forget their loved ones—son, brother, brother-in-law, uncle, and his wife and daughters, the granddaughters, nieces, cousins. They thought about them, but not every minute of the day. Everyday life went on, and this everyday life, even in neutral Switzerland, was hard enough and growing harder all the time. In the end, you couldn't simply sit around all day and wait for the mailman if he was never going to bring anything, day after day and week after week—at some point you stop waiting.

Everyone in the family agreed that Otto's last card to Leni, with the early birthday wishes, was a hint that "we in Amsterdam" were looking for a place to hide and therefore would no longer be able to "correspond with I. and with you all . . . She must understand." And they did understand it, because they had no choice. Then, in 1943, came a letter from the Dutch Opekta Company. Johannes Kleiman, an old friend of Otto Frank's and the current head of the company, wrote a formal letter that was limited to purely business matters. But a comment surfaced that led to long discussions in the house on Herbstgasse: "Our 'little girl' has meanwhile got as tall as my wife, we can hardly believe it." Kleiman didn't have any young daughters anymore—his children were all grown, and they knew that. In that case, was this comment a secret hint about Anne? And if so, did this other sentence mean that the Franks were getting enough to eat in their hiding place and so were healthy? "Although there are difficulties everywhere in keeping house during the war, we do not suffer from serious shortages of anything essential and everyone is altogether in good health." And what about "Not one of us caught

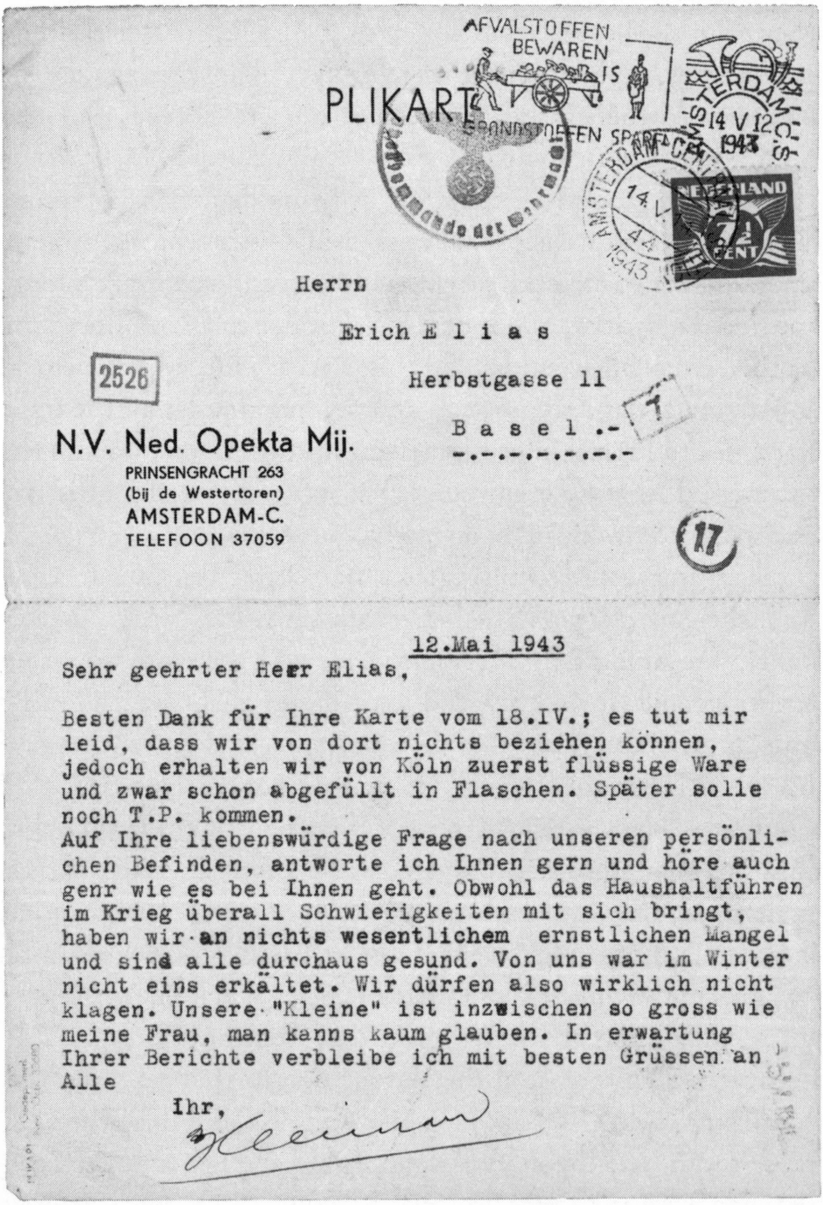

PLIKART

AFVALSTOFFEN BEWAREN IS GRONDSTOFFEN SPAREN

AMSTERDAM C.S. 14 V 12. 1943

AMSTERDAM CENTRAAL 14.V. 44 1943

NEDERLAND 7½ CENT

Herrn

Erich E l i a s

2526

Herbstgasse 11

B a s e l .-

-.-.-.-.-.-.-

N.V. Ned. Opekta Mij.
PRINSENGRACHT 263
(bij de Westertoren)
AMSTERDAM-C.
TELEFOON 37059

17

12.Mai 1943

Sehr geehrter Herr Elias,

Besten Dank für Ihre Karte vom 18.IV.; es tut mir leid, dass wir von dort nichts beziehen können, jedoch erhalten wir von Köln zuerst flüssige Ware und zwar schon abgefüllt in Flaschen. Später solle noch T.P. kommen.
Auf Ihre liebenswürdige Frage nach unseren persönlichen Befinden, antworte ich Ihnen gern und höre auch genr wie es bei Ihnen geht. Obwohl das Haushaltführen im Krieg überall Schwierigkeiten mit sich bringt, haben wir an nichts wesentlichem ernstlichen Mangel und sind alle durchaus gesund. Von uns war im Winter nicht eins erkältet. Wir dürfen also wirklich nicht klagen. Unsere "Kleine" ist inzwischen so gross wie meine Frau, man kanns kaum glauben. In erwartung Ihrer Berichte verbleibe ich mit besten Grüssen an Alle

Ihr,

Letter from Johannes Kleiman to Erich Elias, May 12, 1943

cold this winter?" Did that mean the Opekta employees, or Kleiman and his wife, or did it mean Otto, Edith, Margot, and Anne? They believed the latter—or they told themselves that that's what it meant for so long that in the end they believed it. Here, too, they had no other choice.

Life went on, and for Erich and Leni other problems came to the fore. Their sons, Stephan and Buddy, were growing up and required a lot of care and attention, and the economic situation was not exactly rosy. Then there were worries about Paul, Erich's brother. Erich and Leni tried everything to get him a travel permit to Switzerland, but in vain. Buddy recalls: "Somehow Paul could flee to France. There he managed to get hold of a visa for Bolivia, I don't know how. But he wasn't allowed to go from France to Bolivia, it was only possible via Switzerland. We applied to the authorities here so that he could transit through Switzerland; there would be no financial burden on the country whatsoever, we would pay everything. But they denied it, and gave as their reason that the continuation of his journey was not guaranteed." Switzerland rejected all the applications in this matter, as they did the applications of many other Jews, apparently for fear of being "overrun by foreigners." In cases like this as well, the disgraceful politics of the time continued to follow the "boat is full" principle.

Johanna Elias, circa 1911

Grandma Ida was in despair. She had had three children, and only Erich was left. Her daughter, Johanna, had been a beautiful girl, and there were still a few photographs of her in the house on Herbstgasse. She had fallen in love with a Christian military officer and had let him seduce her. But when Johanna became pregnant, the officer was not willing to marry a Jew and simply abandoned her. An everyday story, one might say, the kind you hear about all the time. But for Johanna it was the end of the world, and she took her own life in 1911, when she was eighteen years old.

Grandma Ida and Erich never kept this story a secret; they always spoke openly about Johanna and her unhappy fate.

So Ida had already lost one child, and now she was tormented with fears about a second, her son Paul. With every refusal from the immigration police, she grew more silent and cleaned house more furiously. How justified her fears were came to light only after the war: Paul Elias was murdered at Auschwitz.

The family also had to worry about Herbert. Erich and Leni tried to get him a residence permit, and there is a letter to the Jewish welfare authorities from January 18, 1943, pertaining to the matter, in which the undersigned, "Mrs. Alice Frank-Stern and Mr. Erich Elias-Frank," guarantee "to be responsible in every sense" for the support of their son and brother-in-law Mr. Herbert Frank "and to see to his emigration elsewhere from Switzerland by whatever means are possible." A handwritten note at the bottom of the document says: "To Herr Gretschel, requesting him to determine whether this counter-guarantor will be sufficient for obtaining a guarantee from the immigration police."

Apparently, it was sufficient for the immigration police. But it might also be the case that Herbert Frank, by that point made stateless like other German Jews abroad, entered Switzerland with false papers, because among the cache of documents in Basel there is a *carte d'identité* with Herbert's photograph but made out in the name of his dead cousin Jean-Michel Frank, a French citizen.

Herbert stayed in the house on Herbstgasse for two and a half years—letters and a handwritten autobiographical statement ("1942–1945 in Basel") are proof—and he left Switzerland to return to France only after the end of the war.

Leni had further worries about feeding the family. In 1943 she moved out of her "flea market" into a real store on Spalenvorstadt, on the corner of Schützenmattstrasse, where she began to sell antique furniture as well as used clothing, shoes, lamps, and all sorts of odds and ends. Many emigrants were forced to sell their furniture, including valuable antiques, which they had stored somewhere—either to raise necessary money or because they were emigrating farther and could not or would not bring it with them. These individuals now turned directly to Leni, if they were already in Switzerland, or wrote her letters and asked her, if sending their belongings onward was not practical, to take care of the stored items and sell them. It was no longer possible to conduct the business from the room in lower Basel and she had hired an assistant, since her activities had grown too extensive to manage alone. Leni had turned into a businesswoman, to the extent that she could. Her methods were unconventional—she had never owned a cash register, but always sorted the money coming in into envelopes bearing the names of the respective owners—but one way or another it seemed to work for her, and of course she also had Erich to help with the bookkeeping.

There is a story about Leni that seems typical of her. Gerti, her daughter-in-law who later worked in the business with Leni, told it: One day, Gerti said, two newlyweds showed up in the store—two students who wanted to furnish their first apartment and were actually just looking for a little wardrobe. They came across a set of china and were sad that they couldn't buy it, but it was far beyond their means. Leni listened to them talk for a while, then interrupted them and said: "You can have the dishes, just pay me when you have the money." The couple came with a little handcart, packed the china on it, and quietly took it away to their apartment. It took a year, Gerti said, before they started

ÉTAT FRANÇAIS
CARTE D'IDENTITÉ N° 3528
Nom Franck
Prénoms Jean Michel
Domicile 54, rue du Perron Oullins
Profession Comptable
Né le 13 octobre 1891
à Beauvais Dpt Oise
fils de Michel
et de Ternier Alice
Nationalité Française
Signature du titulaire,
Empreinte digitale
TIMBRE FISCAL
IMP. CHAIX 19, CRS VITTON LYON

SIGNALEMENT
Taille 1,67
Visage ovale
Teint coloré
Cheveux bruns grison.
Moustaches brune
Front bombé
Yeux marrons
Nez ordinaire
Bouche moyenne
Menton pointu
Signes particuliers néant

Changements de Domicile
Timbre humide
Timbre humide

Oullins le 14 mai 1942
Visa de l'autorité ayant établi la carte,

French *carte d'identité* in Jean-Michel Frank's name, with a photograph of his German cousin Herbert to pay off the dishes in monthly installments of just a few francs each, and by the time they were done paying for them, they had already had their second child. "That's how Leni was," Gerti says. "And despite that, she somehow managed to earn what the family needed."

Even in the bad years, Leni persisted in her Wednesday afternoon bridge games and in inviting people over to eat. According to Buddy, she always said about people whom she didn't like, in a light Frankfurt accent, "I hope he doesn't let the door hit him on the way out," and about people whom she found sympathetic, "He can come to eat." Many people did. Buddy remembers that Wilhelm Herzog, an art history and literary scholar almost forgotten today, was a regular guest at the house on Herbstgasse as an emigrant. In the family, they called him "le duc." Buddy remembers that another guest, "Ivor Gregoritsch or something like that," worked at the Yugoslavian consulate, maybe even as vice-consul, in any case he was there every Saturday for the boiled beef. He sat at the table and waited for Erich to slice the meat. Erich always found something to criticize about it—sometimes it was too fatty, sometimes too lean—and then Ivo would start to grumble until Erich said: It isn't that bad, I didn't mean it. "We liked him a lot," Buddy says. "Then he went back to Yugoslavia and we never heard from him again, unfortunately. During the whole war we always had guests who came to eat with us, refugees."

Leni couldn't cook, everyone knew that. It was all the more surprising to Gerti when she heard her mother-in-law say years later that she had once graduated from cooking school. "When I asked her why she went," Gerti says, "she answered that it was normal in her youth. That's how girls from good families were prepared to be married. She showed me her cookbook with countless handwritten recipes, full of pride. But she never cooked. Later she came into the kitchen a few times and asked me to show her how to cook. I tried to teach her a couple of things, but after just a minute or two she suddenly remembered that she had forgotten to take care of something extremely urgent. And that was that." But even if she had known how, she would not have had any time to cook, since she spent her days at the business and often overextended herself as it was.

Leni's Sunday tea parties were famous, and she carefully chose the guests to invite. The large table in the dining room was pulled out so that there was room to seat twenty people at it, and Leni set the table herself—at that, she was a master. Marvelous lace tablecloths that Alice had made went onto the table, then porcelain china that came from Cornelia, and silverware from Elkan Juda Cahn, silver candlesticks, and flowers.

Vreni served tea and snacks, nothing grand, in fact quite modest given the magnificently laid table. When the two silver teapots, on a silver tea tray with a matching sugar bowl, were empty, Leni pulled on the bell that was attached to the light fixture above the middle of the table and Vreni came to refill them. Many emigrants would have felt themselves transported back to a time that they thought had been long forgotten, which no doubt gave rise to various melancholy remarks over the years.

And of course there were conversations at the table: that was what one did, among cultured people; one belonged to the upper middle class, and one put one's social position on display even if it was more like the position one used to have, in earlier times.

Probably they talked mostly about their families. And of course they sometimes competed with their stories, started to brag a bit. Alice might have said: "My cousin, Dr. Alfred Stern, was Albert Einstein's professor in Zurich, yes, yes, Albert Einstein, who won the Nobel Prize for Physics in 1921. My cousin stayed in contact with Einstein later too, I've seen letters from this famous man with my own eyes."

"So many of the German Nobel Prize winners were Jewish," someone remarks, and then the names are counted off: Richard Willstätter, Fritz Haber, Gabriel Lippmann, Alfred Fried, Paul

Ehrlich, Otto Meyerhof... Everyone nods, and some of their luster is reflected onto Jews in general and Alice and Leni in particular.

"Does your cousin still live in Zurich?" someone else might ask, and Alice would answer: "No, he died in 1936, and none of his three daughters have married. None of them had any children, unfortunately."

And then everyone would start to talk about relatives they were worried about, or relatives they wished were a little more worried about them. At some point the conversation would turn to Holland, of course, as it always eventually did to every European country where there were relatives.

"I'm glad I got out in time, right after the invasion," someone might say, perhaps the nephew of an old established Basel Jewish family—a strong young man who was up to fleeing over the Vosges Mountains to France and thence to Basel. His doctorate of law was of course worth nothing here in Switzerland.

"My brother is still there," Leni says. "He's gone underground." "Underground"—a new word, in this sense, which the refugees from Holland have brought. It comes easily to Leni's lips now. "At least we think he went underground with his family."

And so the conversation was back on the topic that everyone actually would have rather avoided in a social situation like this. "Where can people hide there?" Alice asks. "Dutch buildings don't even have basements. And what happens if someone gets sick? Or gets a toothache?"

The jurist shrugs his shoulders. "It's definitely not easy for people who go underground, or for their helpers. And they say the Germans pay seven and a half marks for every Jew in hiding to the person who betrays them." He pauses meaningfully, long enough to let anyone who wants to call to mind the thirty pieces of silver, then continues: "There are more than enough Dutch who are willing to do it. Then the captured Jews all go to Westerbork and are sent on to Poland, to the camps. And Westerbork used to be a refugee camp for Jews from Germany; back then, it was even paid for by the Jewish communities in the Netherlands."

At this point, if not sooner, Alice stands up and leaves the room, and her footsteps can be heard on the stairs—slow footsteps, for she has become an old woman.

Leni knows that she will find her mother upstairs later in her room. She will be sitting there in the armchair, letters or photographs in her hand—letters from Margot and Anne that she rereads over and over again, and photographs she never stops looking at—and her eyes will be red and swollen.

It is especially bad on birthdays. Alice doesn't even come downstairs to eat, and Vreni has to carry up a tray for her. When Leni visits her later in the day, Alice shows her a photograph and says, on June 12, 1943, "Anne is turning fourteen today. I wonder how she looks now?" And on June 12, 1944: "Anne is turning fifteen today." Or it is February 16, 1943, and she has a photograph of Margot in her hand: "Margot is turning seventeen today. When I was that age, I went to concerts and to the theater and already had suitors." On January 16, 1943, she might say: "Today Edith is forty-three years old. She doesn't deserve this, she's still so young."

"It can't last much longer," Leni then says, because nothing else occurs to her to say and because she wants so badly to believe it herself. "We'll definitely all be together again next year."

"That's what you said last year, and the year before that too," Alice says, and she starts to cry.

Leni gives her mother a kiss and leaves her alone. She knows that consoling words do no good on days like this. The birthdays are the worst.

Maybe she also pictured to herself how sad the birthdays must have been in their hiding place, and wondered if there was any way anyone could come up with a present for the birthday girl. At the very least Otto would have written his daughter a poem—he had always liked writing poems, like all the children in the family.

And in fact, among the cache of documents that was found in the attic on Herbstgasse, a poem was discovered that Otto wrote for his wife Edith's forty-third birthday. The poem was probably one of the few items left behind in the Secret Annex, like the photographs on the wall and of course Anne's diary. Otto must have brought the poem to the house on Herbstgasse when he moved there later, because it was bound up with his memories of his murdered wife, Edith. Here is the poem:

No flowers, no smoked herring,
No pastries, not one earring,
No stockings, no tasty treat,
Not even a little sweet—
No bonbons, no chocolate
*No cookies from Verkade**
Nothing to read, nothing to wear:

How did it used to be out there?
If only we had a little something!
But other than two packs of cigarettes, nothing.
That's all we have, there's nothing more,
And there's nothing to buy in any store.
Anyway, you were not in the mood
To celebrate, just to sit and brood
In silence. So that's what we'll do,
And everyone will understand too.

The old companions, the bygone friends,
The brothers living in foreign lands,
All are thinking of you today.
But there's no pile of gifts out on display,
No card for you, no telephone call.

---

*A shop in Amsterdam.

It's like there is no birthday at all.
And yet: cut off in our Annex today
We nonetheless celebrate your birthday,
Even if there's no bouquet
Of flowers in our room on display,
We're not alone, in fact the care
And faithful aid we are given here
Are worth more than all the presents in
The world. Every morning, again and again,
Our dear friends take good care of us,
bring news and food they spare for us,
They are always ready with head and hands.
No one can know how much that means.

What more can anyone want from life
Than all your children by your side
—And Pim as well—who want to bear
The burden with you, and friends who share
In everything with all their might.
We "four" are together from morn till night.
All we ask is to keep our health
And get through the hard times—we don't need wealth.
We hope that peace soon be here
And next birthday will be full of cheer,
Without a care, and we'll be free:
That's what we hope—and what will be.

The peace they longed for was more than two years away, and there were to be no more birthdays free and without a care. Edith would never turn forty-five, Margot would just turn nineteen, and Anne would never reach sixteen.

8.

Uncertainty

Germany capitulated on May 8, 1945—Japan only on September 2, after the atomic bombs were dropped on Hiroshima and Nagasaki—but in Europe the war, which had cost roughly sixty million lives worldwide and changed the map of Europe for a long time to come, ended on May 8. Obviously, the sense of relief was great, including in Switzerland. At last people would be able to hear news of their relatives again—the sons, the brothers, the uncles, the cousins. Herbert left Herbstgasse and returned to Paris, presumably with the passport of his deceased cousin Jean-Michel Frank, which he had probably used more often than not during the war.

A long period of waiting began. "Can't you call Amsterdam?" Alice asked every day, and every day Leni and Erich explained to her that it wasn't yet possible, there were no connections yet, neither by telephone nor by telegraph. "You know how it is after a war," Leni said. "It can take months before the railroads are running again, before the post office is working. Remember how long we had to wait for Otto in 1918, long after the armistice was declared. Everyone else was back home except him."

Buddy wanted to know what they were talking about—he hadn't heard this story before—and Alice explained: "Otto came home many weeks after the war ended. First he took the horses that the troops had requisitioned back to their owners, a bunch of farmers in Pomerania. And we sat there in Frankfurt and waited and didn't know what had happened to him."

"It was two months," Leni said, "and I think it was Alsatian or Luxembourg farmers, but it doesn't matter, in any case we didn't know what had happened to him for two long months. And now you're anxious after only a couple of days."

Weeks went by, and the anxiety and fear on Herbstgasse grew stronger. The first pictures of the mounds of corpses traveled around the world, and the weekly newsreels at the movies showed spectral, starved men and women who staggered and collapsed after their liberation and were often in such wretched condition that they could not be saved. Then the names: Dachau, Bergen-Belsen, Auschwitz, Treblinka, Majdanek, Belzec, Sobibor. And the rumors, passing by word of mouth, of unimaginable numbers: a million, two million, three million murdered, they said, maybe even more. It struck you speechless.

They didn't repeat these numbers at home, trying to keep the information vague in front of Alice and Grandma Ida. What they were hearing on the radio was bad enough, there was no need to trouble them further. And the truth was, there were so many people whose whereabouts were unknown: Otto and his family were no doubt somewhere in the Netherlands, but where was Paul, Ida's son and Erich's brother? No one knew what had happened to him after Switzerland had refused all his requests for an entry permit even after Erich had guaranteed Paul's journey onward to Bolivia. The pictures they saw, and that filled Leni and Erich with horror, came mostly from Germany, from Bergen-Belsen—a camp on the Lüneburg Heath that had been liberated by the British—and Dachau, which the Americans had liberated. But people were saying that the worst things had happened far to the east, and news from there, from the Russian zone, only trickled out. Who could know where Paul was, where they had taken him? Leni and Erich talked about it as little as possible at home—what would be the point of frightening Ida and Alice, two old women, more

Anne Frank's great-great-grandparents Elkan Juda Cahn and his wife, Betty

Anne Frank's great-grandmother Cornelia Stern née Cahn as a child, circa 1844

Alice Frank as a child by Professor Schlesinger,
the Frankfurt painter, circa 1869

Michael Frank, around seventeen years old, circa 1868

Alice and Michael Frank
(from their betrothal announcement and invitation)

Portrait of Leni Frank, around five years old

Michael Frank, circa 1908

Margot and Anne Frank with the neighbourhood children, circa 1930. Left to right: Buddy Elias (their cousin), Maitly Könitzer, Gertrud Naumann, Anne, Marianne Stab, Werner Beck, Margot, Hilde Stab, Irmgard Naumann, and Butzy Könitzer

Cornelia Stern with her granddaughter, Leni, circa 1910

Alice Frank with her daughter-in-law Edith and grandchildren
Margot and Stephan, Frankfurt, 1927

Stephan and Buddy Elias, 1934 (photograph owned by Anne Frank)

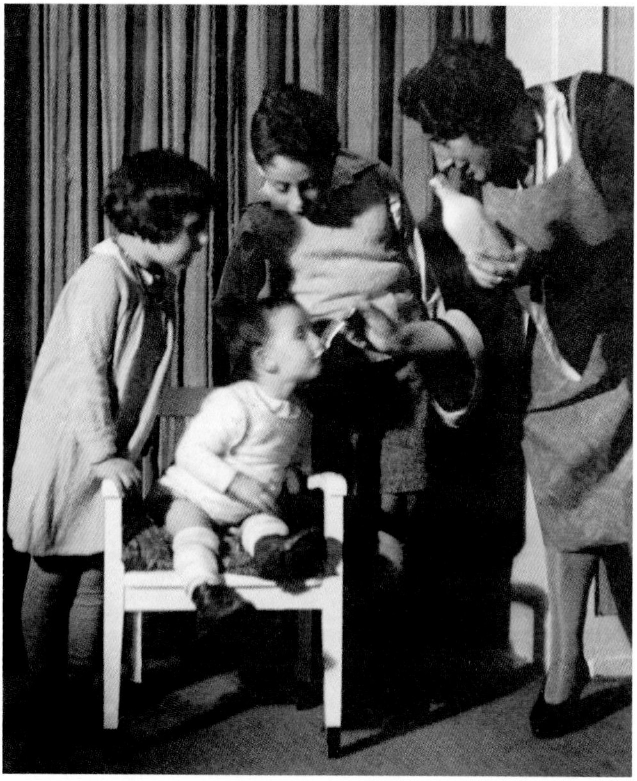

Margot, Stephan and Anne being fed by Edith

Margot Frank, circa 1941

Anne Frank, circa 1941

Buddy and Gerti Elias's wedding, February 1, 1965, in the Basel Art Museum. Left to right: Otto Frank, Herbert Frank, Fritzi Frank, Stephan Elias, Thesy Wiedner (Gerti's sister), Buddy Elias, Erich Elias, Leni Elias, Karl Wiedner (Gerti's father), Gerti Elias, Ado Wiedner (Gerti's sister)

than necessary? But you could sense their anxiety and concern. It filled the house and left everyone silent and afraid.

Leni threw herself into her work, leaving the house early in the morning and coming back only for a short lunch, during which she avoided her mother's and mother-in-law's gazes. She told them something about her day at the store, described a lamp that someone had brought in or a painting, and tried to act as though nothing was wrong, before hurrying back to the store after the meal. She kept all the horrors that people were telling her to herself, just as she had during the war, as well as the rumors that kept popping up. "Propaganda," Erich had said, "it's all just vicious propaganda." And they had believed it all too willingly. Now it turned out that they had been fooling themselves—and not only them: everyone in Switzerland had felt safe and sound. They hadn't known anything, and Leni now had to ask herself whether that was because they had not wanted to know. Not only for their comfort, but also out of helplessness, because after all what could they have done?

Leni was at the store most of the time, Stephan had started to work, Erich was usually on the road somewhere, shoring up his old business connections and striking up new ones, and Buddy was in acting school. The two old women were alone all day in the house on Herbstgasse, alone with Imperia, the new Italian housekeeper. Grandma Ida knit or sewed or cleaned, the way she had always cleaned, wiping and dusting where there wasn't a speck of dirt to be seen as if the rags and dust cloths could clear away her troubled thoughts. Alice, who was starting to have difficulties climbing the stairs—her old bones were just not cooperating, as she always complained—sat upstairs in her room most of the time, in an armchair, some needlework in her hands, looking out of the window at the trees every now and then. It was summer, the first summer of peace after this terrible war; the birds were hopping on the branches, and if Alice leaned out the window, she could see the geraniums blossoming in the flowerpots on the veranda. A peaceful, happy view that she had always enjoyed, but it was empty and cold in her heart. Until she heard news of her sons, she would not find any peace. Even though Leni thought it was pointless, Alice wrote a postcard to Kleiman and asked him if he knew anything about what had happened to Otto. Leni took the card to the post office on her way to work.

The first news came from Herbert. He had arrived safely in Paris, he wrote; life there was not exactly rosy, but he had found work at an American postal office and, since they gave him lunch for free, he only had to worry about one other meal a day. The next bit of news came from England, from Robert and Lotti, who, despite Robert's imprisonment on the Isle of Man, had survived the war safe and sound. Lotti was working with Robert now, she wrote, after having had jobs as a secretary at various companies during the war years.

Then, in late May, there was finally a sign of life from Otto: a telegram addressed to Erich Elias, Herbstgasse 11, Basel. Imperia, who knew of course how anxious the family was for news, took the telegram right to Leni at her store. That night they sat around the table happy and relieved, even if they couldn't understand why the telegram had come from Marseille. "ARRIVEE BONNE SANTE MARSEILLE PARTONS PARIS BAISERS—OTTO FRANK." "Arrived in Marseille Good health Leave for Paris Kisses—Otto Frank." There was, it's true, no mention of Edith and the children, but Alice repeated over and over again, "It says *partons*—'*we*' are leaving for Paris—who else could it be besides Edith and the children? They're alive; they're fine. But why are they going to Paris? What do they want to do there? You have to tell Herbert, Herbert will ask around, maybe he can find something out."

For the first time in weeks they were glad at heart. Even Grandma Ida saw it as a good omen for her own son; she would definitely hear from Paul any day now.

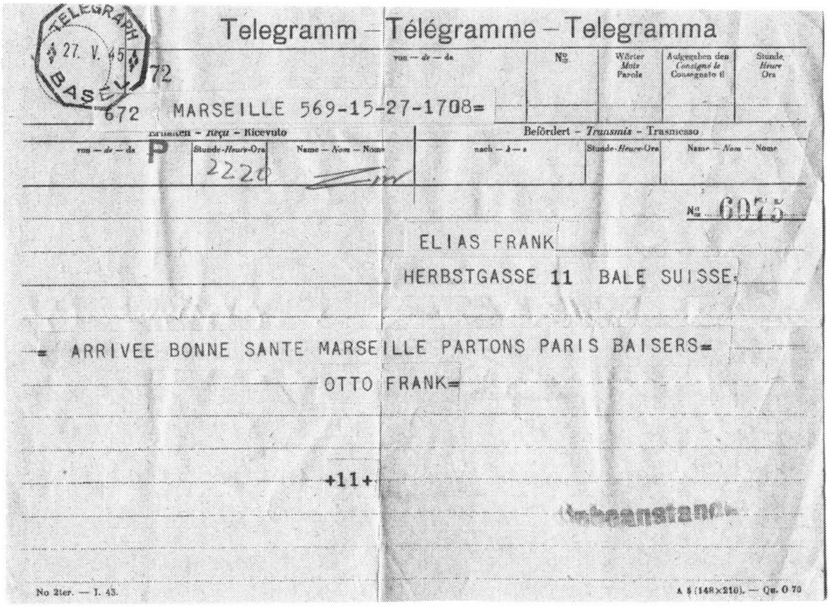
Telegramm – Télégramme – Telegramma

TELEGRAPH 27. V. 45 BASEL

72

672 MARSEILLE 569-15-27-1708=

Erhalten – Reçu – Ricevuto

P 2220

Befördert – Transmis – Trasmesso

No 6075

ELIAS FRANK

HERBSTGASSE 11 BALE SUISSE=

= ARRIVEE BONNE SANTE MARSEILLE PARTONS PARIS BAISERS=

OTTO FRANK=

+11+

No 2ter. — I. 43.

Telegram from Otto Frank in Marseille, May 27, 1945

It took four weeks for a letter to arrive from Otto, and when it did, it shattered their sense of relief in an instant. They felt as though the ground had been yanked out from under their feet. They sat at the table in the dining room, as usual, and read out loud to each other the letter that Otto had written on May 15, 1945, on the New Zealand steamship *Monowai* that was bringing him from Odessa to Marseille.

Dear Mom,
Dear everyone,

Tomorrow we will be in Marseille, and then this letter will hopefully be forwarded to you. I assume I'll be able to telegraph right away too so that you'll know that I've returned safe. We sailed from Odessa. Did you get my news from Kattowitz & Czernowitz?! For now we don't yet know if we can go back to Holland or if we will have to go to England for awhile first. For me the main thing is that we got out of Russia, and so we can be reunited with our loved ones. You have no idea how much I long to see you again. All my hopes are for the children. I cling to the firm belief that they are still alive and that we will be together again soon. They will hardly expect their Pim to still be alive—they experienced too much, and they must know how everything was in the "Auschwitz extermination camp" where I was. It's a miracle I survived. I don't want to write about it for now. Sadly the strain was too much for Edith. She died of malnutrition in the hospital, on Jan. 6, 1945. Her body could no longer withstand a flu. I heard this from a woman I met in Kattowitz after the liberation. I was also in the hospital myself, since 11/19, with "bodily weakness," but I was able to recover.

The closer we get to home, the greater our impatience to hear from our loved ones. Everything that's happened the past few years! Until our arrest—I don't know exactly what caused it, even now—at least we still had contact with each other. I don't know what's happened since then. Kugler and Kleiman and especially Miep and her husband and Bep Voskuil provided us with everything for 2 whole years, with incomparable devotion and sacrifice, despite all the danger. I can't even begin to describe it. How will I ever be able to repay everything they did.—But what has happened since then? To them, to you, to Robert. Are you in touch with Julius and Walter? All our possessions are gone. There won't be a pin left, the Germans stole everything—not a photo, letter, or document remains. Financially we were fine in the past few years, I earned good money & saved it. Now it's all gone. But I don't think about any of that. We have lived through too much to worry about that kind of thing. Only the children matter, the children.—I hope to get news from you immediately. Maybe you've already heard news about the girls.—What are your boys doing, and all the various friends? Is Herbi still there with you?—What about Paul? Where is Helen? But I can't list everyone I want to hear about. I'm writing to Robert directly, I don't know if the letter will reach his old address. London suffered a lot too, of course.—*

---

*Edith's brothers, who had fled to America.

I will stay with the Dutch since aside from a tattooed number on my arm I have no papers & I'll only be able to try to come see you later. Anyway, the main thing is that we are in contact. We hope to see you soon.

With warmest greetings and kisses, love,

Your Otto

Only then did Alice and the others realize that the whole family had been at Auschwitz—a word they shuddered to hear and had avoided saying out loud during the entire period of uncertainty. Auschwitz, the concentration camp in Poland that was to become a synonym for the monstrous actions of the Third Reich as a whole. According to everything they had heard, Otto must have been through true hell. But he was alive. There was no news of the children, so there was still hope, but Edith was dead. Alice sobbed out loud. "She didn't deserve that," she said again and again, "not that."

"Stop it," Erich said. "No one deserved that."

Alice could not be calmed down. She grabbed the letter again and read the horrific sentence out loud to the others: "She died of malnutrition, her body could no longer withstand a flu." The letter trembled in her hand, her voice failed.

Leni put her arm around her and tried to console her. "Otto is alive," she said. "We have to be grateful that at least our Otto is alive. And I'm sure he'll find the children soon, that's all that matters now."

"We have to do something," Erich said. "I'll submit a search request to the Red Cross. We have to find the children."

"We have to write to him," Alice said.

"Where would you mail it?" Leni asked. "We don't know where he is. All we can do for now is wait until we hear from him again."

"We have to talk to Dr. Iller," Alice persisted. "He's waiting for news about his mother, he must know what we can do, we'll ask him for advice."

Grandma Ida stood up and went to her room. Maybe she didn't want to bother anyone; maybe she just wanted to be alone with her own fears. Edith was dead, and what about her son, what had happened to Paul?

The next morning, Alice sent another postcard to Kleiman and asked him if he knew where Otto was staying. And again, Leni took the card to the post office.

It took a while before the letter they were craving arrived. Otto had written it on June 8, 1945.

Dear Mom, dear everyone,

Mother's card dated 5/20 arrived at Mr. Kleiman's today. It made me very happy to see your handwriting. At last we are in contact again! Since my various letters haven't arrived here yet, I don't know what's reached you there, but I assume that my telegram from Marseille arrived. I heard here only that there was no more contact with you after June '44, so you must have been absolutely thunderstruck when you received the telegram. I am writing this here in my office. It is all like a bad dream, I cannot find my bearings in reality yet. I don't want to write much either, so here is a very quick summary.

On July 6, 1942, Margot received a summons from the Gestapo to report for a transport to Germany. I didn't want to let her go, of course, so we decided to disappear. You probably gathered from the last lines I sent you that I had already prepared something. We stayed hidden up in the attic of the Opekta building, where we also had the three van Pelses and later Dr. Pfeffer, the dentist, join us. So there were 8 of us and our people devotedly looked after us, despite all the danger involved. We never once went outside. Nevertheless, we were apparently betrayed, because the Gestapo came and arrested us in July 1944 and after a month in the Dutch camp sent us on to the "Auschwitz extermination*

*Actually, the Franks and the others living in the Secret Annex were arrested on August 4.

camp" in Poland. I won't go into details here. The last time I saw Edith and the children was on Sept. 5, in Birkenau, and the children—from what I've heard from other people—must have been sent to work in Germany or Czechoslovakia in October. I don't know where they are and I never stop thinking about them. In November 44 I was so weak from work and lack of food that with the help of a Dutch doctor I was admitted to the hospital, and I regained my strength there until the Russians liberated us on Jan. 27, 1945. On the 26th we were taken out by the S.S., to be killed, but someone called the S.S. away before they could do it—it was a miracle! Whoever could walk had been taken by the Germans before the 16th. Now we had enough food. From there in early March it was Kattowitz, Czernowitz, and eventually Odessa, in stages, then through the Dardanelles to Marseille and direct to Holland. The initial plan to send us to Paris was not carried out.

Edith had it harder, apparently. I heard that she lost more and more weight, suffered greatly from being separated from the children, and passed away of exhaustion on Jan. 6. She didn't suffer. I am alone, I surely don't need to say more.

I found my old friends again here. Kleiman was in jail and in a camp for 7 weeks. Kugler was released after less than two weeks. All because of us. The company still exists, obviously there are no raw materials but there is a foundation for rebuilding. Everything in our home was stolen. I had stored a few things in other places, but not much. I have no hat, no raincoat, no watch, no shoes, except what other people have loaned me. And it's impossible to get anything here either, there's nothing in the stores. I'm living with Miep Gies. I have money for now, since I don't need much.

I want so badly to be with you all. Please write me with the boys' address. I'm waiting to hear from you about all the many things we haven't been able to hear about for so long. I also wrote only a short letter to Robert, I'm unable to write in more detail. I'm not back to normal yet, I mean that I haven't been able to regain my equilibrium yet, physically I'm doing fine.

[The letter is written on a typewriter, but Otto added the following at the bottom, by hand:]

Enough for today, it is all still too upsetting for me, the main thing is that the children turn up again. I have to be patient. Write soon. Many 1000s of hugs and kisses

Your Otto

One can only imagine how they reacted to this letter on Herbstgasse, how they went over every last point, how they blamed themselves for having lived in such comparative comfort while Otto, Edith, and the children had had to suffer so much. But he was alive, Otto was alive. Leni would have asked, "Why did he write that Edith 'passed away,' why did he write that she 'didn't suffer'?" But to protect her mother, she probably asked the question only after Alice had withdrawn to her room. The doctor had said that her heart was strong, but she was after all almost eighty years old. And presumably, Leni answered her own question: "He wanted to soften the blow for Alice, he wanted to give I. the impression that Edith had simply died." And Erich, who was tormented by constant worrying about his own brother and who may have been able to imagine Otto's feelings better than Leni could, might have said: "Or himself. Maybe he wanted to talk himself into it. It must be easier to remember someone who just died than someone who you know was tortured and starved to death."

The next evening, Alice wrote a letter to her son that he would only receive much later. She read it out loud to the family before putting it in the envelope.

My dearest Ottel, There are no words to say what I felt when we read your letter from the steamship Monowai*! We had no idea what a horrific fate had befallen you all & imagined you all together even though* *we kept hearing with horror from the newspapers & the radio everything that was happening. We totally misunderstood yr first telegraph & thought* "partons" *meant the family! not a transport, which we had no idea about. What a dreadful mistake & what a blow for me & for all of us here! We tried right away but couldn't reach you by telegr. & it's only today I got your address in Amsterdam from Robert! To know that you are alone in your grief for Edith and with no news of the dear children is probably the most horrible thing I have ever felt in my whole life with all its difficult moments. How Edith must have suffered without you & the children, I don't dare to even think about it, & here we all were with no idea! We never got any news from Kattowitz, but still through the whole time when we didn't hear anything my thoughts were with you every single day and my deepest wishes & hopes which now alas I see were not fulfilled. We have submitted a search request to the international Red Cross in Geneva & the consulate here, and we spoke with Dr. Iller today, who unfortunately had no advice for us and is also without any news of his relatives & his mother. The fate of so many of our friends & acquaintances is so terrible, but how you suffer in your heart when it's about your own flesh & blood is indescribable. And after all the suffering in body and soul you've been through the uncertainty about the whereabouts of the girls is the worst of all! I sincerely mourn for Edith with you—she was such a great support in your life & the girls' best friend & tireless mother. If only I could be with you & tell you all the love I feel for you. It wouldn't help, but it would be a consolation for me, to see you & be with you. My strength would be enough for that & you would at least feel that you have your mother with you, and you couldn't even know if you would ever see her again! I am in constant contact with Julius and Walter, it was a serious and difficult decision to send them a copy of your letter but I couldn't keep it from them either. They will suffer terribly from the news . . . Herbie was with us for 2½ years & very dear company for all of us, we miss him very much & he telegr'd in despair when we told him the news about you all! His address is still Hotel d'Edinbourg, rue d'Edinbourg 8, Paris 8ieme. We will send him your address today so he can get in touch with you right away. Helen*

[Schuster] is in Paris for now & also hoped so much to see you, but what are hopes & wishes worth! Leni is writing to you separately, and the Schneiders, whom we see very often. You've probably already seen Mr. Kleiman, Mr. Kugler, & the loving women who were so ready to help you? & where are you staying? There's so much we want to know, but the main thing is everything about you & if you really feel healthy & how your nerves are holding up to do everything in your power to find the children. Letters back and forth to Holland seem to be very slow and unreliable so I am sending this registered to try to be sure that you get it. Goodbye for today, I say it with a heavy heart & I want to tell you again & again how warmly I & everyone here are thinking of you & want to support you & help you in your unspeakable suffering. Don't lose hope & courage, my dearest Ottel, & know for sure that I'm holding you with all my love in my heart. Your Mother.

Erich told Leni when he came home one evening a couple days later that he had written to Otto as well. A postcard, because people said it was better to write postcards, they got past the various censors more easily. The censors were a great hassle, everyone agreed, but people also understood that the victorious nations had to control what went through the mail. They must have been concerned that the German capitulation was only a pretense; it certainly seemed unlikely that everyone would be reconciled to having lost the war. There might still be pockets of resistance somewhere, or plans being made in secret against the occupying forces, sabotage conspiracies, murder plots. Erich said he wrote the card in French, which was definitely more innocuous and would get through the censors more easily—German was, after all, the language of the ones who had started the war and were responsible for the whole mess, you couldn't know how whoever it was whose hands the postcard fell into would react.

"What did you say?" Leni asked.

"I said how horrified we were and how much we hope he will

find the children again soon. I also gave him Herbert's address in France and gave him some suggestions that might be useful for making a fresh start in business."

"It's not about a fresh start in his business," Leni said. "All that matters is the children."

"But you have to live on something," Erich countered. "And the situation in Holland is terrible, everyone who knows about it says so. The Germans plundered the country, there's nothing left, the stores are empty. You heard what this man just said about the Hunger Winter there, lots of people simply starved to death. They said people were grinding up tulip bulbs for flour to make bread."

Even though Otto had not written any details about his time in Auschwitz, enough information about the Nazi death machine was circulating by then that the family on Herbstgasse could imagine what Otto had lived through while they had thought he was safe in hiding. Leni clearly saw in her mind's eye the images from the weekly newsreels, and when she thought about her brother, she pictured those skeletal figures. When she wrote to him on June 22, 1945, these pictures were still haunting her:

Now that Robbie has given us your Amsterdam address I want to try to write a few words to you. You can be sure that all of us will do everything in our power to learn news of the children, I've now tried going through diplomatic channels too. But everything goes at a snail's pace—except for the atrocities of these German villains! To just sit here, unable to help you & powerless, is probably the worst thing—we just hadn't heard anything & had hoped that you would be spared, to some extent, since it was okay until 1944. Poor, dear, good Ottel, what did we do to deserve being spared? It was sheer luck. No letter has reached us from Holland until now . . . We can't even imagine your life there & please please tell us what you need—more and more people are going to Holland and they could bring you things. Can you get a hold of anyone in America? And, I hardly dare ask, can you come here to us?? Everything I'm writing is so stupid, ach, Ottel, maybe you can feel what I can't get down on paper the way I want to!! Mom can much better than I can. It was great having Herbi here for 2½ years & he was a great help to me. It was especially hard for Mom when he left. But none of that matters, all we want is to help you find your children & is that really true about poor Edith? There's no trace of Paul & there are millions of other people whose relatives are looking for them.

Otto's answer was a long time coming. Alice grew more and more impatient every day, and Leni didn't know how to calm her mother. Again and again Alice said that she wanted to go to Amsterdam and see her son, hold him in her arms.

"It's just not possible," Erich said. "We have no passports, we can't just get on a train and go."

"Maybe Otto can come here," Buddy suggested.

His father shook his head. "Otto is just as stateless as we are," he argued. "None of us are Germans anymore."

"I'm glad," Stephan said. "I want to be Swiss, I don't want to be a German."

"Maybe the Netherlands is different from Switzerland," Buddy said. "Maybe they'll just give their Jews who come back from the camps citizenship, it could be."

"Maybe," Erich said, but you could see that he didn't believe it himself.

And Leni said: "Well, the Netherlands couldn't be worse than here, Switzerland is the worst. I'm sure Otto will be naturalized there soon."

That was not how it turned out. The Netherlands, where so many people had helped the Jews and often risked their lives for them, turned out to be in no way willing to welcome the returning survivors with open arms after the war—never mind that only a few returned, around 5,200 out of the roughly 107,000 who were deported.* In addition, there was a state of emergency after the war in the Netherlands, with economic recovery still years away. When Otto wrote that he had no raincoat, no hat, no watch, and no shoes, aside from what other people had lent him, that was only the barest hint of the universal shortages: they had neither enough to eat nor enough places to live. Otto was actually very lucky to have been taken in by Miep and Jan Gies.

Of course they didn't know that in Basel, but they did hear one thing or another from the people who had managed to make it from the Netherlands to Switzerland. They heard about returning survivors who found strangers living in their apartments who refused to move out, and about others who had given their friends their valuables before being deported—not true friends, as it turned out, since they suddenly didn't remember anything about any valuables. It was reassuring to know that Otto's helpers seemed to be true friends who helped and supported him.

So life went on in Basel. Buddy had finished his acting school and was hoping for his first role. There was no word from Otto, except for that one letter. Mrs. Belinfante, an acquaintance, was planning to travel to Amsterdam and said she could take letters and presents for Otto. Alice complained in her letter of July 6 that she couldn't picture Otto's life there, and how he was bearing his life without Edith and the children. The hope of finding the girls again soon must be sustaining him. She said there was still no word from Edith's brothers Julius and Walter either. Then she said that they were in a similar situation on Herbstgasse, since they hadn't heard anything about Erich's brother, Paul. As with Margot and Anne, every possible step was being taken to look for Paul, but unfortunately with no results so far. And she wrote that while she was knitting the sweater that she would pass along to Mrs. Belinfante, she had not once stopped thinking about him,

*Wolfgang Benz, ed., *Dimension des Völkermords: Die Zahl der Jüdischen Opfer des Nationalsozialismus* [Scale of the Genocide: The Number of Jewish Victims of National Socialism] (Munich: R. Oldenbourg, 1991), p. 165.

Otto. She had already started the socks, hoping that she would be able to give them to him herself.

In the same letter, Leni wrote:

Dearest Ottel, Mrs. Belinfante, a magnificent woman, will give you this letter as soon as she possibly can & I hope that you can talk with her a little. Our thoughts are with you every minute & only hope is sustaining us all here. How much I'd love to be there for you, but this terrible world has not got any better & even though we're not really that far apart from each other in miles, almost impossibly high barriers are separating us. We can't even reach you by letter or by phone! But I'm sure that it's only a matter of time. Just try to send us a few lines with one of the Kindertransports to Switzerland! If I didn't have my work, I couldn't possibly bear it—This powerlessness over everything! So, dear brother, warmest kisses from your old Lunni.*

Buddy, just twenty years old, wanted to write to Otto too, but felt that he couldn't. "Anything you write is so horribly shallow, compared to what he's been through," he said.

"So what," Leni countered. "He should know that you're thinking of him. You could tell him, for instance, what your final exams at acting school were like, Otto always liked the theater." And when she saw Buddy's uncertain face, she added: "It doesn't matter what you write, the main thing is that he get a letter from you."

So Buddy wrote to his "dearest Ottel":

After all these years of horrible uncertainty about your fate, the certainty has turned out to be just as horrible. Our thoughts are with you as always and your dear Edith will live on in our hearts. All of our hopes

---

*Between December 1938 and May 1940, Kindertransports (Children's Transports) rescued thousands of Jewish children, sending them by train and ship to Britain for the duration of the war.

Buddy Elias and Otti Rehorek as "Buddy and Baddy" on the ice

are focused on Margot and Anne's return. We mustn't give up hope until their safe return, or until there is certain news that they are not alive, but we don't even want to think about that. Well, now that the terrible times are basically over, better times will come for you as well. I know that it's easy for me to say "Chin up!" and hard for you, but that's why it's so important. Sometimes I'm simply ashamed when I think about how we've lived here in Basel during the years of your martyrdom—never once leaving the table hungry, just doing our work and enjoying our pleasures; the fact is, aside from constant air raids (with no bombings), minor rationing, and some artillery fire from Alsace, we haven't felt the war at all. We had no idea how lucky we were. And it's just as impossible for us to picture the afflictions you were living through. There are lots of horrifying reports in the papers and we see pictures in the American newsreel of the horrifying "extermination camps." But sitting in our plush seats watching a few terrible pictures on the screen there is still no way we can imagine what life i.e. languishing in that hell was really like.

Anyway, I do want to write and tell you a little about myself. You'll definitely be interested in what I'm up to. I finished my acting school three weeks ago and now I'm an actor. I've wanted this career from when I was a little boy. The final performance, which was a test at the end of my course of study to see what I could do in various scenes and roles, was a great success for me. I played the following roles in individual scenes from the following plays: 1) The First Gravedigger in Hamlet. *2) Vansen in* Egmont. *3) Fabian in* Twelfth Night. *4) Sosias in Kleist's* Amphitryon *(my greatest success!). 5) Arnold Kramer in Hauptmann's* Michael Kramer. *At the moment I'm in negotiations with two Swiss theaters for an engagement for next season. Last winter my Comedy on Ice routine was a success on all the skating rinks in Switzerland—my partner and I appeared as "Buddy and Baddy." My stage name is probably going to be "Elias Frank." We're not Swiss citizens yet, Steph and I very much want to be and will keep trying to get citizenship. The requirements are unbelievably strict. At the moment I'm studying typing and English. I want to visit you, and Robbie and Herbi, as soon as I can, of course. But obviously we expect you to come here to see us before that, and hopefully soon! Come as soon as you can. Well, I have to stop for today, 1000s of hugs and kisses from Your, Buddy.*

Then there followed a few lines from Stephan expressing his sympathy:

How much you must have suffered and must still be suffering. But you have to build a new life for yourself, in spite of the pain you feel in your soul. If only we could help the rebuilding a little! It is nice to be with someone today who will see you and talk to you soon. Mrs. Belinfante will be able to tell you the important things about us.

Leni gave Mrs. Belinfante these letters, along with presents for Otto, and settled down to a long wait. It must have seemed to her by that point that her whole life was practically nothing but waiting. Then, suddenly, the postcards arrived at Herbstgasse that Otto had written in February and March: from Auschwitz, from Kattowitz, from Czernowitz. And only a day later came Otto's letter of June 15, the letter in which he enclosed a copy of Lien Brilleslijper's testimony about the fate of his children. It was a cruel and terrible coincidence.

They read the letters and card that Otto had written right after the liberation. They had learned by that point that Auschwitz had been liberated on January 27, 1945; they knew that over a million people had met their deaths there, most of them killed with poison gas, Zyklon B, and that along with the corpses more than seven thousand survivors had been found. And that one of the survivors had been Otto Frank, their son, brother, brother-in-law, uncle. His first postcard came from Auschwitz itself, written on the back of a blank form with regulations from the camp commander.

"Look at these regulations," Erich said bitterly. "What cynicism! They act as if Auschwitz was a place where the prisoners had any rights, as though they weren't being brought there to be exterminated."

Then he turned the letter over. "Dearest Mom," he read out loud.

Hopefully this letter will reach you and give you and all our loved ones the news that the Russians have saved me, I'm healthy and in good spirits and well taken care of in every way. I don't know where Edith and the children are, we were separated on Sept. 5, '44. I heard only that they were transported to Germany. We have to hope that we'll get them back healthy. Please tell my in-laws and my friends in Holland that I'm safe. I can't wait to see you all again and I hope that it will be possible soon. If only all of you are safe and sound. When will I be able to get news from you? All my love and warmest hugs and kisses,

Your son Otto

The sender's name and information were written on the letter: "Otto Frank, born May 12, 1889, Pris. #B9174." Leni felt a chill run

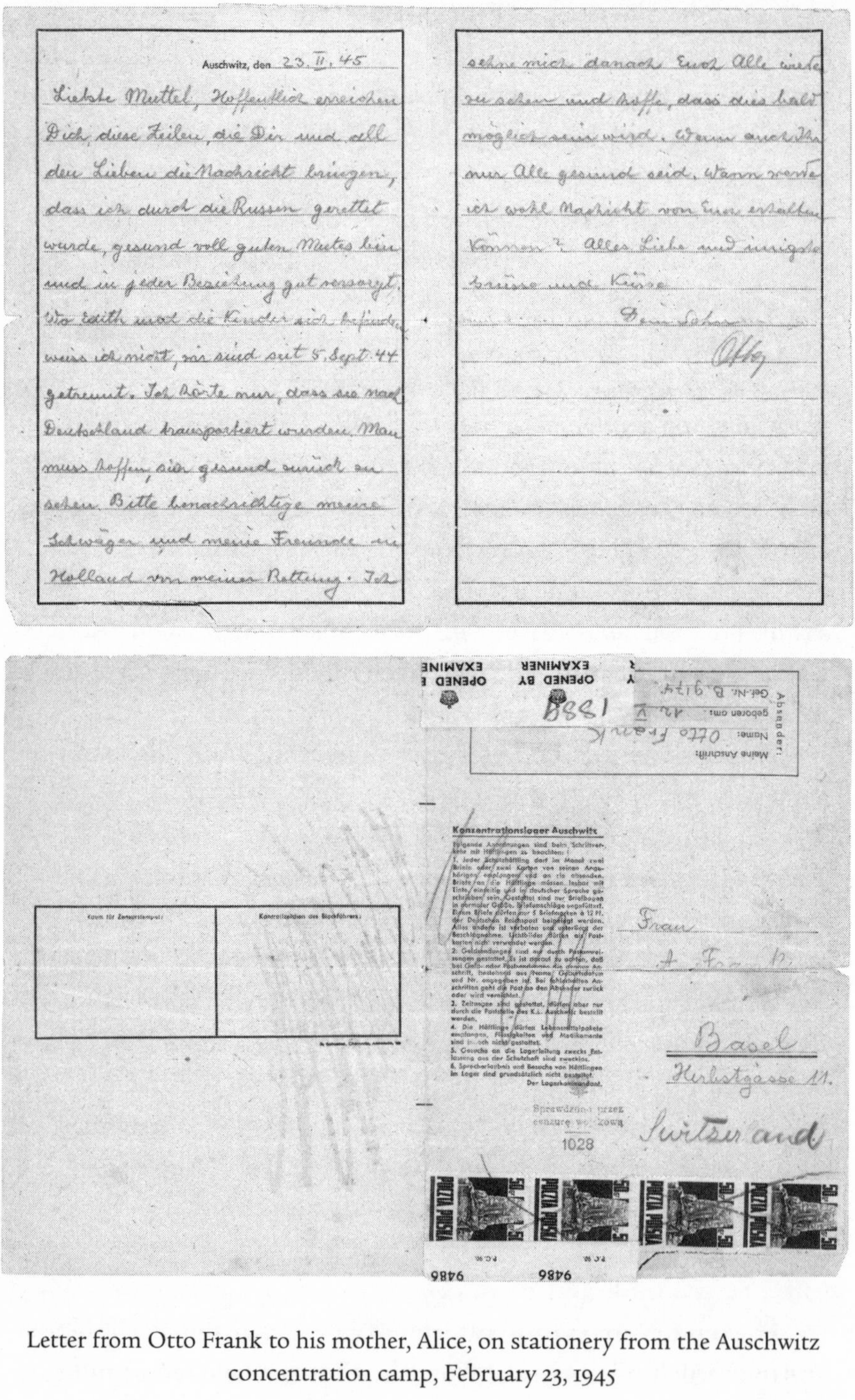

Auschwitz, den 23. II. 45

Liebste Muttel, Hoffentlich erreichen Dich diese Zeilen, die Dir und all den Lieben die Nachricht bringen, dass ich durch die Russen gerettet wurde, gesund voll guten Mutes bin und in jeder Beziehung gut versorgt. Wo Edith und die Kinder sich befinden weiss ich nicht, wir sind seit 5. Sept. 44 getrennt. Ich hörte nur, dass sie nach Deutschland transportiert wurden. Man muss hoffen, sie gesund zurück zu sehen. Bitte benachrichtige meine Schwäger und meine Freunde in Holland von meiner Rettung. Ich sehne mich danach Euch Alle wieder zu sehen und hoffe, dass dies bald möglich sein wird. Wenn auch Ihr nur Alle gesund seid. Wann werde ich wohl Nachricht von Euch erhalten können? Alles Liebe und innigste Grüsse und Küsse

Dein Sohn

Otto

Letter from Otto Frank to his mother, Alice, on stationery from the Auschwitz concentration camp, February 23, 1945 up her spine. She guessed that this number must mean that they had tattooed her brother's left arm when he arrived at Auschwitz. She had seen pictures of these numbers, and she would see many more people with those numbers in future. Alice started to cry. "He didn't know anything about Edith's death yet."

No, he hadn't known anything about Edith's death at the time. In his next letter, too, from Kattowitz, he still spoke of his hope to find Edith and the children again.

I still can't bring myself to describe all my experiences at length, the main thing you want to know is that I am alive & well. You will understand how much it tortures me not to know where Edith and the children are. But I still hope to see them all safe and sound, and I don't want to let myself get depressed. . . . I can hardly imagine normal life and don't want to think about the future yet. I am a beggar here and look like one too . . . I will always be grateful to the Russians for the liberation. If I hadn't been taken to a hospital—I was weak and weighed 52 kg [less than 115 lb.]—there is no way I would still be alive. I was lucky & I had good friends. Peter van Pels, who was with us in hiding in Amsterdam for 2 years, was like a son and did everything to help me. Every day he brought me extra food. And what our Amsterdam friends—Miep Gies, Kleiman, Kugler, Bep—did to take care of us, despite the danger, while we were in hiding, we can never repay it. The Gestapo arrested Kleiman & Kugler with us and they ended up in a concentration camp too. The thought of that is a constant torment to me, I can only hope that they are free by now. In case you can correspond with Amsterdam, send news. . . .

Miep Gies, Johannes Kleiman, Victor Kugler, and Bep Voskuijl were the employees of Otto Frank's company who had taken care of the Frank and van Pels families and Dr. Pfeffer during their two years in hiding, at great risk and sacrifice. Miep Gies and Bep Voskuijl had taken on the difficult task of obtaining the necessary food, which was extremely difficult with the wartime rationing. But all four, it goes without saying, were absolutely necessary helpers without whom it would not have been possible for the Franks and the others to go underground. They belong to that category of people who act humanely in inhuman times. Jan Gies, the man Miep had married in 1941, is in that category as well. Leni knew these helpers—she had met each and every one of them when she had visited the Franks in Amsterdam before the war. Alice knew them too. "May God repay what they did for Otto, Edith, and the children," Alice said. "We can't."

In the next letter from Otto, also sent from Kattowitz, it said:

I can't write much, I just got the news of Edith's death on 1/6/45, and it has hit me so hard that I am not entirely my old self. Only the thought of the children keeps me going. Edith died in the hospital, she was too weak from malnutrition to withstand the intestinal problems that came up. In truth, another German murder. If she could have held out only two more weeks then the Russians would have liberated her too and it all would have turned out differently.

"If she could have held out only two more weeks," Leni repeated Otto's words, in shock.

It was true for so many: if only they could have held out just a little longer . . . Later they would learn that for Peter van Pels—who, Otto wrote, had done everything to help him, "like a son"—just one or two more days would have been enough. He survived one of the most infamous death marches only to die in the Mauthausen concentration camp in Austria on May 5, 1945, the very day it was liberated by the American soldiers. He was not quite nineteen years old.

On still another card that Otto sent from Kattowitz, he told them that he was waiting for transportation back to Holland, but no one knew when it would happen. "It looks like the war ended in a hurry. I am healthy and doing all right, in spite of the sad news of my wife's death. As long as I find the children."

Then there was a card from Czernowitz, dated April 11, with only the information that their transport had brought them there and that they were hoping to be able to continue to Amsterdam soon.

"The war was still going on on April 11," Buddy might have said. "In the rest of Europe battles were still taking place and bombs were still falling. There's no way they'd be able to keep traveling anytime soon."

They looked at each other, torn inside between their grief over Edith, worry about the children, and happiness that Otto had survived the horrors.

The next day came the fateful letter with the news that both children, Margot and Anne, were dead, that they had died months before in a German concentration camp. Just a few days before the letter arrived, Alice had written to Otto: "We are such a short distance apart & yet so separated from each other & we need to be with each other so badly." And Leni had asked: "Can't you try to come here to us? But of course you still need to wait until you learn further details—it's all so horrible, we can't even think reasonably about it." The realization that Otto already knew of the death of his children when he read these lines was now unbearable for Leni. At the same time, Leni also had to worry about her mother—she was afraid that Alice would not be able to survive this turn of fate.

The search for the missing was an urgent concern for many people in the months after the end of the war. Everywhere in Europe, people were desperate for a sign of life from their loved ones; people everywhere were waiting for a miracle. For years after the end of the war, there was a special office of the Red Cross to handle search requests, and sometimes—but rarely—the miracle really happened. One of the people waiting for news of her relatives was

Fritzi Geiringer, originally from Vienna. In Auschwitz she was separated from her husband and son, and she and her daughter, Eva, the same age as Anne Frank, had survived. Otto met Fritzi on the long voyage back to Amsterdam and eight years later he would marry her.

Otto tirelessly asked everyone he met who had returned from the camps if they knew anything about his daughters. He read the lists that the newspapers published, and inquired at the Red Cross again and again, where they kept a list of the survivors and collected eyewitness testimony about the victims.

It was a terrible time of waiting to see who would come back—who might have managed to escape death when everyone had thought they were gone. A time of hopes, of rumors, of suppositions, and of horrible certainties. Finally, on July 18, 1945, Otto found out what had happened to his children. On a list at the Red Cross he discovered the names Margot Betti Frank and Annelies Marie Frank, with the fateful cross after their names. And he obtained the name and address of the woman who had made that report.

The doubts that Otto must have long had were now certain. He informed his family and included a translation of the testimony that Lien Brilleslijper had given—she and her sister Jannie had been in Bergen-Belsen and had met Margot and Anne there.

After we had something to eat, we found a faucet where we could wash up a little, which we hadn't been able to do since Auschwitz. We wrapped ourselves up in our blankets again. Then we saw two thin, bald figures that looked like freezing baby birds. We fell into each other's arms and cried. It was Margot and Anne Frank. We asked them about their mother. Anne said: "Selected."

Then the four of us went past the barracks to the parade ground. We saw several big tents there. They looked like circus tents. We were assigned to one of them and lay down on the straw. We cuddled up with each other under our blankets. The first few days were peaceful, we slept a lot. Then it started to rain. Even under our blankets we could not get warm. And there were the lice too.

Then we were called up to work. We had to tear the soles off of old shoes. For that, we got some soup and a little piece of bread. Soon our hands started to bleed and got infected. Anne and I had to stop first, Jannie and Margot were able to keep going a bit longer.

After a few days, heavy winter storms started. The tents couldn't withstand the storms and fell apart. There were wounded people. We were herded into a shed where rags and old shoes and other things like that were stored. Anne asked: "Why do they want us to live like animals?" Jannie answered: "Because they are man-eating wild animals themselves."

One day, in December, we received a tiny piece of cheese and some jam. The S.S. and the female guards went away to celebrate. It was Christmas. We were three pairs of sisters: us, Margot and Anne Frank, and the Daniel sisters. We wanted to celebrate St. Nicholas Day, Hanukkah, and Christmas in our own way. Jannie had met some Hungarian girls who worked in the S.S. kitchen. With their help we got two handfuls of potato peels. Anne managed to get a hold of a stick of celery. The Daniel sisters found some red beets. I sang and danced for some guards and got a handful of sauerkraut. We had saved our bread, and with all this together we made a surprise present for the others. We roasted the potato peels and quietly sang Dutch and Yiddish songs, and imagined what we would do if we ever got home. Anne's idea was: "Then we'll have a party, a celebratory meal at Dikker & Thys," one of Amsterdam's most expensive restaurants. For a little while we were almost happy.

Then Jannie and I were assigned to another barrack. We asked Anne and Margot to come with us, but Margot had terrible diarrhea and had to stay in the old barrack because of the risk of stomach typhus. Anne took care of her as well as she could. We visited them during the next few weeks and now and then we were able to bring them something to eat.

It must have been March when we went to see them again, the snow had melted. But they weren't in the barrack anymore. We found them in the sick house. We told them they mustn't stay there, because whenever you gave up hope the end was near. Anne said: "Here we can both lie on one bunk, we are together, and it's peaceful." Margot could only whisper. She had a high fever. The next day we went to visit them again. Margot had fallen out of the bunk and was barely conscious. Anne had a fever too, she was friendly and sweet. She said: "Margot will sleep well and when she sleeps I won't need to get up again."

A few days later we found their bunk empty. We knew what that meant. We found them behind the barrack, wrapped their thin bodies in a blanket, and carried them to a mass grave. That was all we could do for them.

Lien Brilleslijper and her sister Jannie were deported first to Auschwitz, then, like Anne and Margot, to Bergen-Belsen, where they were liberated by the British. Lien Rebling-Brilleslijper and her husband, Eberhard Rebling, a successful pianist and musicologist who had immigrated to Holland in 1936, later returned to Berlin, where she became a well-known performer of Yiddish songs and workmen's ballads in East Germany.

She and her sister had survived the Holocaust, but Margot and Anne Frank had not.

9.

You Can't Let Yourself Get Depressed

Margot and Anne were dead. They presumably died in late March 1945 in the Bergen-Belsen concentration camp on the Lüneburg Heath. When British soldiers liberated the camp on April 15, 1945, they found approximately sixty thousand emaciated prisoners. The British military doctor who was later put in charge of the rescue and rehabilitation efforts, Hugh Llewelyn Glyn Hughes, described the situation like this: "The conditions in the camp were really indescribable; no description nor photograph could really bring home the horrors.... There were various sizes of piles of corpses lying all over the camp.... [The huts] were filled absolutely to overflowing with prisoners in every state of emaciation and disease."* The absolute overcrowding and utterly insufficient food and supplies in the camp had taken the lives of more than thirty-five thousand people between January and mid-April 1945 alone, including Margot and Anne Frank.

Alice reacted with shock to the death of her granddaughters, as is apparent in the letter that she wrote to Otto on August 4:

My dearest Otto, Your letter of 6/15 with the copy & 9 cards so far have reached us . . . There are no words to tell you what I feel & every minute

*Quoted from Raymond Phillips, ed., *Trial of Josef Kramer and Forty-four Others (The Belsen Trial)* (Edinburgh: The University of Edinburgh, 1949).

Liebster Ottel, es sind jetzt sehr viele Deiner Karten eingetroffen – wir sind gesund, bleib Du es auch! Alles Liebe
Leni.

Stephan und
Bernhard P. Elias

Basel, den 5. August 1945

Mein lieber Ottel,

Überflüssig, Dir zu schreiben, wie sehr wir alle in diesen schweren Stunden in Gedanken bei Dir sind. Du bist jedoch gezwungen, das grosse Leid alleine zu tragen. Wir können Dir nur das allertiefste Mitempfinden zum Ausdruck bringen. – Doch mit Deiner alten Energie wirst Du nun wieder arbeiten, und in nicht zu weiter Ferne werden wir uns wiedersehen. – Die Erinnerung an die Amsterdamer Tage wird mir zeitlebens im Gedächtnis bleiben.

Alles Liebe wünscht Dir Dein Neffe Stephan

Mein lieber Ottel,

auch ich möchte Dir noch schreiben wie furchtbar leid mir Dein schreckliches Schicksal tut. Ja ich glaube ich darf sagen: unser Schicksal. Die gut kann ich mich noch an die schönen Tage mit Dir und Margot in Adelboden erinnern. Auch Edith und Anne habe ich natürlich noch gut im Gedächtnis und werde sie ewig dort behalten. Ich weiss, dass Du nun schwer zu kämpfen hast, um alles zu überwinden und frisch aufzubauen. Wir können Dich ja leider vorläufig nur so wenig unterstützen ich wünschte Du wärest schon bei uns, oder wir

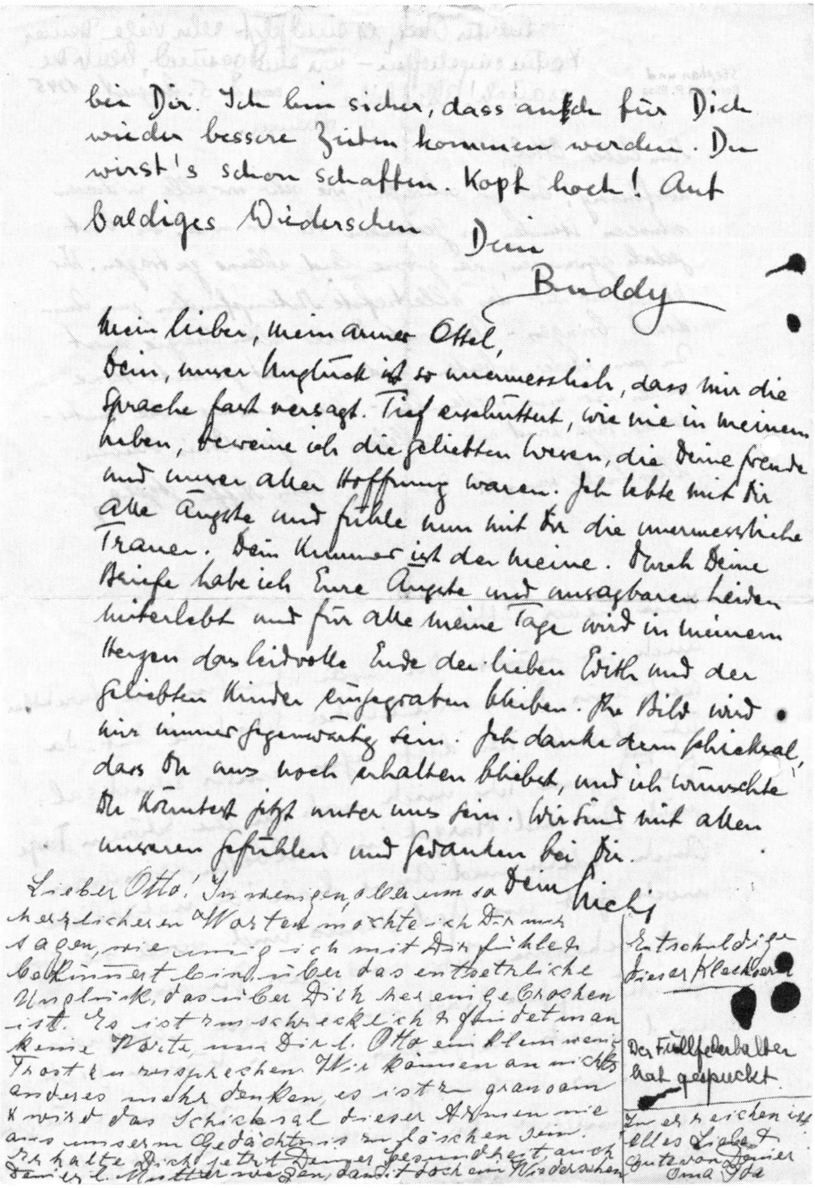
bei Dir. Ich bin sicher, dass auch für Dich wieder bessere Zeiten kommen werden. Du wirst's schon schaffen. Kopf hoch! Auf baldiges Wiedersehen

Dein
Buddy

Mein lieber, mein armer Ottel,
Dein, unser Unglück ist so unermesslich, dass mir die Sprache fast versagt. Tief erschüttert, wie nie in meinem Leben, beweine ich die geliebten Wesen, die Deine Freude und unser aller Hoffnung waren. Ich lebte mit Dir alle Ängste und fühle nun mit Dir die unermessliche Trauer. Dein Kummer ist der meine. Durch Deine Briefe habe ich Eure Ängste und unsagbaren Leiden miterlebt und für alle meine Tage wird in meinem Herzen das leidvolle Ende der lieben Edith und der geliebten Kinder eingegraben bleiben. Ihr Bild wird mir immer gegenwärtig sein. Ich danke dem Schicksal, dass Du uns noch erhalten bliebst, und ich wünschte Du könntest jetzt unter uns sein. Wir sind mit allen unseren Gefühlen und Gedanken bei Dir.

Dein Leni

Lieber Otto! In wenigen, aber um so herzlicheren Worten möchte ich Dir nur sagen, wie innig ich mit Dir fühle. Bekümmert bin ich über das entsetzliche Unglück, das über Dich hereingebrochen ist. Es ist zu schrecklich & findet man keine Worte, um Dir l. Otto ein klein wenig Trost zuzusprechen. Wir können an nichts anderes mehr denken, es ist zu grausam & wird das Schicksal dieser Armen nie aus unserem Gedächtnis zu löschen sein. Ich halte Dich jetzt Deiner Gesundheit, auch Deiner l. Mutter wegen, damit doch ein Wiedersehen

Entschuldige dieser Klecksen
Der Füllfederhalter hat gespuckt.

Inzwischen ist alles Liebe & Gute von Deiner Oma Ida

Joint letter from the family to Otto Frank, August 5, 1945

I am with you in feeling the unspeakable suffering in body and soul that you now have to bear alone. We can't even help you, me with my great love for you & with the unspeakable sorrow I share with you. I don't want to & I can't write about any details today, it's beyond my strength, but it isn't necessary either, is it, the facts are so horrible & nothing I could say about the facts could possibly show you how I feel. Maybe someday later I'll be able to ask everything I want to know about Edith too but anyway now it's all for nothing & you seem to be being brave, that's the only thing I can hope & wish for now. Did you get my telegram, all it's trying to say is that we have one thought now & that is you . . . Olga L. has come back from Theresienstadt, she seems to have partially lost her memory & is living in a home, she doesn't know anything anymore about little Irma since she got to Birkenau. Sig. G. died in Theresienstadt, we haven't had any news of Louis for months. I'm writing you about all this because you asked about everyone in one of your cards & they're also so near and dear to us! I also just now got a nice card from Bep Voskeul & Helene. Both are so nice to write, I thank them & I'll answer soon. I telegraphed Herbie, I also heard from Robert & Lotti yesterday, they didn't know about our great loss. Lotti seemed completely "down." Did you get their package yet & also see the Goldsteins, they had various things for you too.—If only I could be with you, but I'd still have no way to express our great pain, I could only put my head on your shoulder & cry! Stay healthy, send our love to everyone there, they were such faithful friends to you, & warmest thoughts as always from Your, Mom.

Everyone on Herbstgasse was completely stunned. The finality of the news left them nothing but helplessness and despair, especially Alice, who fell apart. Leni tried to be supportive, to give her courage. "Life goes on," she said. "You always told us that we have to keep our sights set on the future."

"What future?" Alice asked.

Leni wished she could take back her thoughtless words, because Alice was right, what future was there for her? She was almost eighty years old, and Otto was fifty-six. Was there still a future for him?

"We have to write to him," Leni said at last. "Everyone needs to write to him. That is the only thing we can do for him—show him that he's not alone in his suffering, that we're by his side."

The letter they all wrote to Otto demonstrates how great their grief was. They all expressed their sympathy, including Grandma Ida, who was affected by the news in a different way than the others, since it supplanted her worries about Paul for a time.

My dear Ottel,
We don't need to say how very much you are in our thoughts in these difficult times. You are nevertheless forced to bear this great sorrow alone—all we can do is express our very deepest sympathy.—But I'm sure that you will work hard with your old energy and we will be able to see you again in the not so distant future.—The memory of our days in Amsterdam will stay in my memory for the rest of my life.

Wishing you all our love,
Your nephew Stephan

My dear Ottel,
I also want to write how terribly sorry I am about your horrible fate. I think I can say: our fate. I remember so well the lovely days with you and Margot in Adelboden. Edith and Anne are fixed in my memory as well, of course, and will be treasured there forever. I know that you have a hard battle ahead now, to recover from everything and make a fresh start. We can only give you so little support now, I wish you were here with us already, or we were with you. I'm positive that better times will come, for you too. You'll do it. Chin up! See you very soon—

Your Buddy

Poor, dear Ottel,
Your sorrow, our sorrow, is so enormous that I am almost speechless. I am shattered like never before in my life, and weep for the dear

creatures who were your pride and joy and carried all of our hopes. I felt all your fears with you and now I feel the enormous grief with you too. Your sorrows are my own. I experienced your fears and unspeakable sorrows alongside you when I read your letters and dear Edith's and the dear children's sad end will stay engraved in my heart for the rest of my days. Their image will always be there before me. I am grateful to fate for keeping you here with us, and I wish you could be here with us now. We are with you in all of our thoughts and feelings.

Yours, Erich

Dear Otto! I want to tell you in just a few words, but all the more heartfelt, how deeply I feel for you & am affected by the horrific misfortune that has burst upon you. It is too terrible & there are no words to console you even a little bit, my dear Otto. We cannot think about anything else, it is too monstrous & the fate of these poor girls will never leave our memory. Keep your health now, also for your dear mother's sake, so that we can finally see you again.

All love & best wishes from your Grandma Ida

They wrote their letter on August 5. This time, they did not have to wait such a long time for an answer: Otto's letter is dated August 19. The postal service was up and running at last, though still irregular, which made it easier for the family to draw together—a need they must all have felt very strongly. Their tight family bonds were only strengthened by their shared sorrows. Otto Frank seemed to feel that way as well. He wrote:

My dears,

I received your family letter from the 6th and Leni's card and I understand how hard it must have been for Mother to write to me. I have got so many letters from every side and I can't answer everything at once. Besides, I'm trying not to think about things too much, but just stay busy. I mostly manage to do it and I am overcome with shock only every now and then. I already wrote that you have to try to sum-

mon me on business so that the consulate has support for my application, and after my conversation with Goldstein I am convinced that very extensive discussions are going to be necessary here if anyone is going to be able to rebuild what's needed. More on that separately.

Now I have to say something to Buddy in particular. He has no idea how often Anne talked about him and how much she longed to visit you and talk about all sorts of things with Buddy. The pictures you sent of the ice-skating are still here; she had a burning interest in his progress, since she herself loved skating so much and dreamed of one day being able to skate with him. Shortly before we went into hiding, she got a pair of figure skates, just what she wanted. Buddy's style of writing also reminds me in so many ways of how Anne used to write, it is really amazing. Stephan has a very different way and both of them seem to be as good and well behaved there as our two were here. I read poems by Goethe and Schiller with Anne, and William Tell, the Maid of Orleans, Maria Stuart, Nathan the Wise, The Merchant of Venice, etc. She especially liked reading biographies, e.g., of Rembrandt, Rubens, Maria Theresa and Marie Antoinette, Charles V and the great men of Dutch history, and also Gone with the Wind and lots of good novels.

Edith and Margot were both keen readers too.

Except to you all I am writing to almost no one about Edith and the children. What would be the point? . . . I hope that Erich will get better soon, I don't know what arthritis is and have to ask about it. Goldstein told me about Leni's business competence, Herbert wrote about it too, it's hard for me to imagine! G[oldstein] was especially attentive and kind to me, he gave me a pair of boots as well & I stayed with him in Rotterdam for two nights last week. He is less kind to his wife, which I didn't like at all. My feelings weren't wrong. I have gathered a lot of information here and I have the impression that he currently has mistaken ideas about the local market here. A merchant who sells to factories always has a different outlook from someone who deals in proprietary materials. I also went to The Hague because of Hanneli Goslar and so the time flew by. I do basically nothing in terms of actual business and am working only on new plans. Business in another letter. All my love and warmest greetings.

It was Leni who read the letter to the family. When she lowered it, she saw how pale Buddy's face was. "Anne," he said, in a strangled voice, "suddenly I could see her clear as daylight before my eyes." It was visibly hard for him to regain his composure. Leni put a consoling hand on his. Then he jumped up and ran out of the room. She could hear the water in the bathroom running, for a long time, and she knew he was washing his face with cold water to calm himself down. When he came back to the dining room, Imperia was just serving the soup, but no one had an appetite. "My letter must not have reached him yet," Alice complained, "even though I wrote to him first, before any of you."

"You know how unreliable the post office is still," Erich said soothingly.

Then they talked about Hanneli Goslar, Anne's friend from before. She and her younger sister, Gabi, had survived the Bergen-Belsen camp; her father had died there. Her mother had died in childbirth before the deportation, together with the baby. So Hanneli and Gabi were now alone, and it was good that Otto was looking after the girls. He and Edith had been friends of the Goslars'.

Three days later, a letter from Otto arrived for Alice confirming that now he had received her letter too. "Dear Mom," Alice read out loud, then her voice failed her, and she passed the letter to Leni to read.

I've now received your letter from the 4th too. I know how upset you are, how much you are thinking about me, and how you share my grief. I am not letting myself go and am distracting myself as much as I can. I don't have any pictures from the last few years of course, but Miep was somehow able to save an album [actually a few albums] and also Anne's diary. I still don't have the strength to read it. From Margot, there's nothing except her Latin exercises. Since they ransacked our whole house, there aren't all the little things that we were used to and that Edith or the children had. Obviously, it's useless to immerse yourself in such things and thoughts, but of course a person isn't always reasonable. I received your telegram, and it won't be long before we can use the telephone again, but I'm afraid that I won't be able to speak. In any case, write and give me your phone number.

Again and again, Otto reported that people had written to him or visited him. Once, for example: "In May 42, Leni Leyens lived with us with husband and child, a good friend of Edith's (from Wesel). I know that a brother, 'Erich Leyens,' was in Switzerland and I'm looking for him since Leni's child was saved while there's no word of the parents after they were sent off from Westerbork to Poland. Is there an office in Switzerland where you can inquire where someone is?"

And he returned to the topic of how difficult it was to travel: "There are still giant complications about visiting, I can see it in my efforts for Hanneli and Gabi . . . The world hasn't got any smaller and closer together, but rather split even farther apart! Still I hope that now that the war with Japan is over there will be better connections soon and all the censors, passport difficulties, and transit visas will fall away. But we have to be patient."

The postal service was definitely still unreliable, since only now did Otto's answer to Buddy and Stephan's letter of almost two months before arrive. Their letter was written back when they had still hoped that Margot and Anne might be alive, though one or the other must have had his doubts sometimes. It was Erich who would insist in such moments that there must be many, many people still alive but incommunicado in the Russian zone, and Leni might have believed him too. And if Stephan or Buddy dared to say "We would have heard from them a long time ago if they were still alive," Leni was the first to cut him short. "Hope is the last thing to go," she said over and over again. "We can't give up hope." Then Stephan and Buddy, so as not to make their mother more anxious, fell silent and clung to their hopes, at least outwardly.

And now it turned out that Otto already knew of his daughters' deaths when he had answered Buddy and Stephan. "Dear boys," he had written:

I'm very happy to have got word from you two as well. You are the only ones remaining of the younger generation, after all, & you have no idea how often we talked about you & the plans we came up with in our Secret Annex for when we would see you again. Your photographs were in our hands often, because we took almost all our photos with us. The rogues accidentally missed a bunch of photos when they ransacked the Annex so I still have them. Today I no longer make plans. My desire to see you is as strong as yours to see me but circumstances are even stronger & we have to submit and wait. I was very interested to hear all the details from Buddy, and I don't yet know what Stephan is up to. Unfortunately, there is so little you can fit on a postcard. I am being well provided for here, nothing is missing in terms of daily life—it's just everything is so empty, but I am staying on my feet & I don't let much of anything show on the outside. Warmest regards to everyone there,

Your Otto

It wasn't only Alice who was desperate to see her son Otto again: Leni also thought constantly about her brother. But they had to be patient. They could tell from Otto's letters how difficult his situation was. He said that he had taken a trip to see Hanneli Goslar and the trip to Maastricht took several days: no trains were traveling south yet, so he had had to take a truck and it took fourteen hours, just on the way there. Next week he was planning to go to The Hague. Goldstein also thought that Otto should try to get to Switzerland, to discuss business matters. If Unipektin would send him a document attesting that his trip to Switzerland was urgently necessary for the pectin trade, then he could take the necessary steps at the consulate to apply for a visa. Even so, he didn't know if he would be able to get a travel permit.

Otto's complaints about the authorities sounded all too familiar in Basel, since Erich and Leni had had corresponding difficulties themselves. Leni in particular kept getting worked up about it. "Anti-Semites!" she said when she read Otto's letters. "There are anti-Semites in all the bureaucracies, everywhere, not just here in Switzerland. It's no better in the Netherlands, it seems."

One Mrs. Auerbach from Amsterdam, who had managed to come visit relatives in Basel, said that she was willing to bring things back for Otto. Leni started shopping—they had heard so many stories, on all sides, about how bad the economic situation was in the Netherlands, how you couldn't get even the most necessary things, never mind any luxuries, so Leni bought everything she could think of that she thought Otto might need and added some clothes for Miep Gies and Bep Voskuijl as well.

Otto wrote that he had got the things:

Everything is great, and it was chosen with so much love. I have almost everything I need personally now, and I am writing to Julius for a few smaller things, he can send them. There are still some sheets and blankets here. I'm sure you understand how happy I am to be able to help my friends a little after all the endless things they've done for me and since they don't have any relatives. Suspenders, garters, and the like are just as welcome here as thread and elastic. The little dress fits Miep like a glove. I can't give anything to Bep until Monday, since she's on vacation. My old razor was beyond help so I was glad to get that too. I'll give something to Mrs. Kleiman too, since Mrs. Kugler doesn't need anything. She is back at home again. Kugler never said a word to his wife during the whole two years! He kept it all to himself and bore everything alone; he is a nervous person himself and suffered from it. His wife had to go to a sanatorium when she heard, and she is back there now. There is a lot more that I can't write . . . I'll do everything I can to come soon. But I'm also a bit nervous about traveling. I cry very easily these days and get excited over little things, as I'm sure you can imagine. But I assure you that I'm in perfectly good health. In fact I now weigh over 150 pounds! I brood about things as little as I can and I am sleeping well. It goes without saying I still think about Edith and the children, but I am trying to look more on the bright side rather than be sentimental.

He also told stories about the many different people he was meeting, and about Hanneli Goslar, in whom he took a particular interest since she was, for him, a connection with Anne. Margot had had a lot fewer friends than Anne—one friend had not come back, and another was in Sweden, he would talk with her later. For the first time, he mentioned Anneliese Schütz, the future translator of Anne's diary into German: "Fräulein Schütz is over 50, almost blind, and very alone, which is why she is trying to make friends with me, she was a journalist and was always very interested in the children. Margot took a literature class with her."

"Margot was always reading, all the time," Buddy said to Alice. "I still remember exactly how she used to sit at the window and read when she was visiting. Back when you still lived on Schweizergasse."

"Margot was a very clever girl," Alice said, and she started crying again, as she always did whenever anyone said anything about Margot or Anne.

Leni cast a reproachful glance at her son and quickly said: "Otto seems to really have a lot to do, with all the friends and acquaintances he's meeting and then his work."

Otto wrote about people he knew in his later letters, too, and said what had happened to them, and also wrote a lot about business matters. For example, he asked Erich once if it was worth buying Opekta "dry" and making it "fluid" in the Netherlands, and he talked about a competitor's product that was so cheap it must be made from something other than pectin.

Leni could clearly see how hard her brother was trying to make a new day-to-day life for himself. In a letter to Erich, he wrote about a baker, one of Kleiman's customers, who was a forward-looking man. Erich told Leni about it. "This baker, Otto says, wants to try to bake bread you can store. He heard that in America they make bread that stays fresh for weeks without losing its taste. Apparently, he asked Otto if you can use pectin as a preservative. Because someday bakers are not going to want to work on Sundays and holidays anymore, that's going to stop. Otto wants to know if anyone in Switzerland has already tried anything along these lines."

"And, has anyone?" Leni asked.

Erich didn't know but thought the whole thing was a good idea and a business opportunity.

"Otto desperately wants to act as though his life is like normal," Leni said to Erich. "Don't you think he's putting on an act for us? It can't really work, in the end, running away from reality into an imaginary world. Reality forces itself back in on you, it's ruthless and merciless."

Erich shrugged his shoulders. "Maybe, but he doesn't have any choice, does he? Life goes on one way or another. He can't just sit home and cry."

Then, at the beginning of September, Stephan fell ill. It started harmlessly, in any case Leni thought it was harmless at first, maybe a flu. Stephan had been cutting peat in the national service (students' mandatory service working on farms); maybe he had caught something there. He complained about backaches, sore hips and legs, everything vague. He had a fever, which confirmed Leni's impression that it was a flu. But naturally they called Dr. Brühl, their doctor, who also said that aching limbs often accompanied a bad case of the flu. He prescribed a syrup for the fever and a powder for the aches and pains, and said that a compress would be good for his leg; he should drink a lot of fluids, especially chamomile tea. Alice immediately took over the nursing, Imperia made the tea, Leni made the compress and sent Buddy out of the sickroom because she was afraid he might catch it. But nothing helped. Stephan said the pain was unbearable; he burned with fever and barely reacted when anyone spoke to him. Leni sent for the doctor again, who was shocked when he saw Stephan's condition and immediately sent him to the hospital. The doctors there couldn't say anything yet, only that they would have to wait and see.

On Herbstgasse they were in despair, especially Alice, seized with fear that she might lose another grandchild. Leni tried to keep calm. At the hospital, the doctors said it was an inflammation of the hip joint, possibly also a sepsis, of an unclear cause, and they mentioned a new medicine, penicillin, that people were saying worked miracles. They wanted to try it on Stephan.

Leni sat at her son's bedside. They had put him in traction. He had a fever and kept sinking into a restless sleep. She wiped off his forehead now and then with a moist washcloth, but whenever he grew calmer, she was plunged deeper into her own panic. The uncertainty, this battle between hope and fear, created a tension in her that was almost impossible to bear. This was how Otto must have felt before he learned the terrible truth.

To distract herself with something to do, Leni took a writing pad out of her bag and wrote a letter to her brother, telling him about Stephan's illness:

He is in unspeakable pain & all of us with him. How Mother can withstand all these worries is a mystery to me, but she always was & still is the most amazing woman & I hope with all my heart that you can come soon and at least feel for yourself her enormous love. She is basically healthy but 80 years old is 80 years old. Ottel, now I'm adding my cares to everything, yours & all of ours are already big enough.

The Goldsteins couldn't tell you much about Stephan, because Mr. Goldstein was in the national service for six weeks & we're afraid he caught something by the end, he is much too conscientious. I think our children were similar that way, Stephan like Margot & Buddy like Anne. Stephan frightfully reliable & hardworking, honest, strange like Robert, but fundamentally good. Buddy lively, egotistical, intelligent, artistically gifted, superficial, but also a good soul. We don't have problems with either. Erich is devastated, he is staying home for a few days. Stephan is being tormented terribly with injections etc. Hopefully, they won't have to operate. On top of it all, business is booming with two huge estate liquidation orders & I'm working, which Stephan always says he wants too.

Continued on Sept. 5. Dearest Ottel, Today is so difficult for you too—I don't need to say another word . . . I was surprised that you wrote so little about Frida Belinfante, she was completely fabulous when she was here & Mrs. Auerbach too, who will bring you lots more things, with some things for Miep and Bep from me too . . . It's my opinion that we're not going to see Paul again either, we've heard too many reports. You can tell Miep that I hate them just as much as she does, but unfortunately that doesn't help anything.

Just a couple days later a letter came from Otto, but not in answer to Leni's letter about Stephan. It made correspondence so difficult, Leni felt. You write on one topic and receive a letter about something totally different. This time Otto had burst out with his grief and sadness after all. The letter, dated September 6, was addressed to Alice but was of course read by everyone in the family, as usual on Herbstgasse:

I know that all your thoughts are constantly with me, but you can't let yourselves wallow too much in such feelings. We have to do what we can for the living, the others are beyond our help. You know that that's how I always felt. We had an unusually harmonious life together and I have no reason to blame her or myself for having made our time together harder than it needed to be. That makes it even harder to bear this fate, but that's how it has to be. A letter came from America for Margot and

Anne a few days ago, from a girl who was corresponding with both of them, without having ever met them. The girl wanted to start up their old correspondence. I answered her in a long letter—with many tears. Something like that is very disturbing, of course, but it doesn't matter.

Even in this letter, he quickly changed the subject:

I hope Bernd had the success he was hoping for. In a career like that, the path is full of pitfalls. I can never say his name without thinking of Anne. I can well imagine that Stephan wants to leave. How is his English? And his ice hockey! What is he doing? The boys are now the only ones who count as the younger generation for me . . . I imagine that you often picture Grandma, I remember her all the time too. And today is the anniversary of Father's death too. You just can't give yourself over to your thoughts, life demands more. I am sure that Leni gets along very well with her customers. And still I'm always afraid that the expenses will be too high—all the prices have skyrocketed everywhere & the household there is so big.

Leni Elias, around sixty years old

"He's worried about my business, with everything he's going through himself," Leni said. "We should really be ashamed of ourselves, writing about our own problems when he has lost his wife and children. Still, we can't pretend that everything is fine here just to protect him."

Leni hardly had time to think, she had so much to do, but that was the way she wanted it. Her business truly had taken off, unexpectedly, and without Frau Thomsen, whom she had hired at first only to clean up and keep an eye on the store, she would not have been able to manage, especially now that Stephan was in the hospital, with no sign of improvement. It wouldn't have worked without Alice too. "But all of us & all our friends," Leni wrote to Otto, "are thinking of you with the greatest love & respect for your greatness—yes, Ottel, there is no other word for it, you are a model for us & so I am trying to complain as little as possible & just do my duty for the family & everyone else. Mother is wonderful, as she always is in these crucial moments, she is at Stephan's bedside whenever I don't have time to be there myself."

Leni left the house at seven in the morning, rode her bicycle (an old one, but sturdy) to the hospital to look in on Stephan, then to her store to give instructions to Frau Thomsen, and finally to the large villa owned by Dreyfus-Brodsky, where she had been hired to appraise and sell off all the contents. It was all possible only because she knew that Alice would be at Stephan's side for hours, taking care of him, since Erich spent almost all his time traveling around by train trying to chase down any kind of business—usually in vain. Sometimes she had to make a special effort not to show her irritation. Did she think in such moments about Ernst Schneider, and the passionate love letters he had written to her? Against his express wishes, she had not destroyed them. Why not? Out of vanity, because it flattered her to be the object of such extreme feelings? Or did she want to read them now and then to lose herself in her memories? A marriage and an affair, those are two different pairs of boots—a saying she would have often heard in Frankfurt, and might well have said to herself in Basel. If she compared the two men in her mind—Erich and Ernst—Erich would probably not have come off badly at all: he was one of those men who age attractively, he still looked very handsome, and his friendly, conciliatory personality must have been good for her, must have brought out a sort of tender pity in her even if she sometimes got annoyed at him.

Life, in any case, was now not what they had hoped for. They did their duty as well as they could–some better, some worse–it wasn't a question of blame. Sometimes Leni couldn't believe how well she herself was handling all this slaving away. "Sometimes I take my head in my hands & can't believe that it's really me," she wrote to her brother Otto. "Buddy got a part and we were there for his debut performance, it was good, he is almost an old hand at it, it was a small part in any case. He has to read a script on the radio too & this winter he will probably be busy all the time. Erich fasted. Stephan is leaning toward being a little more religious, everyone does what they want here. I closed the shop on the holidays."

It took more than two weeks for Otto's letter to finally reach Leni. Stephan was not much improved in the meantime–the doctors had not got his sepsis under control and did not rule out the possibility of needing to operate after all. "Dearest Lunni," Otto wrote:

I just received your letter of the 4th/5th and am really worried about Stephan's condition. What terrible extra worry for you all and for Mom. Personally, I am shutting it out as much as I possibly can and am doing my best to bear up under my own fate. But you know how I always saw it as my task to help the "living" and do something for them and so I'm now thinking more about Stephan than about my two dear Butzens. You can't let yourself get depressed or else you can't do anything. I can picture Mom perfectly well, even though she is 80. If only the boy doesn't suffer too much and everything turns out fine, I still see him in my mind as a young boy, soft and a little dreamy. I'm sure you're right with your comparison between them and my children. I have so much to tell you. I inquired about my passport yesterday and next week I am traveling to The Hague to try to resolve the situation more quickly. I very much hope and think I'll be able to come in November.

I haven't heard anything from Herb and Rob in a long time, but Julius and Walter write a lot. The packages from the U.S.A. take a long time to get here, and the main packages from London, from June, still aren't here. Your things were wonderful, as I wrote already . . . I was with Hanneli for the New Year [Rosh Hashanah]. I probably won't go to synagogue for the Day of Atonement [Yom Kippur] either. There is no Reform service yet—if there was, I would have gone—and I have nothing to do with the other kind. I know that Edith didn't think so narrowly. She also never wanted me to fast and she knew that I went only for her sake. With her or the children I would have gone, but alone it's pointless and hypocritical. I will stay home and I have definite plans that I'll write and tell you about later. Mom knows my views about this and she doesn't need to act any differently from how she is. It all has to stay on the inside and our feelings are no less strong for that . . . I am amazed at your business abilities. I only hope that you're also happy doing it. And I can picture exactly how you treat your customers! You always did like to have lots of people around you and a set routine.

Now first the boy has to get better. I'm anxious and in suspense waiting for further news.

Alice took affectionate care of Stephan but otherwise withdrew more and more into herself. Leni felt that her mother was visibly aging by the day. And not only her—Grandma Ida seemed to get more inconspicuous every day, more like a shadow than a living person. Every morning she stood in front of the house and waited for the mailman, and when once again the mail brought no news of Paul, she quietly went upstairs and looked for something to do. Leni no longer thought that Paul would come back, and

Alice Frank at about eighty, on the garden steps of the house on Herbstgasse

Erich's doubts were growing too; even Otto had written: "I have hardly any hope left for Paul and I don't believe the reports that there are still lots of people with the Russians." They didn't know what Grandma Ida was really thinking—no one dared to talk with her about it. At least she was healthy, just like Alice, who had nothing worse than trouble climbing the stairs. At least Leni didn't have to worry about the state of her mother's health—which was a relief, she certainly had enough else on her mind. In one way or another, everyone on Herbstgasse was preoccupied with themselves, with their own fears and worries. And with waiting for their son, their brother, their brother-in-law, their uncle.

Otto wrote that he had no doubt he'd be able to come, but they had to be patient:

Everything takes such a long time, I have to wait three weeks before I'm even admitted to see the authorities. Then they start their investigation into whether I can be trusted politically, but since I was in a camp and have excellent references besides, that should all be a formality. But it still has to happen. I can imagine how Mom is waiting, but I'm waiting too. She is certainly a great help for you again, despite her age, and still does so much. I can't even imagine it.

Julius wrote that he fasted too, I can see what a great support religion gives people, but there's nothing there for me. If Stephan is so inclined, he should definitely read more about Jewish ethics, it's very interesting to me too.

It's easy for me to imagine Buddy onstage. I found in Anne's diary the description of a waltz on ice that she performed with him in a dream. What I read there is indescribably upsetting, but still I read it. I can't describe it to you, I'm not done reading it yet and want to finish reading through the whole thing before I make any excerpts or translations. Among other things, she describes her feelings in puberty with unbelievable self-awareness and self-criticism. Even if it wasn't Anne who had written it, it would still be so moving. What a terrible shame that this life was snuffed out! I will have hours and hours of stories to tell you when I come visit.

"I don't know if it's good for him to read the girl's diary," Erich said, and Leni secretly agreed. Spending time with what his daughter had written must be upsetting him, must be tearing open all the wounds again. But she preferred to keep her opinion to herself.

It wasn't long before Otto wrote again about Anne's diary. First he told the family about the packages he had received from Julius and Robert:

It's very fine that I now have a raincoat, since you need one here all the time . . . I went to the synagogue yesterday for Purim. Anne and Margot always used to participate, even in Aachen. On the outside I was smiling, on the inside I wept. I can't stay away from Anne's diaries and they are so unbelievably moving. I'm having her book of stories copied now since I don't want to let the only copy out of my hands, and I'll translate some things into German for you. I can't let the diaries out of my hands, there is too much in them that is not intended for anyone else, but I'll make excerpts. In my letters I don't say much about Berndt, but that doesn't mean that I'm [not] thinking of him and his work. It's only that we have to deal with Stephan at the moment. I have to set aside some time to answer Erich properly and it's amazing how little free time I actually have. It's a fact that there's quite a number of people stuck in the Russian zone, so we have to keep our hopes up for Paul. Warmest greetings to all of you, and all my thoughts. I'm doing everything I can to come soon.

"I'm doing everything I can to come soon," Alice repeated. She looked pale and exhausted, but this sentence seemed to revive her. Leni reached out a hand for the bell hanging above the table, and when Imperia opened the door, Leni asked her to make a peppermint tea for her mother. Alice looked at her. "The war has been over for almost half a year already," she said. "Why won't they let him visit his family? He doesn't have anyone else left."

"I'm sure he'll manage to be here for your and Stephan's birthday," Leni reassured her. But Alice shook her head. Leni knew that Alice was in no mood to celebrate anything, she just wanted to see her son.

Otto sent Buddy a copy of a page from Anne's diary, of October 18, 1942:

Bernd is busy teaching me figure skating and I am going to be his partner because his partner happens to be away, we make a lovely pair and everyone is mad about us we sent five photographs to the office 1 Anne doing a turn 2 Anne arm in arm with Bernd left foot forwards 3 Anne waltzing with Bernd 4 Anne with Bernd doing the swan 5 Anne from the left, Bernd from the right blowing a kiss to each other. There will be a film later for Holland and Switzerland, my girl friends in both Holland and Switzerland think it's great. It's in three parts.

1st part. Anne on skates.

First you see her entering from one side while her partner enters from the other side with a blue skating dress trimmed with white fur with zipped pockets and a zipper and a belt with a bag.

Then they do the swan together and Anne does a tremendous leap in the air. Later they waltz and joke about the lessons.

2nd part. Anne making a visit and at school. Busy at the tea table in the small room with Kitty and two boys including Bernd then at school surrounded by a noisy crowd of children and all sorts of silly scenes e.g. in bed with Daddy and at table.

*3rd part. Anne's wardrobe the 8 new dresses skating dress which is a present a white one and shoes.**

Buddy gulped as he read what his little cousin had written, and when he looked at the awkward little drawing. Anne was nine the last time he saw her and thirteen when she wrote this page—a child, with a child's dreams. She would have been sixteen now, he

**The Diary of Anne Frank: The Revised Critical Edition* (New York: Doubleday, 2003), p. 303. This passage did not appear in the original edition.

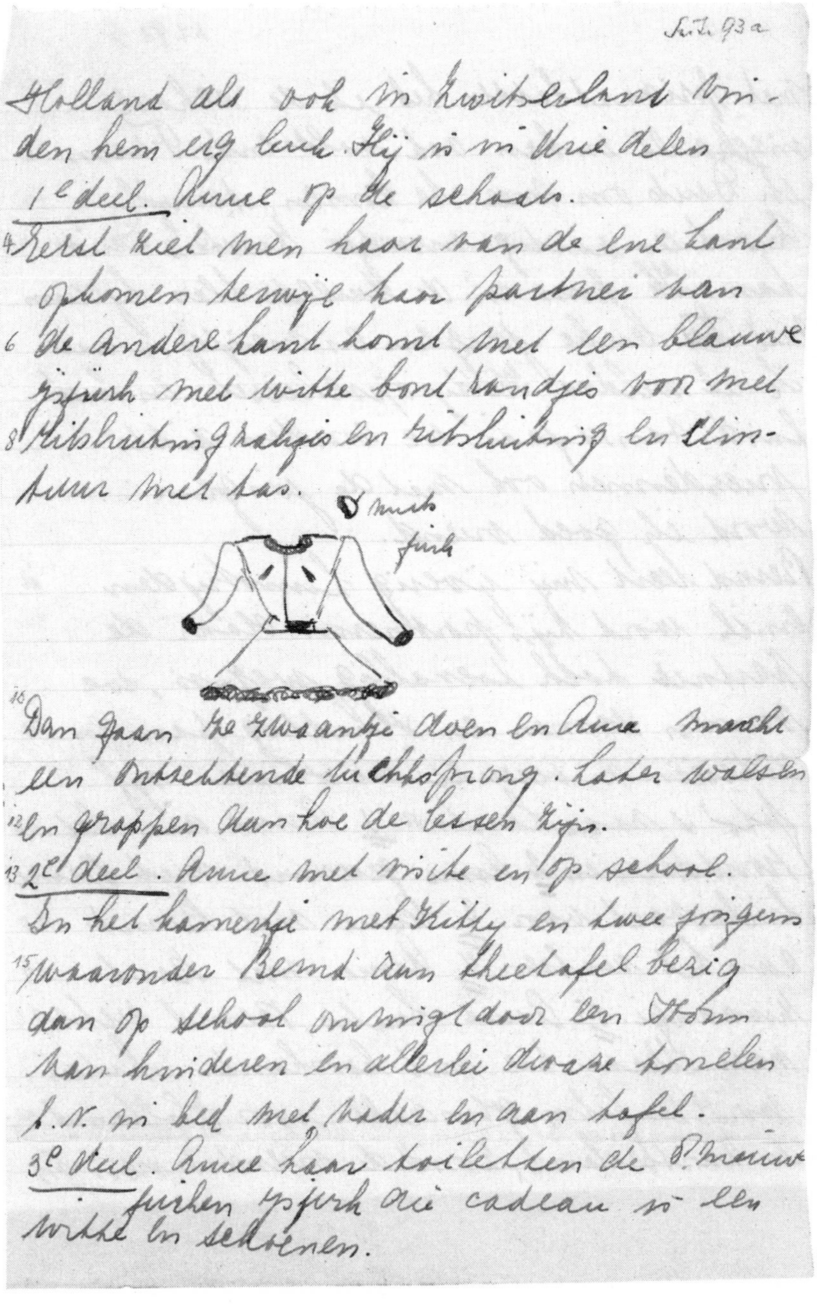
Holland als ook in Zwitserland vinden hem erg leuk. Hij is in drie delen
1e deel. Anne op de schaats.
Eerst ziet men haar van de ene kant opkomen terwijl haar partner van de andere kant komt met een blauwe ijsjurk met witte bont randjes voor met ritssluitingzakjes en ritssluiting en klimtuur met tas.
Dan gaan ze zwaantje doen en Anne maakt een ontzettende luchtsprong. Later walsen en grappen daar hoe de lessen zijn.
2e deel. Anne met visite en op school.
In het kamertje met Kitty en twee jongens waaronder Bernd aan theetafel bezig dan op school omringd door een storm van kinderen en allerlei dwaze trucjes z.v. in bed met vader en aan tafel.
3e deel. Anne haar toiletten de 8 nieuwe jurken ijsjurk die cadeau is een witte en schoenen.

Anne's diary entry, October 18, 1942

couldn't imagine it. He thought about the sixteen-year-old girls he knew, who were definitely no longer children, and felt rage inside him, a helpless fury over the fact that he would never know how Anne would have looked at sixteen, would never know how she would have danced.

He loved to dance himself and took every opportunity that offered itself. There were afternoon dances at teatime at several local establishments, and some nights he also went to the Regina Bar, where many American GIs used to go as well. The soldiers came from nearby Germany to spend their leave in Switzerland and brought lots of new dances from back home, like boogie and swing, that Europe had never seen before. Anne would surely have liked dancing as much as he did; as children they had always liked the same games, rough games that Margot and Stephan didn't join, since they felt too big for such child's play. "Do you remember the set of cards I drew for Anne that time?" he asked.

Leni smiled. "Yes, of course. It was in Sils-Maria. She was very happy with them and kept showing them to everyone."

They were playing cards with pictures of the members of the Elias and Frank families. Next to Anne's picture, Buddy had written, "Anne the rascal." "She laughed at that," Buddy said now. "She laughed loud, she clapped her hands and hopped all around me." That is how she would always remain in his memory: a slightly gawky, sprightly, imaginative child whose admiration he enjoyed. Would she still have looked up to him? He would never know. Grief at his loss tightened his throat. He handed Leni the letter without a word, for her to read out loud, and silently left the room. Leni heard him go upstairs and then heard the sound of his door shutting. She knew that now he would lie in bed and stare up at the ceiling until his eyes hurt.

"Read it," Alice said.

Stephan needed an operation after all. Leni stayed at the hospital until the doctor told her that it had gone well, and returned

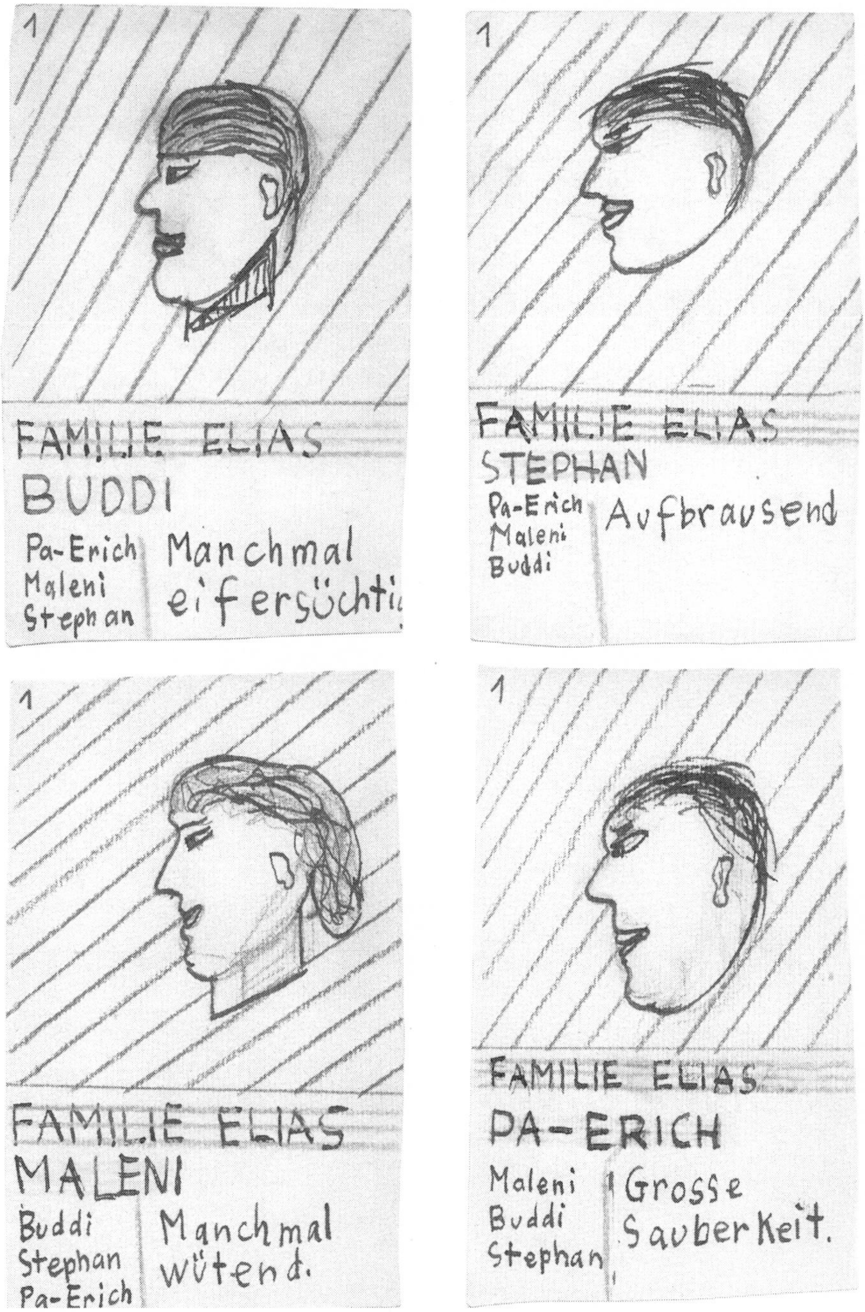

Buddy's sets of cards for the two families

A. Elias Family

Buddi: Jealous sometimes
Maleni: Very angry sometimes
Stephan: Short-tempered
Pa-Erich: Great cleanliness

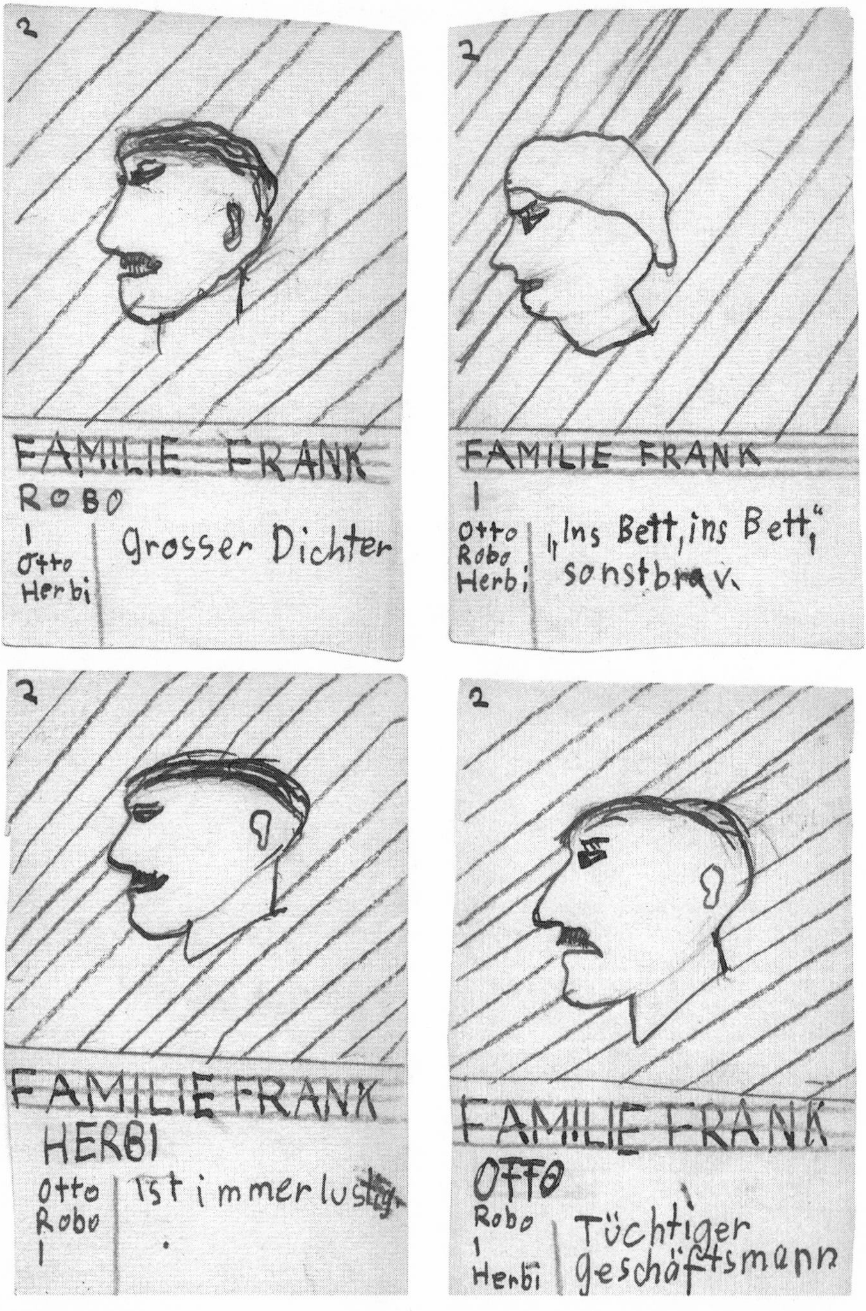

B. Frank Family

Robo: Great poet

Herbi: Is always in a good mood

I. "Go to bed, go to bed," otherwise great

Otto: Hardworking businessman

C. Otto Frank Family

Edith: The good mother
Otto: Good head of the family
Anne: The rascal
Margot: Doesn’t let you kiss her

home only after she saw her boy in person. The next day, Alice showed her the letter she was planning to send to Otto. Stephan's condition seemed hopeful, she had written. There were still "ups & downs," she wrote in English, but things were improving. It was just a month earlier that the doctors had given the family little hope for him. Then she turned to Anne's diary. Otto had apparently sent them a few excerpts.

I can't tell you how much the lines from Annelein's diary mean to me & to everyone here. They are so darling & so incredibly insightful, I read them constantly & they put me right into the thoughts and feelings of that sweet, warmhearted child. I have the little picture with Grandma Holländer too, up til now I was too sad to look at it, maybe that wasn't right but all the same I just couldn't. How terrible that we didn't find any more of Margot's writing, but maybe she didn't have the same gift of expressing herself & kept her feelings more to herself. We'll have so much to talk about about the children, Edith was a quiet type, but so infinitely good & considerate. There are pages and pages of things to write but I don't want to, it gets me so worked up & I <u>have</u> to keep a hold of myself. I sent a telegram to Robert yesterday with the good news, I wrote him a few days ago. I also want to write Herbie for his birthday, you know his two last birthdays were spent here with us, we miss him very much. But he is working now and that counts for a lot. Leni worked very hard the employer was very satisfied and tomorrow morning she is off again, to Zurich & she hopes to be able to make some money there too . . .
Bernd has a lot planned but everything is still up in the air & he is still hoping.

Stephan recovered slowly, and the bodily injury would stay with him for the rest of his life. His days playing his beloved ice hockey were over. For a young man so enthusiastic about sports it was of course a hard blow, but Leni didn't care as much about the sports, she was just glad that he had survived the sepsis. "It's thanks to this new medicine, thanks to penicillin"—that's what the doctors emphasized over and over again.

Leni traveled to Zurich four or five times a week. It wasn't easy for her, though she was happy to have these new assignments. Even in Switzerland the first few years after the war were hard, you had to scramble for every penny, nothing was given to you without a lot of hard work, and she was responsible for a lot of people. Erich earned hardly anything, Stephan was sick, and Buddy hadn't found an engagement yet; then there were the two old women, who brought in no income at all, and Imperia the housekeeper. A letter Leni wrote to Otto shows how hard it was for her at times: "I never complained, about anything at all, it's only the cold that I really don't like. My business started doing better in the last few months & I used to have a business, now it has me. But I just keep going."

And so she did, as she had all year. Erich's pains grew worse; he was suffering badly with arthritis and spent several weeks at the spa at Baden, near Zurich, taking mineral baths. He wrote a long letter from Baden to Otto:

My dear Ottel, I am always wanting to write to you, since my thoughts are with you & of you every hour. The nameless misfortune blankets everything else and I suffer deeply along with you. Edith and the children, I have their suffering before my eyes always. Everything else seems so meaningless to me & I am almost ashamed to tell you that I've been at a spa in Baden near Zurich for two days, and am supposed to take sulfur baths for three long weeks. I don't know if I will have the patience for it, my minor pains seem too insignificant for this endless fussing.

He told Otto about his "arthritis or arthrosis" and two injured vertebrae, then discussed business matters at length and in great detail: Unipektin, Opekta, the company organization. He again mentioned Goldstein, who was trying to organize something similar in the Netherlands. It is a very long letter, a bit scattered, full of plans and ideas and descriptions of various products, preservatives, sweeteners, and so forth. It almost seems as though Erich was trying to forcibly, even violently, drag Otto's thoughts onto another track. Or maybe he was just bored by his forced stay at the health resort.

While Erich was sick, the burden on Leni was even greater. She noticed that she had a quicker temper and wasn't sleeping well at night. She was also crashing her bicycle rather often, luckily without seriously hurting herself. Some days, when it was too cold to ride her bicycle, she had to take public transportation to get to the hospital, and her store, and her clients. And of course she wanted to see Erich once a week. Sometimes she had the feeling that she was in over her head, drowning under the house, all the people, the business, which of course was even busier now that it was approaching Christmas. And on top of it all, Imperia had fallen ill. Luckily, Grandma Ida was able to help out, as she usually did on Imperia's days off too, but of course it wasn't the same. And then the news from Amsterdam was not exactly encouraging. Leni was worried about her brother.

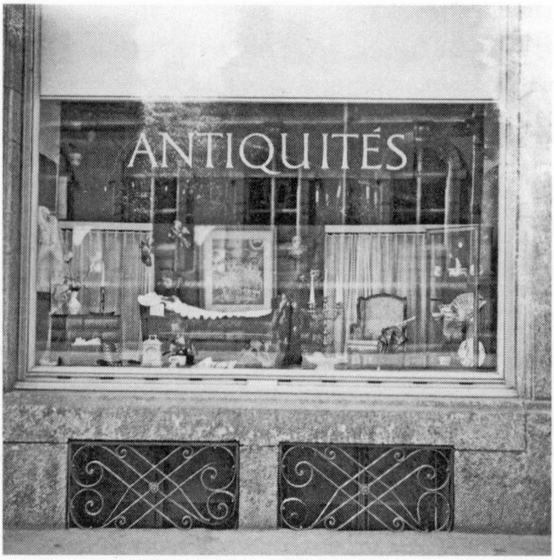

Leni Elias's antiques store in Basel, Spalenvorstadt 3

Otto Frank was apparently working extremely hard to try to get his business going again, but without much success. Fortunately, he had friends—Nathan Straus Jr. had sent him money from America, Otto wrote. Along with the economic problems, he continued to have problems with the authorities too.

But all that was supplanted by his daughter's diary, which seemed to be taking up more and more of his life. He talked about it with friends and acquaintances. For example, he wrote to Basel that he had seen the Cahns on Friday,

and I started to read to them from Anne's diary, to get Werner's opinion about publication. He has worked at Querido Press for years, you know, where Jetty worked too. To be continued next Friday, but already he says: Absolutely publish it, it is a great work! You can't even imagine everything in it, I can't translate it at the moment unfortunately, but it'll happen and it will also come out in German and in English. It's about everything that happens in a group of people while they are in hiding, all the fears and conflicts, all the arguments, the food, politics, the Jewish question, the weather, moods, education, birthdays, memories: everything. Miss Schütz, whom I visited yesterday, wants to translate a fairy tale for you—"Blurry the World Explorer"—a bear story . . . Monday I see Hanneli again, who is due to leave on an airplane with the two Neuberg girls on December 5. I hope that everything will go smoothly now. She is still bedridden and I am constantly comparing her to Anne, who was so much farther along in everything.

Leni could easily picture that, since she also always compared young girls she saw on the street to Margot and Anne, and sometimes, when a thin dark-haired girl was walking in front of her, she would walk faster to pass her and look at her from the front in the sudden, irrational hope that maybe, just maybe, everything was not what they thought. How must it be for her brother! Hanneli Goslar must be sixteen now, like Anne, if Anne were still alive. Leni was not sure if she could have summoned up the inner strength and selflessness to take care of Hanneli if she were in Otto's place. As it happened, Hanneli Goslar's flight to Switzerland went smoothly; she stayed in a sanatorium there for three months, then in a children's home until she immigrated to Palestine in 1947.

Otto kept writing about his own desire to come to Basel: "If only I was there myself! Everything is going so slowly here, it never ends. I saw a lawyer to poss. try to apply for naturalization, but they advised against it, since measures to make things easier were definitely in preparation and expected soon." On December 12 he wrote: "I was at The Hague yesterday, to work on my passport situation some more, for now everything seems to be on track but you can't rush the gentlemen so it is more than questionable whether I will be able to be there by the 20th. Aside from the fact that I also have a lot of business matters to attend to & my stay would be limited. So we have to reckon with the possibility that I won't be there until January. Who knows if it isn't better that way, the anticipation will last longer! as they say."

Otto Frank was still officially stateless. He had applied for Dutch citizenship, but the process turned out to be more difficult than he had realized, and it would take four more years before he became a Dutchman.

"Meanwhile, Mr. Kleiman is very sick again," his letter went on,

with another stomach hemorrhage. How he would have liked to meet you and to come with me, except for the business matters. Since he desperately needs orange juice and you can't get anything like that here, I decided to call Robert! So we talked the night before last, the connection was excellent and we were both very glad to hear each other's voices. Lotti too of course. So I hope to be getting something from them soon . . . I've given Edith's muff to Miss Schütz! She is suffering greatly from the cold and I think that Edith would have wanted me to give it to her too. Miss Schütz will probably be sending you a translation of Anne's fairy tale "Eva's Dream" that she did for me for my birthday this year. I also visited Margot's best friend, Jetteke Frieda, in The Hague. She is almost totally alone here, her father was gassed, brother shot by a firing squad, mother (whom she didn't get along with) is with another man in Switzerland. Tomorrow I'm going to Laren and taking Abe and Isa [Cauvern] Anne's diary to transcribe and correct. I'm done with it for now and I want to have a clean copy to show to publishers. Enclosed is a translation of a letter about Grandma. She also wrote about you, though not much—about your velvety soft crow's-feet that she almost thought she was getting herself. She also wrote that she got your 1942 letter exactly on her birthday. I can't get all of this out of my mind—and don't want to either . . . I have to force myself to do things often enough, an unscalable mountain of correspondence has piled up and I can't bring myself to write, plus it's cold in my room and I can almost never write unless I'm alone. We don't have any heat and there's a stove in only one room.

So Otto, encouraged by friends, was planning to have his daughter's diary published. One of these friends was Dr. Kurt Baschwitz, lecturer and later professor of journalism in Amsterdam. He would later characterize Anne's diary as "the most heart-wrenching document of the era that I know of, and an astonishing literary masterpiece as well. It shows the private experiences of a girl growing into maturity, her impressions stuck in close quarters with her father (whom she tenderly loves), mother (with whom she is often in conflict), sister (whom she discovers as a friend), and the other family in hiding, including the son, whom she starts to fall in love with. It must be published, in my opinion."*

Leni wanted so badly for Otto to come for Alice's eightieth birthday, but it seemed less and less likely with each letter. And Alice was also in no mood to celebrate, as she insisted again and again and even expressed to Otto. He wrote on December 15 to his "Dearest Mom":

Today I received your postcard dated the 11th and I completely understand that current conditions combined with Stephan's long illness have dampened your thoughts of celebrating your 80th. We all imagined everything so differently, didn't we! Still, you mustn't think that my mood here is constantly depressed, I don't let myself feel that way and

**Diary of Anne Frank* (New York: Doubleday, 1989).

also have so much to do most of the time that there's no question of sitting and brooding. How I wish I was with you and the family in these days, but yes, there is so much one needs to do and so little one can do, we have to be content with the thought that I will be able to come soon, it won't be long . . . An 80th birthday is certainly a time to look back and it's important to think about the good things, not grieve about the past. All things considered you must be satisfied with the life you've led, everyone has ups and downs, but when you look back at your life as a wife and mother and weigh everything in the balance, you can't be dissatisfied with it. As sad as much of it was, in the end we were together for a long time, and even though your children are scattered across various countries, in spirit they have all remained "the children."

Just like we had "Grandma" here, Lenerich and the boys have their "IIIiii." That is a lot, and you can still do a lot, and be a help and an inspiration to them. ***Who else can say as much? . . .*** *It's especially bad luck that our good Stephan has had to suffer for so long, but hopefully his recovery has begun at last and one has to keep one's courage and patience. This too shall pass. Just be brave and above all stay healthy. If everything keeps getting better, then our reunion will take place under a better star as well. I can't write any birthday wishes—it all sounds too banal compared to the remembrances we all have predominating inside us. There were so many times that we talked with the children about how we would all try to spend their 20th birthdays with you. Enclosed is a little picture of Anne that Kugler copied, eventually I hope to be able to have some of Margot and Edith made too . . . With warmest wishes, constantly thinking of all of you, and with an especially loving birthday kiss to you.*

Baroque dresser, still in the Herbstgasse house today

As 1945 drew to a close, Otto did in fact manage to come; he was in Basel for New Year's. For the first time, Alice saw her son again, Leni her brother, Erich his brother-in-law, and Stephan and Buddy their uncle. And Grandma Ida the man who symbolized more than anyone else the hope that her son Paul might also still be alive: if Otto had survived everything they heard about on the radio and read about in the papers, then Paul might also have survived it, he was younger too.

It must have been very moving, and heart wrenching, when Otto finally stood in front of the door with Erich, who had fetched him from the train station. It would surely have been on everyone's mind that he never stood there alone in the years before the war—there were always one or two children with him, shouting for their grandma. Leni flung open the door and threw herself into her brother's arms. Then she led him in to his mother. Buddy stood and watched. Otto seemed taller and thinner than he remembered, and much, much older. They hugged him one after the other, and everyone cried.

Finally, they sat down around the dining room table, which Leni had set especially festively. Otto hesitantly stroked the lace tablecloth with his finger, picked up a knife and looked at the initials EJC on it, then a fork, and put it back on the knife rest. No less slowly and hesitantly, he picked up the napkin and looked at the napkin ring. Leni, watching her brother, fought to hold back the tears—she knew what must have been running through his head. Erich opened the bottle of wine, a good red that he had kept for a special occasion. They drank from the engraved glasses that they had used back in Frankfurt, and used napkins that Cornelia, many years before, as a young woman, had embroidered her monogram on. They sat surrounded by the mahogany Louis XVI sideboard with the marble surface and the Biedermeier china cabinet that contained Cornelia's glasses, a tea service with an Asian floral motif, a French Biedermeier tea set that had also belonged to Cornelia, crystal bowls and glasses, and the walnut baroque dresser with three drawers, turned legs, and exotic wood inlays—furniture that they knew from Mertonstrasse—and looking down on them from the walls were Cornelia as a child, Cornelia as a widow, Elkan Juda Cahn and his wife Betty, Alice as a child. Through the open door to the salon, they could see more pictures: Leni as a child, and a photograph of Erich's sister, Johanna. They sat there, looked at each other, and were so overwhelmed by conflicting feelings—their joy at seeing one another again and their grief at their loss—that at first no one could speak.

Otto, always the most practical, pulled himself together first. He asked about Leni's business, about Erich's troubles, about Stephan's health and Buddy's prospects, and gradually everyone relaxed and started to talk.

Only they suddenly fall quiet sometimes, we can easily imagine, and cast helpless looks at one another. Then maybe it's Leni who holds her face in her hands and says in a strangled voice: "Those criminals, those criminals . . ." or "If only you had gone to America in time."

"Who could have known?" Otto said softly. "Who could have imagined something like this?"

Then Erich would have said that they *should* have known; the Nazis had never made a secret of their hatred for the Jews. "By the Nuremberg Laws, at the very latest, we had to have known. The road to Auschwitz led straight through Nuremberg. And even earlier, Hitler laid it out clearly and unambiguously in *Mein Kampf*. A client showed me the page, even before the war, and I still know it by heart today. He said it loud and clear: 'The Germans are the master race and are destined to rule over, enslave, or exterminate the lesser races.' " Erich fell silent, then added: "It was clear that he meant the Jews, of course it was clear. Still, no one could imagine that a people who had brought forth a Goethe and a Schiller could be capable of such barbarity."

Otto also went to the city hospital, of course, to visit Stephan, who seemed to be on the road to recovery. A deceptive recovery, since he had not yet overcome his sepsis; he was still to undergo a staph infection. They could not know that it would take months before he was well enough to leave the hospital. On New Year's Eve they drank punch (which was actually mostly tea) and wished each other a healthy new year. Leni noticed that the others also avoided words like "happy" and "merry," since the year just past, which had brought them so much sorrow, was still all too present. They could not imagine having a "happy" year ever again.

Otto had brought several excerpts from Anne's diary with him, and he read them to the family on the long winter evenings. Buddy remembers that Alice broke out in tears again and again, and stammered: "That we had to lose her so early . . ." She also regretted that nothing remained of Margot's diary. "She was such a good child, such a serious child." Then Otto said what he would always say when his older daughter came up in conversation: "Margot was an angel."

Baroque furniture, Herbstgasse, Basel

Buddy also remembers the constant mention of people's names, often people he didn't know, followed like clockwork by the question of whether this one or that one had been taken, or had disappeared. Arrested. Deported. Murdered.

Once, when Buddy was describing an ice-skating routine that he and his partner, Baddy, had memorized, Otto started to cry and told him, in tears, about Anne's dream to someday skate with her cousin. "She talked about you so much, Buddy. She was a child, she worshipped you."

"She would have been sixteen now," Leni said. It was what they would say again and again in the years to follow, on every birthday or holiday: "Anne would have been seventeen, eighteen, nineteen . . ." or "Margot would have been twenty, twenty-one . . ." or "Edith would have been forty-seven, forty-eight . . ." No birthday would pass without their falling into despair, and especially Alice would start crying every time. But at least they had the certainty of Anne's and Margot's deaths—Grandma Ida would only be able to say "It's Paul's birthday today. Is he still alive? Where could he be? Does he have enough to eat?"

One time, Otto told them about a visit to the police: they wanted to find out who had betrayed the families in the Secret Annex. They showed him, Kugler, and Kleiman photographs of different people and asked whether any of them had been there when they were arrested, because they might be able to learn from them who had turned the families in. "And we recognized two men," Otto said, "two men who were in prison. You can imagine how I felt. Maybe we would find out who the betrayers were, the murderers who had the deaths of Edith and my children on their conscience. But a lot of the time these guys were nobodies, they only acted on the orders of their superiors who always kept their hands clean."

Then, soon, he would talk about Anne's diary again, and that he wanted to ask his old friend Cauvern, who worked at a radio station, to edit the diary for grammatical mistakes and take out any Germanisms. For example, Anne wrote in one place that Peter had got a lighter for his birthday even though he didn't smoke, and she had used the word *vuurtuig* as an overliteral translation of the German word *Feuerzeug*, even though the real Dutch word would be *aansteker*. Obviously, that would have to be fixed. After Cauvern had checked everything, Otto would try to find a publisher for the diary.

Otto stayed in Basel for around three weeks—weeks that were full of both joy and grief, of memories spoken and unspoken. Weeks of sudden hugs and sudden tears. But the weeks passed.

When he left, early one morning, they didn't know what they should say. Alice stayed in bed, having made it known that she could not bear to see Otto walk out the door and not know when she would see him again, or even if she would ever see him again, you could never be sure at her age. Otto hugged and kissed Erich and Buddy, then hugged Grandma Ida, who had come downstairs to say goodbye. He wished her good health and said that he hoped she would hear about Paul soon, because this uncertainty was worse than anything, he knew that from his own painful experience.

Grandma Ida would have to live with this uncertainty, however—it was only long after her death, even after Erich's death, that Buddy received official confirmation that his uncle Paul had been murdered at Auschwitz. Grandma Ida never knew for sure. At some point she would stop waiting at the door every morning for the mailman, and would give the two sweaters she had knit for Paul to her other son, Erich, who could use them. In the course of time she would utter Paul's name less and less often, and she would never knit him any more sweaters.

PART THREE

Buddy Elias, Anne's Cousin

(b. 1925)

Buddy Elias, circa 1928

10.

Starting Out

Buddy, not yet twenty-one years old, is sitting in his little room in Bern. Actually, it's more like a crawl space up under the roof, but that doesn't matter, he has an engagement—that's the only thing that counts now, after the tiny role in *The Merchant of Venice* at the Basel City Theater. An actor can't live on that no matter how young he is. It's not exactly what he expected, or rather dreamed of, but as an aspiring actor you have to take what you can get, and in any case now he is out on his own. Financially, everything's fine: he makes his own breakfast in his room—bread, coffee on a little hot plate—and eats lunch and dinner in the restaurant downstairs. He pays seven francs for room and board together; that's amazingly cheap, he was very lucky. And maybe he'll get more roles soon, if another member of the acting company leaves.

The room is cozy, even though it is small and rather more sparsely furnished than he's used to at home. But so what, he'll be able to work well here—he has brought home parts to memorize, and has his English textbook and a grammar book. He has more time here, more peace and quiet. At home there is always something going on. It's hard to go back to his room and work when someone is visiting somewhere in the house, or when there's tea on the table, or when Leni comes back from the store or Alice has a letter to read that came from Otto or that she wrote to him. He is in a very different situation from Stephan, his poor brother. Buddy feels so bad for him: he has another abscess now, his pain is just not getting better. Buddy thinks back to when he and Otto visited Stephan in the hospital, and again he has the uncomfortable feeling that he can't quite get rid of, that he might not have acted toward Otto the right way. He goes over to the window and looks out. Everything here is a bit cramped, but the old city center in Bern is beautiful, that makes up for a lot. The sun has come out, and he wonders if he should take a walk along the Aare; that would be good for his health and would help calm the restless mood that sometimes comes over him.

But then he sits down at the table after all, the table that takes up so much space in the room that Buddy has to cram himself into his bed at night. A pile of scripts sits waiting for him on the far corner of the table; there are his English books in the other corner, plus notebooks, pencils, pencil sharpeners, erasers, a pen, and a folder with stationery that Alice gave him, probably so that he would not forget to write to his family. There was no need—he wouldn't forget in any case. He flips open the folder and picks up the pen.

"Elias Frank," he writes as the sender's name. That is what he decided on as his stage name: it sounds more mature than "Buddy Elias," more serious somehow, and in any case the name Buddy is already reserved for his ice show with Otti, "Buddy and Baddy." The address sounds good too: "Cactus Cabaret, Corso Theater."

"My dear Ottel," he writes, and hesitates, puts down the pen, chews his lower lip. But then he picks up the pen again after all:

We didn't have enough time while you were here in Basel, I'm afraid, to talk about everything we have in our hearts . . . Maybe you think that I'm not very interested in your life before and during the catastrophe, or in Anne and Margot, because I didn't talk much about them. But you'd be very wrong. It was only that I didn't want to make you talk about it too much, I know how painful it must be for you. It was upsetting every time. I didn't want to ask anything. Now I suddenly feel the prick of conscience and I'm afraid that you'll think I don't care. You must know how eager I am to hear you tell me about everything—your life in the Secret Annex, your arrest, Auschwitz, etc.—but to be honest, I was afraid to tear open old wounds. I hope that I'm wrong and that you don't think I don't care about everything.

I'm here in Bern now and have a charming little room where I can work brilliantly, undisturbed . . . My one great worry is Stephan. He has to be terribly, terribly patient, and has to suffer a lot of pain. I hope the pectin business in Holland is coming back to life and that you can find good work. It would make me very happy if you would write to me. I'll stop here for today. All the best and see you soon.

He reads the letter through again before folding it, putting it in an envelope, writing out Otto's address, standing up, and pulling on his coat. He is so relieved to have finally written this letter that he is taking it straight to the post office.

Buddy Elias as a young man

Buddy liked appearing onstage in Bern, even though the theaters were only half the size of the ones in Basel and at first he had a lot of trouble getting used to it. He would have been glad to stay in Bern, but it didn't work out, his engagement was not extended. Instead, he received an offer from a small theater in Winterthur, with performances in the three summer months of 1946.

In May, when he visited Stephan in the city hospital and told him the news, Stephan laughed and said:

"In *spring*, Buddy from *Herbst*gasse [Autumn Lane] was hired for the *summer* theater in *Winter*thur!" Buddy laughed too, he was so happy to see his brother in a good mood at last. Stephan was usually more serious and depressed every time Buddy visited. Buddy loved his brother, and if he had ever felt jealous of the "handsome boy with his dark locks," that time was past. Stephan was the firstborn, and born on his grandmother's birthday on top of that, and Buddy had come to terms with the division of family roles. In this respect as well, he felt that he had something in common with Anne: both were second children, neither was an easy baby. Leni said often enough that Buddy was a "screecher," and Anne was certainly his equal. In addition, Buddy had suffered from eczema as a child, which probably helped to make him a more difficult child than Stephan had been.

In any case, the brothers had a good relationship, and Buddy visited Stephan as often as he could during Stephan's long stay in the hospital. They now decided to send Otto a letter together. It seemed to be very difficult for Otto to be in Amsterdam, so far away from his family. Both brothers had read the letter he had sent to Alice at the end of January. The return trip had gone well, he wrote, and Bep had fetched him from the station. He was flooded with questions, and there had been so much to discuss that he had not even read the mail that had come while he was away. The next few sentences were deeply moving to Buddy, and probably to Alice too: "My first thought this morning was: 'I wonder how Mom slept?' And I constantly have Stephan in my mind—I feel for him with all my heart. As for what I should try to do myself, I have no idea."

This time, unlike last year, Buddy could clearly picture Otto while reading the letter: the corners of Otto's mouth curving slightly downward, the wrinkles, the unfathomable sadness in his eyes . . . He always felt a stab of pain when he read Otto's letters now. And he could equally well understand Otto's homesick thoughts first thing in the morning: Buddy had those too. He thought with special intensity about home in the mornings when he woke up, and not only because he had to make his own breakfast now, without an Imperia to make it for him—he was seized with a kind of longing for home in the mornings. But the new demands placed upon him forced all such thoughts aside soon enough.

Buddy propped another pillow under Stephan's back and handed him a pen and a writing pad. He observed with pity how difficult it was for his brother to write in his cast.

My Dear Ottel, One of the first letters I can write by myself is for you! Do you know how often I think of you and your friends. Papa has told me so much about you all and his impressions of Holland were only positive. How I would have liked to go! Buddy is visiting me today. It's good that he has something lined up for the next few months. As for me, I find myself once again in a cast from top to bottom. Hopefully, I'll be able to stand up after it's taken off. Otherwise there's nothing new to report. I often think how nice it would be to see all three of you brothers reunited here with us. Maybe my wish will soon come true after all. Enough for today, dear Otto, and heaps of greetings to you and the Gieses, with a special extra kiss for you. Your old Stephan.

Stephan held out the pad to Buddy, exhausted from the effort. There was not much room left on the page so Buddy wrote only: "Dear Ottel, I'm in Basel for just 6 hours and I don't want to miss the chance to send you my warmest greetings. I've been given an engagement for the Winterthur summer theater and I'm really looking forward to that. 1,000 kisses Yours, Buddy."

"I. is always talking about Anne's diary," Stephan said. "Otto sent her the opening pages, in Miss Schütz's translation of course, and she's in a state. She's said a hundred times already how every word and every sentence makes her see Anne right there in front of her. But she thinks that only people who have an understanding of what happened should read it, she's afraid it might not mean anything to anyone else. Have you read it yet?"

Buddy shook his head. "No, just the bits I. has read to us," he said. Alice had asked him to read everything that Otto had sent, but he was too shy to, for reasons he couldn't fully explain himself. Of course he would read what his little cousin had written at some point, someday . . .

Then he said goodbye to his brother, put the letter in his pocket, and promised to mail it that day, at the station, before getting on the train to Winterthur.

Buddy's new job was absorbing. He was engaged for 250 francs a month, and in the second year he would get 280 francs, maybe even 310; today, after more than sixty years, he no longer remembers. But he does remember that the demands placed upon him were great: almost every week there was another premiere. On Mondays there was the blocking and first rehearsal, then rehearsals on Tuesday, Wednesday, Thursday, and Friday and the premiere on Saturday. When the weather was nice, Buddy went to the swimming pool for fifteen cents to learn his lines. He had lunch at the Peacock Restaurant, which cost only a couple of francs, and had bread and cheese for dinner. He paid eighty francs a month for his room.

Still, it was a happy time, he says today—he studied, studied, studied, and learned a lot. Some good actors gave guest performances, for example, Leopold Biberti, who starred in a production of George Bernard Shaw's *Arms and the Man,* where Buddy played Nicola. "Biberti was a brilliant actor. He was born in Berlin, but he always felt Swiss, and he had to flee Germany because he had spoken out loud and clear against the Nazis. He was quite a character, a man with an amazingly deep voice. Women were crazy about him, he always had to fight them off."

The economic situation was still very difficult in 1946, and you had to do what you could to make ends meet. Alice wrote to Otto in November and said that they didn't have enough wood and coal for the winter. Leni's store was struggling. Luckily,

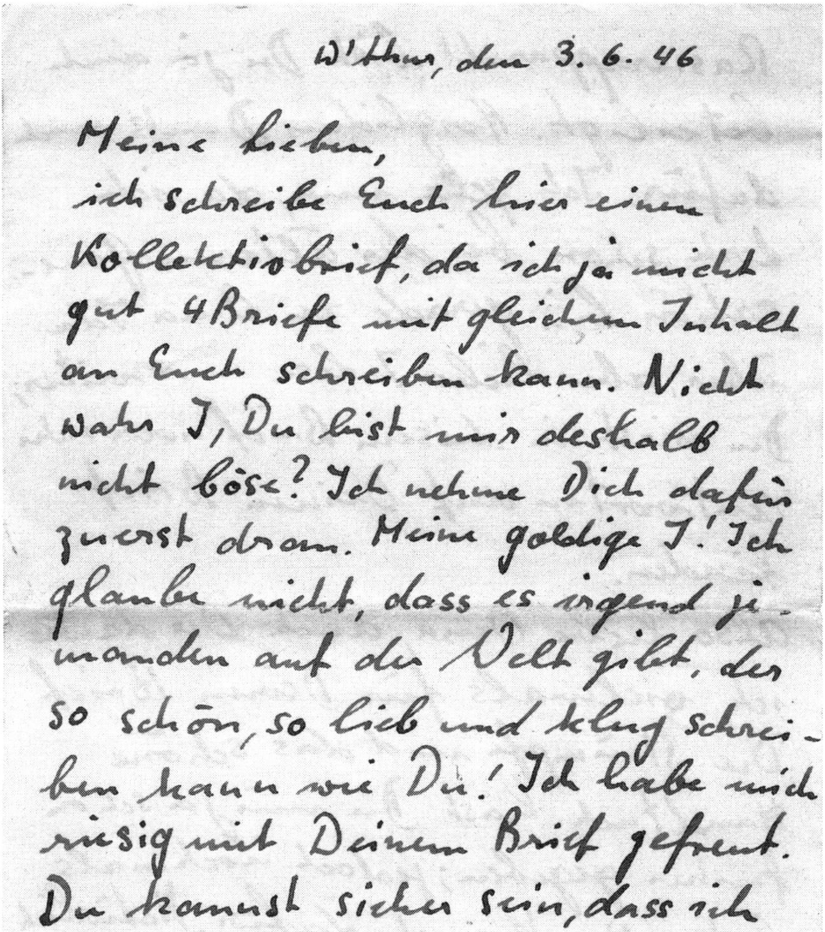

W'thur, den 3. 6. 46

Meine Lieben,
ich schreibe Euch hier einen Kollektivbrief, da ich ja nicht gut 4 Briefe mit gleichem Inhalt an Euch schreiben kann. Nicht wahr J, Du bist mir deshalb nicht böse? Ich nehme Dich dafür zuerst dran. Meine goldige J! Ich glaube nicht, dass es irgend jemanden auf der Welt gibt, der so schön, so lieb und klug schreiben kann wie Du! Ich habe mich riesig mit Deinem Brief gefreut. Du kannst sicher sein, dass ich alles daransetzen werde, Euch nicht zu enttäuschen. Mein Beruf ist mir heilig und ich fasse ihn mit dem nötigen Ernst an. Am

Letter home from Buddy Elias, June 3, 1946

Stephan was getting better, slowly, but he still had the constant itching under the cast to deal with. In Amsterdam, a city that had suffered so terribly under the German occupation, the situation was even worse than in Basel: Otto Frank's business just could not get going, and in fact it would not be until the early 1950s that it would make a regular profit. Until then, it was a time of scarcity and need. There were still shortages of food, of clothing, of everything, but especially of fuel. The electricity and gas came on only certain hours of the day. Still, everyone was very relieved that the terrible war was over—things could only get better.

Buddy would not have thought about it too much: he concentrated on his work, his acting. On June 2, 1946, his twenty-first birthday (and the first one he didn't celebrate with his family), Buddy received letters and a package from Basel. The very next day, he sat down and wrote a "collective letter" back, since, he said, he couldn't very well write four letters with the same contents:

Isn't that true, I., you're not mad at me for that? To make it up to you, I'll write to you first. Sweet I.! I don't think there is anyone in the world who can write such beautiful, loving, and clever things as you can! I was tremendously happy to read your letter. You can be certain that I will do everything I can not to disappoint you. My career is sacred to me and I am approaching it with all the necessary seriousness. The electric shaver is partly from you too, so thank you very much for that. Now I will pass to Grandma Ida, to stay with the older generation for now, but please read on, I., you will find answers to your other questions farther down in this letter.

So, dear Grandma Ida! thank you very much as well for your letter. You already gave me the socks and the beautiful towel before, but thank you for them again. I was definitely sorry not to be able to see you all on my birthday, but unfortunately there was no way around it.

And now to you, dear Leni and Papa! (saving the best for last) Thank you both very much for all the wonderful surprises. All the beau-

tiful ties were chosen brilliantly. The visiting cards are perfect, the handkerchiefs charming, and the socks lovely. Needless to say, your letter was wonderful and nice as always. I haven't received the stationery yet, I'm sure it will come soon. Thank you very much in advance. Please forward the enclosed letter to little Marie! And thank you both too for the shaver. I have never felt what family really is more than now. I feel how much I belong with you, Leni and Papa, and especially with you, my dear Steph, like never before. For the first time, I can see what our family really is! For my whole life, together with you and having the inconceivably great good fortune never to be apart, I took your presence for granted. Now that for the first time I am away from home for an extended period, no longer fed and sheltered by my beloved parents, I feel for the first time what it really means to be homesick! But I don't want to get too sentimental—and there's no real reason to, since everything is excellent here and countless people would be happy to have it half as good as me. And now [in English], "last but not least," to you, my dear Steph! How happy I was to get the first of your letters in your own handwriting again! Thanks very much to you too for your contribution to the shaver. I am tremendously happy to hear that you will be out of your cocoon soon, and I would so love to be there when you get up for the first time! My dear Steph! There was a time when I was extremely worried about your illness and very pessimistic (who wasn't?). But I have to tell you that I'm exactly the opposite now. I'm sure that if (to assume the worst!!) you still have any aftereffects (which I don't think you will!), that it won't make a difference in your future life. I know that you will be just as successful at whatever you do as you would have been if you didn't have these health problems. I am certain, dear Steph, that with all your intelligence, your superb noble character, and your education, you will find your way! Needless to say, you can always count on my moral + whenever possible material support. And now I will tell you a little about myself. The last few weeks were very stressful. I left for Winterthur early every morning and came back home to Läppli *[a dialect play] in Zurich only at night . . . Rehearsals for* Arms and the Man *will probably start at the end of the week. Bibi is playing the lead role, I don't know what part I will have yet. I have Pentecost off . . . and will be in Basel Monday morning, until Tuesday 7:13 a.m. Hopefully nothing will come up in the meantime! I really look forward to seeing you. I hope Bit will be there until then. Hugs and kisses to everyone, Yours, Buddy.*

"Bit" was the family nickname for Herbert—the "problem child" who had fallen upon further difficulties in Paris. He had lost his job again, and once again Alice was receiving letters from friends and acquaintances who were worried about his situation. It was the usual story: he had never held down a job for long. Alice was upset and Leni muttered curses that it was high time her brother finally grew up. Erich wrote to Otto that Herbert was lacking direction above all, lacking a goal in life and work to do, and the worst thing was that it constantly kept Alice on tenterhooks when the poor woman needed all her strength for herself. Even so, Erich and Leni did everything they could to bring Herbert to Switzerland, and in the end they succeeded, although not for another few years.

Buddy had also received a loving and friendly letter for his birthday from Otto, of course, and before he went to bed, he also dug up the birthday letter that Anne had written to him in 1942, a few weeks before she and her family went into hiding in the house on Prinsengracht. He had kept it at the time—in the ordinary way one does, without really thinking about it, maybe it was even by accident—but ever since he found it again while going through his things in preparing to move out of the Herbstgasse house, he had preserved it as a relic, and brought it with him. Four years earlier it was an ordinary birthday letter; now it was something he treasured. For many years he would continue to read it on his birthday, just for himself, without anyone else, even though he soon knew it practically by heart. He always tried to read the Dutch text, not to understand the words, but so as not to forget Anne's handwriting. He would always keep this letter as proof of her affection for him.

Dear Bernd, Many happy returns on your birthday (all birthday letters start like that) and many more to come. I hope you're all healthy there like we are here. We had five days off for Pentecost, that was great and I've been very busy. I don't get home before 10 at night, but usually a boy walks me home. How is it going with the girl you sent us a photo of? Do write and tell me, I'm very interested in things like that. Margot has a boyfriend too but he is even younger than mine. This epistle didn't turn out very long but I also don't have any more time to write, since I'm going with Father to a film showing at some friends'.

Best wishes to everyone. Write me back. Anne

It was a letter from another world, another era, although only four years separated then and now. Anne had written him shortly before her own thirteenth birthday, and he, Buddy, was turning seventeen. "Write me back," she wrote. And now he never could. He folded the letter and placed it back in the little folder where he kept all his important papers.

After the Winterthur summer theater, Buddy performed in Wilfried Seyferth's Zurich theater, in William Saroyan's *Time of Your Life*. Seyferth was looking for a young actor who could also dance. Later, Buddy accepted from Kurt Götz the role of the oldest son in his play *The House in Montevideo*. Götz had just returned from America and was planning a tour through Switzerland; it was not a great role, but Buddy was happy to get it.

But it turned out that that would be his last tour. Totally unexpectedly, an offer came from his ice-skating partner, Otti Rehorek, who was working at the time as a graphic artist in England. Otti had met Tom Arnold, the producer of the biggest English ice show, and showed him photographs of "Buddy and Baddy." Tom Arnold, Rehorek wrote, had said: "I need comedians, you can start straightaway." Otti was enthusiastic, and it sounded exceedingly tempting to Buddy too—they would be able to see a bit of the world simply by doing, for a lot of money

Lieve Bernd,

Welgefeliciteerd met je verjaardag (zo begint een verjaardagsbrief altijd) en nog vele jaren. Hoplijk zijn jullie allemaal gezond. net als wij.

Wij hebben 5 dagen Pinkstervacantie gehad, het was erg fijn, en ik ben erg bezet met mijn dagen. 's Avonds kom ik niet voor 10 uur thuis, maar meestal wordt ik wel door een jongen thuisgebracht. Hoe gaat het met dat meisje? waarvan je die foto gestuurd hebt? Schrijf daar eens over, zulke dingen interesseren mij wel. Margot heeft ook een vriend maar hij is nog jonger dan de mijne.

Het epistel is niet erg lang uitgevallen maar ik heb ook geen tijd, daar ik met vader naar een filmvoorstelling bij kennissen ga. De groeten aan allemaal.

Schrijf eens aan mij terug

Anne

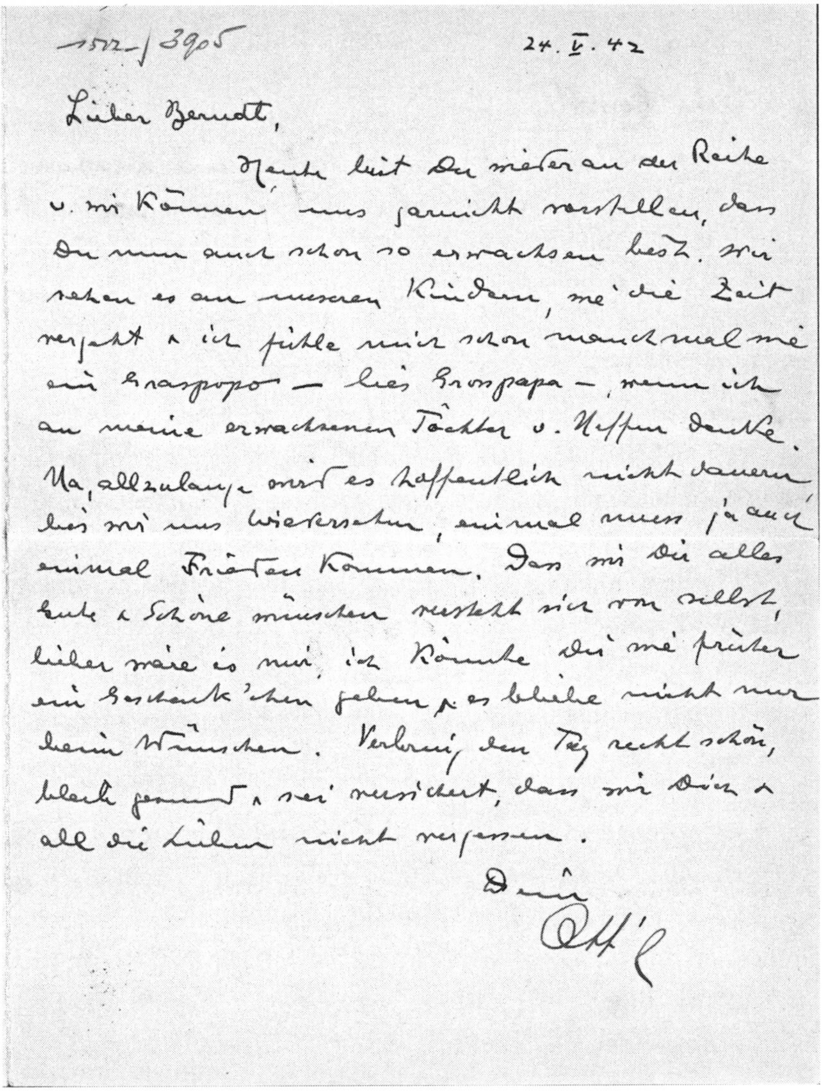

1512/3905 24.V.42

Lieber Berndt,

Heute bist Du wieder an der Reihe u. wir können uns garnicht vorstellen, dass Du nun auch schon so erwachsen bist. Wir sehen es an unseren Kindern, wie die Zeit vergeht u. ich fühle mich schon manchmal wie ein Graspopo – lies Grosspapa –, wenn ich an meine erwachsenen Töchter u. Neffen denke. Na, allzulange wird es hoffentlich nicht dauern bis wir uns wiedersehen, einmal muss ja auch einmal Frieden kommen. Dass wir Dir alles Gute u. Schöne wünschen versteht sich von selbst, lieber wäre es mir, ich könnte Dir wie früher ein Geschenk'chen geben, so es bliebe nicht nur beim Wünschen. Verbring den Tag recht schön, bleib gesund u. sei versichert, dass wir Dich u. all die Lieben nicht vergessen.

Dein

Ott'l

Birthday letter to Buddy from Anne and Otto, June 2, 1942

abroad, what they had been doing for not much money at all in Switzerland. It probably also contributed to his decision that his father was somewhat skeptical about Buddy's engagements in Bern and his small guest parts in the local dialect productions like *Läppli* in Zurich. "I simply can't get used to the idea that what you are doing is supposed to be art," he had said, and in truth Buddy had to agree. Small parts in light comedies, playing the fool in dialect plays—for Buddy, too, it was not exactly what he saw as the art of the theater.

At the same time, he liked making people laugh. He knew that he had a talent for comedy, and when he thought back to his auditions two years earlier, he still had to suppress a grin. Adolf Manz and Ellen Widmann, two good people, had started an acting school in Basel in addition to the conservatory. It was perfect timing for Buddy and he applied, choosing as his audition piece a speech by Faust . . . that he performed in Hessian dialect. "Ellen Widmann laughed till she cried," Buddy says with obvious pleasure even today, "but she didn't accept me, she said I was welcome to audition again, but not in Hessian. So I did, and then she accepted me. Those were two great years."

He hesitates when he says that, then adds: "While they were stuck in hiding in Amsterdam, and then when they were arrested, while they had to go through all of that, I went to acting school and had a great time." But Anne did get word of it; in her diary on June 30, 1944, it says: "We've heard from Basle that Bernd took the part of Innkeeper in *Minna von Bernhelm*. Artistic temperament Mummy says." Apparently, Erich, who sometimes had business correspondence with Kleiman, occasionally let something personal slip into his letters, hoping that Kleiman would be able to pass the information along to Otto, Edith, Margot, and Anne. It was never expressed openly, and Erich and Leni never actually knew anything about the Franks' going into hiding, Buddy is positive about that. But it seems to be some consolation to him that Anne did hear he had become an actor. Their "artistic temperaments" were obviously something that bound Anne and Buddy together.

He had always dreamed of becoming an actor, ever since he had first gone to plays with Alice, who took him and Stephan to all the children's theater performances: fairy tales like "Puss in Boots" and "Hansel and Gretel." Sometimes she brought her grandchildren along to the opera too. *The Bartered Bride* was the first opera that Buddy had ever seen, and it made a big impression on him—he remembers it to this day. Still, opera couldn't hold a candle to the theater. He loved being in the German equivalent of Punch-and-Judy shows, called Kasper Theater—it was with great delight that he slipped into the roles of Kasper, Seppl, and Grandma, but his favorite part was the Devil. He gave the Devil the bickering voice of one of his teachers whom he couldn't stand, and when he spoke in the trembling voice of Grandma, it always sounded like the old woman in the stationery store, with her wobbly head on a skinny neck. Buddy would have liked to put on a show for his family every day, but at some point they said no, once a week would be enough, twice at most. At least when his cousin Anne came to visit Basel, she could never get enough of his playacting. It was especially hilarious for her when the crocodile wanted to eat Grandma, and Kasper stepped in and beat the crocodile with his club while pouring out a flood of the most terrible, unbelievable curse words—words they were absolutely not allowed to say, and that they would never have dared to repeat if anyone else was there. Buddy was always given to comedy and exaggeration.

He was only fourteen when he and a friend memorized a few comedy numbers on ice—clown routines that they then performed in ice variety shows at the numerous Swiss resort towns. They didn't make much money at it, but they liked it. Buddy recalls that he didn't have to think for long when the offer came from England. He could do it for a year, he thought, with no idea that he would actually do it for more than fourteen years.

In November 1947, Buddy and his friend and partner, Otti Rehorek, performed as "Buddy and Baddy" for the first time in Brussels. The premiere was something of a disaster, since they had been talked into appearing together with another clown, but they rehearsed their routine overnight, improved it, and then it was a success.

Buddy wrote home on November 29 that he was making more and more contact with the ensemble, and he had the feeling that he and Baddy were welcome there, especially by the stage hands, since they, unlike the English, spoke perfect French. "Today Len Stewart told us that the head of the theater came by and said that during the premiere he didn't clap once and cursed us, but when he saw the swing number today, he burst into spontaneous applause and thought it was wonderful! . . . I'd love it if you could see the show. It's quite an experience. The crowd goes crazy every night." In this letter, he also mentioned his citizenship: he had submitted yet another application to be recognized as a Swiss citizen and receive a Swiss passport, but unfortunately he couldn't pursue it himself at the moment; they should try to see if they could put a little pressure on the authorities for him.

Buddy (with fiddle) and Baddy in *Holiday on Ice*

Buddy had rented a small apartment together with Otti and his wife, Bimbo, so he wasn't entirely alone. That was some consolation, since he missed his family and felt homesick in spite of all the new impressions and experiences. The many letters home he wrote show how much he was still thinking about Basel and worried about his family. For instance, he once offered to send Leni money for the rent.

At the end of 1947, Otto Frank came to Brussels to see Buddy. Buddy fetched him from the train station. It was an especially cold winter, and he was wearing many layers of clothing but was still freezing, and his fingers were frozen and numb despite the new gloves that Grandma Ida had knit for him. The cold was not all that was making him feel uncomfortable, however. He was looking forward to seeing Otto, of course he was, Otto had always been his favorite uncle, and the blows of fate had only brought them closer together; still, he felt a little awkward and shy standing there at the station waiting for the train from Amsterdam. He didn't know if he could talk normally with Otto, the way he did with everyone else in the family—tell him about the show and his plans and hopes, and maybe his fears. Was it possible? How could you expect anything normal from someone who had lived through such terrible things and lost his wife and daughters in the most unimaginably dreadful way? And this time he would be alone with him, for three days, without any support or distraction from Alice and the other members of the family—just him and Otto.

At last the train arrived and Otto stepped out. He seemed to have put on some weight in the two years that they hadn't seen each other, he looked better—still too thin, but his shabby coat didn't hang loose on his body the way it did then, back when he came to Basel. He looked distinguished, in spite of his humble clothes, the thick scarf, and the old hat with earmuffs peeking out underneath. A gentleman, Buddy thought, definitely a gentleman, who had seen better days. When Otto caught sight of Buddy a smile spread across his face. He put his little cardboard suitcase and brown briefcase down on the platform and opened out his arms. Buddy ran to him and threw his arms around Otto's neck and they hugged and kissed, the way they always had, and Buddy knew that his nervousness and fears were unwarranted, that everything would be fine.

He had rented a room for Otto in a simple pension, and they took the streetcar there. He had suggested a taxi, because of the cold, but Otto refused. A streetcar was good enough for him, he said. Later too he would only take a taxi when it was absolutely necessary—not because he was stingy (Buddy says today that he was never stingy) but out of modesty. He never liked to show off.

On the way to the pension, Otto asked about Alice, his sister, his brother-in-law, Grandma Ida, but above all about Stephan, who had finally recovered after months in the hospital and was back at work. "His hip joint is stiff," Buddy said, "and Leni is afraid it will stay that way. I talked to her on the phone, she says he is constantly washing his hands now too, because of bacteria. His fear of another sepsis has given him an obsession about cleanliness, Leni says."

"Does he have a limp?" Otto asked.

Buddy shook his head. "No, no limp, but he has a strange stiff way of walking, like he's always about to fall on his face. I saw him before I left. But I thought it would go away by itself. Doesn't seem as if it will, unfortunately."

"Poor boy," Otto said. "So it's over for him with sports then."

Buddy almost said that sports didn't matter, what mattered was that he was still alive, but luckily they had just arrived at their stop and had to get out of the streetcar. "In the house of the hanged man you don't discuss rope," Leni would have said.

Later, after they had been to a simple local restaurant for an even simpler meal, Otto opened his briefcase, took out a book, and put it next to Buddy's plate. Buddy gave a start when he saw the cover: *Anne Frank*, he read. *Het Achterhuis: Dagboekbrieven van 14 juni 1942–1 augustus 1944.*

"There it is," Otto said. "Anne's diary, her *Secret Annex*. Just how she would have wanted."

Buddy had always imagined it slimmer, less of a "book," as he put it. He carefully ran his fingertip across the rough texture of the cover, across the letters of her name, and felt strangely bashful. "It's too bad I don't know Dutch," he said, to have something to say.

"It will come out in German," Otto said, "and in English too. Maybe even French, who knows."

The waiter cleared the plates and asked if they wanted anything else. "A beer," Otto said. "And one for you, Buddy?"

Buddy nodded. He hesitated, then asked the question after all: "Did you ever think about whether it's right to publish her diary? It's so private, so intimate. Alice says . . ."

"I know that Alice has misgivings," Otto interrupted him. "She thinks that anyone who's not in the family might not be able to understand it the way it should be understood, or might even think it's boring. Just a child's thoughts and feelings."

Original Dutch edition of Anne Frank's diary

The waiter brought the beer, and Otto took a sip before continuing: "Anne was a child, it's true, but she had an intellectual maturity that most adults don't have and maybe never will have. I didn't know my own child until I read her diary. That's painful. I never knew her, and you, Buddy, you never knew her either, none of us knew what was really going on inside her. She was a child to me, and I loved her the way you love a child. She annoyed me a lot of the time too. I made her feel better when there was an air raid and she cried with fear, I stroked her hair and let her sleep in my bed. I laughed at her jokes and got mad at her when she was fresh and turned everyone else against her. She was a noisy, carefree kid to me, I never saw her inner depths. And now I can't show her that I see who she is. I can't show her how much I admire her, how proud I am. It's very painful to realize that. She was a very special person, and I only ever saw her as a child. I felt the same way about her diary: at first I thought it was only a child's private thoughts, which I reacted to so strongly because I was there and had lived through everything with her, and now I could suddenly see the whole situation and everything in the Secret Annex through her eyes. But then I showed part of the diary to my friend Albert Cauvern, and to Dr. Baschwitz, and read excerpts to Werner and Jetty Cahn. All experts. It was only from their reaction that I realized this was more than a young girl's diary, much more. Anne was wrong a lot of the time, she was often unfair and too quick to judge others, but she wrote something of universal significance, about living together in difficult circumstances, about humanity itself, and about believing in life. Yes, my opinion changed and now I'm sure of it, it was right to publish her diary. And I'm not the only one who's sure." Otto's voice had grown softer and softer; now he opened his briefcase again and took out a crumpled piece of newspaper and showed it to Buddy. It was written in Dutch, and the headline, in big black letters, said, "Kinderstem."

"*Kindersstimme*?" Buddy guessed at the German translation. " 'The Voice of a Child'?"

Otto nodded. "A very intelligent man wrote this article for *Het Parool*, a Dutch newspaper. Dr. Jan Romein, Professor of History in Amsterdam. Should I translate some parts for you?"

"Yes, please do," Buddy said, and Otto read him what the article said, translated into German. He read so smoothly, without hunting for the right words or correcting himself, that Buddy knew he had read it many times already and translated it many times, not only in his mind.

By chance a diary written during the war years has come into my possession . . . If all the signs do not deceive me, this girl would have become a talented writer had she remained alive. Having arrived here at the age of four from Germany, she was able within ten years to write enviably pure and simple Dutch, and showed an insight into the failings of human nature—her own not excepted—so infallible that it would have astonished one in an adult, let alone in a child. At the same time she also highlighted the infinite possibilities of human nature, reflected in humor, tenderness and love, which are perhaps even more astonishing, and from which one might perhaps shrink, especially when they are applied to very intimate matters, were it not that rejection and acceptance remain so profoundly childlike.

*That this girl could have been abducted and murdered proves to me that we have lost the fight against human bestiality. And for the same reason we shall lose it again, in whatever form inhumanity may reach out for us, if we are unable to put something positive in its place. The promise that we shall never forget or forgive is not enough. It is not even enough to keep that promise. Passive and negative rejection is too little, it is as nothing. Active and positive "total" democracy—politically, socially, economically and culturally—is the only solution; the building of a society in which talent is no longer destroyed, repressed and oppressed, but discovered, nurtured and assisted, wherever it may appear. And with all our good intentions, we are still as far from that democracy as we were before the war.**

Otto fell silent, as though exhausted after hard work, and Buddy suddenly noticed that he had been stroking the book the whole time, the way you stroke a child's head. Otto had apparently noticed it too because he reached out his own hand and placed it on Buddy's, so that now two hands were on Anne's diary.

"This article got a lot of attention," Otto said. He carefully

***The Diary of Anne Frank: The Revised Critical Edition* (New York: Doubleday, 2003), pp. 67–68.

refolded the newspaper clipping and tucked it back into his briefcase. "A lot of people read it and wanted to know who this child was. And now here is the book."

Otto returned to the topic of the diary several more times in the next few days. He told Buddy how hard it had been tó find a publisher: the big presses had turned it down, they didn't see a market for it, they presumably thought that so soon after the terrible war no one would want to read the thoughts and feelings of some Jewish girl who spent two years in hiding with her parents, her sister, and four other Jews. "To some extent they're right," Otto said. "A lot of people just want to enjoy themselves now, to make up for the hard times they have behind them. But not everyone is like that. Not everyone acts as though nothing happened, as though this hell had not taken place. The book has been on the market for six months, and I get more and more letters from people, especially young people, who have read Anne's diary and write to tell me how much it moved them. It changed their lives, they say. And I answer every single letter. I see it as my duty to contribute to a better understanding between people, in Anne's memory." After a short pause, he added: "That is the only thing I can do for her now." All of a sudden he looked unfathomably sad again.

Buddy wondered if it wasn't better to let old wounds heal rather than constantly reopen them. He had the feeling that Otto was spending a lot more of his time and energy on Anne's diary than on his company. He cautiously raised the question with Otto.

"Yes, it's true," Otto said, and he explained: "It was like a whirlpool. Once I started, I was more and more sucked in. I spent almost all my time on it. It took a lot of work to make a readable text out of the two versions."

"Yes, you told us that Anne wrote the diary twice," Buddy said. "And I remember you saying something about a government minister's speech."

"We had a radio," Otto said, "even though of course it was prohibited—the Jews had been ordered to turn in their radios a long time before that. Anne always said that the radio went into hiding just like us. But since everything was illegal anyway, it didn't matter that we listened to the illegal radio station, Oranje. The Dutch government had fled to England at the start of the occupation and spent the whole time there as a government in exile. They used Oranje to keep the Dutch people informed about the events on the front, the battles, the resistance. And they said over and over again that we had to hang on, liberation was right around the corner. Especially after the Allies landed in Normandy." Otto fell silent for a moment, then went on in a quieter voice: "We believed it too, that liberation was right around the corner, but it wasn't, at least not for us. For us it came too late." His voice had grown so soft with these last words that Buddy could barely hear them. He didn't say anything. What could he have said?

Otto pulled himself together and went on: "In early 1944, one of these ministers in exile, Bolkestein, gave a speech on the radio. I still know what he said, I've read a transcript in the meantime but I would have remembered it perfectly anyway. 'History cannot be written on the basis of official documents alone.' That's true, Buddy. It's only when people tell and write down what they experienced, they themselves personally, that other people, who weren't there and didn't have those experiences, might be able to understand or at least have some idea about what happened, what they did to us Jews. How else could anyone even conceive that it was possible? Never in the history of the human race has there been anything like this, this organized, mechanized, assembly-line murder of millions of people. It must never happen again, Buddy, but anything that has happened once can happen again . . ." Otto was crying, and Buddy held his hands, helpless and full of sympathy. He would often see Otto cry.

"You know," Otto went on after he had dried his eyes, "the idea that my loved ones were only three out of millions is no consolation. It doesn't make it any easier for me. And I have a hard time believing what happened—even me, who saw it all with my own eyes and went through it in person. Auschwitz was another world, another planet. I've heard that said many times—many of us talk about 'Planet Auschwitz.' And Auschwitz wasn't the only one, of course. We have to tell this story, every one of us, even if, in truth, it can't be told, because there are no words for it, words like 'horrible' and 'monstrous' are not enough to describe it. I sometimes think we need to invent a new language for it."

Neither says another word. Otto gives himself over to his thoughts, and Buddy does not know how he can console him. There is no consolation. "Come on, let's take a walk," Otto says at last.

He continues his story while they walk. "This Minister Bolkestein had said that they would have to found an institute after the war to collect, prepare for publication, and publish everything that showed how terribly the Dutch people had suffered under the German occupation. He mentioned as examples pastors' sermons, letters from forced laborers, and diaries. All of us in the Secret Annex knew that Anne was keeping a diary, and after this speech we rushed over to her and said that maybe her diary would be published one day too. To tell you the truth, we clutched at any new topic of conversation like a lifeline that might save us from drowning in an ocean of boredom—there was nothing new in the Annex, we had squeezed the life out of every possible topic long ago, there were no new stories, everyone knew everything about everyone. Or at least that's what we thought. We didn't take it seriously, this idea of publishing her diary. But Anne was different—she took it seriously, she took everything much more seriously than I realized. Now I know that she had been writing in her diary for a long time that she wanted to be a journalist and a writer. In any case, she soon began copying out her own diary onto carbon paper that Miep brought up from the office. So there are two versions of the diary, her original one and a second one that she wrote with an eye to publication."

In putting together the second version, Anne did not limit herself to little corrections or leaving out passages that she thought were uninteresting: she combined entries and expanded the diary after the fact by adding more to existing entries or writing entirely new ones. So there were two more or less different versions, and Otto used both to create the edition he published.

It would not have been possible to do it differently. A year was missing from Anne's original diary—one or two of the notebooks must have been lost when the residents of the Annex were arrested by the German secret police, the "Green Police," and their Dutch accomplices. By writing out a second version, she had saved these lost entries after all. And even aside from that year there were many important entries missing that were written only later. So they couldn't publish only the first version, but publishing only the second version would have been a great loss as well, since there were interesting scenes in the first version that Anne herself had decided not to carry over, and because Anne had not finished recopying and rewriting the diary: the entries in the second version ended in March 1944, while the original diary went up to August 1, 1944, three days before their arrest. So five crucial months would have been missing. For these reasons, Otto saw no other option besides using both versions.

"How can you be so sure that she really wanted to publish the second version?" Buddy asked. "That she thought about publishing it at all?"

"Why else would she have copied and rewritten her diary?" Otto said. "Another thing is that she included a list of names and fictional names. She assumed that we would all survive and would not want our real names used, so all the characters were supposed to stay anonymous. Anne wanted to call herself Robin, van Pels was supposed to be van Daan, Pfeffer would be Dussel, Kleiman would be Koophuis, and so on."

"And? Did you use those names?" Buddy asked.

Otto Frank nodded. "Most of them."

Only in the new reader's edition that would be published in 1991 (known as *The Definitive Edition* in English) did the Anne Frank-Fonds in Basel decide to use the real names, at least of the men and women who had helped the Franks, to give them the honor that they deserved.

When Otto Frank finished putting together the manuscript, he asked Albert Cauvern, an old friend who was working at a radio station at the time, to check the diary for grammatical mistakes and correct any stray Germanisms. Cauvern did so and added a short conclusion: "Anne's diary ended here. On August 4, 1944, the 'Grüne Polizei' made a raid on the 'Secret Annex' . . . In March 1945, two months before the liberation of Holland, Anne died in the concentration camp at Bergen-Belsen."*

What Otto Frank perhaps did not discuss with his nephew Buddy was that he had made cuts in the diary. For example, he took out places where Anne had talked too explicitly about her bodily changes as she developed into a woman, and he had also—out of an understandable loyalty to his dead wife and the other people in the Annex who had not survived—cut sentences and phrases where Anne expressed herself too cruelly about her fellow residents. Naturally, Anne Frank was sometimes unfair. What thirteen- or fourteen- or fifteen-year-old isn't in her diary, especially in conditions like that, where it was impossible to avoid her mother or anyone else she was fighting with or even to vent her anger behind their backs? Some of her comments about people who could no longer defend themselves must have been too much for Otto Frank, this man of the utmost civility, equanimity, and understanding. That was surely the reason for many of the cuts that he made. In any case, in putting together a text from

*These details are taken from *The Revised Critical Edition.*

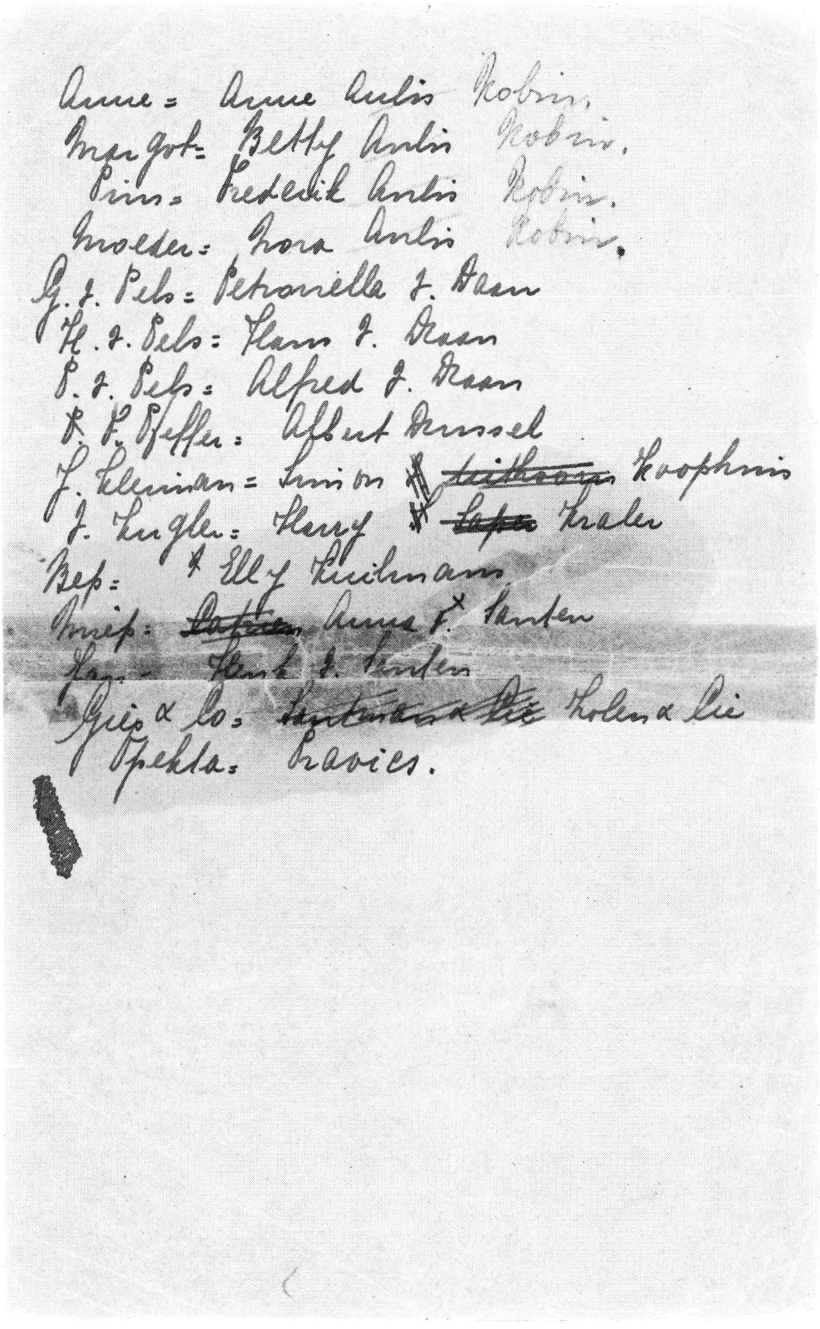

Anne = Anne Aulis Robin.
Margot = Betty Aulis Robin.
Pim = Frederik Aulis Robin.
Moeder = Nora Aulis Robin.
G. v. Pels = Petronella v. Daan
H. v. Pels = Hans v. Daan
P. v. Pels = Alfred v. Daan
F. Pfeffer = Albert Dussel
J. Kleiman = Simon ~~Stiphoorn~~ Koophuis
V. Kugler = Harry ~~Lapa~~ Kraler
Bep = Elly Kuilmans
Miep = ~~Tatia~~ Anne v. Santen
Jan = Henk v. Santen
Gies & Co. = ~~Kastman & Co~~ Kolen & Cie
Opekta = Travies.

Anne's list of pseudonyms in the diary

the two versions, he very skillfully and sensitively drew out "the essential things," as he always put it, to do justice to his daughter.

Otto stayed with Buddy in Brussels for three days, a visit that Buddy would never forget and that made his relationship to Otto that much deeper and stronger. They were days of great closeness. "But we didn't only have serious conversations," Buddy says today. "We also laughed together. I told him about the Ice Revue, about my partner and his wife. Otto came over for dinner once and also came to watch the show. He sat in the first row, and I could see him laughing, laughing hard. And afterward he told me how proud he was of me."

Gerti, Buddy's wife, says: "Otto was interested in Buddy's career his whole life, he followed everything."

"Those were three great days," Buddy says, "and when he left, we both cried."

11.

Years on the Road

Buddy's years on the road had begun. After Brussels was London. How exciting it must have been for this young man to go out into the wide world and leave the narrow confines of Switzerland behind him. But there were difficulties too: he was still stateless, even now, and his "labour permit" would run out at the end of October. But he was lucky. In early October he flew to Basel to pick up his new passport—at twenty-three years of age, Bernhard "Buddy" Elias, having lived almost his whole life in Switzerland, was finally a Swiss citizen. Erich and Leni had still longer to wait before they reached this goal.

London was the first truly metropolitan city that Buddy lived in. It fascinated him. He always entered enthusiastically into new experiences, he loved it when people laughed at their revue numbers, he loved the success, the applause. He also saw his uncle Robert and Robert's wife, Lotti, in London, of course, who welcomed him with open arms. He was amused to realize that Robert and Lotti were more English than the English, in their clothing, their way of speaking, their way of moving. Lotti had an aristocratically quiet drawl of a voice, and Robert, in his bowler hat, topcoat, and umbrella, practically looked like a caricature of an English gentleman. They were both a little eccentric, but kind. Nonetheless, Buddy's relationship with his English uncle would never be as warm as with Otto or as friendly as with Herbert.

Buddy got a driver's license in London too and wrote to Herbstgasse: "After I passed my driving test last Monday, I got my car right away. You can't imagine a happier man. Your 'little one' with his own car! . . . Robo and Lotti are thrilled too. Yesterday, I drove Robo to an auction and took Lotti for a drive in rush hour through Piccadilly to Regent street. Lotti was sweating blood but I hadn't passed my driving test for nothing."

When their contract was up, "Buddy and Baddy" were hired by a new Danish group, the Scan Ice Revue.

Buddy felt right at home in the Scan Ice Revue. He was especially impressed by one of the managers, Volmer Sørensen, a conductor who had been a celebrated pianist before the war and had played under many great conductors, such as Weingartner in Basel in 1932. When the Germans invaded Denmark, he joined the resistance and took many Jews to Sweden at night, in his tiny rowboat. Until the Gestapo caught him. He was captured and tortured, and they crushed his hands so that he would never be able to play the piano again.

This man was one of the few people whom Buddy told about his uncle Otto and about Edith, Margot, and Anne in those days. He didn't keep it a secret that he was Jewish, but he didn't emphasize it either—he didn't feel sure of his Jewish identity, both because he was not at all religious and because he had stayed safe in Switzerland while millions of Jews were being killed elsewhere in Europe. It would take a long time before he worked through what had happened to him and his family, enough to be able to talk about it with any distance.

The happy birthday letter that he wrote to his mother in September 1949 shows how well Buddy was doing with the Scan Revue. Sender: "Scan Is Revy [Danish spelling for 'Ice Revue'], 16, Enighedsvej, Charlottenlund, København."

Dear "Leniköppche,"

. . . Happy birthday!

Yes, yes, I know, it was a long long time ago. Now you're already 56 years old, a very big little girl. And "your little lads" are old enough to be daddies too (or maybe they are already!)

Yes, my dear Clownmama, the times are changing. I don't think Mr. Old Bank Director Frank in Frankfurt could ever have dreamed that his grandson would one day entertain the public with his green hair. What would he say if he could look down from Heaven and see me now? "Il n'a pas de sale métier!" and then silently sit down at the card table with Kaiser Wilhelm and lose of course, since his thoughts would be so preoccupied with his meshuggah descendant. But even if his family has broken with the ancient traditions of the Franks, he can't really complain. Yes, his good wishes fall even now upon the members of his family. Full of pride, he takes the Kaiser by the hand and points down at a little shop in a beautiful country: "There, Willie, won't you look at that! With that little thing my daughter is getting 7 people through difficult times. I know the situation will get better soon, but she's been doing it for years and all the boys, never mind the girls, should take a lesson from her!" And a tear of joy from one eye and a tear of pride from the other eye roll down his sunken cheeks.

The Kaiser, too, is not unmoved by what he sees down here on earth. After dear Grandpa turns away, and the Kaiser thinks no one is watching him, he bows a deep bow to this little Leni who is walking out of Spalenvorstadt 15 and getting on her bicycle. And after one last look of recognition and deep respect at the old banker, he returns to his heavenly hermitage to give our dear Lord a written report of this new paragon of love and sacrifice.

You know what I hope for for your birthday. May it come true immediately. And don't buy any groceries or pay the rent with the enclosed money, buy something nice for yourself!

We'll be here 10 more days and then we're off to Norrköping and then 6 weeks in Stockholm! Nov. 15 or so we're back in Copenhagen. It would be lovely if you could visit me. Think about it. I'm making better money here in Denmark too. [In English:] Give my love to everyone and a special big-kiss for you! Buddy.

After the Scandinavian tour they were off to Cairo. Buddy was afraid he would have problems as a Jew in an Arab country. Even though the manager of the tour had explicitly looked into it and assured Buddy that he had nothing to fear, Buddy wrote to Basel: "It will be better if I say I'm Protestant while I'm staying in Egypt, in case anyone asks. I don't like denying my religion, but for 5 months it's not too bad. Better safe than sorry."

Egypt—his first Middle Eastern country—was very exciting for Buddy, who was enraptured by everything there that was new to him: the foreignness of Cairo and Alexandria, the landscape, the desert, the Oriental voices, colors, and smells, everything that he was seeing for the first time. He wrote enthusiastic letters home: "Cairo—city of noise—city of smells—city of riches—city of poverty, city of beauty and of horrors. My head is throbbing and my eyes hurt. You'd need 100 eyes to take everything in here." He wrote long and beautiful letters that must have sometimes reminded Alice of the lively and vivid letters that Robert used to write to his parents. She might have drawn this comparison herself, but the family's letters to Buddy have not been preserved. It seems clear from his answers, though, that Buddy was kept fully informed about everything—that Alice was in poor health, and that Otto had received Dutch citizenship.

During this period, the family also decided to buy the house on Herbstgasse. The owner had given them the choice to either move out or buy the house. They all felt a connection to the house—it had become a home for them, a fixed center for the family, the way the house at Mertonstrasse 4 in Frankfurt had once been—and they did not want to lose it under any circumstances. Buddy sent the money for the down payment, just as he would always send money later for the mortgage, repairs, and other necessary purchases. He made comparatively good money, and he was the only one at the time who was in a financial position to save the family home. "I only hope that I stay healthy so I can keep earning money, otherwise I'm screwed," he wrote in a letter to his father.

View of the house at Herbstgasse 11, from the garden. Otto Frank and his second wife, Fritzi, lived for seven years on the top floor, on the right. The room beneath it, whose window is also in the roof, was occupied for decades by Alice Frank.

When the Ice Revue got to Alexandria, the artists were put up in a splendid hotel, but it soon turned into a hospital for Buddy when he came down with jaundice. Luckily, he recovered by the time of their planned return to Oslo, in May. He wrote to Basel on April 28 that he had got out of bed for the first time and felt perfectly fine, although he was still a bit shaky and "a little yellow in the eyes."

In the summer of 1950, Buddy returned for a week to Basel, to Herbstgasse. Only then did he fully realize how badly he had missed them all the whole time he was away—Alice, Erich, Leni, Grandma Ida, Stephan, and Herbert, who had returned from Paris again and now had to live in Saint-Louis, near Basel but on the French side of the border, since Switzerland had refused to give him a residence permit. That meant he had to continually commute back and forth between his little apartment and the house on Herbstgasse.

Alice had grown thin, almost never left her room anymore, and rarely came downstairs for meals. She had never been a large woman, but now she seemed to Buddy downright shriveled, and he hugged her very carefully, afraid he might break her bones. She had grown old and looked her eighty-four years. Sometimes she was attentive and interested and asked Buddy about her oldest son, Robert, and his wife, Lotti—she wanted to know how they looked, how they lived, and what they talked about.

Once, she said: "It's too bad that they never had children."

Buddy nodded, and Alice went on: "Sometimes I think that we're a very unlucky family. Klärchen and Alfred died without grandchildren, Robo and Herbi have no children, Margot and Anne, God curse their murderers, are dead, all we have left are you and Stephan. Stephan's not making any effort to get married, and what about you?"

"I'm still so young," Buddy said. "I'm not ready to get married yet, you'll have to wait a little."

She turned aside, to the window, and said: "How long do you think I can wait, then?"

Buddy gripped her hand, which had got shockingly delicate and fragile, and kissed it. And suddenly it struck him how long it had been since he had seen her with needlework in her hands.

Sometimes Alice sat in her chair for hours at a time, looking out the window and reacting only with a vague smile when someone said something to her. Then she would ask Buddy to tell her about the Ice Revue, about the foreign cities he had seen and the many people he had met. Buddy was always ready to tell anecdotes and stories, for instance, that both the day porter and the night porter at the Cairo Hotel were Jewish. He tried to paint what he had experienced in the most vivid possible colors, describing the Nile, the desert, the pyramids, the bazaars, the luxuries at the Alexandria hotel, the veiled women entirely covered except for their eyes, but what eyes! and so on, and he was happy when he could make his grandmother smile.

It was touching how Herbert took care of his mother: he saw her every wish in her eyes, brought her her meals, and ate upstairs with her himself when she couldn't or didn't want to go downstairs; he read to her and, when she wanted, helped her down the stairs and back up again later. "He is making up for all the worries he caused her over the years," Leni said, and Erich said, "It's about time he made up for some of it."

Grandma Ida was as sweet and inconspicuous as ever. She had knit Buddy new socks and a scarf from the leftover wool, although actually it was much too brightly colored for a young man. Leni and Erich were in good health and good spirits, fortunately: Erich was counting on getting a position at Maypro AG in Weinfelden. Stephan had recovered from his bad illness too—his hip was still stiff, but he had started to work again and even appeared in "Cock-a-Doodle-Doo," a Basel cabaret. And was good too, Buddy heard.

Something else happened in 1950: Anne's diary appeared in German, in Anneliese Schütz's translation, under the title *Das Tagebuch der Anne Frank*. It was published by the relatively small press Lambert Schneider Verlag in Heidelberg, after several bigger publishers rejected it. The first printing was forty-five hundred copies, and it sold only moderately well.

The diary also appeared in France in 1950, as *Journal de Anne Frank*, published by Calmann-Lévy; in Great Britain in 1952, published by Vallentine, Mitchell, and in the United States, also in 1952, as *Anne Frank: The Diary of a Young Girl*, published by Doubleday with an introduction by Eleanor Roosevelt. In the United States too, it had been rejected by about ten other publishers. Only after the success of the play in 1955, and the movie version in 1959, did Anne Frank's diary become a permanent bestseller worldwide.

The family in the garden at Herbstgasse 11. Front, from left: Herbert Frank, Alice Frank, Leni and Erich Elias, Ida Elias. Rear: Stephan Elias.

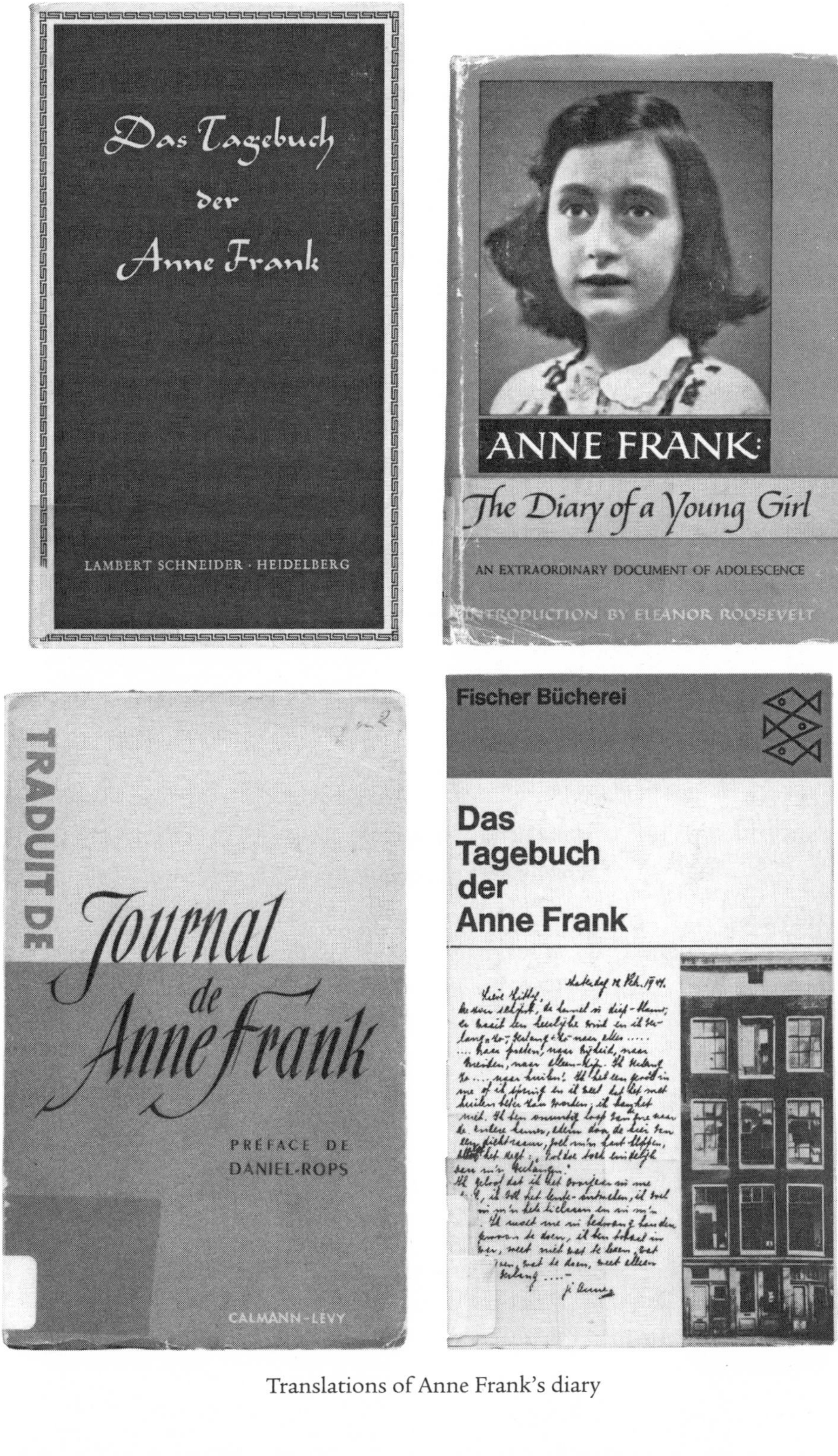

Translations of Anne Frank's diary

Buddy, who until then knew only the short excerpts that Alice had read him, could no longer avoid reading the diary itself. He started to read it and was deeply moved, shaken. He had to keep putting the book down because he could not bear the confusion and disorientation it stirred up inside him. Now it was clear to him why Otto had said that he had never really known his daughter; Buddy felt the same way. He sometimes had the feeling that Anne was so close to him he could hear her voice, her laugh, her boisterous cry of "I won! I won!" Other times, it was a new, strange Anne who appeared from the pages of her diary, an Anne he would have loved to meet in person. In the past few years he had said goodbye to the child Anne, cried for her and mourned for her, but his grief at the loss of this new Anne struck him unexpectedly hard. Every sentence brought her closer, every period at the end of the sentence took her away again. But through all his admiration and all the shocks of emotion he felt, the thought still forced itself upon him that the generous sentence she had famously written—"In spite of everything I still believe that people are really good at heart"—was written before she was sent to Westerbork, Auschwitz, and Bergen-Belsen, before she had really got to know the other side of human nature, the abysses. What would she have written after these experiences? This thought was so painful for him, though, that he quickly pushed it aside. Take it as it is, he told himself—her belief in human goodness is admirable, even if it turned out, at least for her personally, to be an illusion.

He had another thought too: the book had come out in German in precisely the year that Anne would have turned twenty-one and become an adult. Alice had said that too: "She would have been twenty-one. I got married when I was twenty-one."

Buddy talked with his mother about his strange reactions to Anne's diary, and Leni told him that it was exactly the same for her. She too kept having the feeling that there were two Annes, just as Anne had described it herself. "Like they always say about Geminis," Leni said, "although I usually don't believe that nonsense." Buddy didn't talk about the diary with Alice: he was afraid to upset her. Alice was so old by that point that everyone was gentle with her, even Leni, who usually loved to make pointed comments.

One evening they talked about a certain Elfriede Geiringer, whom Otto called Fritzi and was mentioning more and more often these days. He had told Leni a bit about her on the telephone; she was a "fellow sufferer," he had said. She was originally from Vienna and had fled the Nazis to Amsterdam; she too had been in Auschwitz and had lost her husband and son. She and her daughter, Eva, who no longer lived with her mother, had survived the horror.

A faint hope sprang up in the house on Herbstgasse. They knew Otto, knew how dependent he was on a familial environment. He was not a man born to live alone, or at least not raised to—he needed to be close to other people. And Fritzi seemed better suited to him than any other woman: she understood Otto's sorrow, they would be able to prop each other up, support each other. That's how Leni saw it, and the others were only too ready to believe her. They hoped that Otto and Fritzi would become a couple. The more they talked it over, the more sure of it they became.

Buddy's time at home with his loved ones passed, and it was even harder this time to say goodbye, because this time Buddy was traveling even farther away from Basel. He was off to America. Starting at the end of the year, "Buddy and Baddy" would be appearing in *Holiday on Ice*. They had got in touch with the most famous ice show in the world through a former colleague in London, and in Basel itself, where the show was performing, they auditioned their number. When they were offered a contract, they were thrilled to accept, and on December 14, Buddy was off to New York. He had become a real globe-trotter, as Leni put it, with pride but also a little sadness. America was far away—who knew when they would see him again. When Buddy said goodbye to Alice, he kissed her especially tenderly, as though he knew that this farewell might be their last.

12.

The Globe-Trotter

So began Buddy's time with *Holiday on Ice,* which would last fourteen years. He got to know many countries, many cities, many people, and everywhere he went he wrote letters back to Herbstgasse, telling stories about his experiences and his success. For a few years it was all new and exciting, and it filled Buddy with a certain pride, of course, that he was earning comparatively good money, though it also depressed him, as he wrote once, that after five years of a good income he didn't actually have enough cash to be able to pay the accumulated interest on the mortgage without difficulties. "If only the house turns out to be a good capital investment! Does it have fire insurance???!"

In 1952, Erich and Leni at last received the long-hoped-for letter of citizenship. Erich Elias had written to the lawyer, Dr. Naegeli, back in October 1946:

From my numerous experiences over the course of almost 17 years, I know that the Bern authorities are anti-Semitic on principle and act accordingly. It used to be different. A good friend of ours, Jewish, was the Swiss consul general in Frankfurt in the '20s. For a Christian it's enough to live here for a few years and have a bank account, but for us Jews they impose almost impossible requirements, and if they don't have a reason to reject our applications then they simply invent one. First they said that seven years' residence was insufficient, I should reapply in two years;

then, after another two years, etc. In Basel, where people know me, my family and I were considered "well assimilated" after only seven years, but in Bern on the other hand, where they don't know me, I am rejected after sixteen years in the country "due to insufficient assimilation." Still others fulfill the necessary requirements for Swiss citizenship after only six years, by giving the authorities valuable paintings as presents.

What a bitter conclusion to come to; there is hardly anything to add. But finally they had managed it. After more than twenty years!

When Buddy heard that his parents had become citizens, he sent them a delighted letter of congratulations, dated March 20, 1952, and written in thick Swiss dialect. As in his early audition for acting school, Buddy used dialect to express his humor and high spirits.

Life with *Holiday on Ice* was so new and exciting for Buddy at first that he no doubt spent less time thinking about Anne and the diary. But he did write in July 1952: "Otto should be careful and not sell the rights to Anne's book too cheap."

This comment was in reference to the news that Otto Frank was planning to travel to America to negotiate about a stage adaptation of Anne's diary and movie rights. Buddy, on a European tour at the time, wrote a letter from Valencia to "Dear Ottel": "I wish you all the very best from the bottom of my heart for your trip to America! My thoughts are with you and I'm in huge suspense to hear how everything goes. Take care and don't get ripped off. When the Americans really want something, they'll pay any price. I assume that you have a good lawyer. You have relatives in New York as far as I know, don't you? . . . I hope to hear from you soon, but you don't need to write specially to me, I'll hear everything from Basel. If you need any money over there, my account in New York is at your disposal, though there's not much in it."

Leni was sorry that Otto wanted to travel alone; she thought that Fritzi could have easily gone with him. And in one letter Buddy raised the possibility of playing "Peter" if the book was turned into a movie or play. He asked the family in Basel to ask Otto if that might not be possible. But already in his next letter, he wrote that he was probably too old to play "Peter."

Anne's diary had come out in the United States in June 1952 to great and immediate acclaim. Even before that, a journalist and writer named Meyer Levin had got in touch with Otto Frank: he had read the diary in French and was convinced that it had to be adapted for the stage, he was ready to do the job himself, as a Jew he was no doubt the right man for the job. He also said that you needed a producer for a play, and he suggested Cheryl Crawford. Otto Frank agreed to Levin's suggestions, and so the disastrous relationship between the two men began. The trip he undertook in late September 1952 on the *Queen Elizabeth* was supposed to be a chance to arrange everything and wrap up all the issues of theater and film rights.

On October 1, Otto wrote that the crossing had been pleasant and he had been treated "fabulously" aboard the ship. Then he expressed his admiration for the hotel: "a fine room, with a bath of course. Everyone attentive to their guest, a little sewing kit, washcloths, shoe shines, soap, fruit—everything perfect." Buddy understood exactly what Otto meant—he too had been impressed, at first, by the luxurious arrangements in the better hotels. But in the meantime he had lived for years in hotels—more or less good, more or less expensive, more or less sophisticated; it was not that the differences were entirely insignificant to him now, but a hotel was, in the end, just a hotel. It wasn't easy, never mind comfortable, to live out of a suitcase all the time, not to mention the never-ending restaurant meals. In any case, he had had more than enough opportunities, while waiting for a meal he had ordered to be brought to the table, to think back to the dining room on Herbstgasse and how everyone would spoon up their soup and then Leni would ring for Imperia, who would come in, and Leni would say, "You can clear the table now, please," and then Imperia would take out the soup plates and come back in with potatoes, vegetables, and meat that his father would set to carving.

American prosperity and its ostentatious display must have been astounding to Otto Frank for another reason as well. In Europe the economic situation had improved, and Otto's business was going relatively well, but there was no question as yet of the real prosperity that ruled in the American middle and upper classes. The difference between everything that you could buy in America and the things that slowly made their way onto the shelves in Europe must have been astonishing to him.

Otto described Doubleday: "The company has more than 4,000 employees, a gigantic office of 3 floors in a big building. Marks has the idea that all the publishers of Anne's book should buy the building at Prinsengracht 263 together and set up a library for young people in the Secret Annex. That's how they think here. The young people have 'Anne Frank clubs.' " This was certainly the first time that Otto Frank experienced the kind of "fuss" about his daughter's diary that he would have to get used to in the years to come. For now, the issue was the theater and movie rights.

Buddy and Leni's concern that Otto might not be able to stand up to the Americans was justified, even if Otto was not as alone there as Leni had feared. Nathan Straus, whom Otto continued to call Charley even after he had changed his name, looked after him. In addition, Otto saw Edith's brothers and lots of old acquaintances and distant relatives.

The business negotiations, though, were not going well, and before long Otto felt the first stirrings of doubt about Meyer Levin. With good reason, as would soon become clear. Cheryl Crawford, the theater producer Levin himself had suggested, didn't like his play and turned it down. Another producer, Kermit Bloomgarden, who had made his name with Arthur Miller's *Death of a Salesman,* was also unwilling to produce Levin's play.

But Levin was working like a fiend and did not give up. A burdensome and unpleasant tug-of-war developed. Buddy's premonition that his gentle, cultivated uncle might not be quite up to the American business world had come true.

In a letter to Fritzi, Otto described the situation in this way:

I saw the lawyer and he foresees serious difficulties: anything another writer writes will no doubt have echoes of Levin's script and no good, well-known writer will take on the job of delivering a script unless Levin is paid off first. There have already been long, tangled, nasty court cases in situations like this. That was this morning. This afternoon Levin came and explained that even though he doesn't have any money he will not accept any payment for a play that is unacceptable. He says that as a writer, his name is at stake and that we need to give him the chance to find another producer if Crawford and Bloomgarden don't like it. Since the information that he is writing the play has been published, it would give the impression that it's no good and he is not convinced that it is. The problem is that Crawford never signed a proper contract with him, so there's no clear agreement that lays out how to proceed. I am trying to keep myself out of it and explain over and over again that I am not in a position to judge. The truth is, I'm caught in the middle, so I proposed that Levin, Crawford, my lawyer, and I have a group meeting. I can't tell you everything that's going on in my mind and by the time you get this letter everything will have changed again anyway. I do nothing without a lawyer.

Even that was not much help. He had landed, inexperienced and naive, in a situation that would have consequences for him for a long time to come.

Otto stayed in America for six weeks and met many people who were involved in the planned adaptation. There was already talk of a movie. Fritzi supported him from Amsterdam by letter: "So you're doing Meyer Levin a favor & showing his script to another producer. It can't hurt, but if Bloomgarten also doesn't think it's good enough, then you have to be firm and say enough is enough, and leave it to Crawford to find a famous author who can write a real play that will work onstage. Will Crawford keep her word and compensate Levin for his work?"

But the negotiations were not easy. Meyer Levin clung to his adaptation and was convinced that he was the only writer who could do justice to Anne Frank's diary. Eventually, in 1973, he would write a book about everything concerning the diary that was going on at the time—a book called *The Obsession*, with good reason. He was truly possessed. Otto decided "to sort things out" with Levin and then try to find a new writer for the dramatization. Fritzi commented on the situation from Amsterdam, on October 26: "I find it horrible that this situation has dragged on like this. What does he want?! Are you supposed to go hawking his play from door to door until you find a madman who is willing to risk putting it on? He doesn't have another producer who wants it. I'm glad that it's in the lawyers' hands now."

In the letters that Otto and Fritzi exchanged during his stay in the United States, hints repeatedly surface that they had decided to marry and move to Switzerland. For example, Otto advised Fritzi in one letter not to rush into anything with the apartment, and in another he mentioned that he still had to pack up everything at Miep's in the large trunk. He showed Fritzi's picture to all of his friends and said that they were getting married. "You know that everything takes a rather long time with me, but then it turns out well in the end, right?"

Still, the major topic of their many letters was the conflict with Meyer Levin. On October 20, 1952, Otto wrote:

The discussions about Levin continue and now it's actually Doubleday that's warning me and in a certain sense "stirring up trouble," which I'm resisting. I don't want any unnecessary bitterness or drastic mea-

sures, under no circumstances do I want there to be a lawsuit, either against me (which I don't think will happen) or against Doubleday or Miss Crawford. Levin is now trying to find a home for his script with Peter Capell, who was in Amsterdam, and so a letter (very proper) arrived from him to negotiate the matter. I refused and discussed it with my lawyer, who will write the appropriate letter. I insist on the view that I am still tied to Crawford (and also want to be) and that Levin needs to understand that all his dealings with anyone else whatsoever are pointless if he and Crawford haven't come to an agreement. He is fixated on the idea that his play is the only one that can possibly be performed. He needs to come to his senses and think things over.

Fritzi wrote and asked if any progress at all had been made in these more than three weeks, and carefully expressed the opinion that Otto would have to be a bit more energetic about it. Otto replied on November 13: "A few quick lines. Very busy the past few days and it looks like at least a partial agreement will be reached in the eleventh hour. Levin will be allowed to show his script to a few other producers, all the details will be laid out, it's a long contract but it lays out a clear path for the future course of events with or without Cheryl Crawford." This contract also gave Levin the rights to have his play performed in Israel.

The play ended up going forward without Cheryl Crawford, as it happens, who pulled out of the project in irritation. Otto Frank gave the production rights to Kermit Bloomgarden, who hired Albert Hackett and Frances Goodrich Hackett, experienced scriptwriters (and married to each other), to write the theatrical adaptation of the diary.

That was the end of the conflict for the time being, though there were still further consequences to come.

Otto returned to Amsterdam. On November 10, 1952, Otto Frank and Fritzi Geiringer were married and began in earnest to arrange their move to Basel. Especially Alice was very anxious to see him.

She was not doing well, and the following poem, found with her letters, must have been written during this period of waiting:

No:
They say that I always refuse and deny
And miss out on lovely things thereby
But I say "no" when it's right for me
Though I hate that word as much as can be!
Like when someone wants to visit me,
I say "no" and very vigorously,
Because I can't stand those idle questions
It gets on my nerves and upsets my digestion.
I'm never hungry when it's time to sup
So I say "no" when the food comes up,
And send at least half of it back down
And bravely swallow the other half down!
When the paper comes and they say I should read it
I say "no," I don't understand it or need it,
I have no head for politics and news
And say "no" to all the fuss and to-dos.
I would like very much if I could say "yes"
And not complain about every behest.
If only Ottel were here to take me
Into his arms & not forsake me,
To that I would not say "no,"
& I would be content, I know.

Everyone in the house on Herbstgasse was glad that Otto had found another wife, and they were ready to welcome her with open arms. They were not disappointed. Buddy and his wife, Gerti, still talk about how happy Otto and Fritzi were with each other, how warmly and tenderly they treated each other to the very end. Everyone, including Alice, felt deeply grateful to Fritzi for giving Otto a new life after everything that had happened to him. And of course in the other direction as well.

Buddy was also very happy for Otto when Otto wrote to tell him that he was planning to remarry. The first time he heard about Fritzi, their relationship struck him as rather like two children clutching each other in fear in a dark forest, but later, when he saw Otto and Fritzi together, he understood it better. Two people had found each other who were not only bound together in suffering but also deeply drawn to each other.

One time, he asked Otto if it was their shared past that connected him to Fritzi. "Not only that," Otto said, "but that is part of it. I couldn't have married a woman who wasn't in a concentration camp. We had similar experiences–she lost her husband and son, I lost my wife and daughters. When she talks about it I understand her, and vice versa of course."

By December 1952, Otto Frank was already in Basel. He was staying in a hotel but spent his days at the Herbstgasse house and spent a lot of time sitting with Alice and Grandma Ida, as he wrote to Fritzi. On December 10, Fritzi asked in a letter: "Is our room nice, warm, and cozy? Describe it to me a little? Have you unpacked and 'rangschikked'* anything yet?" Fritzi meant the room on the top floor of the Herbstgasse house, where she and Otto would live for many years. She ended the letter with these words: "So my darling, take care in the meantime, these are your last days as a bachelor so make good use of them."

After moving to Switzerland, Otto took less and less part in his pectin business, though he remained a director for some years, until he had set all the financial matters in order. He wanted to live with his family in Basel and dedicate himself to the "legacy" of his daughter, which he understood to be his personal duty.

On December 15, 1952, he wrote to Fritzi, who was still in Amsterdam:

*Fritzi uses the Dutch word *rangschikken,* meaning "organize, put in order," in quotation marks and with a German ending.

The baggage came today and so I'm sitting in my (not very comfortable) room and writing a couple of very important letters, because I went to a tax adviser this afternoon and it seems that we won't be able to avoid the income tax, and it is very high here too, though of course not nearly as high as in Holland. The defense tax is 10% everywhere and then there's the normal income tax and local taxes. You can minimize the latter two if you move to a canton with a lower tax rate, and the adviser suggested Schwyz. I need to look into that, but you can see how it's possible to save your pennies and let many thousands slip through your fingers. So don't drive yourself crazy about little things. I just wrote to Barbara and will try to get paid in installments so that the amount will be lower for the time being. Now we wait. You see how desperately I need you here to discuss everything, since everything affects both of us together! . . . I haven't spoken to anyone except the Schneiders and Max Lindner's family, whom I had dinner with last night. I went to the Lindners' on purpose because I wanted to find out the name of a good tax adviser. We'll go there again when you're here. Now it's off to Immigration tomorrow.

A comment in one of Otto's other letters is also interesting: "I mentioned Hanukkah and no one here knew anything about it." Clearly, Alice, Leni, and Erich were far removed from religion.

Otto and Fritzi lived in the room under the roof—an extra floor added onto the house that was reached by a narrow, steep flight of stairs. The bathroom was down a flight, and Fritzi and Otto set up a hot plate and some dishes on a dresser in a little vestibule room that led to the toilet. This was where they usually made their breakfast. Their lodgings were not very spacious and were in no way luxurious: the most valuable pieces of furniture were a Biedermeier secretary with a flip-top desk and a bowed armoire, both from Frankfurt. Otto had given them to friends to store before the family went underground, and now had taken them with him to Switzerland. Sitting at this secretary, Otto answered many thousands of letters and inquiries about Anne's diary that arrived over the course of the years to come.

"The letters came by the sackful," Buddy says. He also says that, in retrospect, this room reminded him of the rooms in the Secret Annex where the family in hiding had lived in similarly spartan and cramped conditions. Maybe that is why Otto never needed anything special. Gerti, Buddy's wife, says that this comparison struck her too. Here in the Herbstgasse house, Otto also had a tree outside his window, another similarity to Prinsengracht—though here it was a beech, not a chestnut.

Otto and Fritzi came downstairs to the dining room and salon for meals and tea, of course, like the other members of the family, but they spent most of their time in their tiny room. It must have been a very harmonious life that they led, for all its modesty; Buddy, at least, doesn't remember there being any fights or arguments. He says that the first time he came home after Otto and Fritzi had moved in, it was as though they had lived there always, everything went so smoothly.

On Alice's birthday, her eighty-seventh, they were all together: all four children. Robert, who according to Buddy only rarely came to Basel, had made the trip for his mother's birthday. Buddy, unfortunately, was missing, but he had sent a lovely letter and a present: a silk scarf. They all sat in the dining room; Herbert and Stephan had helped Alice down the stairs for dinner. She was wearing her new scarf, and Stephan was sitting next to her—the grandson who was celebrating his birthday too. Alice revived in the circle of her loved ones, although she had grown very weak by that point and everyone noticed how shaky her voice sounded when she recited the poem that she had written for her birthday.

In all my 87 years
I've had much laughter and many tears

And always did everything I could
To make our lives be as they should
Your father, whom we so loved so much, he was honored by all of us very much,
There were many things that he was spared,
He and so many others about whom we cared.
I thank you today for all your favors
With all my heart—may your love never waver,
And may your mother's blessing always
Accompany you on your paths and byways.
I cannot write many words today, calm & reasonable I must stay.—
It means so very much to me
To have the "four" all here with me.
It's also a special treat for Stephan, I'm sure he feels in seventh heaven!
My wishes apply to him as well;
With him too I will not always dwell.
I end with hugs and kisses forever,
Otherwise my tears would flow like a river.
Your Mother

This flood of tears was probably avoided, but surely a few of the people at the table quietly wiped away a tear or two, in a premonition of the farewell that they must have realized was fated to come sooner or later.

Buddy was in Antwerp with *Holiday on Ice* when Leni wrote to him, in early March 1953, with the news that Alice was sick: she was bedridden and had probably caught pneumonia. The news frightened Buddy, and he wrote back: "I am very worried about I. I hope she gets better soon . . . At her age a pneumonia is very bad, of course. I'm keeping my fingers crossed. Let me know any further details."

Otto, in London at the time with Fritzi visiting Fritzi's daughter, Eva, flew back to Basel right away when he heard the news. He

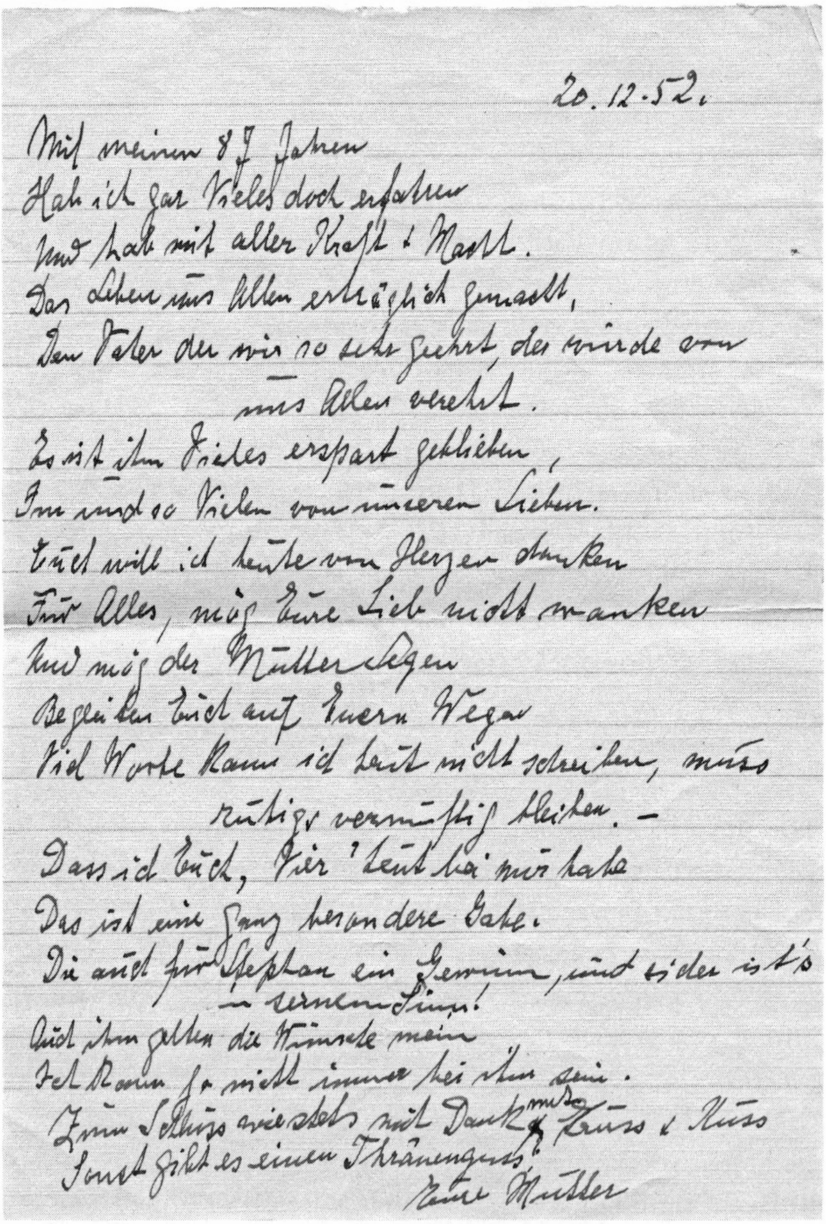

20.12.52.

Mit meinen 87 Jahren
Hab ich gar Vieles doch erfahren
Und hab mit aller Kraft & Macht
Das Leben uns Allen erträglich gemacht,
Den Vater den wir so sehr geehrt, der würde von uns Allen verehrt.
Es ist ihm Vieles erspart geblieben,
Ihm und so Vielen von unseren Lieben.
Euch will ich heute von Herzen danken
Für Alles, mög Eure Lieb nicht wanken
Und mög der Muttersegen
Begleiten Euch auf Euern Wegen
Viel Worte kann ich heut nicht schreiben, muss ruhig & vernünftig bleiben. –
Dass ich Euch, Vier heut bei mir habe
Das ist eine ganz besondere Gabe.
Die auch für Stephan ein Gewinn, und sicher ist's in seinem Sinn!
Auch ihm gelten die Wünsche mein
Ich kann ja nicht immer bei ihm sein.
Zum Schluss wie stets mit Dank und so Gruss & Kuss
Sonst gibt es einen Thränenguss!
Eure Mutter

Alice's poem on her eighty-seventh birthday

spent a week with his mother, and she seemed to be doing better, so he returned to London to continue his visit.

Alice died on March 20, 1953. Leni was crying so much on the phone when she told Buddy the news that he could hardly understand her. "A stroke . . . she was gone just like that . . . put out like a candle . . . snuffed out." She couldn't say another word. But what was there to say, it had happened.

Buddy had no words either. He did not say that life goes on, or that she won't suffer any more now, or that we have to take care of the living, there's nothing more we can do for the dead, the way Otto might have said. He went to his room, lay on the bed, and stared at the ceiling. He could not imagine life without Alice, his beloved I. From now on everything would be different, nothing would be the way it used to be.

All four children of Michael and Alice Frank—Robert, Otto, Herbert, Leni—were together once more for their mother's funeral. It was to be the last time.

Buddy couldn't come. He wrote on March 24:

Dear everyone,

I hardly need to tell you how terribly I will miss I. Her goodness, her sense of humor, her wisdom and intelligence, just to name a few of her good qualities, have made her a remarkable person in my life who was very important for me. Her loss is irreplaceable.

My nerves have somewhat abandoned me in the last 5 days, probably because of I.'s death; I threw up several times for absolutely no reason, and I have no idea how I managed to get through the clown routines. But I'm better again now.

Alice, the woman who had experienced so many heights and depths in her life, and who had shaped her family like almost no one else, was dead. Born in Frankfurt, and with an accent that always gave away where she came from, she was buried in the Jewish cemetery in Basel. To this day, the living room in Basel, Leni's "salon," is dominated by the painting of little Alice, and when a guest sits on the sofa, drinks her tea, and looks at the painting, she might well have to fight off the strange feeling that Alice's spirit has never left the house.

Life went on, as it always does, although the next bad news followed shortly after, in May: Robert had died, two months after his mother. When Buddy learned of his death, he thought: At least I. was spared that.

Leni, Otto, and Herbert had lost mother and brother within two months, and even though they were no longer young themselves, they felt orphaned. Leni had inherited a difficult burden, because Alice, before she died, had said to her: "I always had to worry about Herbert, and when I'm not here anymore, you have to take care of him. He can't manage on his own."

Leni had promised. Just as Alice had accepted as a given the responsibility of looking after Cornelia, Leni took on the responsibility for looking after her brother.

There was only one woman from the older generation left in the house on Herbstgasse: Grandma Ida. Although she was eighty-five years old by that time, she never stopped cleaning and dusting, even where there was not a speck of dust to be seen.

13.

The Play

Buddy focused on the concerns of everyday life once more. He sent money home to Basel for the house and asked how much he should send for the burial costs. His professional life changed too: Otti Rehorek, his partner, retired from ice-skating and moved back to Basel after he and his wife, Bimbo, had a second child. Steve Pedley, Buddy's new partner, turned out to be a stroke of luck—he became just as good a friend as Otti had been, and the new "Buddy and Baddy" were just as successful as the old team. They continued to tour with *Holiday on Ice*—in Italy, in Japan. Buddy wrote from Japan that he had met Mr. Washio, the publisher there of Anne's diary, and that the Japanese edition was already in its eighteenth printing.

The diary came up more and more often in Buddy's letters in general. For example, he wrote that he had suddenly come upon a large photograph of Anne in the shopwindow of a bookstore in Kyoto, and how moved he was. Another time, he wrote: "Just recently I walked into the room of someone in the show and he was reading Anne's book, without knowing that I was her cousin. I have a feeling that when the play comes out the book will sell even more strongly." How right he was would soon become clear.

The Japan tour was also an important and happy one for Buddy because he became close with a *Holiday on Ice* soloist, Irene Braun, whose name began to be mentioned often in his letters home. The show had traveled onward to Manila when Leni, at the bottom of a letter from Erich that was mostly about the house, finances, and taxes, wrote the following: "Just a few words from me, we're doing well and I'm happy beyond words about our newly redone bedroom with the mattresses on the floor, carpets, curtains, built-in closet! I sold the leather armchairs from the dining room and put in I.'s wing chair, reupholstered. We're happy for your successes and it looks like things will be getting better here too. You have 'strangely' a lot to say about this Irene! Is she your true love?? Just another of your mother's indiscreet questions!! you don't have to answer me."

What had Buddy written about Irene? That she was beautiful, intelligent, good-hearted, and that men were all crazy about her—every day she got dozens of calls, letters, and flowers "from millionaires and philistines."

After the Asia tour, Irene Braun's mother in Munich wanted her to come back home. Buddy, back on tour with the show in America, toyed with the idea of marrying Irene, but her mother wouldn't let Irene go, and the daughter gave in. Buddy was disappointed and depressed. Later, when Leni asked how his love life was going, he answered: "I could write a whole book on the topic . . . Nowhere in the world are the girls as spoiled, stupid, degenerate, and uneducated as the ones I always meet . . . It's better to just sit in my room and listen to my records . . . Apropos of girls, that's why I miss Irene, she was pretty as a picture, smart, educated, and sweet and had the same interests as me."

Meanwhile, there was progress with the play. Albert Hackett and Frances Goodrich Hackett had written a first draft that Otto so disliked he was even sorry he had agreed to a dramatization of Anne's diary at all. In his opinion, the play conveyed nothing of Anne's ideals, of what he understood to be her "message." After all the editions of the book and the countless letters he had received, he knew what people were most moved by: Anne's difficulties going through puberty, the conflicts with her mother, and the love story with Peter. They were impressed most of all with Anne's "optimistic approach to life," as Otto Frank emphasized again and again.

In other words, Otto didn't want it to be a "Jewish" play—he felt that it should be "universal," not directed only to a Jewish audience. Still, the conditions in the Secret Annex were obviously and unambiguously based on the fact that they were Jews who had gone into hiding. If Meyer Levin's version, according to the general consensus, was "too Jewish," the Hacketts' version was perhaps too non-Jewish, too light and cheerful. The director, Garson Kanin, backed the team of writers and said that he had never seen the diary as a sad book; as he said in one interview, he didn't want to depress the public. He felt that the specifically Jewish aspect should be suppressed "to allow for a better identification with the theme and the characters." So he changed Anne's line "We're not the only Jews who have to suffer. Right through the ages there have been Jews who have had to suffer" to: "We are not the only people who have to suffer. There have been people who had to suffer for centuries, now this race, now that one."

Otto, the father, was to be played by Joseph Schildkraut, an actor born in Vienna who had started out as a child star and over time had become a well-respected character actor. Edith, the mother, would be played by Gusti Huber, also from Vienna, who had married an American in 1946 and followed him back to the States. This casting gave rise to fierce debate, from the beginning, since it was rumored that Gusti Huber had had close ties to National Socialism during the war—too close. That she of all people was to play Edith Frank unleashed a storm of criticism, especially in Jewish circles. But Garson Kanin insisted on her despite all the attacks. The young actress Susan Strasberg was to play Anne.

To make the action of the play more dramatic, the Hacketts, at the director's request, added a scene in their revised draft where Mr. van Daan (who was called van Pels in the diary and thus in the play) stole some bread. As Buddy related later, that didn't seem right to Otto himself, since obviously no such theft had taken place. Anyone who only saw the play without having read the book would think that Anne had described this scene, he said, and he repeatedly expressed his regret that Dussel (Pfeffer) as well as van Daan (van Pels) were being presented as not very sympathetic characters. In his opinion, the play showed them in a false light. He nevertheless let himself be talked into agreeing every time, when Bloomgarden and Kanin argued that it was crucial for the play.

The premiere of *The Diary of Anne Frank* took place on October 5, 1955, in New York's Cort Theatre. The play was an overwhelming success. Only two days later, Buddy wrote to Herbstgasse from Dayton, Ohio:

I have just read the absolutely glowing articles about the play and am stunned, but happy. I almost cried my eyes out. The whole situation has been on my mind for months, much more than I realized. If there are critics in New York papers writing things like that, then it must really be [in English:] "top quality." If only I could see it. Of course I know that for me it would be anything but a pleasure to watch! Congratulations to Otto, to Fritzi, and especially to dear Anne, who has created such an indelible monument to humanity. Like so many other great individuals, she had to die so that the world could profit from her genius.

Since I assume you will get all the N.Y. articles from the Hacketts, I want to keep for myself the newspapers I bought. But I'll send you the article in Billboard that will be out next week. Billboard and Variety are the newspapers of the theater world.

Ottel, what about translating the play into German. Maybe it can be performed in Switzerland, Austria, or Germany. I would be terribly happy to try to translate it and I think I could do it too.

This suggestion from Buddy most likely arrived too late; in any case, it was never mentioned again. The Hacketts' play was translated into German by Robert Schnorr.

In Basel they were obviously also following the news of the play's unexpected success. Anne's diary became one of the main topics of conversation in the house on Herbstgasse, where at that point, in 1955, eight people were living (now that Herbert, after many failed attempts, had succeeded in getting a residence permit for Basel): Leni and Erich, Grandma Ida, Otto and Fritzi, Stephan, Herbert, and Imperia the housekeeper. The success of the diary that their "little Anne" had written astonished them. They almost couldn't believe the good reviews that were appearing everywhere and the worldwide interest in Anne's book that resulted. They listened, amazed and moved, as Otto read them letters that people from the far corners of the world had written to Anne's father after reading the diary. Otto, who, as he himself put it, "was built right near the water" when it came to anything having to do with Anne's diary, was often moved to tears, especially by letters from young people, and when he read sentences like "Anne Frank changed my life." Sometimes, he would say, a little depressed: "Everyone only talks about Anne, but I had two children. No one talks about Margot." Since there was little else to say, he would then add, as though to console himself, the sentence that he always said when Margot came up: "Margot was an angel."

Naturally, they all read the letters that Buddy sent to Herbstgasse; he knew he didn't need to write to individuals in particular. His greeting, "Dear everyone," was meant literally. In the numerous letters that he wrote in the following weeks and months, the main topic was the play. As early as October 10, 1955, five days after the premiere in New York, he wrote to them from Illinois, full of excitement:

Hurrah, it's what I've been waiting for! I will send you the reviews that are out from Time, Newsweek, New Yorker, *and* Billboard.

HOTEL Moraine

DAYTON, OHIO

10. 10. 55

Hurrah, auf das habe ich gewartet!

Ich werde Euch noch die Kritiken aus „Time" „Newsweek" „New Yorker" und „Billboard" schicken sofern was erscheint. Bis jetzt habe ich „New York Times" „Telegraph" „Dayly mirror" „dayly news" und „Journal American". Habt Ihr die alle?

Meine Kollegen sind alle der Meinung, dass das Stück jahrelang spielen wird. Walter Windell, der bekannteste Radio kommentator, dem ganz Amerika jeden Sonntag zuhört, sagte heute: „Best Drama on Broadway is „Anne Franks Diary", a play which will stay in your hearts forever! A new star is

FIREPROOF – 130 ROOMS WITH BATH AND SHOWER

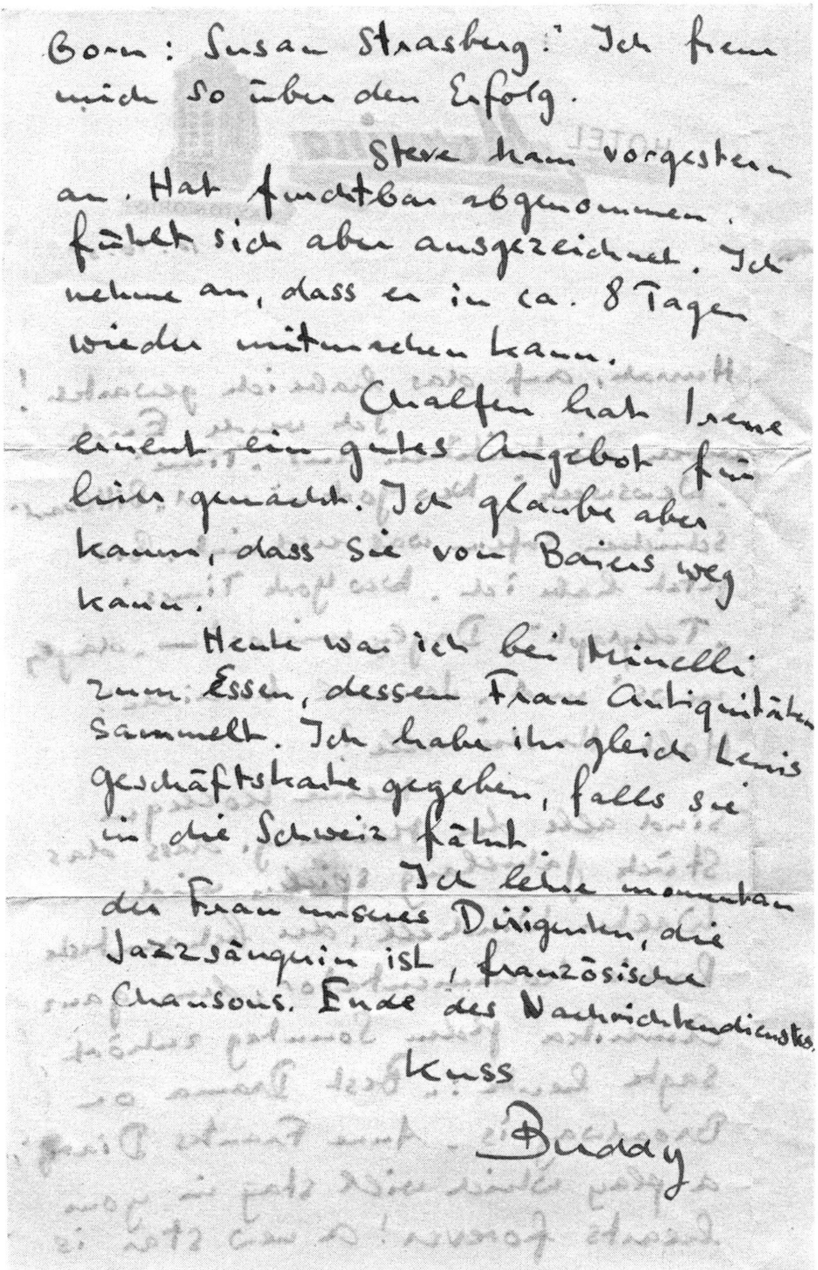

Born: Susan Strasberg! Ich freue mich so über den Erfolg.

Steve kam vorgestern an. Hat furchtbar abgenommen, fühlt sich aber ausgezeichnet. Ich nehme an, dass er in ca. 8 Tagen wieder mitmachen kann.

Chalfen hat Irene ~~einen~~ ein gutes Angebot für Lilis gemacht. Ich glaube aber kaum, dass sie von Baiers weg kann.

Heute war ich bei Minelli zum Essen, dessen Frau Antiquitäten sammelt. Ich habe ihr gleich Lenis Geschäftskarte gegeben, falls sie in die Schweiz fährt.

Ich lehre momentan der Frau unseres Dirigenten, die Jazzsängerin ist, französische Chansons. Ende des Nachrichtendienstes.

Kuss

Buddy

Buddy Elias's letter from Dayton, Ohio, October 10, 1955

So far I have the New York Times, Telegraph, Daily Mirror, Daily News, *and* American Journal. *Do you have all of those?*

My colleagues all think that the play will run for years. Walter Winchell, the most famous radio commentator in America, whom the whole country listens to every Sunday, said today: [Buddy's English:] "Best Drama on Broadway is 'Anne Frank's Diary,' a play which will stay in your hearts forever! A new star is Born: Susan Strasberg!" I am thrilled about the success.

Another five days later he was already sending his next letter to "Everyone and especially to Ottel":

I've enclosed some clippings that you might not have already. Especially the magnificent article in Life . . . *I don't want to be indiscreet, but I'm burning to know if Ottel will also get his share of the truly major financial success of the play and the movie. If I had been at the premiere I would probably have gotten to meet Marilyn Monroe, and I certainly wouldn't have objected to that! I can hardly wait to go to New York.*

The play's success really did exceed all expectations, although even then there was the occasional criticism that the Hacketts' play was too light—the word "kitsch" even turned up here and there.

Buddy had mixed feelings about attending the play: on the one hand, he was greatly looking forward to it; on the other hand, he realized that it would be "anything but a pleasure" for him. He could completely understand, he wrote to Basel, that Otto did not want to see the play, although he could imagine nothing better than meeting up with Otto and Fritzi in New York. And when he came home, hopefully that summer, he would be very happy to read some of the letters that Otto had received.

By the end of 1955, the time had come, and Buddy saw the play. He wrote on December 26: "That unforgettable evening at the Cort Theatre is still on my mind and I will be turning it over in my head for a long time. Of course I'll tell you everything about it in this letter."

This was when he started to tell people who he was, how he was connected with the Anne Frank whose name everyone had now heard, and slowly the news got around. Today, Buddy says: "I was happy about the success, and I was proud to be Anne Frank's cousin, I have to admit it . . . Yes, well, the truth is I was a little conceited about it." In interviews that he gave for *Holiday on Ice,* he would answer whenever asked about it: "Yes, I am the cousin." The play's success was so unexpected and so overwhelming that it couldn't help but affect everyone who had had anything to do with Anne.

Buddy's next letter, of January 4, 1956, shows how much the play really was on his mind:

Some more things about the play. Not much can be changed in the directing or the staging at this point, but what absolutely needs to be changed, in my insignificant opinion, is the following: After van Daan steals the bread, Edith has a practically hysteric fit of rage and orders the van Daans to leave the Annex immediately. However humanly understandable this outburst is, the scene has an embarrassing and repellent effect on the audience and makes Edith look like a monster, when we all, and the audience too, have only seen her good side. The outburst is improbable and feels wrong. It's also much too long. It's what bothered me the most in the whole production. Van Daan's theft is not connected with Judaism. In general the whole issue of Judaism is treated wonderfully throughout until then. He makes up for the theft with serious, heartfelt regret. Still, he is shown throughout the whole play as a rather unpleasant person. It makes sense that Mrs. van Daan wears a gold lamé dress, she is a woman who pays a lot of attention to her appearance and even in tragic surroundings doesn't want to let herself go, which the scene with the fur coat highlights. The gold is appropriate in my opinion. That Anne makes herself look pretty when she visits Peter is maybe a little exaggerated but it's sweet and I would take out only the part where she pads her bra. The audience's laughter absolutely does not bother me. It's not the laughter a comedian gets, it's a liberating laughter like a child's when you give her a doll after she's been through something painful. The laughter doesn't take away from the audience being moved, attentive, and sympathetic, not even for a second. Susan is a little too wild in the first act.

This letter makes it very clear that Buddy, despite his skating career, remained in his heart of hearts an actor. In the following months and years he wrote about all sorts of things and experiences, obviously—for instance, he was worried about Stephan and advised him to take better care of himself, or he sent money for the house—but Anne's diary and the play occupied him wherever he went. He was sucked ever deeper into the whirlpool that emanated from Anne's diary and continues to be to this day.

An additional reason for his immersion in what his cousin had written might well have been that he often felt isolated and lonely. He always suffered from homesickness and loneliness, says his wife, Gerti, having to live so far away from his family and so rarely seeing his loved ones. It's true that Buddy met a lot of people, but the friendships and relationships always remained on a superficial level. It could hardly have been otherwise given his unsettled life, always on the move. No matter where he was, he took every opportunity to meet relatives, even distant relatives. For example, when he was in Los Angeles, he saw Dora and Emma, two of the daughters of Alfred and Klärchen, Alice's favorite cousin. These childless old women, already over eighty, lived together in an apartment filled with old furniture and pictures, two of which hang in the Herbstgasse house today.

At Otto's request, Buddy also visited many people with whom his uncle had corresponded, whether readers of Anne's diary or actors such as Joseph Schildkraut. He visited the Hacketts, too, the authors of the play. In a letter from June: "I hope you got the card that we sent you from the Hacketts'. It was a very nice visit.

The Diary was obviously the main topic of conversation. Mrs. Hackett also told me: "I fell in love with your father, your mother, and your brother. She showed me a newspaper clipping from a Hamburg paper that said Dorit Fischer (from Basel) would play Anne there."

In April, Buddy wrote: "I'm glad that Anne's play won the Tony Award. It more than deserves it. I only hope that the productions in Europe go as well as here. It will be hard to find another Susan Strasberg."

Mexico was the last stop on this tour, and Buddy wrote from Mexico City on May 16, after *The Diary of Anne Frank* had won the 1956 Pulitzer Prize for Drama:

Most of all, congratulations Otto on the Pulitzer Prize! It is really tremendous, everything that's happening, and wonderful. I wrote to the Hacketts . . . Mexico City is fantastic. An ultramodern city. Spanish and American combined. It's a relief to be back in a sophisticated city with real atmosphere and not to have to see yet another endlessly identical, boring, uninteresting Amer. city for once . . . The premiere went very well but there were lots of obstacles. Since Mexico City is 8,200 feet above sea level and the air is so thin, lots of us had terrible problems breathing. Some of us fainted, Ted Roman as strong as he is had to come off the ice even today because of pains in his side and shortness of breath, and Steve and I could only barely drag ourselves to the oxygen machine after our number.

The play's success was unstoppable, and in late August 1956 the European premiere took place in Göteborg, Sweden. Then, starting in October, *The Diary of Anne Frank* was performed in Germany too, first in West Berlin, Düsseldorf, Hamburg, Karlsruhe, and Konstanz, then in other cities as well, and of course in Vienna and Zurich too. Productions in many other European countries soon followed.

Especially in Germany, the play was an overwhelming success.

Sometimes the audience sat in deathly silence for many minutes after the play ended, before leaving the theater without a sound; sometimes the applause went on longer than anyone had ever seen at a play. *The Diary of Anne Frank* helped to break the silence that still blanketed the Nazi era. Young people in particular poured into the theaters in great numbers; the play had long runs in sold-out theaters everywhere. One reason for its success might have been that there were no monstrous, horrifying acts portrayed onstage; another was presumably sentences like "In spite of everything I still believe that people are really good at heart"—so forgiving and non-accusatory—which even perpetrators and collaborators could identify with, although Anne had clearly not meant them that way. In fact, there were only a few critical voices in Germany, as in America. Hannah Arendt, the philosopher, who grew up in Königsberg and had been living in exile since 1933, called the universal admiration for Anne Frank a form of "cheap sentimentality at the expense of great catastrophe." It was of course completely reasonable to analyze a mass phenomenon critically and ask whether the public reaction was the sign of genuine sympathy or simply the idealization of a girl who made it easy to avoid asking deeper questions of guilt, responsibility, and individual bad conscience. But so soon after the war it could hardly be expected that such questions would be discussed by the general public. In any case, Hannah Arendt was an exception to the general enthusiasm.

Everyone living in the house on Herbstgasse went to see the play performed in Konstanz, except for Otto, who never saw *The Diary of Anne Frank*. Leni and Erich talked with Anja Römer, who played Anne, and invited her to visit them in Basel. She met Otto there and became a frequent guest of the family.

Buddy wrote in October 1956: "I don't know if you realize how much all this stirs my emotions and occupies my mind. The public's reaction in Germany must really be unbelievable. It almost scares me and I would really like to know what the majority of the people there really think . . . In any case the name Anne Frank will live forever, and if humanity will take her message to heart, as we all hope, then Ottel will really have achieved what he wanted."

In a later letter, he wrote: "These overwhelming reviews from Germany. I read them last night and am still flabbergasted. What is there to say?! Little Anne has really made world history. I'll take these clippings with me to New York and show them to Schildkraut . . . I have so many questions I would love to talk to Otto for a few hours . . . The movie plans don't seem to be very secret after all . . . This all must be terribly agitating for our good Ottel."

In Germany there would soon be schools and youth centers named after Anne Frank. Buddy would write in June 1956: "It's wonderful, that news about the Anne Frank School, and I would love to hear about the celebrations in Frankfurt from Herbert, since he was there at the opening."

Buddy also wrote that in his opinion everyone in the family, except for Otto, should see the play, even if it obviously would be painful. They should do it for Anne's sake. Ultimately, it was her work there onstage.

His letter of December 3, 1956, was about another New York production:

We had a wonderful but difficult evening last Thursday. Steve, Dolores Pallet, and I went to the theater. Five of the actors were new, and the girl playing Anne is magnificent. Better than Susan. Susan was technically brilliant but little Dina Doronne is so natural, and acts with so much heart, that she reaches the audience better, in my opinion. The new Peter is better too. It was a wonderful production and for the first time in my life I saw Steve cry . . . I couldn't control myself either of course . . . After the performance we went backstage. The whole ensemble was there and they were expecting me. They had intentionally not told little Dina that I was in the theater, and when I came backstage, hugged her, and was introduced as Anne's cousin, she burst into tears. Then, when I said how magnificent I thought she was, she ran sobbing from the stage . . . We had to go into Schildkraut's dressing room, where a press photographer took pictures of us that would come out the next day. They turned out brilliantly and I'll bring them with me . . . After the performance we went out to eat with Schildkraut, his wife, Dina, and some of Sch's friends. Little Dina is so enchanting that I fell in love with her right away. So natural and sweet. Totally charming.

A week later, he wrote: "Yesterday I went out to eat with Dina (the new Anne). So enchanting. Very religious, and a burning patriot for Israel. When I think that this delicate little creature was in the Israeli army, carrying a gun—just unbelievable."

The play's great success also ignited Meyer Levin's anger. He could not be dissuaded from thinking that his version of the play was the one that deserved to be performed, not the "Broadway hit." In late 1956, he filed a lawsuit against Otto Frank and Kermit Bloomgarden in New York Supreme Court. He, Levin, had been assigned to write the play, he attested, and had suffered serious losses due to fraud and breach of contract. He had settled with Otto Frank in 1952 only under duress, therefore their previous verbal agreement was still valid, he claimed, otherwise his rights to a production in Israel were in jeopardy as well. Furthermore, he claimed that the Hacketts had used Levin's ideas in their version, and sought damages.

Otto Frank declared in writing that Levin was wrong on every point and asked for the case to be dismissed. In addition, he said, Levin had no further rights with respect to the production in Israel because he had taken no steps in the meantime to realize his plan. In short, the situation with Meyer Levin was far from over. However, until a judicial decision was reached, Otto's royalties for the stage production remained frozen. With the help of wise men from the Jewish community, an agreement was eventually reached on October 26, 1959: in return for a payment of fifty thousand dollars, Otto Frank would receive from Meyer Levin all copyright in Levin's stage adaptation. But that resolution lay far in the future.

As Buddy had predicted, the success of the play had consequences for the sales of the book. Fischer published a paperback edition in Germany in 1955 that went through more than a dozen printings in the following years. Anne Frank's diary had touched people, had got them to stop and reflect on their own memories of the catastrophe, which was not yet far in the past. It had awakened questions of guilt and responsibility, which most people would have gladly avoided but which were unavoidable once they read the book. To that extent, it really had changed people's lives. Its effects remain visible to this day.

Of course the diary that had influenced and changed so many strangers also had effects on Buddy, as is clear from this letter he wrote from South Africa in February 1957:

So now I've seen The Diary *here too. When you take into account that Cape Town is not exactly the theater capital of the world, the production here is remarkably good . . . The best thing about the production was without question the young man who played Peter. He is sensational and belongs on Broadway. Absolutely phenomenal. One of the greatest talents I have ever seen onstage. He was so mature and at the same time so touching, childish, awkward, and shy, just what the role requires . . . In general there were good directorial decisions throughout, e.g. when Miep came in and Anne said she could smell the fresh air in Miep's coat. She stuck her little head in Miep's coat and stayed there for a few seconds like that while Miep looked sadly at Kraler [Kugler]. It was not a very important scene in the script, but thanks to the direction it turned into one of the most impressive and moving scenes . . . We had a very unpleasant incident backstage that's typical of how things are here. Some negroes work for us as stagehands and we always have hot tea during the break. I overheard one of our white African musicians tell another: "That bloody nigger tried to get a cup of tea, but I showed where his place was, I threw that tea right in his face!" I turned beet red of course but didn't say anything. Just then another negro came up and*

I didn't know if he wanted some tea or was just walking by. In any case this white musician suddenly grabbed the negro by his collar and threw him to the ground. I jumped up of course and yelled at him to stop, and he answered: "We have to do this in this country, it's the rules and if I wouldn't do it you wouldn't be here."

You can imagine what I wanted to tell him, that I spit on his rules of the country, *that I follow the* rules of humanity *and see no reason to spend any time in a country where these conditions etc. etc. And what did I actually say to him? Nothing! I thought about how it might cause problems not just for me but for Steve and for the whole show and I would be acting thoughtlessly, but I could have kicked myself for my own cowardice and I swore a vow if anything like that ever happened around me again not to keep silent whatever the consequences. Too many people have put blinkers on in recent times and shut their eyes when human beings were persecuted and damn me to hell if I do it too. I couldn't live with my conscience. Brotherhood of man is more than an empty phrase for me.*

Earlier, before his tour of Egypt, Buddy had written that it was probably better to say he was Protestant during his stay there; now he was taking an unambiguous stand. And leaving aside the word "negro," which was still used at the time, in 1957, this letter shows another effect that Anne Frank's diary had and, hopefully, still has today—namely, awakening a sense of the consequences that follow when people only look out for their own well-being, their own comfort. Without these—in Buddy's word—"blinkers," the Nazis would never have been able to carry out their program of exterminating so many human beings.

14.

Our Reason for Being Here

Otto and Fritzi traveled to New York in 1957 to be present at the trial that Meyer Levin had instigated. Now it was Fritzi's turn to write long, detailed letters to the family from on the road. On November 18, 1957, she wrote to the house on Herbstgasse:

All my darlings, The time flies by, tomorrow it'll already be two weeks that we've been here and even though I've seen a lot of beautiful and interesting things we haven't made the slightest bit of progress when it comes to our reason for being here. We now hope that things will start happening on Wednesday. In any case, the jury selection will take at least a day, if not two . . . Yesterday morning we were at the lawyer's again and he told us that he could not understand why Levin's lawyer had not requested a pretrial hearing with Otto, which he had the right to do and which is always done. He could have also insisted on seeing all the documents and files that we have and he doesn't have, but he didn't do that either. They think he will still try to settle out of court, today or tomorrow. I personally don't believe it, I'm afraid that instead it will mean that tomorrow there might still be another delay. Levin is giving a public lecture today, "Authors and Producers," and our case is sure to come up . . . At 2 this afternoon we are supposed to go back to the lawyer's and Crawford's lawyer will be there too. Otto will get his final instructions and will go through answering all the questions again that the opposing lawyers might ask. But he is already very well prepared.

You know how he can always hold everything exactly in his head. Stay healthy and very warmest wishes and kisses from Your Fritzi.

Fritzi wrote unbelievably long, elaborate letters with many precise descriptions of the people she saw, how their apartments looked, how their children behaved, and so forth. She had a lot to report and ultimately had more than enough time to report it, since everything was proceeding "at a snail's pace." On December 14, she wrote:

Levin began his testimony on Wednesday, continued on Thursday and Friday, and only now has he gotten to August 1952. It goes like this: His lawyer asks him a question that he is only allowed to answer completely concretely and specifically. If he doesn't, our lawyer says "Objection" and the judge usually agrees. Meanwhile, letters are read out loud, there is a whole procedure for that and it takes a long time. Sometimes the lawyers disagree about something and then they go up to the judge and quietly talk it over & so nothing moves forward. He's telling the same old story that we also already have in writing, the alleged meeting in fall '50, with the verbal agreement, etc. We are already looking forward to his being unmasked.

On December 30, she sent news of the breakthrough in a telegram to Basel: "Judge rejects claim as baseless in all particulars Plagiarism and countersuit will take another week Regards FritzOtt."

Of course, the satisfactory conclusion of the affair with Levin still lay far in the future. Fritzi wrote on January 4 in reply to the congratulatory letters she had received: "Only the plagiarism case is a very dangerous matter, because if Levin wins he could sue the Hacketts and Foxfilm and the damages would be incalculable. The lawyers and we ourselves are very optimistic, since we know for a fact that no one told the Hacketts the slightest thing about Levin's script, but you can't imagine the methods the other side is using, it's exactly what you're used to seeing in gangster movies. Our lawyer catches most of it, he's wonderful, and counteracts it, and also the jury is very much on our side, which is also important."

Otto was on the witness stand for only half an hour, and Fritzi wondered if it was worth traveling all the way to New York for that. He came across well, very calm and dignified, but they had asked him hardly anything, only whether or not he had shown Meyer Levin's script to the Hacketts or to Kanin. The situation looked very good, from Fritzi's point of view. All the more unexpected was the verdict, which hit them hard. She wrote to "All our darlings" on January 9:

I'm sure you got the telegram with the bad news, we are still utterly stunned about this outrageous injustice, and I will quickly tell you how it happened.

Tuesday morning all the way until 3 in the afternoon our lawyer gave a fabulous speech and we were all convinced that everyone would understand that the Hacketts had no direct or indirect knowledge of the Levin script and that every similarity between the two scripts came from the book. Levin's lawyer started from 3 to 4 and continued the whole next morning, & really in such a nasty way that you've only ever seen in gangster movies. He called the Hacketts skillful thieves who had done what a car thief does: given the car a new paint job and license plate so that it couldn't be recognized. In other words, they changed his ideas so that they were not technically identical but only similar . . . So the lawyer claimed that either Otto or Bloomgarden or Kanin or someone else had told them about it. They couldn't prove it, of course, but they deduced it from the similarities between the scripts. And that was enough to award Levin, the so-called collaborator on the script, $50,000, which of course Otto has to pay on top of his legal fees.

Not only our friends were crying—they were all with us until half past midnight in the court while we were waiting for the jury's verdict—but our lawyer too, who is hardly a child. He is hardened enough, but he was as stunned at the injustice as we were. We don't know what will happen next. The lawyers are looking into the possibility of an appeal. But it's possible that Levin will also appeal the other decision, or try to get more money from this, we have no idea. We also think that the Hacketts will have to do something, since it's their honor at stake too. We also don't know to what extent the film is involved too now.

The news struck the family in Basel like a bomb, of course. Fifty thousand U.S. dollars was an amount of money that sent a chill up the spine of everyone who heard it—the times of shortages and hunger, when you had to count every penny, were not that long ago.

Buddy was furious too. On January 22, 1958, he wrote "Dear everyone: I just got your horrifying letter with the enclosed letter from Ottel and Fritzi. I already saw the news in *Time* magazine but had no idea that it was that bad, and that Otto has to pay $50,000. I very much hope that an appeal will be granted. Justice must be done! . . . You can't imagine how deeply I feel the news. Poor Otto and Fritzi, who are totally innocent and who want to do so much good with the money . . . Is the movie jeopardized?"

Otto and Fritzi stayed another couple of weeks in the States. George Stevens, the director of the planned movie adaptation of the diary, had arranged everything for their visit to Los Angeles. "We are traveling by train and will have a sleeping car as well as a lounge car in the train, all paid for by Fox [Twentieth Century Fox]." Financially, Fritzi wrote, they were in bad shape. The film company withheld the installment of their payment that would have been due in January, which was within their rights according to their contract. "It doesn't make any difference for our personal, modest life," Fritzi wrote, "but it makes things difficult for the Foundation and so Otto will definitely try to pry loose some money while we're here. It is all very stressful and I would really like to know when we will ever have any peace."

But there was not to be any peace for some time. Buddy's

comment that Otto and Fritzi wanted to do so much good with the money, like Fritzi's saying that Otto would definitely try to get some of the money while they were still in the United States, was in reference to the Anne Frank Foundation in Amsterdam.

After Pectacon and Gies & Co. were sold, the companies moved from the Prinsengracht into new office spaces, and the Anne Frank Foundation was established, on May 3, 1957, with the goal of "preserving the Prinsengracht 263 building in Amsterdam and in particular the Secret Annex thereof, as well as advancing the ideals that Anne Frank left behind for the world."

Otto Frank had never forgotten the idea that Joseph Marks from Doubleday had expressed in 1952: that they should buy the house at Prinsengracht 263 and establish a library for youth in the Secret Annex. He decided to set up a foundation that would manage the house. With many donations, state support, and the help of the City of Amsterdam, they were able to buy the building and the adjoining houses, although they were in dilapidated condition and first had to be thoroughly renovated.

Otto planned to use the front of the house—the former office rooms—for exhibitions on Nazism and various aspects of the Holocaust and the German occupation, and to keep the Secret Annex empty. After the arrest on August 4, 1944, the Nazi officers had hired the Puls moving company to empty the Annex and confiscate all clothing, furniture, and personal belongings for distribution to bombed-out families in Germany. That is what happened to all the apartments of arrested Jews. Luckily, before the moving company arrived, Miep Gies and Bep Voskuijl saved Anne's diaries and notebooks.

Johannes Kleiman represented Otto Frank on the new foundation's board of directors until his death on January 28, 1959. From then on, Otto Frank would devote much of his time and energy to the Anne Frank Foundation.

Three years after the foundation was established, the Anne Frank House opened its doors. The Anne Frank House organizes traveling exhibits; develops educational material, and designs activities for the advancement of tolerance and mutual respect in society; houses a documentation center on Holocaust pedagogy, racism, discrimination, and the radical right; and hosts seminars and workshops for schools, businesses, and associations. The Secret Annex itself receives countless visitors year after year. Nine thousand people visited the Anne Frank House in the first year, 1960; ten years later the number was 180,000; and in 2007, for the first time, there were more than a million visitors: 1,002,902, to be exact. Along with the Madame Tussauds wax museum in London, the Louvre, and the British Museum, the Anne Frank House is one of the ten most visited museums in Europe.

Otto Frank was guided by the idea of doing something in memory of his daughter to promote the mutual understanding of young people and tolerance between different religions. He never wanted anything else, and he dedicated all his energies and all the time that remained to him to this task.

"Otto never wanted anything for himself, he was always there for others," Buddy and his wife, Gerti, say today. "He devoted the rest of his life to his daughter's work. The success of the diary was also a business, of course, but the money was not important to Otto, it wasn't about that. He always said, 'The money isn't my money, it's Anne's money,' and he never kept it for himself. He lived modestly his whole life long. The only thing that mattered to Otto was spreading Anne's message."

15.

The Movie

Filming began on the movie version of the diary in the spring of 1958, and kept not only Otto and Fritzi busy but the whole family on Herbstgasse and of course Buddy as well, who was kept informed about everything. The Hacketts had again written the script, and to produce and direct the film, Bloomgarden had got George Stevens, who was famous for many films, including *Shane* and *Giant*. From South Africa, Buddy wrote that it was totally unbelievable what was happening: "I am on the edge of my seat to hear about Ottel's meeting with Stevens. I hope Stevens is sensitive enough not to turn it into a Hollywood blockbuster . . . Please keep me up to date on the latest developments. I can hardly wait for your letters. You can't imagine how involved I feel with everything that has to do with Anne."

Audrey Hepburn originally intended to play the role of Anne, and Buddy was enthusiastic: "I'm glad Audrey Hepburn will be playing Anne. I'm convinced she'll be good for the part." She even visited Otto and Fritzi on Herbstgasse—there is a postcard from Hepburn to Leni, and one from Mel Ferrer, who was married to Audrey Hepburn (his fourth marriage), to Otto and Fritzi. But in the end Audrey Hepburn withdrew from the project, saying that she had too many doubts about whether she could withstand the emotional burden of the part. And in her late twenties (she was born in 1929, the same year as Anne Frank), she was in truth too old for the role. Buddy was very disappointed. He wrote: "I didn't know that Ottel and Fritzi met Audrey and Mel Ferrer. I'm jealous . . . So who will play Anne, if Audrey can't?"

A letter that Otto Frank wrote to George Stevens in English on October 21, 1957, about the curtains in the Secret Annex, shows how important every detail was to Otto:

Dear Mr. Stevens,

Through our dear friends Frances and Albert [Hackett] we heard how busy you were all the time working with them on the script und preparing the picture.

In their last letter they have asked some questions concerning our curtains in the hiding-place you had and I want to give you my answer directly. Please don't hesitate to ask me whatever details you want to know. I am only too pleased to be of help whenever I can.

1. the net curtains: As Anne wrote we had net curtains in all our rooms. We had sent old curtains to the hiding-place before we came, but as the sizes did not fit, we had to arrange them and sew some of them together. Of course these curtains always stayed.

2. Before getting dark we put before all the windows our black-out. This consisted of an ordinary wooden frame on which strong cardboard was fixed. This frames were made to fit in every window and if you look at the photo showing the window of Anne's room, you will notice small wooden turnable handles on every side which had to hold the black-out. On the bottom of the windows small wooden pieces were fixed so that the black-out could not slip down. Of course these frames were taken down in the morning. To be quite sure that no light could get through on top or on the sides, we fixed stripes of black paper there as you can see also on the photo. Besides we had clothcurtains, not because it was necessary for the blackout, as this was safe with what we had, but to make the rooms look nicer.

3. In our rooms no window was painted. However there were some windows bluepainted. If you look at the map of the house shown in the book, the windows of the storeroom second floor behind, facing the secret annexe, were painted. Besides the windows of the landing were treated in a manner to prevent people from looking through. A sort of transparent paper with a pattern was glued on the glass, so that light could come in, but you could not see through.

In the front office first floor there were very heavy, lined dark red wool-en curtains which were sufficent. In the front rooms, they stopped work before dark and in the rear office ordinary black paper rollcurtains were used.

I hope these descriptions will be useful to you.

You certainly will have heard that my wife and I are due to arrive in New-York November 5th and we hope to have the opportunity to meet you.

We are thinking of you many a time remembering the hours we spent together.

All the best to you from both of us and kindly give our regards to George.

Yours sincerely
Otto Frank

This letter, describing the measures that the occupants of the Secret Annex were forced to take in order to prevent anyone outside from noticing that there were Jews in hiding there, is impressively precise. These precautions are also an indication of the occupants' fear, which must have been ever present, even though the daily handling of the blackout curtains must have quickly become routine.

On February 20, 1958, Otto Frank recorded his impressions of Millie Perkins, the actress who had accepted the part of Anne Frank in the movie. Again he wrote in English:

When I first met Millie we both felt the importance of the meeting, and she was rather shy and wouldn't speak very much. She impressed me as a very modest sensitive girl who felt the importance of representing Anne in a picture.

Her eyes first impressed me—dark eyes—very tender, with faith and sincerity. You think they are dark eyes, but they are blue. Anne's eyes were very similar and were very noticeable. She did not have brown eyes—they were grey.

Later, Millie and I had a serious talk about Anne, the conditions in hiding etc. She asked very clever and intelligent questions.

My general impression of Millie: she looks very young—a charming, natural girl, and she does not act like an "actress." I think she is very suitable for the role.

The second time we met she was much more free in her behavior, which I felt was more or less a sign of confidence. I think we both had the feeling of confidence in each other, and I remarked that we were both born on the 12th of May. So we compared characteristics—we are both very handy in finishing things, like electrical and mechanical things. We have a certain kind of nervousness and sensitiveness.

Millie has a movement of her hands, like Anne had—and she has a little trick of bending her fingers backward, just as Anne did. She takes care of herself (her personal grooming), just as Anne did. Anne would not go without having her hair combed, nails done—she was very soignee—very neat, as Millie seems to be.

When we first met, Millie said—"when I read the script and the book I knew it was all real. After speaking with you, I really felt the reality of it all."

I am confident that Millie will represent Anne in a very natural way because she now identifies herself with Anne. She is trying to entirely live the role. She has asked me many questions about everything so that she will understand how Anne felt about everything—all of her inner feelings, and her personality.

I think that the casting of Diane Baker for the part of Margot is just wonderful. She is so very much like Margot was—the other day as I looked at her profile, I was struck with the great resemblance. She has the same sweet, quiet dignity. I think the casting of Millie and Diane as sisters will be perfect as there is the same difference between them as there was between Anne and Margot.

It must have been difficult for Otto Frank to compare the two actresses, Millie Perkins and Diane Baker, to his daughters, Anne and Margot. All the more remarkable is the openhearted friendliness with which he treated them, especially Millie Perkins. Once again he showed the trait that must have been so characteristic of him: withdrawing his own personality from the situation and always being ready to engage with other people.

So Otto was very fond of Millie Perkins, and of Diane Baker too. He met everyone involved in the filming, of course. He traveled with Fritzi to America to advise George Stevens and the actors about the details. Buddy was kept informed about everything too, as his letters show. He wrote in February 1958: "I'm not surprised that Otto and Fritzi like it at the Hacketts'. It's beautiful there." In April: "I can only partly understand why Ottel would not like Schildkraut. He is a typical actor, the way little Moritz would imagine an actor. Completely taken with himself, puffed up, ambitious, and as they say in English 'a big ham.' But he was always extremely nice friendly and sincere with me."

Joseph Schildkraut played the father, as he had in the play, and Gusti Huber again took the role of Edith Frank. The young actors who would play Anne, Margot, and Peter were not entirely appropriate, because of their ages: Millie Perkins had just turned twenty when the movie was shot, so she was five to seven years older than Anne when she had written the diary; Diane Baker was also twenty, three to five years older than Margot; and Richard Beymer, twenty as well, was a little older than Peter, who died in the Mauthausen concentration camp when he was eighteen.

The settings also didn't correspond to the diary. Stevens shot the exterior scenes in Amsterdam, but a set of the Secret Annex was built at the Fox studio and constructed as a single room so that it would seem more like an attic. The movie clearly differed from the diary in another regard as well: in the movie, only Miep Gies and Mr. Kraler (Kugler) protected and cared for the occupants of the Annex—Bep Voskuijl and Johannes Kleiman were written out.

The movie premiered in 1959. Although it won three Oscars the following year—Shelley Winters for Best Supporting Actress as Petronela van Daan (van Pels), Lyle R. Wheeler for Best Art Direction, and William C. Mellor for Best Cinematography—the reviews were less positive, and the movie was not a great commercial success. Possibly this was because people did not want to hear anything more about the Holocaust—the argument that is always made. In any case, the attendance figures left something to be desired. Another reason might have been that the movie was ultimately too superficial: as a British journalist wrote in the *Daily Mail*, "*The Diary of Anne Frank* is an outstanding instance of a subject being diminished by filming . . . The girl who wrote the diary must have had something more than the perky charm of a New World Junior Miss . . . These were European Jews in a European situation. But as presented here, especially by Shelley Winters and Ed Wynn they become stock figures from any tragic-comedy of Jewish life in Brooklyn."

The *Lexikon des Internationalen Films* (Dictionary of International Film) says: "The restrained, matter-of-fact style of Anne Frank's famous diary entries is given a largely conventional dramatization. The convincing performances and seriousness of the presentation, however, do force the viewer to confront the true story that is the basis for the film and among the most moving testimonies we have from the National Socialist period."

Buddy saw the movie for the first time in September 1959, in Tours in the Loire valley in France, during his European tour. He wrote to the family on Herbstgasse:

The Anne movie is on the whole excellent. Stevens's direction brilliant. It still strikes me a bit too much like a stage play on-screen, but that is probably just my personal critical opinion . . . Little Perkins is sometimes charming, especially in the love scenes, when you can feel Stevens's firm hand. Other times, she doesn't reach the audience. Also I have to say that for me she is a bit too much like a typical modern American teenager, which you notice especially in her speech since almost all the other actors talk in some kind of slightly foreign accent, which is good. Shelley Winters is especially excellent with her very faint Yiddish accent. Gusti Huber is better in the movie than onstage, Schildkraut is the opposite. The actor who played Dussel onstage was better than Bert Lahr [actually Ed Wynn] in the movie. Jakob brilliant, Margot brilliant too and the most like our real Margot. Peter was okay but could have been better. Kraler and Miep were good. I still would have rather seen Dina Doronne. The background music was exquisite, very beautiful, and there is nothing to criticize about the camera work either.

In this letter too, Buddy is above all an actor passing judgment on his colleagues. His reaction has a greater distance than he was able to maintain when reading the diary itself, and his judgments were amazingly accurate, when you compare them with those of the British journalist who had described Millie Perkins as having "the perky charm of a New World Junior Miss," and the academy that awarded Shelley Winters the Oscar for Best Supporting Actress. In all his years on the ice, Buddy never lost his sense for the theater and acting.

16.

Homesick for Herbstgasse

In the spring of 1958, *Holiday on Ice* traveled to South America, a tour that according to Buddy's descriptions must have been exciting and beautiful. In Lima, he attended a rehearsal for a stage production of *The Diary*. He described the director as gifted and serious, and Anne as the weak point of the production: the actress was too old, looked too old, moved as though she were too old, and screamed loud enough to make the auditorium shake, he said. Here too, in Lima, he met with a distant relative: Frau Holzer-Holländer, a cousin of Edith's. With his friend and colleague Denny he took a side trip to the Incan village of Pachacamac with Frau Holzer's brother, Richard Holländer, and Richard's wife. It was not far from Lima, so they could eat lunch at the Holländers' house, and Buddy had never seen such a house: it moved him to write, "A palace! Oh, it must be wonderful to be rich." Aside from the chauffeur, the Holländers had servants, a cook, a maid, and a rose garden illuminated at night with different-colored lights. The kitchen was as big as the whole ground floor of the Herbstgasse house, he said, and furnished in the most modern way possible, of course.

Despite the beauty, excitement, and success of the tour, Anne's diary came up again and again in his letters. For example, on May 2, 1958, from Lima: "Since one of our shows was canceled, I had the opportunity to see the premiere of *The Diary* here . . . I am happy to report that the performance was quite extraordinarily good for an amateur production. I can say in good conscience that it was absolutely professional. The production is on the whole better than the one in Cape Town, though of course there are some problems . . . But the most important thing is that the message of the play comes across perfectly and doesn't miss its mark in the audience."

He also didn't miss a chance to ask about the diary's sales in all the various cities he visited. Everywhere the play was performed, the diary also sold well, he wrote. "In Santiago, they also sold a lot of copies in German, since there is a large German colony there. In Brazil, I saw it displayed in Spanish."

In June he describes his apprehension about Bogotá, which lay more than 8,000 feet above sea level. He remembered only too well the serious problems he had had in Mexico City because of the altitude. And then came a sentence that showed how homesick he felt: "Even though I really do like it in South America, I've had enough, and I miss Herbstgasse and Switzerland terribly. [In English:] There's nothing like it!!"

He had had enough of hotels, of living out of a suitcase, of restaurant meals and strange beds. In Bogotá he rented a small apartment, which he was doing more and more frequently whenever the troupe had a longer stay somewhere. "It's good to get out of the hotels for a while and eat some home cooking again," he wrote home. "I'm sharing the apartment with Denny (I live in sin!!) and she's totally involved in the apartment too."

And yet barely two months later they were already in Colombia, in Medellín. Leni had written her son a letter from Sils-Maria, and Buddy had such a strong reaction that he went around crushed for a day or two. He was battling against homesickness, against his memories. He saw before his eyes the beautiful house, the park with the swing, and thought about how lovely and carefree those weeks were that he had spent there with Anne. They had played hide-and-seek and never dreamed that the game of hiding would one day turn deadly serious. They had still believed that the future lay before them like a picture book with one brightly colored page after another, and that they had only to turn the pages, rest their finger on something, and say, "That, there"—and it would happen. But it had all turned out so differently. Buddy sat down at the desk, in a hotel room that was as boring and arbitrary as every other one, and nothing compared to the elegant, well-furnished rooms at Villa Laret, and he wrote: "Many thanks for Leni's letter from Sils. I want so much to be with you all and I'll be there on August 1. I'm tired of traveling again and want to be home again for a few days. How I look forward to being at home."

In late 1958, *Holiday on Ice* went on a European tour, and on December 17, Buddy wrote home that they had been to Amsterdam. "With a heavy heart I visited the Prinsengracht house, where dear Miep showed us around. I didn't know that there was so much renovation in progress. We had to clamber up a chicken ladder to get to the Annex. There are two wreaths hanging in Anne's room from German youth groups."

What Buddy didn't write was how deeply the visit upset him. It was almost fifteen years earlier that Anne had lived in this room, the kind of room that Leni would probably have described as "a dump." He saw the photographs of movie stars that Anne had pasted to the wall above where her bed used to be, and felt a stab of pain in his heart. There was Heinz Rühmann, who throughout the war was allowed to pursue his acting career undisturbed since officially he was a "nonpolitical" star. In fact, he had divorced his Jewish wife in 1938 and appeared in numerous movies during the Nazi period because as a "national actor" he was exempt from military service. After the war, he just continued his career. Buddy felt rage and bitterness at the thought of him as he looked at the photograph and imagined how happy Anne was back then, in July 1942, when they moved into the Annex, to stick his picture on the wall in an effort to make this shabby room a little nicer.

In January 1959, with *Holiday on Ice* in Frankfurt, Leni visited her son. They had not seen each other in person for a long time and were overjoyed. Leni came to the show, of course, and was happy to see how well received "Buddy and Baddy" were by the audience. As Gerti repeatedly emphasized, Leni was always very proud of her son and collected all the newspaper clippings with reviews and notices that Buddy sent home, to show them to her friends and acquaintances. When Leni went back home to Basel, Buddy wrote: "I was so happy to see you on your visit and was glad you liked the show so much." In the same letter, he brought up a newspaper report that had made him angry: "Again the article about me has things in it that I really don't like and that I never said. Above all I never said that Otto is blind to everything except the foundation now. I said that his life is now entirely dedicated to Anne's work and especially to the foundation in Amsterdam."

On February 4, Buddy sent a letter to his loved ones from Frankfurt in which he describes having met Elvis Presley:

It was really strange to see Elvis Presley. Little Joyce was beside herself. She worships him and wrote him to see if he would like to come see the show. She always said to us: If I ever see him in person, I'll die!! Then, when he came backstage and even had his picture taken holding hands with her, the expression on her face was something to see. She was almost crying with joy and excitement. It was really moving. He spent the whole last show on Saturday backstage and brilliantly talked with everyone, and then later went back to the hotel where he plucked at least one of our girls to do justice to his manly sentiments. Sadly not our little Joyce.

Denny, the woman Buddy was "living in sin" with in Bogotá, decided at the end of 1959 to give up show business, "not because it was too difficult for her," Buddy wrote from Munich, "but because she couldn't stand the constant changes of climate and food." So there was no reason for her to go on tour again. That didn't change his own plans, he said; he planned to keep going for two or three more years.

In May 1960, Buddy was in Casablanca. On Otto's birthday,

he wrote: "Especially to Ottel, a heartfelt happy birthday and very best wishes for the success of the Anne Frank Foundation. I pray to God that this incredible work achieves what you, Fritzi, and countless other people are living for . . . I look forward to coming home and hearing all about the opening celebrations and your trip to Israel."

Today, Gerti, Buddy's wife, says, "It is too bad that Buddy didn't keep any of the letters he got from Otto. Otto wrote him so many."

Nineteen sixty, with *Holiday on Ice* back in America, was a decisive year for Buddy, who began planning his retirement from skating. In June he wrote from Miami: "So this is a memorable letter: my last from abroad . . . or in any case my last from my skating rink. I have 14 years behind me, the kind that are probably granted only to very few people, and you can't imagine what's running through my head right now. Joy, worry, hope, trust, regret, memories, fears, dreams."

He must have thought long and hard before coming to this decision. Buddy had been very successful with *Holiday on Ice*; the successes were less and less important to him as time went on, but would it really be so easy for him to leave? He had lived a life with *Holiday on Ice* that most people could only dream of, had had all sorts of experiences he would never forget, and met all sorts of people he would not have wanted to miss the chance to meet. He had seen incredible landscapes and fascinating cities. But even variety eventually turns into a routine and leads to boredom and satiety. Later, in a birthday letter to his wife, Gerti, he would put it this way: "Fourteen years of the ice show, fourteen years with hardly any culture, no theater, almost no good concerts, a lot of popular culture and countless experiences and impressions in many foreign countries, a lot of unforgettable things, but still, no THEATER. So I wanted to come back."

Buddy had seen a lot of the world, very much—maybe too much, he says today—but in his heart he dreamed of little Switzerland, of Basel, of the house on Herbstgasse. Above all, he dreamed of appearing onstage again and doing what he had wanted to do since he was a boy. But after so many years would he find a way in? Would anyone hire him, a thirty-five-year-old nobody just starting out? Who went into the theater at that age? There were actors who left the theater at that age. Did he have even the slightest chance of being hired by a well-known theater? The decision to try anyway took shape slowly, especially since no one back home except for Leni supported it. Erich advised against it, and Otto felt that he shouldn't take lightly the decision to give up his career as an ice-skater. Buddy wasn't taking it lightly—he was actually quite nervous about it—but he did not want to keep going. He also was feeling the difficulties more acutely than in earlier years, not only the constant travel, which was depressing, and the feeling of being without a real home, but also the falls that were unavoidable in his line of work. It was getting harder and harder for him to cope with his black-and-blue bruises, a sprained finger here, a contusion there. Some days, especially the ones with three performances, he was totally kaput, as he says today.

It nevertheless took a while before he could realize his wish. In October he wrote to "My dear ones": "As for coming home. I'd rather come today than tomorrow. And stay forever too. I am really sick of this but I don't know what to do. I have to think it over well . . . I want to give Steve enough time to look for something else. But I have decided to make the 1961/62 season my last season with the show no matter what. My decision is firm."

He wrote from Portland, Oregon, on November 4, 1960: "I pray to God that he help me get back into the theater. I will get in touch with Breitner as soon as I know for sure that I'm coming home, and ask him if there's any room in his ensemble for me. It won't be easy for me to get used to settling down after 14 years of traveling around. My main concern is whether I can restart my acting career. I don't think that I've lost the talent for it, but I need people who will help get me on my feet."

In his New Year's letter in December, he expressed his deepest wish for the year 1961: to see all his loved ones again and to make the house on Herbstgasse his home at last. He had had enough. Besides, he was thirty-five years old and would have to retire in a few years anyway, the sport was very physically demanding. So why shouldn't he just get out now while he was still relatively young? "I'm still enthusiastic and sure that I can act," he wrote home. "I'm tired of travel. I want to put down roots."

On January 6, 1961, he sent a letter from Lansing, Michigan:

Dear everyone,

I actually wrote to you yesterday but then got Leni's and Papa's letter from the 2nd last night. Many thanks. It's depressing that no one except Leni believes in me. Or do you think the theater situation in Switzerland is so terrible that you think I don't have a chance? Although it's not really a way to judge, still I have to say that if . . . countless other people that I've seen can make it in the theater then goshdarnit I can make something happen too. I may not have star appeal, but I have enough faith and hope for that! Dearest Leniköppchen, thank you for all your moral support.

Later in the same letter he wrote that money isn't everything: "I'm not as materialistic as all that. I don't care whether I have a nice steak or sausage and bread. That sounds arrogant, but I mean it literally. I need to be happy in my work, that and my health are the most important things."

He was no longer happy on the skating rink, that was the decisive factor. And then, finally, it was decided. He had his ticket in his pocket to leave New York on the *Flandre* ocean liner on July 8, 1961, and arrive in Paris on July 15. He sent this enthusiastic letter to Basel, to Herbstgasse:

I look forward
I look forward to seeing you

I look forward to the lakes in summer and the mountains in winter
I look forward to bratwurst with rösti and to the bells of my homeland
To MY bed in MY room without a number on the door.
I look forward to "News from the Swiss Telegraph Bureau,"
To hot sweet chestnuts and a cold glass of beer.
I look forward to simple people and rich people and the Casino Trottoir on the first warm Saturday afternoon in the spring.
I look forward to breakfast with the national paper and Papa's delicious jam,
To the first rehearsal in the theater, to carnival, and tea on the balcony.
I look forward to watching "Frühschoppen" on Sunday mornings.
To Alsatian asparagus and "tasty potatoes, three pounds for a franc!"
I look forward to the Freie Strasse and cold chocolate milk.
I look forward to my car and taking a little drive with you down the Leimen valley,
To the fires on August first, to Swiss chocolate and beef soup.
I look forward to no longer needing to fall on my butt to earn a living.
I look forward to my records and the blue chair in the corner.
I look forward to a symphony concert, a good opera, or an exhibit at the art museum.
I look forward to no more ice-skating conversations.
*To not having to constantly unpack and repack my bags.**
I even look forward to Herbi's singing!
I look forward . . . .

** Stephan's face after a successful day at the office,*
to Leni's energy and Papa's calm,
to Ottel and Fritzi's good cheer + optimism
to Imperia's spaghettis and
even to Herbi's singing.

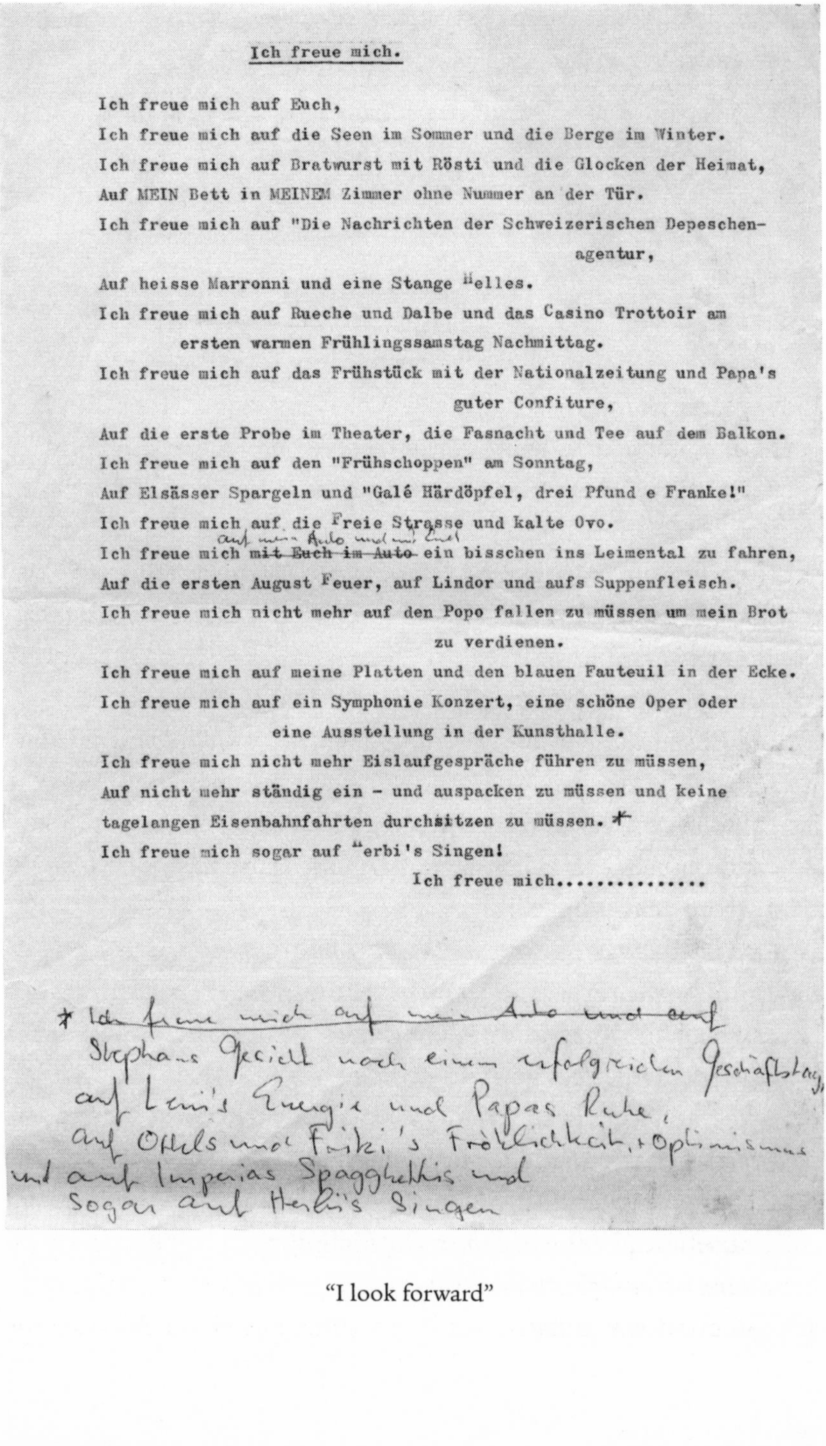
Ich freue mich.

Ich freue mich auf Euch,
Ich freue mich auf die Seen im Sommer und die Berge im Winter.
Ich freue mich auf Bratwurst mit Rösti und die Glocken der Heimat,
Auf MEIN Bett in MEINEM Zimmer ohne Nummer an der Tür.
Ich freue mich auf "Die Nachrichten der Schweizerischen Depeschen-
agentur,
Auf heisse Marronni und eine Stange Helles.
Ich freue mich auf Rueche und Dalbe und das Casino Trottoir am
ersten warmen Frühlingssamstag Nachmittag.
Ich freue mich auf das Frühstück mit der Nationalzeitung und Papa's
guter Confiture,
Auf die erste Probe im Theater, die Fasnacht und Tee auf dem Balkon.
Ich freue mich auf den "Frühschoppen" am Sonntag,
Auf Elsässer Spargeln und "Galé Härdöpfel, drei Pfund e Franke!"
Ich freue mich auf die Freie Strasse und kalte Ovo.
Ich freue mich ~~mit Euch im Auto~~ auf mein Auto und mit Euch ein bisschen ins Leimental zu fahren,
Auf die ersten August Feuer, auf Lindor und aufs Suppenfleisch.
Ich freue mich nicht mehr auf den Popo fallen zu müssen um mein Brot
zu verdienen.
Ich freue mich auf meine Platten und den blauen Fauteuil in der Ecke.
Ich freue mich auf ein Symphonie Konzert, eine schöne Oper oder
eine Ausstellung in der Kunsthalle.
Ich freue mich nicht mehr Eislaufgespräche führen zu müssen,
Auf nicht mehr ständig ein - und auspacken zu müssen und keine
tagelangen Eisenbahnfahrten durchsitzen zu müssen. *
Ich freue mich sogar auf Herbi's Singen!
Ich freue mich..............

* ~~Ich freue mich auf mein Auto und auf~~
Stephans Gesicht nach einem erfolgreichen Geschäftstag,
auf Leni's Energie und Papas Ruhe,
auf Ottels und Friki's Fröhlichkeit, + Optimismus
und auf Imperias Spagghettis und
sogar auf Herbi's Singen

"I look forward"

17.

Home at Last

Buddy was home in the house on Herbstgasse. After fourteen years of hotel life he woke up in his own bed every morning, in the room he used to share with his brother, Stephan. That didn't bother him—it felt homey and comforting. He no longer had to try to figure out in the moment between sleep and waking what city he was in, what hotel. He was home, surrounded by the people he knew and loved. Still, the house seemed strangely empty without Alice and Grandma Ida.

Ida Elias had died on January 15, 1957. Born in Homburg, she spent her life as a wife and mother in Zweibrücken and was buried, like Alice four years before, in the Jewish cemetery in Basel. She had passed away as quietly and inconspicuously as she lived, Leni wrote at the time. Buddy felt that now too. Only now that Grandma Ida was no longer with them did he become aware of how much greater a role than he had realized her caring presence, which they had always taken for granted, had played in his childhood and youth. He missed her the way he missed Alice. Now he had to get used to a house that seemed to have lost some of its warmth without the two women.

Otherwise, everything was the same as always. Imperia ran the household, Leni worked in the store, Erich dropped in to see her there often—much too often, she sometimes complained—and Stephan was busy at his import business handling various consumer products, a business that wasn't very successful. Herbert—yes, what exactly was Herbert doing? He had jobs here and there and sometimes helped out at Leni's store. Other than that, he rode his bike to Kleinbasel at 10:30 every day to have a morning drink in the Leuen Restaurant and was always back in time for lunch. He spent most of his evenings at the pub with his friends. He liked to drink and had one too many now and then. Otto usually spent all day in his room and answered, with Fritzi's help, the many letters that arrived from all over the world.

Buddy applied to various theaters and auditioned in Basel and in Zurich, but in vain. Of course he had known that it wouldn't be easy to find a foothold onstage after such a long time—he didn't think that the German-language theater world was waiting with bated breath for him, Buddy Elias. He was happy not needing to be constantly on the rink, training hard and undergoing the sometimes almost unbearable physical strain of his old career, but after a while it did get a bit boring. Luckily, he got a couple of jobs on the radio, and when Harald Kreutzberg, the famous dancer and choreographer, was looking for an actor to dance the part of the snake in Paradise in a guest production in Bern, Buddy applied and was accepted. "It was from Harald Kreutzberg," he still says today, full of pride, "that I got the greatest compliment of my life. When I danced for him the way I thought the snake should dance, he said: 'There's no way to improve on that.' " Later, Buddy would play the Young Monk in Jean Anouilh's *Becket; or, The Honor of God* under Egon Karter at the Basel Komödie and be noticed by Dr. Herterich, director of the State Theater in Tübingen, in Germany.

That was his breakthrough. Buddy was offered the role of Mephistopheles in the *Ur-Faust.* He went to Tübingen to look for an apartment and found a cheap bachelor pad with coal heating. As the date of starting rehearsals grew nearer, he rented a small truck and drove to Tübingen with Erich and a few pieces of furniture in August 1962. He had a two-year contract in his pocket.

On August 17, he already sent his first letter to "everyone":

Writing letters again! [In English:] It seems to be the story of my life. Anyway, after I said goodbye to Papa with a heavy heart (still, I was very glad he came with me), I headed to my new home . . . First thing after my arrival I unpacked my clothes, then I went to the theater and checked in, and met a few of my colleagues . . . The next morning I woke up early, had a great breakfast with the newspaper that came with my order, and used my day off to go to Stuttgart and go shopping. I bought all kinds of things for the apartment and looked into furniture and a refrigerator . . . This morning was the first read through for Faust. *My ideas 100% matched the director's ideas, while he has already had to have serious arguments with the actor playing Faust.*

Only two days later, he clearly had to tell someone how happy and proud he was: he wrote to Basel that he had rehearsed the student scene in *Faust* and that Loges, the director, had interrupted him several times with the word "brilliant." It must have given him not a little satisfaction to show the members of his family, who except for Leni had so forcefully expressed their doubts about his chances as an actor, that he had been right to take the plunge.

On September 22, he sent Leni and Erich, who were staying in Italy, all the reviews and notices that had appeared so far, along with a note saying that he really couldn't complain, he always got the best applause. And he added: "Take the reviews home please and show Steph, Ottel, Herbi, etc. The important Stuttgart reviews are super, aren't they? People read those! There were people from the Stuttgart radio and TV stations there at the second performance, by the way, and it was in that performance that when I left the stage after getting my solo applause some people in the audience started to stamp their feet. Too bad they started too late."

Tübingen was not so far from Basel, and the whole family came to see Buddy onstage: his parents, Herbert, and Otto and Fritzi, who had recently moved to Birsfelden. They had been looking for a house of their own for a while. Buddy's return might have hastened their decision, he can no longer say for sure, or maybe they just wanted a more comfortable place. In truth, the reasons were irrelevant—what is surprising is not that they wanted to move but that they had managed so long in the cramped conditions on Herbstgasse. Their life there was truly modest; the only thing they permitted themselves was occasional trips, and they usually spent the hottest weeks of the summer, when the heat collected in their added-on rooms under the roof, in Beckenried on Lake Lucerne. Now they had bought a house in Birsfelden, a town in the Basel district but only a good fifteen minutes to Herbstgasse by streetcar. Otto and Fritzi lived on the ground floor and rented out the apartment on the second floor. Later, Birsfelden would be the first municipality in Switzerland to name a square after Anne Frank, in 2009.

They visited Buddy in Tübingen and congratulated him on his success, but not all at once: Erich and Leni went first, Otto and Fritzi somewhat later, in October. Buddy was in fact such a success that he was offered the lead role in *A Model Husband*. On November 13, 1962, he wrote a very happy letter home: "Voilà la situation. I am very content and of course happy with Model Husband. It's a fantastic role, as you know! You can hardly do better in one season than Mephistopheles and the Model Husband."

It hardly *could* go better, since *A Model Husband* was a great success as well and Buddy's reviews were stellar. He wrote in January 1963: "It's going unexpectedly well. Especially for me. The audience roared and hooted with laughter. Applause after the scenes and big applause at the end . . . I met the gentleman from Berlin who has just been hired as a director for South German TV. He has to shoot 9 TV movies and is scouring all the theaters near Stuttgart for talent at the moment. I was really flattered when he told me that an actor at the State Theater in Mannheim and

Buddy Elias and Gerti Wiedner's first stage appearance together, in *The Bockerer* by Ulrich Becher and Peter Preses, Tübingen, 1963

I were the only actors he approached . . . He obviously couldn't promise me any TV parts yet, but he told me I should come to auditions in Stuttgart in March." On top of that, Egon Karter from the Basel Komödie Chamber Theater had seen him perform and hired him for the 1964–65 season in Basel. Buddy had found his feet, won a place onstage as an actor, and proven that his decision to leave *Holiday on Ice* was the right one. Everyone in Basel was very proud of him, especially Leni.

In January 1963, Otto and Fritzi established the Anne Frank-Fonds as a trust under Swiss law, based in Basel. Otto Frank had discussed his plans for a long time and in great detail with his family and friends. It was a question of managing the copyrights in Anne Frank's literary estate as well as the income from the sales of *The Diary* and the royalties from the play and the movie.

There was already the Anne Frank Foundation in Amsterdam, of course, but Otto did not want to send all the money to Amsterdam—he said that no one knew how the foundation would develop. Here in Basel, he had his family and his friends, and wanted to have the money here, under state control, as well. His opinion had always been that it wasn't his money but Anne's money, and his wish was that it be used in accord with her vision.

The new Anne Frank Foundation was intended to carry out social and cultural projects in memory of Anne Frank's message. Otto expressly said: "The foundation will contribute to better understanding between different religions, serve the cause of peace between peoples, and promote international contact between young people."

From the beginning, Stephan and Buddy were members of the foundation's board. Stephan was not very active, however, and Buddy was performing at various theaters in Germany. It was only in 1986 that Buddy would become more involved in the Anne Frank-Fonds.

In the 1963–64 season a new actress joined the State Theater in Tübingen, Gerti Wiedner. Buddy says today that he fell in love at first sight but that Gerti didn't know. They acted together three times, in fact: once in *The Bockerer,* a play by Ulrich Becher and Peter Preses; a second time for a Chekhov evening with three one-acts; and finally in the musical *My Sister and I* by Ralph Benatzky. It still took months before anything developed between them. Buddy mentioned her in a letter home for the first time in February 1964, and in March he brought her to Basel's famous carnival celebrations, supposedly as a favor to her but actually to introduce her to his family.

Gerti still had no idea what Buddy was feeling; for her, Buddy was just a colleague, they had not even started to use the informal form of address with each other. But she was very excited to meet Buddy's family, since everyone at the theater knew that he was Anne Frank's cousin. Gerti had read the diary when it came out in German, when she was seventeen or eighteen years old, and later had seen the play in Graz, Austria. She was already an actress then, but had not acted in *The Diary of Anne Frank*.

They drove in Buddy's car, a sleek Panhard, from Tübingen to Basel, which at the time was around a four-hour drive. Buddy was sunk in thought and said hardly a word to her, she says. Then they arrived at Herbstgasse, and Gerti was overwhelmed by the house and especially by the people.

Gerti had grown up in a large family in Austria, in Oberhaag, a small town in southern Styria not far from the Yugoslavian border. Her father ran the general store. Despite the impoverished years during and after the war, she had a happy childhood, she says. "We had a beautiful house, we had beautiful furniture—no antiques, of course—and we had kilims, the pretty, colorful area rugs they have in Yugoslavia." When Gerti was fifteen years old, her mother, who had suffered from heart troubles since a serious angina in her youth, died giving birth to her sixth child. Gerti's father sent her, the third child, to live with an aunt in Graz so that she could go to acting school there. That was Gerti's deepest wish, and her deceased mother had always supported it. To this day, Gerti marvels at the fact that it all turned out well, that she didn't get into any trouble even at the young age of fifteen and a half.

Buddy Elias and Gerti Wiedner in *My Sister and I* by Ralph Benatzky, Tübingen, 1963

At Herbstgasse, Leni, an extraordinarily distinguished lady, and Erich, an equally distinguished gentleman, received Gerti with a warmth that astonished her. Leni hugged her, even though they had never met, and said, "What a beautiful woman you are!"; Erich kissed her hand and said, "How nice to meet you, my dear lady." Herbert and Stephan too were more than approachable, Gerti says, "they were charming." She carried her bag up to the little room on the top floor next to the stairs that they had set aside for her—the room where Grandma Ida used to live, she would later learn. Then she came back downstairs to look around the dining room and the adjacent salon.

It was all new and fascinating to her. She had never met a family like this and never seen a house with such beautiful old furniture and so many paintings on the walls. One of them made a special impression on her: a strangely serious, dressed-up little girl, maybe four or five years old. "That was Alice, my mother, as a little girl," Leni said, and added: "Buddy's grandmother." And Anne Frank's grandmother too, Gerti thought. "And that is Cornelia, my mother's mother," Leni continued. Gerti could not overcome her surprise: in her house there were only photographs, no painted portraits. "And these two," Leni said, pointing to a small oval painting, "were my grandmother Cornelia's parents, Elkan Juda Cahn and his wife, Betty." Leni brought the guest over to another picture in a carved gold frame: a pastel drawing of a very beautiful girl with slightly protruding ears, dressed in a cloud of tulle and ribbons. "And that was me. My parents were very proud of me, I was the only daughter after three boys."

They sat down in the salon, which was smaller than the living room in Gerti's parents' house. Everyone seemed to have their usual place—one particular chair from the many that were scattered around the room, and which they referred to with the French word *fauteuil*. Gerti sat down on the sofa and answered the questions that came at her from all sides: how she was liking Tübingen, what roles she was playing, which theaters she had acted in before, if she was ever homesick.

Then Mariuccia came in, the Italian housekeeper, a short, round woman with her gray hair in a perm. The whole family spoke Italian with her, and when she said "*A tavola*," they immediately stood up and went to wash their hands, one person after another, before entering the dining room and sitting down at the large table that Mariuccia had meanwhile set with old china, silver knives and forks, silver napkin rings, and lit candles. Everyone unfolded their napkins and laid them on their laps, except for Erich, who tucked his under his jacket, and Mariuccia brought the soup. When the last person, Stephan, put down his spoon, Leni reached for the bell hanging from the light fixture over the middle of the table; Mariuccia appeared and Leni said, "*Abbiamo finito.*" Mariuccia walked around the table, stacked the soup plates, and carried them into the kitchen, then brought in various serving dishes with meat, potatoes, and vegetables. Now it was Erich who stood up, to carve the meat and serve it to everyone before anyone took potatoes and vegetables.

The conversation at the table never stopped. Buddy told stories about the theater and mimicked different actor colleagues; Leni reported on her business and imitated, with raised eyebrows and pursed lips, the words and gestures of one rich client looking for a present for her husband, a tiepin, but it had to be something special, something suited to his position. That prompted Stephan to tell a joke that was just the slightest bit indecent about a married couple, and Erich said that the forsythia buds were about to bloom, you could already see the yellow tips of the flowers. The whole time, Herbert, Leni's brother, drummed on the table with his napkin ring until Leni at one point said, "Herbi, please!" Herbert said, "Yes, yes," and stopped his nervous drumming before starting it again after a minute or two.

Gerti observed it all and thought: What a family! Buddy had definitely inherited his talent as a comedian from his mother.

When they were finished with the main course, Leni rang the bell again, and Mariuccia cleared the table and brought dessert: petit fours and espresso in paper-thin Asian cups. Only after dessert did they all stand up and disperse to their various rooms to relax. Except Erich, who sank into his *fauteuil* in the living room and immediately fell asleep. Gerti headed out with Buddy—he wanted to show her the city, although she already knew Basel, since she had had a short run at the local theater.

They stayed in Basel for only two days, then they had to go back to Tübingen. The farewell was as unbelievable as the visit. Leni said to Gerti: "You are truly a beauty." Gerti was embarrassed and did not know how to react. She would have been much more embarrassed if she had heard what Leni had already told her son, in her cheeriest Frankfurt dialect: "You can marry her, she has beautiful nostrils."

In any case, their relationship developed quickly after this visit to Herbstgasse. Gerti broke things off with her boyfriend in Graz, and she and Buddy grew closer and closer. Buddy wrote that she was "very sweet" and often came over for dinner. Another time:

Many thanks for your dear letter. Gerti has already written you. We are very happy. Aside from the Basel clan I have never met anyone I get along with so perfectly, down to the tiniest detail. It is really unbelievable. We have the same outlook on life, we like the same things and couldn't care less about the same things. To start with, peace and quiet and a newspaper over breakfast (if you think <u>I'm</u> an epicure then you've never seen Gerti!), then theater, art, music, walks, etc. In everything she does, she is the most lovable, friendliest, most upstanding creature, brilliantly educated, 100% the lady. She is certainly no prude but hates bad language. (So no dirty jokes. Off-color jokes are allowed.) Everyone loves her. And she's modest and accommodating too . . . We can't get married right away, since Gerti still has her obligations in Tübingen, but she will try to get out of them sooner.

They got engaged in the summer of 1964, and the ceremony took place at the registry in Basel on February 1, 1965. Grosser, a "totally charming director" in Tübingen, had been very understanding and let Gerti out of her contract early so that she could follow Buddy to Basel, where he had already started his engagement. The wedding party, which Gerti's father and her sisters Ado and Thesy came to as well, was beautiful and moving. Obviously, Otto and Fritzi were there too.

Mariuccia and Frau Baumann, who had worked as a housekeeper in the Herbstgasse house for a while after Imperia's departure, until Mariuccia came, had prepared a feast. They pulled out the leaves of the table far enough so that everyone could fit comfortably, and laid it splendidly with the old china, Elkan Juda Cahn's silverware, the antique silver candlesticks, and the nineteenth-century goblets. Stephan and a friend, René Steinbach, put on musical sketches that they had rehearsed—René was

Gerti and Buddy Elias's wedding photograph, February 1, 1965

an excellent pianist, and Leni and Herbert dressed up in Buddy's clown costumes and danced and sang a song from *Kiss Me, Kate* that Stephan had rewritten for Buddy and Gerti, accompanied by René on the piano.

Gerti was welcomed with wide-open arms and happily threw herself into the family's life together. Buddy's acting career went well too. His first role was Grumio in Shakespeare's *Taming of the Shrew,* with Barbara Rütting, then it was Truffaldino in Goldoni's *Servant of Two Masters,* a role that won the hearts of the Basel public. In Brecht's *Resistible Rise of Arturo Ui* he imitated Hitler in such a horrifyingly accurate way that many people still mention it to him today. Gerti and Buddy lived in the room that had been Alice's, although they bought a new bed, since they didn't want to sleep in the ancient Biedermeier bed, and added a walk-in closet.

The wedding of his younger son was presumably the occasion for Erich to put certain financial matters in order. In any case, on May 20, 1964, he gave his sons the following document to sign:

Herr Stephan Elias
Herr Buddy Elias

Dear Stephan, dear Buddy,

As you know, I have sold our house, Herbstgasse 11, to Buddy, due to fears that turned out not to come true. This sale was notarized on December 1, 1952, and took effect on January 1, 1953. That it took place signifies no preference for him and had no reason other than the aforesaid.

Since these facts are clear and since it is your mother's and my wish that the two of you will have equal claim to the house at Herbstgasse 11, it is our wish that you manage the house together from now on and also that any income from the sale of the house go into a common account. In short, the two of you are equal co-owners of the house.

Because Buddy has spent 45,000 francs of his own money to date on the mortgage, taxes, and maintenance, this sum is to be reimbursed to him upon any sale of the house. If he wants, or if it would be beneficial, this amount may be secured with a mortgage.

Please confirm by signing a copy of this letter that you acknowledge and agree to the contents.

Your parents

Both sons, Buddy and Stephan, placed their signatures at the bottom of this document, and Erich was satisfied.

Gerti soon became an integral part of the family. She was amazed to realize that the ceremony she had so marveled at during her first visit for carnival took place at every meal.

The table was always set beautifully, there were always candles burning, always soup, Erich always carved the meat, especially the Saturday boiled beef, and there was always dessert, fruit with a fruit knife and fork, or a compote, or at least pastries, and espresso to finish. After lunch they dispersed back to their rooms to rest, and Erich fell asleep in his *fauteuil* in the salon. Leni had her afternoon nap as well but was always back at her store punctually at 2:30. In the evenings there was always bread with ham and cheese and sausage, but that too was laid out nicely on a table that was set, with candles lit.

Stephan moved out of the Herbstgasse house in 1964, into his own apartment, but that didn't stop him from continuing to come to most meals. He typically fetched Leni from the store in his car at noon and drove her back to Herbstgasse. They all sat there in the salon, each with a book or newspaper, and no one said anything until Mariuccia called out "*A tavola.*"

Mariuccia did all of the housework and refused all offers of help, so Gerti did not have much to do, and she started to help Leni at the store. She also accompanied Leni whenever she had to go out on an appraisal. Even today, Gerti is full of admiration when she talks about how expert Leni was: how she could identify every piece of furniture, every candlestick, every sugar bowl, even every tablecloth or piece of embroidery, and every carpet—both its period and its value. Gerti helped with displaying the objects on the tables and with taking down the information about each object, including the price.

"Those were gigantic houses," Gerti says, in amazement even today. "Sometimes there were more than four stories, each one full of valuable objects. Here in Switzerland, of course, there had been no wars for hundreds of years, just imagine! Everything was still there, everything they inherited plus everything new they bought. I couldn't believe my eyes when I saw how rich some of the people here were, and what kinds of things they had!" She was fascinated by the work, and admired her mother-in-law for being able to judge and appraise everything without any hesitation. "At a set time, people came and bought things, and you had to keep a sharp eye out to make sure nothing was stolen. Herbert usually manned the desk downstairs and collected the money, and there were another couple of people there as well to pack everything up."

Gerti stopped working with Leni only on April 9, 1966, when her first son, Patrick, was born. Along with the proud parents, the grandparents were crazy about the child. Leni cuddled him and kissed him and said several times: "It's too bad that I. didn't live to see him." Otto and Fritzi visited often as well, and Gerti was always happy to see them. She still remembers it exactly: how tense and even a little nervous she was, how hesitant, the first time she met this man who had had to bear such a terrible fate. And how differently it went from how she had feared. Otto and Fritzi had welcomed her naturally and lovingly. It was a lovely evening, there in Birsfelden, and Otto had laughed a lot.

On their way back home, Gerti had expressed her amazement, and Buddy had said: "What do you expect? Otto has his life under control, he loves Fritzi and Fritzi loves him. And she does everything she can to help him spread Anne's ideals. Otto sees it as his task to work toward a peaceful coexistence of different religions and peoples, as Anne would have wanted. He could never have found someone better to help him than Fritzi."

"Did he ever do anything else?" Gerti asked. "Did he come back from the concentration camp and start working on his daughter's diary?"

"Not right away," Buddy answered. "It took time for the significance of the diary to become clear. I think that at first he only wanted to make it up to Anne, he felt bad that he had never really known her and thought he should have treated her differently. They had divided up the children–Anne was Otto's child and Margot was Edith's, not exactly but you know what I mean. You could tell from when Anne was very young. Margot was a wonderful girl, but very quiet and introverted. I always see her in my mind with a book in her hand, always. Anne on the other hand was a bit wild, funny, and cheeky, as you can tell from her diary too. Otto had no idea what the diary would become, the thing took on a life of its own with the book's worldwide success. Now Otto has something to do about it every day, because people write to him or visit him or invite him somewhere to dedicate a school or give a lecture. But that doesn't at all mean that he has no pleasures in life. He can obviously never forget the loss of his family, but I think that Anne's success and everything that goes with it, and his trips, make him happy, even if it's a strain at the same time. It is very, very important to him to be in contact with young people: I wouldn't say it's fun for him, but it does give him pleasure. What I really think is that he needs people he can talk to about Anne."

Gerti would confirm for herself again and again how right Buddy was in this estimate of Otto's good mood and vitality. Sometimes she did think she could see a shadow pass across Otto's face when he held Patrick in his arms, and that he would suddenly look deeply sad. He must have been thinking about Margot and Anne in those moments, she thought, and she imagined how, if his daughters had lived, he would probably have been able to hold a grandchild of his own in his arms. But she never uttered a word of these thoughts out loud; she was afraid to open old wounds.

Patrick's birth revived many memories in the house. For example, one time when Gerti walked past an open door, she heard Leni and Erich talking about the child. "I always think about I. and Grandma Ida," Leni said. Gerti stopped and listened. "I. had four children, Ida three. Without Hitler and the catastrophe they could have easily had twenty great-grandchildren, or more, but now there's only little Pat, only one single great-grandchild."

"You're right," Erich answered. "It truly is sad. But Buddy and Gerti might still have more children. And maybe Stephan will even get married someday. He's not too old to become a father."

"That would be a real miracle," Leni said, with bitterness in her voice. "Steph has bad luck with his girlfriends, he always ends up with the wrong ones."

Erich gave a deep sigh. And Gerti, embarrassed, as though she had done something wrong, went quietly upstairs.

18.

'Winter on Autumn Lane'

The actor's life is an unsteady one—or at least not much steadier than that of an ice-show star. After his engagement in Basel, Buddy played a few more parts in Zurich, then accepted an offer from Bremen and moved with his wife and son to northern Germany. They found an apartment, not too small and not too large, and Buddy worked at the Theater Bremen on Goetheplatz playing many major roles. Gerti sometimes appeared onstage too. For example, they appeared together in Kurt Hübner's production of *Nathan the Wise,* with Buddy as the Dervish and Gerti as Sittah, Saladin's sister. Gerti sang and played Metella in Jacques Offenbach's operetta *Parisian Life.* Buddy wrote from Bremen in 1969 that Gerti was a smash hit with the *Parisian Life* people, everyone loved her and wanted to give her a permanent place in the ensemble, but she turned them down because of Patrick. Still, she might take a part now and then. In fact she did, but her career was clearly limited, especially when she became pregnant for a second time.

On December 5, 1971, Oliver was born after a difficult pregnancy. Gerti was on bed rest for four months because of the risk of a premature birth. Everyone was very happy that the child was born healthy after all of these fears, particularly the parents of course. Oliver, who had given rise to so many fears and anxieties, would become an especially friendly and lovable child. Patrick and Oliver were the family's hopes for the future, that the family would not die out. Everyone was happy. Leni and Erich came straight to Bremen, and Otto and Fritzi wrote a letter with their congratulations:

You can't imagine how happy & relieved we were to get the news of the happy arrival of your little Oliver and we wish you as much happiness and joy as his big brother has already brought you, and that the 2 brothers will love each other just as much as Buddy and Stephan do.

It was so nice to talk to both of you on the phone and to know that everything is going fine. It's too bad only that we won't be able to see the little one grow up as much as we could with Pat. But if you're in Mannheim next season, we'll have a lot more chances to visit you.

We're doing well here and send you and Pat our biggest hugs and kisses.

Your Fritzi

What Fritzi wrote comes from the bottom of my heart too and I don't have much to add. Just as I sent a sum of money as a present for Pat when he was born, I am now doing the same thing for Oliver.

I gave Papa Erich a check for 1,054.71 francs to deposit into an account for your second child. You'll have to guess how I arrived at the amount.

All my love and warmest greetings,
Your Otto

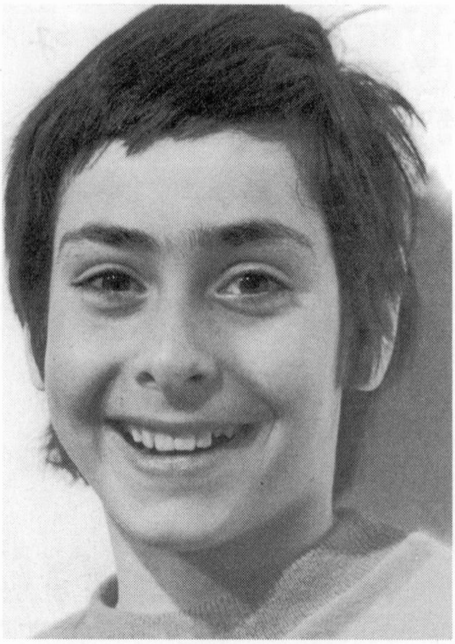

Patrick Elias, around ten years old, 1976

Buddy and Gerti no longer know what the sum meant, and don't remember if they ever knew.

They were happy. They had two children, and Buddy was getting good parts. He was especially successful in a musical version of Chaucer's *The Can-*

terbury Tales, playing multiple roles, including Old January, an old man who gets it into his head to marry the youngest girl in the village. As the date approaches, though, he is overcome with fear about how certain things will go on their wedding night, and someone calms his nerves by giving him an aphrodisiac. Jazz music starts to play, and Old January starts to dance. It was a part that could have been written especially for Buddy. Of course the old man has to pay dearly for his second youth, and he is soon cuckolded by his young wife. Buddy would later be hired for *The Canterbury Tales* in London and Stuttgart, and after Bremen came an engagement in Mannheim, where, as Gerti says, he lived more at the theater than at home, playing one lead role after another. Kurt Hübner brought him from Mannheim to Berlin, where he performed at the Freie Volksbühne, at the Renaissance Theater, and elsewhere. They would spend twelve years in Berlin, interrupted by a several-month run of *The Canterbury Tales* in London in 1979, where Gerti would visit him with the children. Buddy was in Stuttgart for several months as well, then returned to Berlin. Gerti stayed in Berlin and worked hard to give her children "a comfortable home" and always be there for them. She knew that with all the rehearsals and performances Buddy didn't have very much time for his sons, so she only occasionally took on any theater work herself.

As the years went by, Buddy Elias performed onstage with many of the most famous actors in the German-speaking world, for example with Will Quadflieg in *Nathan the Wise,* Horst Buchholz in *Twelve Angry Men,* Maximilian Schell in *Poor Murderer,* and Harald Juhnke as Motel in *Dreyfus,* directed by Helmut Käutner.

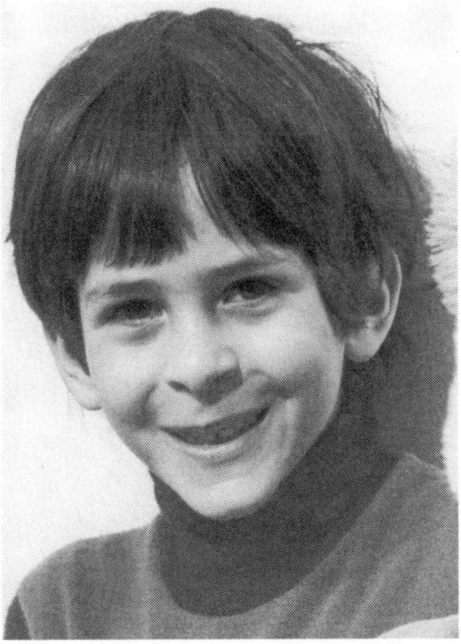
Oliver Elias, around five years old, 1976

Buddy also performed in several movies, including Peter Lilienthal's *David,* Hans W. Geissendörfer's *Magic Mountain,* and Michael Verhoeven's *Mother Courage.*

Buddy and Gerti traveled often to Basel, of course, but they also went to see Gerti's family in Oberhaag, and little Patrick especially loved it there. As Buddy wrote once: "For Pat it's a real paradise here." But the family visited Buddy and Gerti much more often than Buddy and Gerti visited Basel, attending Buddy's premieres in Bremen, Mannheim, Berlin, and Stuttgart. Gerti says: "It was unbelievable how much Otto shared Buddy's life and his successes. Until the very end, when he was too sick to travel, he and Fritzi came to Buddy's performances, often to the premieres. And they always wrote letters."

Otto kept Buddy informed about the three lawsuits he filed in Germany against people who called his daughter's diary a forgery. The first time, he brought charges against an English teacher from Lübeck, member of the far-right German Reichspartei, and one of his fellow party members, for slander, insult, libel, defaming the memory of the dead, and anti-Semitic hate speech. Both men withdrew their statement, and Otto Frank agreed to an amicable settlement. He would later regret his decision, saying: "If I had known that there were people who would not consider a settlement as proof, I would probably have gone ahead with the trial."

Otto Frank filed charges again in 1976 against an architect from Odenhausen who had self-published numerous neo-Nazi brochures and flyers, such as *Anne Frank's Diary: A Forgery* and *Anne Frank's Diary: The Big Hoax.* The architect was forbidden to make or spread these or any other such claims in public on penalty of a fine of up to 500,000 deutsche marks ($200,000). He appealed, but it did not come to a further judicial decision, since the man died before another trial.

A third lawsuit in Germany, with Otto Frank as a co-plaintiff, lasted from 1976 until 1993, thirteen years after Otto's death. It started when a member of the radical right handed out flyers titled *Bestseller: A Fraud* after a performance of *The Diary of Anne*

Frank. He was sentenced by the Hamburg District Court in 1977 to pay a fine of 1,500 deutsche marks ($600) for defamation, and he appealed. During the proceedings, a like-minded comrade distributed the same flyer in the courtroom. The appeal process dragged on so long because the judge wanted to wait for the German translation of the scholarly edition of the diary to come out, and in the end the case was dropped because the statute of limitations had run out. Buddy and Gerti say how much these cases depressed Otto—how the charges of forgery hurt him and how terrible it was for him to have to go before a judge and show the tattooed number on his arm in front of everybody.

But they have happy memories of Otto Frank too. Buddy says: "I can't forget this other time when he and Fritzi were in Sedrun, on a winter vacation, and we visited them there. He was already a very elderly man. When we went out one evening, there was jazz music and people started dancing. Otto stood up and danced with Fritzi; they pulled off a terrific swing dance. Everyone watched, and Otto was the star of the dance floor. It was unbelievable, really incredible."

In the summer of 1980, while Buddy and Gerti were living in Berlin, they received the news that Stephan was sick. At first it seemed that he had suddenly caught jaundice, then there was talk of another sepsis. Gerti went to Basel—Buddy couldn't get away, given his many rehearsals and performances—and had Stephan transferred from a clinic in the Basel district to the university hospital. There they said it was a suppuration of the biliary duct and operated immediately. Gerti went back to Berlin. Buddy would have

Buddy Elias with Maximilian Schell in *Poor Murderer* by Pavel Kohout, Renaissance Theater, Berlin, 1982

time off in August, and they wanted to go to Basel first, then to see Gerti's family in Oberhaag and spend their holiday there.

Just before their departure, though, they got the call that Otto Frank had died, on August 19, 1980. The news hit them unexpectedly hard, even though he had been in poor health for quite some time and they had to be prepared for it. They arrived in time for the funeral, which took place on August 22 in Birsfelden with many mourners in attendance, including Fritzi's daughter, Eva, who came from London with her husband, Zvi Schloss, and their three daughters.

The night after the funeral, they were together again in the house on Herbstgasse: Erich, Leni, Herbert, Buddy, and Gerti. Fritzi, Eva, and Eva's family had stayed in Birsfelden. Leni said little, as if paralyzed, while Herbert was the opposite: he was utterly broken and kept saying over and over, "What are we going to do without him? How can we go on?"

"He was generous," Erich said, "a good person. He loved to give."

Buddy reached for Gerti's hand. They both thought back to when they had wanted to travel to Israel, years before. Fritzi and Otto had come by to give them a few tips before the trip and some addresses. They were sitting in the dining room, and Mariuccia had just cleared the table, when Otto gave Buddy and Gerti a signal to follow him into the salon. He carefully shut the double doors before taking a wad of cash out of his pocket and pressing it into Buddy's hand. "Quick, put this away," he said with a meaningful nod toward the door. Buddy stuck the money into the inner pocket of his jacket. They both understood what Otto meant—Fritzi didn't need to know. She was always on the thrifty side, and this quality grew more pronounced as she got older. Otto had given them two thousand francs, which was a lot of money, more than they themselves had set aside for the trip.

"Yes," Buddy said, "he was a good person. We will never forget him."

They visited Stephan, who was still not doing well. He was on an artificial respirator. But the doctor said that his condition was stable, considering the circumstances, so Gerti and Buddy left for Oberhaag with Patrick and Oliver, where the news reached them three days later that Stephan had died. Patrick, who had an especially close and special relationship with Stephan, ran out into the fields when he heard that his favorite uncle had died and reappeared only many hours later.

They returned to Herbstgasse. They had lost two loved ones within the space of a few days.

François Fricker, a good friend of Stephan's, gave the following eulogy at the funeral:

Dear Elias family, dear friends,

In the night of August 19th to 20th, one week ago, Otto Frank, the father of Anne Frank, passed away. Four days later, on Sunday, August 24, at 3:15 p.m., his nephew, our dear Stephan Elias, followed him in death.

Although both of these events are equally sad, we might be tempted to view them rather differently. Otto Frank died in his 91st year, while our Stephan, whom we are here to remember today, was only 59. An age that seems much too young to us, according to the prevailing view. To put it another way: the unavoidable fate we all share has here, it may seem, taken a very unusual course, and so this death seems to be a tragedy.

Nevertheless, I have to say that this line of thought is not entirely correct. As a very, very close friend of Stephan's, I know for a fact that the one thing he absolutely never wanted was to grow old. Whatever the motivation for this wish might have been, Stephan expressed it again and again, and now it has unexpectedly been fulfilled.

After a routine operation on June 15, due to jaundice, there were unexpected complications. Only twelve days later his condition was critical, a fact of which Stephan was perfectly aware.

Reliable studies show that patients can often evaluate, almost instinctively, their difficult situations completely realistically, even if they lack specialized medical training. So it was probably clear to Stephan that should he survive he would have to reckon with certain restrictions in his quality of life, and that he would require assistance in his daily life, even if not constantly. A thought that was surely unbearable to Stephan.

For even though he was always extraordinarily eager to help everyone else, in the other direction he never wanted to cause the slightest inconvenience for anyone.

As a result, the following became crystal clear to all of us who were at his side during his wavering between life and death (starting on June 27, he was continuously in intensive care):

The common wisdom, that as long as there is life in a dying man there is hope and that we therefore have to extend a person's life irrespective of its quality, can have consequences contrary to morality and human dignity.

. . . My dear Elias family, it may be surprising to you to hear me stand here today and utter such reflections. On the other hand, these thoughts are not ones that I can simply suppress, because they arose from my daily visits and conversations with the sick and dying Stephan . . . Looking back, I feel that it was a great mercy that I could accompany Stephan, together with his parents, during the last five hours of his earthly life . . .

The Stephan who had an unbelievable instinct for spontaneous puns and wordplay is known to all of us . . . I will quote a small example here that shows how Stephan could juggle with words: during one of his frequent visits to his dearly beloved and admired brother, Buddy, sister-in-law, Gerti, whom he was so proud of, and nephews, Patrick and Oliver, about whom he was always telling stories—during one of these visits to Berlin, a friend of the family's came by and was introduced to him, one Frau Saile. Stephan noticed lightning fast what nobody had realized until then, that the name Saile is Elias spelled backward . . .

I mentioned earlier Stephan's nephews, Patrick and Oliver, but that was in no way to neglect his nine-year-old goddaughter, Claudia . . . When Claudia heard the news of her godfather Stephan's death, she burst into tears. Her eight-year-old sister, Ariane, whom Stephan always tacitly saw as a second godchild, did not. She said, "God had the right to take Stephan back. Because Stephan made so many people happy. And now God should have Stephan to make him happy too."

After the speech, another friend of Stephan's, Ferdinand Afflerbach, played reveille on the drums, and when he stopped in the middle of the melody, a cold shiver ran over Gerti's spine.

On the evening of October 5, an official memorial service for Otto Frank took place in Basel, which Buddy and Gerti could not attend, because Buddy was not given time off from the theater. Still, they later found in the cache of documents a moving statement from Fritzi about her marriage to Otto Frank. The statement is undated, and it is not known if she read it out loud at this or another memorial service. It bears the title "My Life with Otto Frank."

It began in Auschwitz. Back in February 1945, when the Russians took the camp after the Germans withdrew, the surviving ex-prisoners were ordered to gather together to honor a day of remembrance for the revolution. I noticed a man with a small head who was shepherding some of his sick and weakened comrades and lovingly taking care of them.

I met him later on the transport back to Holland. It was Otto Frank, who took it upon himself in Amsterdam to visit the Jews who had returned or come out of hiding and offer them his advice and support. He visited the two of us as well—my daughter and me. And I had the chance to get to know his extraordinary qualities, his great humanity, for seven years. In 1953 we were married, and the following 27 years were among the happiest of my life.

Otto Frank was a very special person. He had charisma. Everyone who was lucky enough to meet him would confirm what I am saying. Every one of our countless visitors would mention, in writing or verbally, how friendly he was and how sincerely he welcomed them.

He never wrote a book, but the thousands of letters he wrote to friends and to readers of Anne's diary, many of whom became friends in turn, are a monument in themselves. They contain his immense understanding, for young and old, and express his great love of humanity, and his goodness. Practically every recipient wrote to say that they treasured his letters as a unique and prized possession. This voluminous correspondence took up a lot of his time and energy, but he knew only too well how important a friendly written word can be in a world where so few people take the time to be considerate or compassionate. It was his life's work to spread the ideas and ideals that Anne had expressed in her diary, and he gave courage to many people, especially young people, when they were unhappy. Not a few of them have had their paths in life changed, for the better, thanks to him.

The Anne Frank Foundation in Amsterdam, which he and several prominent citizens of Amsterdam founded, incorporated this goal among others into its statutes. Otto Frank spent many years working intensively with the foundation. It was a satisfaction to him to learn that an organization of friends of this foundation has now formed in the U.S.A.

He took people seriously no matter what social class they belonged to. He had a personal word to say to every waitress or bank clerk. He once put his arm around an Italian porter's shoulder like an old personal friend. Honors and riches meant nothing to him, for him there were only "people," whom he wanted to help in whatever way he could.

He had a special love for young people and he would soon become a father figure, later a grandfather figure, for countless boys and girls who gave him their trust and with whom he would continue to correspond for many long years.

Otto also possessed a well-developed sense of family. And so I was very happy to see that he saw my daughter as a blood relative along with his brothers and sister and treated her as another of his children. He also loved the three grandchildren with his whole heart, which they repaid with great affection.

He was an optimist and hate was entirely foreign to him. As early as 1946 he traveled to his hometown of Frankfurt to look for two old German friends, who he knew had not been Nazis. He wanted to show that from his perspective there was no such thing as collective guilt. He certainly said that we must never forget Hitler's and his thugs' crimes against the Jews, but hate doesn't get us any further. He was committed to reaching out the hand of forgiveness to German youth.

I learned a lot from him, and it was enormously enriching for me to work for peace and international understanding, as I did at his side for all those years. Otto Frank was a stimulating personality. Almost to the very end, he took a lively interest in events all over the world. He was especially interested in Israel, where we often visited. The children on the kibbutzim and in the children's villages ran after him as if he were the Pied Piper, since he gave off a warmth and kindness even without words that enchanted young and old. He was very concerned about Israel. He vehemently defended its right to exist despite not always agreeing with its political positions, although he understood those positions to some extent, in light of the deadly threat the country is under. He was not an especially religious person, coming from his liberal cosmopolitan milieu, but due to the events of the age he became more conscious of his being a Jew. Cooperation between the great world religions, especially Christian-Jewish cooperation, lay close to his heart. He was a member of many different groups with ecumenical and reconciliatory goals.

He carried prayers of different religions in his wallet and it was his wish to have them all read at his funeral. That happened. I will end with one of these prayers. His good friend Rabbi Soetendorp read it at the Sabbath service:

Let us commemorate those whom we loved.

Those who were taken from us and have gone to permanent rest.

May everything good that they have done,

Every truth and goodness that they spoke be recognized to the full and may it direct our life accordingly.

Because through that the living award the dead the greatest honor and they are spiritually united with them.

May those who mourn find comfort and be uplifted by the strength and trust in this worldly spiritual power

And the indestructibility of life.

By then, Fritzi was seventy-five years old, Leni eighty-seven, Herbert eighty-nine, and Erich ninety. "Winter had finally come," as Leni said, to Autumn Lane.

19.

A New Purpose in Life

Leni had stopped working, and a manager was running Epoque. "But that doesn't make any difference," Leni said over and over to Gerti, "an employee is always just an employee, the owner has to be there in person. The customers expect personal treatment, and they're right. It's time for you to come and take over the business, Gerti, who should carry it on if not you?"

Leni had grown old. With a paralyzed expression on her face, just as when her brother and older son had died four years before, she now absorbed the death of her husband, on October 2, 1984. Erich was in the hospital for an asthma attack. He was sitting on a chair in his silk bathrobe and having a lively conversation when suddenly he collapsed. The woman who was in his room rang for the nurse, and Erich was revived—successfully, but unfortunately. He lay in bed at home for a few more weeks, needing constant care, and then it was over.

"To revive a ninety-three-year-old man," Buddy said bitterly, "it's irresponsible, it's practically criminal. Especially for my father, who was always so elegant and distinguished, to give him the shame of needing diapers!" And Gerti repeated what François Fricker had said four years before, at Stephan's funeral: "The common wisdom, that as long as there is life in a dying man there is hope and that we therefore have to extend a person's life irrespective of its quality, can have consequences contrary to morality and human dignity."

Leni didn't answer, she didn't cry, she let Buddy and Patrick support her on the path to the cemetery and stared with her face unmoving as her husband's coffin was lowered into the earth. They had been married for sixty-three years. Erich Elias, who had grown up in Zweibrücken, was now, like his mother-in-law, Alice Frank née Stern, and his mother, Ida Elias née Neu, buried in the Jewish cemetery in Basel.

Gerti really did want to take over the business. It had long since been arranged; she and Buddy, after the many years of their wandering life, the frequent moves from one city to another, one apartment to another, longed to be truly at home. But they couldn't move back to Switzerland as quickly as Leni would have liked. To prepare for her new life, Gerti took a distance-learning course in antiques in Berlin. She studied the characteristic features of various periods; learned how to distinguish different styles, painting techniques, materials; memorized the names of goldsmiths and silversmiths, manufacturers, and furniture makers; crammed lists of prices from auction catalogs. She passed her exams, which were far from easy, and slowly started to prepare their move to Switzerland.

Patrick, the older son, moved to Basel first, in 1985, right after his final exams. He wanted to act, but his parents, both actors, had advised him that it was better to learn a serious trade since an actor's life was too dependent on chance—sometimes you have an engagement and sometimes you don't, life as a banker would be much more secure. Patrick

Leni and Erich Elias, circa 1983

let himself be convinced, but in the end it didn't work, and he would go to acting school and become an actor after all, like his younger brother, Oliver, too. Still, in the meantime, Patrick started an apprenticeship at a bank in Basel and lived with his elderly grandmother.

One night, Leni fell in the bathroom. Patrick heard a crash, ran downstairs, and found his grandmother lying on the floor, her face racked with pain. He called the ambulance. Leni had broken her hip and was taken to the city hospital and operated on. The operation was a success and she recovered, but she never returned to Herbstgasse again. Everyone, including the family doctor, Dr. Schlumpf, advised Leni to move into an old-age home. She decided on La Charmille, a Jewish old-age home in Riehen, near Basel, and her brother Herbert, ninety-three years old himself, joined her there soon afterward. Financially, there were no difficulties, since Otto had left them both a legacy in his will. "Even after his death he looked after his siblings," Erich said when he first learned of the provision. He was very grateful, since they may have owned their own house but had never managed to save up any real money for their retirement.

Patrick, the solicitous grandson, took the streetcar every day after work to La Charmille, about half an hour from Basel, to visit Leni. That was naturally quite an inconvenience for an eighteen- or nineteen-year-old young man, but he was glad to do it, for his grandmother's sake.

In Berlin, Gerti was already packing up their books when she got the phone call from a friend in Basel saying that Leni's business had been run into the ground and that she would probably not be able to make very much money from it. "It was terrible news for me," Gerti says. "But we had gone too far, there was no turning back."

They arrived in Basel on March 10, 1986, and on March 11 the big moving truck came with their things. The next day, March 12, Buddy had to go to Stuttgart, where he was performing in

The Canterbury Tales. Gerti was left alone with the moving boxes, with Patrick, who was more and more reluctant to go to the bank, with fourteen-year-old Oliver, who was dealing with a new school, with Leni, who was still bedridden at the time, and with a business that was in fact in desperate shape. The manager, who had agreed to stay until the end of the year and show Gerti the ropes, called two days later and said that she had found another job and would not be coming back.

"So there I was," Gerti says, "and I had no idea how I was going to manage. I was constantly running back and forth between the house, the store, and the old-age home, Oliver was there and he needed me, and there was Fritzi in Birsfelden, I had to worry about her too, and on top of it the business, where I felt totally lost. Everything was dirty, there were no details anywhere about the periods or prices of the pieces there. I was desperate. I had taken a correspondence course in antiques, but I had zero practical experience. For example, baroque or Biedermeier pieces all look different depending on whether the object is from Germany, Italy, or France. The beginning was truly terrible, and right away I got an ulcer too."

Luckily, there was Zita, a neighbor, who offered her help. The two women shut the store and got to work cleaning everything first. The carpets had all been piled up on top of each other, and the creases were stiff with dirt, so that they had no choice but to cut them to pieces and throw them away. They polished the silver and the furniture, dusted everything, and tried to arrange everything to attract possible buyers.

A lot of people actually did come to the reopening, but more out of curiosity than anything else. They wanted to see how "the new place" looked. Still, gradually, they began to buy. In the first year, the business ultimately cost more than it brought in—in the end, Zita had to be paid. Gerti threw herself into her work and took care of her sons, the two old women, Herbert, and the business. And on top of that was the housework, of course. Gerti had no Mariuccia, no Frau Baumann, no Imperia—she had to do everything alone, since Buddy was away most of the time. Because he was no longer a permanent member of an ensemble, he had to take guest roles at various theaters in various cities. Sometimes he had parts on TV too, but these roles weren't so thick on the ground either.

On top of their financial worries, they were worried about Leni, who was getting worse. She died on October 2, 1986, two years to the day after her husband, Erich. It was Patrick who happened to be at her side, visiting his beloved Mona-Grandma, and he held her hand until it was over, which was merciful for Leni but terribly difficult for Patrick, who almost collapsed. Like Erich, Leni Elias née Frank was buried at the Jewish cemetery in Basel. Now only Herbert and Fritzi were still alive from the older generation, and Gerti took on responsibility for them. Herbert died on March 20, 1987, at age ninety-five, in La Charmille.

It was not how they had imagined their first year back home. Oliver was having greater difficulties than his parents had expected with the transition from metropolitan Berlin to sleepy Basel, where everyone spoke this strange Swiss German. He rubbed people the wrong way with his High German and must have seemed arrogant to his teachers. He got along brilliantly with his schoolmates, though. They gave him the courage to keep speaking High German, and some of his friendships from then have lasted until today. Patrick, too, was not happy with his apprenticeship at the bank. One day, when he was visiting Buddy's former skating partner Otti Rehorek and his second wife, and Otti asked how it was going at the bank, he burst out with how horrible everything about banking was to him. He wanted nothing to do with any of it, every day was torture to him.

"What else do you want to do?" Otti asked, and Patrick answered: "I want to be an actor. I've always wanted to be an actor."

Everyone descended on Buddy and Gerti and asked them why they wouldn't let the boy do what he so desperately wanted to do.

The discussion that followed made it clear to Buddy and Gerti that they were wrong, and they gave their permission for Patrick to quit and go to Bochum to attend acting school there. Oliver, too, would leave Basel immediately after graduating and return to Berlin, to take acting classes with Maria Körber.

Things went better starting in their second year in Basel, and Gerti actually managed, with Zita's help, to revive the business. It was a great relief for Buddy, of course, to have Gerti at his back. Life became more relaxed, they got used to things there, and the house on Herbstgasse became their home, just as they had dreamed it would.

Gerti ran the business for fifteen years, paid for her sons' education, and was the primary breadwinner for her family, as Leni had been.

Buddy took parts at various theaters but did most of his work for television. Gerti worked in the store and took care of the household, and especially of Fritzi. She was helped by Oliver and Patrick, who loved Fritzi very much—Fritzi had taken on the role of a substitute grandma for them after Leni's death. Fritzi came over for meals almost every Sunday and sometimes joined the family on vacations to Nax. Eventually, though, Fritzi grew so frail and confused that she could no longer live alone. Eva Schloss, her daughter, brought her to London in 1997, where she died in 1998, at age ninety-three. Her urn was buried in Birsfelden.

After fifteen years, Gerti was sixty-eight years old, and she gave up the store. She arranged a going-out-of-business sale, and describes it as "like Hollywood. People rushed the doors. Two of my sisters were there, and a friend from Berlin, and another from Basel, and the five of us were selling, selling, selling. I was up a ladder the whole time fetching down lamps. It was crazy what was going on. It was really a crowning finale for Leni's business."

Today, Gerti is also on the board of the Anne Frank-Fonds in Basel, like Buddy, who spent more time working with the Fonds

Buddy Elias in Molière's *Hypochondriac*, Komödie Basel, 1997–98

and attended every meeting starting in 1986. He has been president of the Anne Frank-Fonds since 1996, fulfilling Otto Frank's wish that a member of the family always be on the board. Buddy dedicates his energy and all his free time to what he now calls his "life task." Just as the diary became the center of Otto's and Fritzi's lives, it is now the focus of Buddy's and Gerti's. The whirlpool that sucked in Otto works on them as well.

Someone said once that Anne Frank is dead, Otto lives on for her. Now they could say: Anne Frank is dead, Buddy Elias lives on for her.

The most important task of the Fonds is to distribute donations to the many organizations that approach the Fonds for help. Everywhere in the world, projects that promote peace and intercultural understanding can count on its support, especially projects working against xenophobia and racism that are relevant to children and young people. The Fonds also plays a special role for "the Righteous": the non-Jewish men and women who saved Jews during the Holocaust. The Anne Frank-Fonds devotes particular energy to Eastern Europeans, since in the West, where there are obviously also "the Righteous," they tend to be taken care of by the national safety nets. Not so the ones in Poland, Romania, and the Baltic countries. They are old now, often sick, and often without the medicines they need, either because they are not available there or because they are too expensive. The Fonds pays for their medicines, hearing aids, and other assistance. To prevent any fraud or misuse of the funds, Yad Vashem, the memorial and research center in Jerusalem dedicated to victims of the Holocaust, needs to certify that they actually did save Jews. In 2000, the Anne Frank-Fonds put a new plan into effect: endowing a chair in ethics for a professor at the University of Basel, currently occupied by Professor Stella Reiter-Theil from Germany. In the spring, the Institute for Applied Ethics and Medical Ethics was founded in the medical school. One of its high points to date was an International Conference on Clinical Ethics Consultation, about advising on the difficult questions of patient care; over two hundred participants from a wide variety of fields and countries were in attendance.

Buddy Elias keeps the memory of Anne Frank alive by answering letters, giving lectures, and working to help people who need assistance. The many trips that he has to take for the foundation, for Anne Frank, are often difficult, but he does his work satisfied with the knowledge that his cousin is still as important as she deserves to be to so many people, especially to young people, and that her ideals have not been forgotten. He sometimes thinks about the fact that he is the only member of Anne's family left who knew her when she was alive—the real Anne, the mercurial, rebellious, imaginative girl she once was. One day he will take these memories with him to the grave, and when he and the people who knew Anne as a schoolmate and friend are gone, only Anne Frank the icon will be left: a symbol for the one and a half million Jewish children who lost their lives in the Holocaust.

Epilogue

Basel, a gray January morning, 1946. A tall man in a loose, shabby winter coat draped across his thin shoulders leaves the house on Herbstgasse. Knit earmuffs stick out from under a hat that is a bit too big for him. In one hand he carries a brown cardboard suitcase, in the other a shopping bag with a knit jacket, a couple of books, a thermos with coffee, and some sandwiches wrapped in newspaper. A small, fragile woman is walking next to him, wearing her fur coat—not exactly new, but well tailored—and a white hat, white gloves, and high-heeled shoes. She looks positively elegant compared to him. At the garden gate the man turns around one last time to face the two men standing at the top of the stairs and waving—a distinguished middle-aged gentleman and a very young man—then he steps out the gate and follows the woman down the street.

The man is Otto Frank, who has spent three weeks in Basel with his family: his mother, sister, brother-in-law, brother-in-law's mother, and nephews, Stephan and Buddy. Three weeks that were deeply moving for all of them, because for the first time he came to Herbstgasse alone, without one or two daughters with him, as he always had before the war. The woman next to him is Leni Elias, taking her brother to the train station after he said goodbye to everyone and promised to come back again soon. Leni clings to this "soon" as much as Alice, his mother, does.

After the long years of separation, a "soon" is a sign of hope and consolation.

They walk alongside each other through the cold streets to the streetcar stop. It is not yet totally light out, in fact it would never get truly light in Basel that day, the winter sky hangs too low over the city and the cloud cover is too gray. Otto considers all the old houses in this city that was spared the war—buildings standing there as complacently as if there weren't ruins and rubble throughout all of Europe. The buildings radiate security and safety, security that Otto can no longer believe in.

In the streetcar they sit next to each other and look out into the gray, overcast morning. "It'll snow soon," Leni says, just to have something to say, and Otto says that it snows less often in Amsterdam than in Switzerland and melts faster. Then they fall silent again. The other passengers are mostly silent too—men and women with scarves or turned-up collars, even, strangely, the children going to school with satchels on their backs and wool caps pulled down low over their ears. It feels like the cloud cover is pressing down on everyone's mood.

"Erich might be able to go to Amsterdam soon," Leni says next to him. "The company has put in an application, so there's a good chance he'll get a travel permit. Write and tell us if you need anything, he can take it with him."

Otto strokes his fingers along the scarf that his mother has knit him in these three weeks; the gloves and the new socks are from Grandma Ida. "You've all already given me so much," he says.

And Leni says: "I wish there was more we could give you."

The streetcar stops at the train station and they get out, pushing their way to the platform between the other travelers.

The train is not there yet. They stand facing each other, looking at each other. "I am so sorry," Leni says.

Otto nods, then suddenly says: "She had gray eyes. They looked dark, but they weren't brown, they were gray."

"Who?" Leni asks.

"Anne."

Leni puts her arms around him, lays her head on his shoulder, and hears his voice right next to her ear: "If I ever forget that, you have to remind me. Promise me that. They were gray."

Leni starts to cry. Otto takes the glove off his right hand, takes a handkerchief out of his coat pocket, and wipes away her tears, the way he used to do when she was still a child.

"Oh, Leni," he says, "we imagined our lives so differently."

"Completely, totally different."

Then the train comes. Otto takes out the tickets that Erich had bought for him three days before and kisses his sister as sweetly as he always used to, before picking up his suitcase and bag and getting on the train. After finding a seat, he opens the window and leans out. They look at each other. Again neither says a word, but they also don't need to. They are again as close as they used to be, when life still lay before them, when they didn't yet know that it would not bring them only joy, but also so much sorrow. When they didn't yet know that life's most important lessons are endurance and bearing up under the blows of fate.

His face has grown older, his skin is pale, and wrinkles extend from his nose to the corners of his mouth. Even so, she can still see the young man's features in his face. Even the boy's. And she wonders if he can still see the young woman, the girl, in her face. "You can't let yourself get depressed," she says.

Otto wants to answer, but at that moment the conductor blows the train whistle, shrill and unambiguous. The train jerks, steam comes hissing out of the engine's smokestack, and the train starts to move and then pulls out of the station. Otto leans out the window and waves. He calls out something, Leni sees his lips move but can't make out the words. She takes out her handkerchief and waves back, and keeps waving even after the train has left the station and vanished into the gray air.

No, this isn't how she imagined her life. Stephan, it's now

clear, will recover, that's the most important thing, but it will still take a while. Buddy will leave home in the next few days; he has been hired in Bern. Youth goes ever onward, it's the way of the world. It's the old people who are left behind, Grandma Ida and Alice. And Erich. And her. She is fifty-two years old, her youth is behind her. What is left for her to expect from the future? It doesn't matter, she will carry on the way she always has. And anyway, fifty-two isn't that old. Who knows how many years she still has ahead of her? What is it that Jews say on birthdays? "May you live to be a hundred and twenty"? Decisively, she turns around. When she steps out of the train station, she sees a few isolated snowflakes drifting through the air. She shivers and wraps herself tighter in her coat and sets off on the road home.

Afterword

The present book could only be written because I found an enormous cache of letters, documents, and photographs from the Frank and Elias families that had been kept for decades in the attic of our house. There were around six thousand items in total.

When my husband, Buddy, my sons Patrick and Oliver, and I moved from Berlin to Herbstgasse in 1986, I took over my mother-in-law's antiques business. She was living by that point in La Charmille old-age home, along with her brother Herbert. The first few years were difficult ones, since I was responsible not only for the business and taking care of my family but also for running the house. Along with the other tasks I set myself, there was also taking care of the attic. It was packed solid with furniture, crates, boxes, suitcases—I was curious what was in them, of course, especially the two white armoires in which I found wonderful things: sequined dresses, an opera hat, a tuxedo with tails, evening gowns, furs, hats. I also discovered a box covered in floral-print fabric that contained letters, lots of letters, mostly loose but others lovingly tied up with silk ribbons. It took some time before I worked up the courage to read them, and even longer before I understood that these were family letters, since many of the names were unknown to me and some were written in the old Sütterlin style of handwriting that I could mostly read but that was sometimes hard to decipher. My husband too was not always able to help—of course he knew the names of his uncles, Robert, Herbert, and Otto, but other names were as new to him as they were to me.

In the following years I rummaged around in the attic every now and then, but I did not have time to explore everything more carefully until 2001, after I closed the antiques store. By then, all the family members from the older generation had died. I found more boxes and more letters, including letters from Otto Frank, Margot, and Anne, some in suitcases, others in crates. I eventually realized that these were letters that Leni and Erich, my in-laws, and Alice, Leni's mother, had kept for years. And while dusting the house, I found a slim little book in the salon's bookcase—more of a hardcover schoolbook than a book—containing Alice's memories as she wrote them up on the occasion of her seventieth birthday. I found another little volume titled "Klärchen," written by Alfred Stern, Alice Frank née Stern's cousin, a historian and professor. He had written it for his wife, Klärchen, and given it to her on their twenty-fifth anniversary, sketching out the history of his family. Alfred and Klärchen were cousins who had married within the family; that's how it was in the nineteenth century.

I was very surprised one day when I came across a large leather suitcase with hundreds of letters that Buddy, my husband, had sent home to his family from every corner of the world. It was a great joy for me to be able to get to know my husband better through these letters.

And I was especially shaken when I found Otto's letters that he had sent to Herbstgasse after the war, from Auschwitz, Kattowitz, and later from Amsterdam.

It was clear to my husband and me that these treasures could not just stay lying in the attic. It was the kind of material for a family chronicle that you seldom find.

I reported on the find at a meeting of the Anne Frank-Fonds, and it was decided to have a specialist organize and archive the mass of materials properly. An experienced and well-known historian, Dr. Peter Toebak, agreed to do it, and spent two half days a week in our attic for almost two years. He set up his computer in the added-on story where Otto Frank and his second wife, Fritzi, had lived for almost eight years, answering the letters that came from people all over the world who had read his daughter's diary.

When the documents were fully archived, the valuable shipment was packed up and sent to the Anne Frank Foundation's archive in Amsterdam, where every page was digitized or microfilmed. The documents are currently on loan there.

The Anne Frank-Fonds also decided that the letters and documents should be turned into a book, and I was asked to be in charge of that process. It meant I had to go through the many letters and documents and select the most significant and interesting ones, the ones with the most information about the family's life in the nineteenth and twentieth centuries. Dr. Toebak was very helpful and competent assisting me during the two and a half years I spent sifting through the documents. I am very grateful to him.

Lastly, we needed an experienced writer, preferably a literary author, who would be up to the task of turning these letters into a book that would do justice, at least partly, to the history of the Stern, Frank, and Elias families. After all, in truth there was only a one-sided correspondence—only letters sent to the family, not the family's answers.

It was Eva Koralnik of the Liepman literary agency in Zurich who suggested Mirjam Pressler, a writer who had already translated the critical edition of *The Diary of Anne Frank* into German and had put together the new reader's edition (called *The Definitive Edition* in English). This suggestion turned out to be a great stroke of luck, since the collaboration with Mirjam Pressler was not only pleasant and friendly but also interesting and stimulating. I gave her approximately five hundred letters that I had selected, along with numerous documents and photographs. We spent many weekends with each other, during which she asked us many detailed questions. The present book is based on this foundation.

It is a great satisfaction to me to have completed this work. In so doing, I have become very, very close to the wonderful family I married into.

Gerti Elias
April 2009

Abraham Süsskind Stern ∞ Golde b'Herz (1st marriage)
*1764
† 7.5.1838

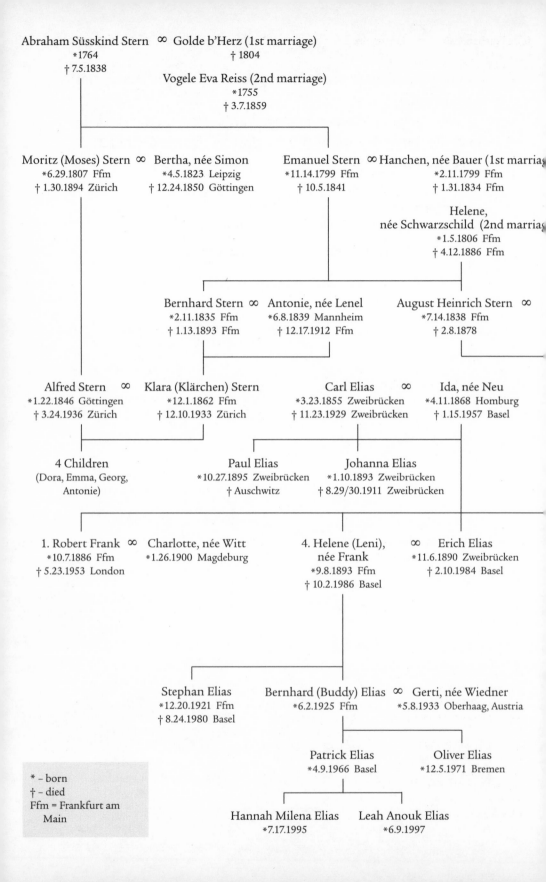

Golde b'Herz (1st marriage)
† 1804

Vogele Eva Reiss (2nd marriage)
*1755
† 3.7.1859

Moritz (Moses) Stern ∞ Bertha, née Simon
*6.29.1807 Ffm
† 1.30.1894 Zürich

Bertha, née Simon
*4.5.1823 Leipzig
† 12.24.1850 Göttingen

Emanuel Stern ∞ Hanchen, née Bauer (1st marria
*11.14.1799 Ffm
† 10.5.1841

Hanchen, née Bauer
*2.11.1799 Ffm
† 1.31.1834 Ffm

Helene,
née Schwarzschild (2nd marria
*1.5.1806 Ffm
† 4.12.1886 Ffm

Bernhard Stern ∞ Antonie, née Lenel
*2.11.1835 Ffm
† 1.13.1893 Ffm

Antonie, née Lenel
*6.8.1839 Mannheim
† 12.17.1912 Ffm

August Heinrich Stern ∞
*7.14.1838 Ffm
† 2.8.1878

Alfred Stern ∞ Klara (Klärchen) Stern
*1.22.1846 Göttingen
† 3.24.1936 Zürich

Klara (Klärchen) Stern
*12.1.1862 Ffm
† 12.10.1933 Zürich

Carl Elias ∞ Ida, née Neu
*3.23.1855 Zweibrücken
† 11.23.1929 Zweibrücken

Ida, née Neu
*4.11.1868 Homburg
† 1.15.1957 Basel

4 Children
(Dora, Emma, Georg, Antonie)

Paul Elias
*10.27.1895 Zweibrücken
† Auschwitz

Johanna Elias
*1.10.1893 Zweibrücken
† 8.29/30.1911 Zweibrücken

1. Robert Frank ∞ Charlotte, née Witt
*10.7.1886 Ffm
† 5.23.1953 London

Charlotte, née Witt
*1.26.1900 Magdeburg

4. Helene (Leni), née Frank ∞ Erich Elias
*9.8.1893 Ffm
† 10.2.1986 Basel

Erich Elias
*11.6.1890 Zweibrücken
† 2.10.1984 Basel

Stephan Elias
*12.20.1921 Ffm
† 8.24.1980 Basel

Bernhard (Buddy) Elias ∞ Gerti, née Wiedner
*6.2.1925 Ffm

Gerti, née Wiedner
*5.8.1933 Oberhaag, Austria

Patrick Elias
*4.9.1966 Basel

Oliver Elias
*12.5.1971 Bremen

Hannah Milena Elias
*7.17.1995

Leah Anouk Elias
*6.9.1997

* – born
† – died
Ffm = Frankfurt am Main

Juda Nathan Cahn ∞ Gütte, née Sänger
*1748 † 4.29.1837
† 5.19.1833

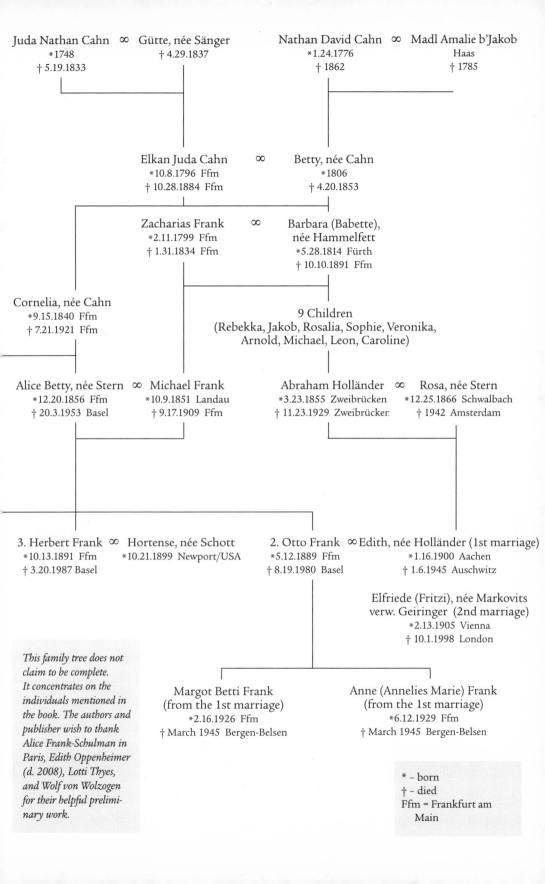

Nathan David Cahn ∞ Madl Amalie b'Jakob Haas
*1.24.1776 † 1785
† 1862

Elkan Juda Cahn ∞ Betty, née Cahn
*10.8.1796 Ffm *1806
† 10.28.1884 Ffm † 4.20.1853

Zacharias Frank ∞ Barbara (Babette), née Hammelfett
*2.11.1799 Ffm *5.28.1814 Fürth
† 1.31.1834 Ffm † 10.10.1891 Ffm

Cornelia, née Cahn
*9.15.1840 Ffm
† 7.21.1921 Ffm

9 Children
(Rebekka, Jakob, Rosalia, Sophie, Veronika, Arnold, Michael, Leon, Caroline)

Alice Betty, née Stern ∞ Michael Frank
*12.20.1856 Ffm *10.9.1851 Landau
† 20.3.1953 Basel † 9.17.1909 Ffm

Abraham Holländer ∞ Rosa, née Stern
*3.23.1855 Zweibrücken *12.25.1866 Schwalbach
† 11.23.1929 Zweibrücken † 1942 Amsterdam

3. Herbert Frank ∞ Hortense, née Schott
*10.13.1891 Ffm *10.21.1899 Newport/USA
† 3.20.1987 Basel

2. Otto Frank ∞ Edith, née Holländer (1st marriage)
*5.12.1889 Ffm *1.16.1900 Aachen
† 8.19.1980 Basel † 1.6.1945 Auschwitz

Elfriede (Fritzi), née Markovits
verw. Geiringer (2nd marriage)
*2.13.1905 Vienna
† 10.1.1998 London

Margot Betti Frank
(from the 1st marriage)
*2.16.1926 Ffm
† March 1945 Bergen-Belsen

Anne (Annelies Marie) Frank
(from the 1st marriage)
*6.12.1929 Ffm
† March 1945 Bergen-Belsen

This family tree does not claim to be complete. It concentrates on the individuals mentioned in the book. The authors and publisher wish to thank Alice Frank-Schulman in Paris, Edith Oppenheimer (d. 2008), Lotti Thyes, and Wolf von Wolzogen for their helpful preliminary work.

* – born
† – died
Ffm = Frankfurt am Main

Bibliography

Amt für Wissenschaft und Kunst der Stadt Frankfurt am Main, ed. *"Früher wohnten wir in Frankfurt . . ."* Frankfurt, 1985.

Anne Frank Stichting, ed. *Die Welt der Anne Frank.* Amsterdam, 1985.

Backhaus, Fritz, Gisela Engel, Robert Liberles, and Margarete Schlüter, eds. *Die Frankfurter Judengasse: Jüdisches Leben in der Neuzeit.* Frankfurt: Societäts, 2006.

Benz, Wolfgang, ed. *Dimension des Völkermords: Die Zahl der jüdischen Opfer des Nationalsozialismus.* Munich: R. Oldenbourg, 1991.

Frank, Anne. *Anne Frank Tagebuch (Leseausgabe).* Edited by Otto H. Frank and Mirjam Pressler. Frankfurt: S. Fischer, 1991.

——. *Tagebücher der Anne Frank (Historisch-kritische Ausgabe).* Edited by Rijksinstituut voor Oorlogsdocumentatie. Frankfurt: S. Fischer, 1988.

Grab, Walter. *Der deutsche Weg der Judenemanzipation, 1789–1938.* Munich: Piper, 1991.

Herbert, Ulrich, Karin Orth, and Christoph Diekmann. *Die nationalsozialistischen Konzentrationslager.* Frankfurt: Fischer Taschenbuch, 2002.

Herlitz, Georg, and Bruno Kirschner, eds. *Jüdisches Lexikon.* 2nd ed. Frankfurt: Athenäum, 1987.

Heuberger, Rachel, and Helga Krohn. *Hinaus aus dem Ghetto . . . Juden in Frankfurt am Main, 1800–1950.* Frankfurt: S. Fischer, 1988.

Historischen Museum der Stadt Frankfurt am Main, ed. *Anne aus Frankfurt: Leben und Lebenswelt Anne Franks.* Frankfurt, 1990.

Kolb, Eberhard. *Bergen-Belsen, 1943–1945: Vom "Aufenthaltslager" zum Konzentrationslager.* Göttingen: Vandenhoeck & Ruprecht, 2002.

Lee, Carol Ann. *Otto Franks Geheimnis.* Munich: Piper, 2005.

Longerich, Peter, ed. *Die Ermordung der europäischen Juden.* Munich: Piper, 1980.

Seifert, Claudia. *Das Leben war bescheiden und schön.* Munich: Deutscher Taschenbuch, 2008.

Stapferhaus, Lenzburg, ed. *Anne Frank und wir.* Zurich: Chronos, 1995.
Stern, Alfred. *Zur Familiengeschichte: Klärchen zum 22. März 1906 gewidmet.* Privately printed. Zurich: Buchdruckerei Berichthaus (formerly Ulrich & Co.), 1906.

Photo Credits

1. ILLUSTRATIONS IN THE TEXT:

Elias Family Archive/Frank and Anne Frank Archive, Amsterdam
Page 2, 5, 9, 16, 16, 17, 19, 20, 58, 60, 62, 67, 68 (top), 70, 71, 73, 74, 78, 81, 84, 87, 91, 96, 97, 99, 103, 105, 108, 110, 113, 114, 117, 118, 121, 126, 130, 131, 136, 137, 139, 142, 145, 149, 153, 160, 163, 164, 166, 168, 171, 176, 180, 184, 186, 190, 201, 213, 216, 224, 225, 238, 241, 245, 252, 263, 267, 271, 276, 277, 283, 291, 300, 301, 316, 324, 325, 356.

Jewish Museum Frankfurt: Page 52.

Jürgen Bauer: Page 17, 25, 26, 29, 41, 68 (bottom), 187, 256, 259, 297

Elias Private Archive, Basel: Page 247, 248, 249, 290, 361, 363, 367, 374, 375, 377, 385, 390.

Universität Heidelberg: Page 88

2. ILLUSTRATIONS IN THE INSERT:

Elias Family Archive/Frank and Anne Frank Archive, Amsterdam:
Number 4, 5, 7, 8, 9, 10, 11, 12, 13, 14

Jürgen Bauer: Number 1, 2, 3, 6

Elias Private Archive: Number 15

We thank Christoph Knoch and the members of the Anne Frank Fund in Basel, and the Anne Frank Stichting in Amsterdam, for their cooperation and friendly support.

A NOTE ABOUT THE AUTHOR

Mirjam Pressler is one of Germany's most beloved authors. She was the German translator of Anne Frank's diary.

A NOTE ABOUT THE TRANSLATOR

Damion Searls is a writer and an award-winning translator of authors such as Rainer Maria Rilke, Marcel Proust, Ingeborg Bachmann, Jon Fosse, Robert Walser, and Hans Keilson.